C is an excellent choice of language for a beginner. It's easy because the language is remarkably compact, so there isn't an enormous amount to remember. C is powerful and also portable. There is an ANSI standard established for C which most modern compilers support, so if you take care to program according to the standard, you can run your programs on virtually any machine with little difficulty.

The Beginners Guide to C is the quickest and easiest way to become proficient in C. The book assumes no previous experience, but doesn't just stop at the basics. Each chapter ends with a useful application of what you have learnt, that teaches you how to put the theory into practice. This is real life programming

The fastest way to programming confidence.

What is Wrox Press?

Wrox Press is a computer book publisher which promotes a brand new concept - clear, jargon-free programming and database titles that fulfill your real demands. We publish for everyone, from the novice through to the experienced programmer. To ensure our books meet your needs, we carry out continuous research on all our titles. Through our dialog with you we can craft the book you really need.

We welcome suggestions and take all of them to heart - your input is paramount in creating the next great Wrox title. Use the reply card inside this book or mail us at:

feedback@wrox.demon.co.uk
or
Compuserve 100063, 2152

Wrox Press Ltd.   **Tel:** **0101 312 465 3559**
2710 W. Touhy   **Fax:** **0101 312 465 4063**
Chicago
IL 60645
USA

The Beginner's Guide to C

Ivor Horton

Wrox Press Ltd.®

The Beginner's Guide to C

Published by Wrox Press Ltd. 1334 Warwick Road, Birmingham, B27 6PR. UK

Library of Congress Catalog Card Number: 94-78391
ISBN 1-874416-15X

Trademark Acknowledgements

Wrox has endeavored to provide trademark information about all the companies and products mentioned in this book by the appropriate use of capitals. However, Wrox cannot guarantee the accuracy of this information.

Credits

Author
Ivor Horton

Technical Editor
Julian Dobson

Series Editor
Nina Barnsley

Technical Consultant
Ian Cargill

Additional Material
Darren Gill
Julian Dobson
Nina Barnsley

Production Manager
Gina Mance

Book Layout
Ewart Liburd
Eddie Fisher
Kenneth Fung
Greg Powell

Beta Testers
Mark Holmes
Gordon Rogers
Paul Wilson

Proof Readers
Joanne Wheeler
Wendy Entwistle
Paula Limbert

Cover Design
Third Wave

For more information on Third Wave, contact Ross Alderson on 44-21 456 1400

About the Author

Ivor Horton has been in the computer industry for 30 years. He has applied and taught most programming languages in a wide variety of contexts. He has design and implementation experience of a wide variety of systems involving mainframes, on-line control systems and PCs. He has extensive knowledge of engineering and scientific applications and systems, particularly in the context of Computer Aided Design and Computer Aided Manufacturing.

CONTENTS

Summary of Contents

CONTENTS

Appendix A: Computer Arithmetic 521

Appendix B: ASCII Character Code Definition 529

Appendix C: Reserved Words in C 533

INTRODUCTION

Why The Beginner's Guide?

If you have picked up and opened this book then you are almost certainly interested in learning to program, and like most things in life, you want it to be painless. There are plenty of computer books out there that claim to teach you C easily, so why choose our book? The simple answer is that we have designed this book with a very clear aim. We understand that it's not just content that people need. C is C and this book won't change that. What we can change is the *way* we teach you C.

Our first assumption is that people don't learn for the sake of learning. Most people want to learn to program so they can achieve something with their programs - just learning C isn't an aim in itself. For this reason, wherever possible each chapter in the book ends with a real life application of what you have learnt. This takes you through a problem and finds its solution in a C program. The method teaches you about designing programs for real. It also shows you how the language works - not just the language constructs. The programs aren't trivial and can be quite tough. The reward is that their effectiveness in teaching you how C is applied in practice is much greater than the average example.

The book is based on the principle that you learn best by doing. If we promised to teach you French just by teaching you the grammar, you might find it dubious if we claimed you would be fluent by the end. The only way you can become fluent is if you use what you learn in a real life way. We make extensive use of complete working examples throughout the book, together with clear and thorough explanations.

How to Use This Book

Because we believe in the hands-on approach you will write your first programs in the very first chapter. Every chapter has several programs to put the theory into practice and these examples are key to the book. We would advise you to type in as many as possible. You won't always find it easy or get it right, but the very act of typing programs in is a tremendous aid to remembering the language elements. When you do get a program to work for the first time, particularly when you are trying to solve your own problems, the sense of excitement and satisfaction will make it all worthwhile.

Each chapter covers a lot of ground. Don't expect to be able to digest it all in a few hours. Take your time and experiment with your own ideas. Try modifying the programs and see what you can do, that's when it gets really interesting. Don't be afraid of trying anything out. If you don't understand how something works, just type in a few variations and see what happens. Making mistakes is usually very educational, unless you are something like a highwire walker. A good approach is to read a chapter through, and once you have a good idea of its scope, go back to the beginning and work through all the examples. For some topics you will almost certainly need to go through the material a couple of times before it really sticks.

You may find the end of chapter programs quite hard. Don't worry if it isn't all completely clear on the first try. There are bound to be bits that you find difficult to understand at first because they often apply what you have learnt to quite complicated problems, so persevere. Some programs take time to understand because they are doing complicated things. If you really get stuck, all the end of chapter programs are designed so that you can skip them, carry on with the next chapter and come back to them at a later date. You can even go through the book right to the end without worrying about them. The point of these programs is that they are useful even after you finish the book.

Who is This Book For?

This book is for both beginners to programming and beginners to C. If you are a complete novice then this book will teach you programming, using C as the vehicle. If you already know another language, but want to learn C this book will teach you all you need to know. It assumes no knowledge, but moves quickly and easily from the basics to the real meat of the subject. By the end of the book you will have a thorough grounding in C, and provided you have used, understood and exercised all the examples, you should have little trouble in writing programs for yourself.

What You Need to Use This Book

The only personal attributes you need to tackle programming in C is a basic knowledge of high school math, and the enthusiasm to get through a 500+ page book. You will also need a computer with a C compiler installed on it so you can run the examples. Many of the current C++ compilers available will also compile C, so if you have one of these it will do just as well.

Conventions Used

To enable you to find your way around this book easily, we have used a variety of different styles to highlight different references, and to enable you to recognise them more easily.

Program Code

All programs in the book are highlighted with a blue background so you can find them easily.

```
#include <stdio.h>

void main()
{
   int salary;      /* Declare a variable called salary        */

   salary = 10000;   /* A simple arithmetic assignment statement */

   printf("My salary is %d.", salary);

}
```

When we use extracts from this code we also shade it so you can spot it quickly.

When we have shown general examples of code or the output from a program we have put it in this style:

```
The is how general code and output will look.
```

When code features in the middle of sentences, we write it in `this_style`.

When for the sake of brevity we haven't printed some lines of code we'll use three periods

...

to indicate a missing fragment.

In the end of chapter programs we repeat a lot of the code. This is deliberate, so that you can see the flow of the program develop. We have shaded lines which are new additions to the program, and left the lines that are repeated unshaded. This will enable you to see immediately where new stuff has been added..

```
This is repeated code.
This is new code.
This is repeated code.
This is new code.
This is new code.
```

Important Bits, Interesting Bits

Bits that you really must read are in this type of box.

Things that are interesting but not essential are in this type of box.

Important words are in **this style**. These are significant words that we are meeting for the first time. Subsequently they will appear as normal text.

File names are in **THIS_STYLE**. All file names appear like this in the text, even when they are conventionally written in lower case inside a program.

Keys that you press are in *this style*, such as *Enter* or *Ctrl*.

Tell Us What You Think

One last thing. We've tried to make the book enjoyable and accurate. The programming community is what we're here to serve, so if you have any queries, suggestions or comments about this book, let us know. We will be delighted to hear from you. You can help us ensure that our future books are even better. Return the reply card at the back of the book, or contact us direct at Wrox. You can also use e-mail:

feedback@wrox.demon.co.uk
Compuserve: 100062,2152

Basic Ideas

Welcome to the world of programming! If this is your first language, or you are new to C, we are going to teach you all the fundamentals of C programming in an enjoyable and easy-to-understand way. By the end of this first chapter you will have written your first few C programs and will have had an exciting taste of controlling your computer.

We are going to have to cover a few basic ideas about computers and look at the jargon to make it clearer, but the hands-on approach means you should try to get writing your own programs as soon as possible. Don't worry if you don't understand everything. The main thing is to get your fingers on the key board and start typing. You will make mistakes, we all do, but that's the quickest way to learn.

In this chapter you will:

- Learn about computer jargon and how computers work
- Understand what a compiler does
- Understand how a C program is made up
- Write your own programs to display text on the screen

Computer Jargon

The computer industry has more jargon than you can shake a stick at. You will find that the professionals, and many of the magazines relating to computing, use so much of it sometimes that they would be just as intelligible to the uninitiated if they were using Sanskrit. However, in spite of its impenetrable appearance to the uninitiated, it's not as hard as it looks, and it often is of genuine value in communicating ideas in a concise form.

Most of the jargon is derived by simply taking the initial letters of the original descriptive phrase to form a sort of shorthand. For example, DOS for Disk Operating System, or ROM for Read Only Memory. It may still be rather opaque if you are not familiar with the subject context of the original phrase, but in the main, you will find you pick it up quite quickly. Throughout the book we will explain any new jargon as we go along.

Understanding Your Computer

To understand your computer, first of all forget all that electronic brain stuff. Your computer is about as much like an electronic brain as the average washing machine. No-one thinks washing machines are clever, yet they work on the same principle as a computer, just far more simply. You tell the machine what to do and it does it.

> The history can be interesting, for instance - did you know that the world's largest computer company used to major in bacon slicers, or that one of the first commercial (as opposed to research) computers in the UK was produced by a company packaging food and running a chain of tea shops? How's that for the cradle of today's information technology?

Do you happen to have an aunt (or an uncle for that matter) with one of those fancy machines for knitting socks, sweaters etc.? Maybe one of those knitting machines with a card with holes punched in it to indicate when it should knit plain and when purl? Punch up the right set of holes and auntie can produce a pair of Fairisle socks in no time at all. Punch up the wrong holes and who knows what may turn out; a Picasso pullover with three armholes and one left foot perhaps, or more typically, a mass of knotted wool with the whole thing jammed up. As we shall see when we get into programming a bit, this is quite a good analogy for what can happen inside your computer when the odd mistake has crept in. So remember - it's as easy as knitting, and if auntie can hack it, so can you.

Your computer is a device which can follow a sequence of instructions you give it, and it follows them to the letter no matter how ludicrous the end result. Not a lot of "brain" in evidence in that. Experience will soon show you, if you are not already aware, that computers do exactly what you tell them to do, not what you want them to do. If you are ambiguous in your language you get strange results.

If you are not careful about how you instruct your computer, it can be entertaining, tiresome, or even downright dangerous as illustrated in the next figure.

"Don't worry, ladies and gentlemen.
The Autopilot computer has FULL control."

Computer Instructions

When your computer performs calculations, it does so by executing a set of instructions. The instructions it is able to execute have to be of a very specific kind. Give a computer something that is not one of the instructions it understands and it won't do anything.

Computers don't speak English. They don't even speak C. They are so simple that the only things they understand are ones (1s) and zeros (0s). Typical of the kind of stuff involved is:

1011 0100 0000 1001 ....

Interesting, isn't it? All computer instructions look like this. They are all collections of numbers, so called **binary** numbers because the only digits involved are 0 and 1. The numbers instruct your computer to perform an action, and where the data can be found that it is to act upon. Don't worry though, nobody in their right mind would want to spend their time producing thousands of binary digits like these, although in the days when computers generated more heat than light, quite a few strange individuals did. Nowadays there is a better way.

Early on in computing, some bright, or possibly lazy individuals cottoned on to a revolutionary idea: if you had a program that could read instructions that were a bit closer to what the average human was happy to deal with, written in a high level language, and then translate them into the weird stuff these glorified bacon slicers required, then computers might be a whole lot easier to use - and could conceivably be quite useful.

This was a brilliant idea and it produced various intermediaries which people could communicate with more easily and which could then convert that communication into something the computer was happy with. C is one of those intermediaries and is one of the most versatile and widely used.

There are now many such programs processing various interpretations of what the average human might want to use as a means of communicating with a computer. They are generally called **compilers**, translating - or rather compiling - a program written in a high-level programming language into binary machine instructions. Since in reality, your computer only understands binary numbers, this process is an essential part of producing a computer program.

In the programming world there are high-level and low-level languages. It simply means that since the native language of a computer is machine code, a single instruction in a low-level language corresponds closely to a single instruction in machine code. In a high-level language, one statement or instruction could correspond to many more lines of machine code. Languages such as Assembler are low-level, and languages like BASIC, Lisp and Prolog are high-level languages. High-level languages are much closer to English, and therefore much easier to understand. C is an odd ball - it is really a medium-level language because it has some features of both types of language.

The Ideas Behind a Programming Language

Let's start putting all this into practice. In the places where the action is specific to either DOS or UNIX we have described both alternatives, just look for the heading that covers your operating system.

Try It Out - A Simple Program

That's enough theory. Writing programs is what it's all about, so let's get typing. For this first program we will take you step-by-step through the process of creating a C program. Don't worry if what you type doesn't mean anything to you at this stage. We will explain as we go along. Let's get started.

1   Switch on your computer.

2   **In DOS**

Load your compiler. To do this from the `c:\` prompt you need to change the directory to the one where the compiler commands are found. This is normally a sub-directory similar to `c:\tc\bin.` (This is for Turbo C but the exact subdirectory will depend on what product you use and where on your fixed disk you install it. The easiest thing is to check your manual. We are assuming your compiler works in a similar manner to Turbo C, and comes with an editor.)

Try It Out!

Next type the command to start your compiler, the command will again depend on which product you are using, but would typically be **tc.exe** or something similar. This process can be summarized as follows:

c:\>

c:\>cd tc\bin

c:\tc\bin>

c:\tc\bin>tc.exe

You will now be in the editing screen where you can type and edit your program. If you are using Turbo C/C++ your screen will look something like this:

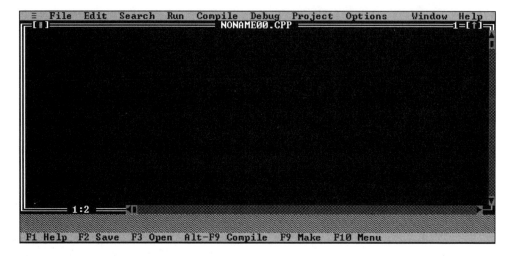

Using the file menu of your compiler select a **New** file. This will then open up an editing screen where you will be able to write your code (refer to your product manual for a full description of how to use your editor). If you are using a command line compiler then you will have to use the DOS edit program to write and edit the program. To do this from the **c:** prompt type **edit**. If you have already created a file and you want to edit it, you simply add the file name. For example, to edit the file **prog1.c** you would type **edit prog1.c**.

In UNIX

Load your editor. There are many text editors available for UNIX, a common one would be the **vi** editor. To use this type **vi prog1.c** and then type your code. For more information on how to use the editor for UNIX refer to your manual. You need to end the name of the file that you produce with **.c** (for example, **example.c**) as this is important for when the computer actually compiles the code.

3 Type in the following program exactly as written below. Be careful to use the punctuation exactly as you see here. The brackets used on the fourth and last lines are the curly ones: {} NOT the square ones [] or the round ones () - take care to get them right! Also, make sure you put the slashes the right way (/) and don't forget the semicolon (;).

```
/* Example 1.1 Your Very First C Program - Displaying Hello*/

#include <stdio.h>

void main()
{
    printf("Hello");
}
```

The following screen shows what it should look like with a DOS compiler.

```
≡  File  Edit  Search  Run  Compile  Debug  Project  Options    Window  Help
┌[■]══════════════════════ NONAME00.CPP ═══════════════════════1═[↑]┐
│/* Your Very First C Program    */                                  ▲
│                                                                    ▯
│#include <stdio.h>                                                  
│                                                                    
│void main()                                                         
│{                                                                   
│  printf("Hello");                                                  
│}                                                                   
│                                                                    
│                                                                    
│                                                                    
│                                                                    
│                                                                    
│                                                                    ▼
└──■── 8:2 ══◄▮                                                      ►┘
 F1 Help  Alt-F8 Next Msg  Alt-F7 Prev Msg  Alt-F9 Compile  F9 Make  F10 Menu
```

Can you guess what this program does?

4   Save the file (call it **PROG1.C** for example).

In DOS

In a DOS environment, go to the **File** menu and then select the **Save** option. Type the name you want to use (remember the **.c** extension) and **OK**.

In UNIX

In a UNIX environment using **vi**, simply quit from the editor, and the file that you have just produced can now be found in your current working directory.

5   Now that you have created your file containing your program code it is time to produce a program you can run on the computer. This is the process of compiling, and linking your file. **Compiling** the file is the process of translating all the code you have written in C into the 1s and 0s of machine instructions. **Linking** is the process of putting all the pieces of program together when there is more than one part to your program. C is designed to enable you to develop your programs in pieces (it is a **modular language**, which means you can break your code into **modules**). The final stage is to run the program. You should get the following output on the screen.

```
Hello
```

In DOS

In Borland compilers, to compile the code you typically select the main menu **Compile**, and then choose the **Compile** option (see the following screenshot). Alternatively you can use the keyboard and press *Alt + F9*.

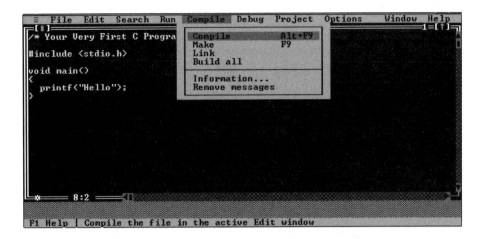

If this is successful, you will get a message to tell you so.

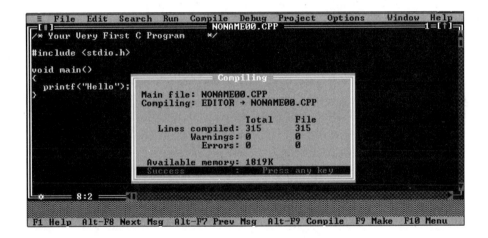

The next stage is to link all your compiled code modules (we have only one here as it is a very small program). To link, you again use the **C**ompile menu, but now choose the **L**ink option. If you have any errors then you must return to the editing stage, find where the incorrect code is and change it. If you have completed both these stages without any errors then you can run your program. There are 2 ways to do this.

One way is to use the menu item called **R**un in the **R**un menu. This means you can compile, link and execute the program in one go. To see the results (the output) you need to use the **W**indow menu to change to an **O**utput window.

The other way is to leave the compiler environment and move to the output directory (you can check where this is by looking in the **O**ptions menu and choosing the directories option). From this directory simply type the name of the executable file (**prog1.exe**) and the program will run. For other types of compiler you will have to check your manual.

In UNIX

The command supplied to compile C source code is **cc**. To compile the code you must type:

```
cc prog1.c
```

This will also link the compiled code, if it is able, and produce a file called **A.OUT** which is the executable version of your program. We recommend that you change the name of this as soon as you have produced it because each time you use the compiler the same name is used and the old program is always replaced by the new.

You've done it! This is your first program, which displayed the word **Hello** on the screen. You could try altering the same program to display your name on the screen. For example, if your name is Mary try editing the program to read like this:

```
/* Example 1.2 Your Very First C Program - Displaying Hello*/

#include<stdio.h>

void main()
{
    printf("Hello Mary!");
}
```

Try running it. A triumph! You have now edited that first program. Isn't it great! You have written a program using the editor, edited it and then compiled, linked and executed it. This sounds complicated but it wasn't bad was it? Let's look again at what happens during each of these phases.

> Execution sounds really violent, but in computer jargon executing a program simply means running it.

Editing

This is the process of creating, or later modifying your **source code** - the name given to the program code you have written, for example in the "Hello" program above. The result of this process is a file containing the source code for your program, the text printed above.

> By convention your C source file has the extension **.C**, so you should use names such as **MYPROG.C** or **TRY_OUT.C** or some other useful name. Most compilers will expect the source file to be named in this way.

Many C compilers will have a specific editor with them which can provide a lot of assistance in managing your programs. Indeed, products from both Microsoft and Borland provide a complete environment for writing, managing, developing and testing your programs. This is called the **Integrated Development Environment**, or IDE. You can also use other editors such as the DOS editor. If you are working in a UNIX environment then you should have the **vi** editor or something similar.

> You could use a word processor, such as Word or WordPerfect, although they aren't very suitable for producing program code. They have no special facilities to help you in this and normally create a lot of hidden codes that will cause havoc in the next phase if you don't ensure they are omitted. They generally provide a save function which will generate ASCII DOS text which eliminates these codes, but it isn't the easiest method to produce your source code.

Compiling

This is the process of translating your original C program into machine language. The input to this phase is the file you produced in the editing phase which is usually referred to as a **source module** (more jargon, I'm afraid), whereas the actual lines of C programming are the **source code**. The translation program, called the compiler, will first send the file to a preprocessing stage which prepares the text for the actual translation into computer language.

The pre-processor carries out instructions to insert text and replace text where it has been given instructions to do so in the source file to be compiled. These instructions start with a hash (#) symbol. If you look, there is one of these in the program above.

The next stage is where actual compilation into machine instructions takes place (remember we talked about translating your file from C into a language the computer can understand). The compiler can detect several different kinds of errors during the translation process, and most of these will prevent the machine language module, usually called an **object module**, from being generated. Various messages are generated by the compiler to tell you what sort of error has been detected.

Try typing in the example again but miss off the semi-colon (;) as shown below.

```
/*Example 1.3 Your Very First C Program - Displaying Hello*/

#include<stdio.h>

void main()
{
    printf("Hello")
}
```

You will see an error message, which may vary depending on which compiler you are using. A typical example is shown below:

```
error C2143: syntax error : missing ';' before '}'
  CL returned error code 2.
HELLO.C - 1 error(s), 0 warning(s)
```

It's hard to believe that all that could be caused by the absence of just one little semi-colon! When you start programming you will probably get lots of errors in compilation that are caused by simple punctuation mistakes. It's so easy to forget a little comma or a bracket - and don't worry, lots of experienced programmers make the same mistake too.

A common cause of confusion initially, is that just one error can result in a whole stream of abuse from your compiler referring to a large number of different errors, as you can see in the example above. After considering the messages carefully, the basic approach is to fix those you know you can, and have another go at compiling. With luck, you will get fewer errors next time around. All errors, at this and later stages, usually mean you have to go back to square one and re-edit the source code. When you finally succeed in compiling your program you will have the object module in a file ready to be input to the next phase.

The steps that you must actually take to compile a program depend on what sort of compiler you are using. In a DOS compiler such as from Borland, you simply have to select the compile option from the drop-down menu. The compiler package will then do the rest of the work for you. Under a UNIX based system you would use the **cc** command with the name of the file you have produced, for example:

```
cc myprog.c
```

The result of a successful compilation stage also depends on what system you are using. A DOS based system will produce a file with the same name as you used for the source file, but the extension will have changed to **.OBJ**. A UNIX system will produce the file **A.OUT** by default. It will be left to you to change the name here to something specific if you want to.

Linking

This process links together all the pieces necessary to make your program complete. The pieces include the object file generated during the previous phase from the C code you have written, and any **library routines** your programs use. Library routines are standard functions you include in your program to carry out a specific task to save you having to write the code for it yourself. All C compilers have an extensive library of functions covering a wide range of facilities - from getting information into, and out of, your program, to mathematical functions. Also, your program may be built up from a large number of parts you have produced separately. These parts are called modules, as we mentioned earlier.

By programming in pieces you are able to break up a large program which is difficult to write into many smaller and more simple ones. The **link editor**, or **linker** as it is sometimes called, will bring in the required library functions and modules automatically. A failure during this phase again means you have to go back to square one and modify the source code. Success will result in a file containing an executable module.

Often you will be working with programs that are made up of a lot of modules. In this case to use the linker on a DOS based system you should use the **P**roject menu option. This tells the linker which modules the program needs to link together to produce an executable module. To actually start the linking process there is a menu option in the drop-down **Compile** menu. If linking has been successful then a message will be displayed, see the screenshot.

In UNIX the required modules are all given together with the **cc** command. For example:

```
cc myprog.c firstmod.c secondmod.o
```

These 3 modules will be linked together. Notice that two of them have the **.c** extension and the last one has **.o**. This is because the final module has previously been compiled to produce the **A.OUT** which has been renamed. The **.o** extension tells the compiler that the module is only waiting to be linked with the others and doesn't need to be compiled.

Execution

This phase is where you run your program, having completed all the previous phases successfully. Unfortunately, this phase also commonly generates a wide variety of error conditions, from producing the wrong output, through sitting there and doing nothing, to crashing your computer. In all cases it's back to checking and editing your source code.

The process described is in practice essentially the same for developing programs in any environment with any compiled high-level language. Once you are experienced in writing and testing C programs successfully, you will find it relatively easy to try another language if you have the inclination.

This whole process of editing, compiling, linking and executing your program is shown in the figure below.

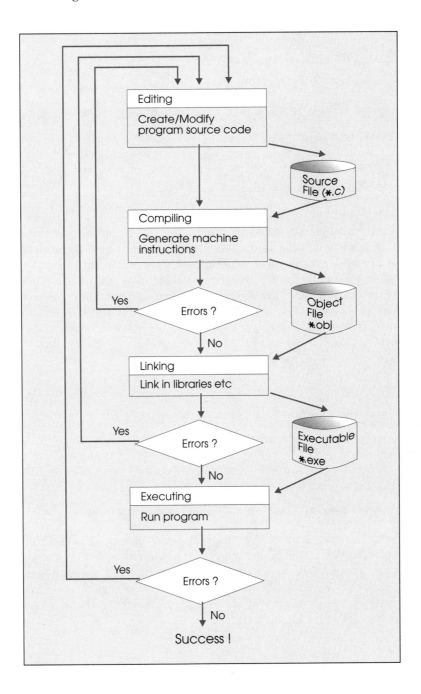

What Do the Program Parts Mean?

Now that you have written your first program let's go through and actually analyze what's going on.

Try It Out - Another C Program

Have a look at this program:

```
/*Example 1.4 Another Simple C Program - Displaying Great Quotes     */

#include <stdio.h>

void main()
{
    printf("Beware the Ides of March!");
}
```

You can probably see similarities with the first program. Can you see what it does without compiling and executing it? Even if you do understand it, type the above code in on your computer and see what happens when you compile and run it. Fingers have a memory of their own which sometimes work when the brain doesn't. And the only real teacher is experience, so we will get you to type in examples as often as possible. If you type it in accurately, compile it and run it, you should get the following output:

```
Beware the Ides of March!
```

How It Works

Let's pick the program to pieces and see what all this means.

Comments

Look at the first line.

```
/* Another Simple C Program - Displaying Great Quotes     */
```

This isn't actually part of the program code, in that it isn't telling the computer to do anything. It's simply a **comment** and it is there to remind you what the program does, so you don't have to wade through the code (and your memory) to remember. Anything between `/*` and `*/` is treated as a comment. Your compiler will simply ignore anything that's a comment and go on to the next real bit of code.

You should try to get into the habit of always documenting your programs using comments as you go along. Your programs will of course work without comments, but when you write longer programs you may not remember what they do or how they work. Put in just enough to ensure that a month from now you, or another programmer, can still understand what the aim of the program was and how it achieved its task.

Comments don't have to be in a line of their own, they just have to be enclosed between /* and */. For example:

```
/* Example 1.4 Another Simple C Program - Displaying Great Quotes    */
#include <stdio.h>          /* This is the first real line of the program */

void main()                             /* This is the main() function */
{
  printf("Beware the Ides of March!"); /* This line displays a great quote */
}
```

Although this is excessive, and probably more confusing than without, you can see that using comments can be a very useful way of explaining in English what is going on.

Pre-Processor Directives

Look at the next line:

```
#include <stdio.h>
```

This is not strictly part of the executable program, but is essential in this case. The symbol # indicates this is a **pre-processor** or **pre-compiler directive**, an instruction to your compiler to do something. There are quite a few compiler directives, and they are usually placed at the beginning of a program's text.

In this case the compiler is instructed to "include" in our program the file **STDIO.H**. This is called a header file because it's usually included at the head of a program. It defines information about functions provided by a standard C library. In this case, as we are using the **printf()** function we have to include the **STDIO.H** file from the library. This is because it contains the information C needs to understand what **printf()** means. We will be using other C library files later in the book.

It is common practice to write the header file names in lower-case in the **include** statement. We will refer to filenames in the text in upper-case for consistency and clarity.

> There is a selection of header files supplied with your compiler and they all have file names with the extension **.H**. They all do certain basic jobs in your program, and to some extent remove programming chores that you may have experienced if you've done any programming in other languages. This particular one contains definitions for the standard input and output functions available. Including this file into our program allows us to use the function **printf()** which occurs a bit lower down in our program.

Defining the main() Function

The next four statements define the function **main()**:

```
void main()
{
        printf("Beware the Ides of March!");
}
```

Every C program consists of one or more functions and every C program must contain a function **main()**. Execution always starts at the beginning of the function **main()**.

```
void main()
```

This defines the start of the function **main()**. Notice that there is *no* semicolon at the end of the line.

Imagine you have created, compiled and linked a file called **PROGNAME.EXE**. When you start your program from the command line by typing **PROGNAME**, it causes your function **main()** to be called by the operating system. (Examples of an operating system are DOS or UNIX.) When execution is finished, when your program has finished running, control goes back to the operating system.

The first line identifying this as the function **main()** has the keyword **void** at the beginning. This defines the type of value to be returned. In this case it signifies that the function **main()** returns nothing to the point from which it was called (the operating system).

There are circumstances when you would want to return something from **main()** to the operating system, an error code for example. In this case a keyword other than **void** would be used. We will see more about this when we come to Chapter 8.

Brackets, Braces and Parentheses

You may have noticed different types of 'brackets' used in the program. The difference is important. We will refer to the symbols ( ) as parentheses, the symbols { } as braces and the symbols [ ] as brackets.

What is the main() Function?

We have talked about the **main()** function and it sounds pretty important, but what exactly is it?

As we mentioned before, every C program must contain a function **main()**. Although a program may consist of more than one function, execution always starts at the beginning of the function **main()**.

The parentheses immediately following **main** enclose a definition of what is to be transferred to **main()** - in our case nothing. The function **main()** can call other functions which in turn may call further functions and so on, all of which may give us a use for the parenthesis. We shall be discussing functions in much more detail in Chapter 8.

Keywords

In C, a keyword is a word with special significance and you must not use these words for other purposes in your program. In our example **void** is a keyword. There are a variety of keywords and we shall accumulate knowledge about them as we go along (see Appendix C).

The Body of the Function

The general structure of the function `main()` is illustrated below.

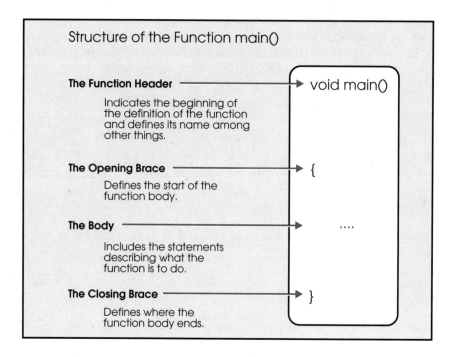

Structure of the Function main()

The Function Header → void main()
Indicates the beginning of
the definition of the function
and defines its name among
other things.

The Opening Brace → {
Defines the start of the
function body.

The Body → ....
Includes the statements
describing what the
function is to do.

The Closing Brace → }
Defines where the
function body ends.

A very simple function body including just one statement is:

```
{
        printf("Beware the Ides of March!");
}
```

The two curly braces, **{** and **}** enclose what is termed the **body** of the function
main(). This is the executable bit which defines what the function actually
does. Every function must have a body, although it can be empty and just
consist of the two brackets, in which case it will achieve nothing.

Empty Bodies

You may wonder what use is a function that does nothing. It can be very
useful when you are developing a program that will have many functions. You
can, initially, leave some of them empty; to be completed when the general
action of your program seems to work - this helps you build your program
piecemeal.

Curly braces are aligned one below the other to make it clear where the block of statements they are defining starts and ends. Statements between curly braces are usually indented by two or three spaces. This is good style, as the statements within a block can be readily identified.

Outputting Information

```
printf("Beware the Ides of March!");
```

The body of our function **main()** only includes one statement, which calls the **printf()** function. As we have said **printf()** is a standard library function, and it outputs information to a display screen based on what is contained between the parentheses immediately following the function name.
In our case it's a simple piece of Shakespearean advice. Notice that this line *does* end with a semi-colon.

Arguments

Items enclosed between the parentheses following a function name are called **arguments.**

If you don't like the quotation we have as an argument, you could display something else by simply including your own choice of words within quotes inside parentheses. For instance, you might prefer a line from Macbeth:

```
printf("Out, damned Spot! out I say!");
```

Try using this in the example, even though it does sound like cruelty to animals.

As with all executable statements (as opposed to defining or directive statements) our **printf()** line must have a semi-colon at the end. As we have seen, a very common error, particularly when you first start programming in C, is forgetting the semi-colon.

Control Characters

If we wanted to display two sentences on different lines, try typing in the following code:

```
/* Example 1.5 Another Simple C Program - Displaying Great Quotes    */

#include <stdio.h>

void main()
{
    printf("\nMy formula for success?\nRise early, work late, strike oil.");
}
```

The output looks like this:

```
My formula for success?
Rise early, work late, strike oil.
```

Look at the **printf()** statement. After the first sentence we have inserted the letters **\n**.

The character immediately following a backslash (\) is interpreted as a control character. In this case it is **n** for newline. There are others. If you wanted to display a backslash itself you simply use two backslashes so, \\. Similarly, if we actually wanted to display quotes we can use \".

For example try typing in the following program:

```
/*Example 1.6 Another Simple C Program - Displaying Great Quotes    */

#include <stdio.h>

void main()
{
  printf("\n\"It is a wise father that knows his own child.\"  Shakespeare");
}
```

The output displays the text:

```
"It is a wise father that knows his own child."  Shakespeare
```

You can use control characters to add a beep to your code to signal something exciting or important. Try typing in the following example:

```
/*Example 1.7 A Simple C Program - Important   */

#include <stdio.h>

void main()
{
    printf("\nBe careful!!\a");
}
```

The output of this program is sound and vision. Listen closely, and you'll hear the beep.

```
Be careful!!
```

The next table shows a summary of control characters.

Control Characters	Action
\n	Starts a newline
\t	Inserts a horizontal
\a	Makes a beep
\"	To display quotes (") on screen
\'	Display single quote (') on screen
\\	To display a backslash (\) on screen
\b	Backspace

Try printing other lines to the screen and alter the spacing in the text, put words on different lines or use \t to tab the text in.

The combination of \ plus another character, is also referred to as an **escape sequence**. We will accumulate knowledge of these as we progress through the book.

Where Do You Start and Where Do You End?

We threw you into that first program without much warning. This isn't a very realistic way of producing a program. Normally you will start with a specification or a plan to do something and then you will go through a series of steps that end with a working program. This is what we did to produce that program, so let's go through that process retrospectively now.

The Process of Writing a Program

Writing programs is an activity like any other. The best way of explaining the process is to use an analogy which is something you are familiar with. Imagine making an omelet and let's compare the process to creating your first program.

```
/*Example 1.1 Your Very First C Program - Displaying Hello*/

#include<stdio.h>

void main()
{
    printf("Hello");
}
```

1   You make yourself an omelet because you are hungry, you want something to eat. You write a program because you want a result. In our first program the result we wanted was to display the word "Hello" on the screen. This, like the omelet, is the output.

2   Next you need to think about what you need to use to get the result. To make an omelet you need eggs, milk, oil, salt, and a frying pan. For the program you need, among other things, keywords (**void**), functions (**main()**), an editor and compiler. The process of making the omelet is to transform these items into a delicious meal. The art of programming is to accurately describe how to successfully transform the input data into output.

3   This leads to the actual design of the process. How do you get from input to output? From eggs and milk to an omelet? This might be:

▶ Put oil in frying pan	Include the C library **STDIO.H**
▶ Whisk the eggs and milk	Call the **main()** function
▶ Add the salt	Let it know that it doesn't return a value (use **void**)
▶ Pour into frying pan	Call the **printf()** function
▶ Leave until cooked	Tell it to display the words "Hello"

4   Now that we know where we are going and how to get there, we can write the program using the design to get the computer to do the task. Computer programs are written in a programming language, in this case using C. In effect the program becomes the recipe for making the omelet. Now that the recipe isn't just in your head, you could pass it to anyone, and whenever you are hungry get them to make your meal for you. Now that's useful!

5   Next we need to prepare the input data. This involves deciding what oil to use, and whether to use full fat or skimmed milk (are we on a diet?). We would also need to make sure the utensils (like the frying pan) are on hand.

6   OK. So you have a recipe. Unfortunately though, this recipe is in English, but your cook is Spanish. You will either have to try to remember your rusty Spanish, or call a friendly neighbor to translate it for you. The same applies to the program. The program is in C but the computer doesn't speak C. That's right, your computer doesn't speak either English or C. For the computer to understand it, it needs to be translated into **machine code** which is the language your computer speaks. This is where compiling comes in. Compiling translates your programs from C into machine code.

7 Once you have it in a form the computer can understand you can actually run it. Running it means stepping through all the processes. You can make that omelet and eat at last. When you run the program you perform all the *doing* processes, so you mix the ingredients, cook them, and of course, devour the omelet.

8 You might think the process ends there, but not a bit of it. Imagine you sit down, finally, to eat your beloved, favorite omelet and horror of horrors it tastes awful. Is it burnt? Does it have too much salt, or not enough eggs?? What can you do? How can you recover?

The simple way is to **debug** your program. Although this term originated from the time a computer wasn't working and an insect (hence bug) was discovered to be the culprit, it now refers to any error in a program. The process of debugging is a powerful way of assessing what went wrong and where.

Functions

The word function, with reference to the **main()** function, has appeared a few times so far in this chapter. We need to explain a little about what this means. Most programming languages, including C, provide a means of breaking a program up into segments which can be written more or less independently of one another. In C these segments are called functions. Each segment, or function, will be designed with a specific interface to other functions in terms of how information is transferred to it, and how results generated by the function are transmitted back from it.

To continue our previous analogy, if we wrote three separate functions, one that makes an omelet, one that makes apple pie and one that makes coffee, we could then use the **main()** function to call all of them (one at a time) and end up with a program that prepares a whole meal. The best thing about it is that when confronted with a tricky task, like making a meal, the easiest thing to do is to break it down into small self-contained pieces and tackle those individually. It makes life much easier and means that if you do run into problems you can quickly locate the problem area without having to check the whole program. This is vital when your programs get bigger. This is called modular programming and is what we were referring to when we talked about modules and source modules earlier.

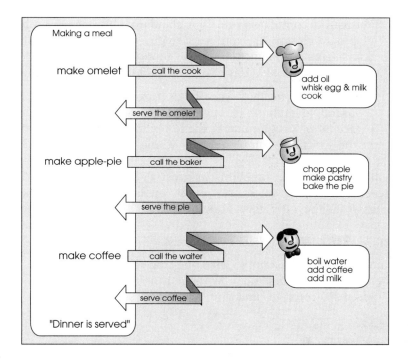

Let's go over the reasons again for designing a language to allow the segmentation of programs in this way.

- Dividing the program into a lot of separate functions allows each piece to be written and tested separately. This greatly simplifies the process of getting the total program to work.

- Several separate functions are easier to handle and to understand than one huge function.

- Libraries are basically just sets of functions that people tend to use all the time. As they have been pre-written and pre-tested you don't have to go to all that trouble. You know they will work and you don't need to bother typing them in. This obviously will accelerate program development and leaves you to just cope with your own code problems. This is a fundamental part of the philosophy of C. The richness of the libraries greatly amplifies the power of the language.

> You can accumulate your own standard libraries applicable to the sort of programs you are concerned with and interested in. If you find yourself using a function all the time (if you are really fond of omelets and eat them every day) you can build this into your own library.

> In the development of very large programs, which can be from a few thousand to millions of lines of code, development can be undertaken by teams of programmers, each team working with a defined sub-group of the functions comprising the whole program.

We will be covering C functions in great detail in Chapter 8. Because the structure of a C program is inherently functional, you have met standard functions from the very first example.

Try It Out - Putting it All Together

Let's now look at an example that puts together what we have learnt. See whether you can understand it without running it and guess what it does. Then type it in, compile, link and run it and see what happens.

```
/* Example 1.8 A longer progarm  */
#include <stdio.h>

void main()

{
    printf("Hi there!\n\n\nThis program is a bit");
    printf(" longer than the others. ");
    printf("\nBut really it's only more text.\n\n\n\a\a");
    printf("Hey, wait a minute!! What was that???\n\n");
    printf("\t1.\tA bird?\n");
    printf("\t2.\tA plane?\n");
    printf("\t3.\tA control character?\n");
    printf("\n\t\t\b\bAnd how will this look when it prints out?\n\n");
}
```

The output will be:

```
Hi there!

This program is a bit longer than the others.
But really it's only more text.
```

Hey, wait a minute!! What was that???

1.   A bird?
2.   A plane?
3.   A control character?

And how will this look when it prints out?

How It Works

The program looks a bit complicated. This is deliberate to help you understand the way the computer views the information you give it. For one thing, it won't put things on a new line unless you categorically tell it to. Let's look at it in detail.

```
#include <stdio.h>
```

We have included the **STDIO.H** file.

```
void main()
```

We then defined the start of the function **main()** and told it not to expect a return value at the end.

```
{
```

This brace tells the computer this is the body of the function.

```
    printf("Hi there!\n\n\nThis program is a bit");
```

This line tells it to print **Hi there!** followed by 2 blank lines and then the words **This program is a bit**.

```
    printf(" longer than the others. ");
```

This code is on a new line but there are no instructions to tell the computer to put it onto a new line so it will simply continue where the last line left off. This means you need to type a space otherwise the computer will display **This program is a bitlonger than the others**, and what is a bitlonger?

```
    printf("\nBut really it's only more text.\n\n\n\a\a");
```

This line starts on a new line, displays the text and then adds 2 new lines and beeps twice.

35

```
printf("Hey, wait a minute!! What was that???\n\n");
```

More text is printed and some new lines.

```
printf("\t1.\tA bird?\n");
printf("\t2.\tA plane?\n");
printf("\t3.\tA control character?\n");
```

These three lines insert a tab, display a number, insert another tab and more text and end with a new line. This is useful for making your output easier to read.

```
printf("\n\t\t\b\bAnd how will this look when it prints out?\n\n");
```

Finally we use a combination to add a new line, two tabs and then backspace twice before displaying the text.

```
}
```

This brace marks the end of the function body. The program doesn't return any value at the end which is why we used **void** with the function **main()**.

Key Points From the Examples

Let's have a quick review of what we have learned so far.

Common Mistakes

As we implied at the beginning of this chapter, programming languages are for human convenience. But since your computer must be able to understand your programs as well, there must obviously be very strict rules governing how the language is used. Leave out a comma where one is expected, or add a semi-colon where you shouldn't and nothing works.

You will be as surprised as we are, at just how easy it is to introduce typographical errors into your program. If you are lucky they will be picked up when you compile or link your program. If you are really unlucky they can result in your program seeming to work fine, but producing some intermittent erratic behavior. You can spend a lot of time trying to determine the appropriate correction.

Other Points to Remember

Let's leave **printf()** options for the moment. They can become rather soporific in too large doses. We will return to them many times throughout this book. It would be a good idea to summarize what we have gleaned from our first program. We can do this by overviewing the important points in the following diagram:

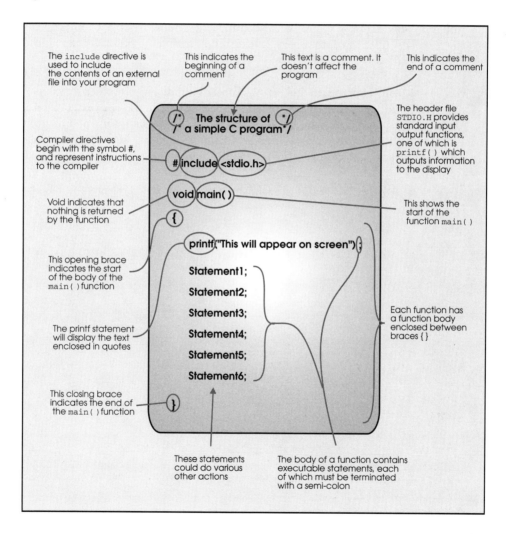

Summary

Well done! You have reached the end of the first chapter and have already written a couple of programs. We have covered a lot of ground. We have tried to give you a sketch map of the land of C. We haven't filled in all the information on the map, we have simply given you an overview. The aim of the chapter was to make you feel comfortable with the C environment. You should be confident about editing, compiling and running your programs. You probably only have a vague idea about how to construct a C program, but don't worry. It is hard to really understand until you have written more complex programs.

Maybe you are starting to get a bit blasé about these simple programs. You may be thinking, "Hey, this is easy. I'm fed up with the `printf()` statement. All it does is repeat what I type". Well, in the next chapter we are going to move on to more complicated things, actually enabling us to manipulate information and get more exciting results.

CHAPTER 2

First Steps In Programming

By now you are probably fed up with using the **printf()** statement and want to start having some interaction with your computer. That is, after all one of the attractions of computers. You don't want to use the program as a glorified typewriter that just displays what you type. For example, suppose we had a program that displayed your salary on the screen. If your salary changed the program would have to be modified, re-compiled and link edited, which could get very tedious.

Ideally, when you ran the program it would ask you to enter your salary before it was displayed. This would make the program much more versatile. Your friends could use it to type in their salaries, or each time you got a rise you could use it to display the even bigger figure on screen. This whole idea of inputting information that varies each time a program is run is key to programming. An item that varies in a program is, surprisingly, called a variable, and this is what we are going to look at in this chapter.

This is quite a long chapter covering a lot of ground, but when you reach the end you will be able to write a really useful program. In this chapter you will:

- Learn about memory and variables

- Look at arithmetic in C (forget school arithmetic, what we're doing is far more exciting)

- Understand conversion and casting

- Understand the different types of variables you can use

- Write a program that calculates the height of a tree

Memory In Your Computer

You may be wondering how the computer deals with the information you type in. To understand this you need to know a little about memory in a computer, so in this chapter, before we go into our first program we will have a quick tour of your computer's memory.

The program of instructions your computer executes, and the data they act upon, have to be kept somewhere while your computer is making its way through them one at a time. The place they are kept at this time is called the machine's memory. It is also referred to as main memory and Random Access Memory (or RAM).

Your PC also contains another kind of memory called Read Only Memory, or ROM. As its name suggests ROM cannot be changed by you, you can only read its contents or have your machine execute instructions contained within it. The information contained in ROM was put there when the machine was manufactured. This information is mainly programs which control the operation of the various devices attached to your PC, such as the display, the hard disk drive, the keyboard, and the floppy disk drive. These programs are called the Basic Input Output System or BIOS for your computer. We won't need to refer to this in detail in this book.

You can think of the memory of your computer as an ordered line of boxes. Each of these boxes is one of two states, either the box is full (let's call this state 1), or the box is empty (this is state 0). Already you see that we are talking binary here (1s and 0s). The computer sometimes thinks of these in terms of **True** and **False**: 1 is True and 0 is False.

> Even though we're talking about memory, if you can't remember about binary, don't worry. It's computer memory we're talking about, not yours. The important point here is that the computer can only deal with 1s and 0s, Trues and Falses. These can be grouped into sets of 1s and 0s (for example, 10010011) but they are made up of the same building blocks.

For convenience we group our boxes in sets of 8. To get to the contents we label each of the groups of 8 boxes with a number, starting from 0 and going up to whatever number of groups of boxes you have. To return to the real world situation, each box is a **bit** and each of these groups of boxes is a **byte** of storage. To summarize we have our building blocks (called bits), in groups of eight (called bytes). A bit can only be either 1 or 0.

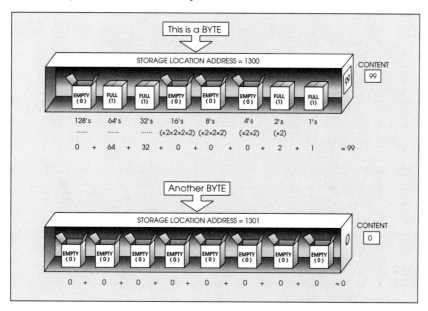

This storage is the computer's memory. But, you may think, how does the computer know where each byte is? The information is there somewhere, but where? There clearly has to be a way for the computer to get at information stored in its memory. The way the computer solves this problem can be compared to the way the post office deal with your mail (only the computer should be a lot more efficient). When you post your letter you don't just abandon it in the mailbox and hope it will arrive safely, you use an address. This means the post office will be able to find where the letter should be delivered without any problems.

Similarly, in your computer each byte of memory has a number which is used to reference it, this is called its address.

Memory is often expressed in terms of so many kilobytes, megabytes, or even gigabytes. But just what do these terms mean? Simple.

- 1 kilobyte (or 1K bytes) is 1024 bytes
- 1 megabyte (or 1M bytes) is 1024 kilobytes which is 1,048,576 bytes
- 1 gigabyte (or 1G bytes) 1024 megabytes which is 1,073,741,841 bytes

Wait a minute, I hear a strangled cry - why all these weird values rather than simply one thousand or one million or one billion? Once again it's very simple. There are 1024 numbers from 0 to 1023, and 1023 happens to be 10 bits in binary - 11 1111 1111, so this is a very convenient binary value. On the other hand, 1000 is a very convenient decimal value, but it tends to be inconvenient in a binary machine. The kilobyte is defined in a manner that's convenient for your computer, rather than for you. Similarly for a megabyte we need 20 bits, and for a gigabyte we need 30 bits.

So without further ado, let's see how we can use this memory in our programs.

What is a Variable?

In the introduction to this chapter we talked about a program that displays your salary. If we assume your salary is $10,000 we can already write that program very easily.

```
/*Example 2.1 What is a Variable */
#include <stdio.h>

void main()
{
    printf("My salary is $10000");
}
```

I am sure you can guess what the output is. It works on exactly the same principle as the programs in Chapter 1. So how can we modify it to allow us to customize the message depending on the input? There are, as ever, several ways of doing this. What they all have in common though, is that they use a variable. This is a place in the computer's memory where it stores the information we type.

In this case you would allocate a piece of memory called **salary** and store the value **10000** in it. When you wanted to display your salary you would use the variable name, **salary**, and the value stored in it (**10000**) would be displayed. Wherever you use the variable name, the computer uses the value stored there, so you can use it several times in one program. Then, when your salary changes you simply change the value stored in **salary** and the whole program updates.

The value each variable contains at any point is determined by the instructions in our program. The value isn't fixed and can change many times as a calculation progresses.

Number Variables

There are a few different kinds of variables, but we'll start off by looking at variables that you can store numbers in. At the end of the chapter we will have a look at storing letters using character variables. However, they are a bit more complicated than numbers, so we'll start with something simple.

Integer Variables

First of all we are going to look at **integer variables**. An integer is any whole number without a decimal point. Examples of integers are:

    1
    10,999,000,000
    -1

Examples of numbers that are *not* integers are:

1.234
99,999,999,999.9
-0.0005

Before we discuss variables in great detail (and believe me, there is a lot of detail!) we'll see a simple variable in action in a program, just so you can get a feel of what they are used for.

Try It Out - Using a Variable

Let's go back to your salary. Have a go at writing the previous program using a variable:

```
/* Example 2.2 Using a variable   */
#include <stdio.h>

void main()
{
    int salary;                     /* Declare a variable called salary */

    salary = 10000;             /* A simple arithmetic assignment statement */

    printf("My salary is %d.", salary);

}
```

Type in the program, compile, link and run it. You will get the following output:

```
My salary is 10000.
```

How It Works

The first three lines are exactly the same as in all our previous programs. Let's look at the new stuff.

```
int salary;              /* Declare a variable called salary */
```

Notice that the variable declaration ends with a semicolon. Miss it off and you will generate an error. This is an easy mistake to make, so be careful.

This is what is known as the **variable declaration.** Here we declare the type of variable we are going to use and then its name. We use the keyword **int** to signify an integer variable since we know for salaries we are unlikely to need anything other than a whole number (hopefully!). The keyword is followed by the name of the variable, in this case, **salary**.

Remember, keywords are special C words that mean something specific to the compiler. You mustn't use them as variable names or your compiler will get confused.

The next statement,

```
salary = 10000;
```

is a simple **arithmetic assignment statement.** It takes the value to the right of the equals sign and stores it in the variable on the left of the equals sign. Here we are declaring that the variable **salary** will have an initial value of **10000**. We are storing the value on the right (**10000**) in the variable on the left (**salary**).

We then have the familiar **printf()** statement, but it is a little different to what we have had before.

```
printf("My salary is %d.", salary);
```

There are now two **arguments** inside the parentheses, separated by a comma. These are:

➤ Firstly, a **control string,** so called because it controls how the output is presented. This is the line inside the quotes which we have used before.

➤ Secondly, the variable `salary` which is new to us.

The control string is fairly similar to our previous example in that it contains some text to be displayed, but if you look carefully you will see a `%d` embedded in it. This is called a **conversion specifier** for our variable. Conversion specifiers determine how variables are displayed on the screen. In this case, we have used a **d** which is a **d**ecimal specifier which applies to integer values (whole numbers). It just means that the integer value you include in your program will be output as a decimal (base 10) number.

Try It Out - Using More Variables

```
/*Example 2.3 more varibles */
#include <stdio.h>

void main()
{
    int brothers;              /* Declare a variable called brothers */
    int brides;               /* and a variable called brides       */

    brothers = 7;          /* Two simple arithmetic assignment statements */
    brides = 7;

    printf("%d brides for %d brothers", brides, brothers);
}
```

If you run this program you should get the following output:

```
7 brides for 7 brothers
```

How It Works

The program works the same way as the previous example.

```
    int brothers;              /* Declare a variable called brothers */
    int brides;               /* and a variable called brides       */
```

We declare two variables, **brides** and **brothers**. These are both type **int**.

Try It Out!

Notice that they have been declared separately, each line ending with a semicolon. Because they are both the same type, we could have saved a line of code and declared them together like this:

```
int brothers, brides;
```

The variables are separated by a comma and the whole line ends with a semicolon.

As long as variables are of the same type you can declare them together on one line, separated by commas and ending with a semicolon.

```
brothers = 7;            /* Two simple arithmetic assignment statements */
brides = 7;
```

Then we initialize them with a value (in this case 7 for each).

```
printf("%d brides for %d brothers", brides, brothers);
```

We have a control string that displays a line of text and replaces the **%d**s with the values stored in the variables that appear after the comma. They are replaced in order, so the value of **brides** goes in the first specifier and the value of **brothers**, in the second. This would be clearer if we changed the variables to **brides = 4**, **brothers = 8** (a rather dubious scenario). The resulting **printf()** statement would know which variable was which and would output:

```
4 brides for 8 brothers
```

Naming Variables

So far we have covered some important things with regard to naming variables. The name we give to a variable, conveniently referred to as a **variable name**, can be defined very flexibly. It is a string of one or more letters and digits beginning with a letter, and where the underscore counts as a letter. Examples of good variable names are:

```
Radius   diameter   Auntie_May   Knotted_Wool   D666
```

It cannot include any other characters and must not start with a digit. So **8_Ball** and **6_pack** are not legal. Neither is **Hash!** or **Mary-Lou**. This last example is a common mistake. **Mary_Lou** would be quite acceptable (remember not to type in any gaps though). Don't use the underscore as the first letter of your variable, as it could clash with a standard system variable in your compiler and create mayhem. For example, **_This** or **_That** is best avoided. Although you can call variables whatever you want (within the above constraints) it is worth calling them something that gives you a clue to what they contain. A variable named **x** that stores your salary may be confusing, far better to call it **salary** and leave no-one in any doubt.

The number of characters permitted in a variable name depends on your compiler. Commonly up to 31 characters are acceptable, so we suggest you don't make your variable names longer than this.

Another thing to remember when naming your variables is that C is case-sensitive which means that capitals and small letters are completely different. Try changing the **printf()** statement so that the variable names sometimes start with capitals.

```
/*Example 2.4  More Variables again */
#include <stdio.h>
void main()
{
    int brothers;                   /* Declare a variable called brothers */
    int brides;                          /* and a variable called brides */

    brothers = 7;           /* Two simple arithmetic assignment statements */
    brides = 7;

    printf("%d brides for %d brothers", Brides, Brothers);
}
```

It won't work and you will get an error when you compile. C thinks the two variables **brides** and **Brides** are different, so it doesn't understand what **Brides** refers to. This is a common error. As we have said before, punctuation and spelling mistakes are one of the main causes of errors, particularly for beginners.

Remember, C is case-sensitive. The variable names **republican** and **Republican** are quite different. Just to repeat again, this kind of spelling mistake is a common cause of errors.

Using Variables

You now know how to name and declare your variables, but this isn't much more useful than what we learnt in Chapter 1. What else can you do? Let's try another program. This time we take the values in the variables and do something other than just print them.

Try It Out - Doing a Simple Calculation

This program does a simple calculation on the variables stored.

```
/*Example 2.5 Simple calculations */
#include <stdio.h>

void main()
{
    int Total_Pets, Cats, Dogs, Ponies, Others;

    Cats = 2;                   /* A simple arithmetic assignment statement   */
    Dogs = 1;
    Ponies = 1;
    Others = 46;
    Total_Pets = Cats + Dogs + Ponies + Others;      /* Another assignment */
    printf("We have %d pets in total", Total_Pets);
}
```

How It Works

As an aside, look at how the statements in the program body are indented. This makes it clear that all these statements belong together. We will discuss layout a little later, but for now try to organize the programs the way we have, indenting blocks together. It makes your programs much easier to read.

For a full understanding of what's going on, let's look at what's happening.

```
int   Total_Pets, Cats, Dogs, Ponies, Others;
```

First we define 5 variables of type **int**. Again, these variables are definitely going to be whole numbers. As you can see, because they are all type **int**, we can declare them all on one line, separated by commas and ending with a semicolon.

```
    Cats = 2;               /* A simple arithmetic assignment statement   */
    Dogs = 1;
    Ponies = 1;
    Others = 46;
```

The variables are given initial values in these four assignment statements. Notice however, that the variable `Total_Pets` doesn't have an initial value. It gets its value as a result of the calculation on the other variables.

```
Total_Pets = Cats + Dogs + Ponies + Others;   /* Another assignment  */
```

In this arithmetic statement we calculate the sum of all our pets on the right of the equals sign by adding the values of each of the variables together. This total value is then stored in the variable on the left of the equals sign, `Total_Pets`. The order of events is important. If `Total_Pets` already had a value (perhaps we initialized it to 25), this value would be overwritten by the calculation on the right.

```
printf("We have %d pets in total", Total_Pets);
```

The `printf()` statement shows the result of the calculation by displaying the value of `Total_Pets` on the screen. Try changing the numbers of the animals, or maybe add some more of your own. Remember to declare them, initialize their value and include them in the `Total_Pets` statement.

Arithmetic Statements

The previous program was the first one that really *did* something. It was fairly simple, just adding a few numbers, but think of the potential. You are now starting to really control your computer and make it do more complicated things. Let's look at some other calculations you can do.

Basic Arithmetic Operations

In the example above we encountered an arithmetic statement for the first time. Hopefully, you shouldn't have had too many problems understanding this, as it just used the basic mathematical symbols. In C, an arithmetic statement is of the form:

```
Variable_Name = Arithmetic Expression;
```

In the example this was:

```
Total_Pets = Cats + Dogs + Ponies + Others;
```

The effect of this statement is to calculate the value of the arithmetic expression to the right of the equals sign, and store that value in the variable specified on the left hand side. In C the = symbol is an active thing. It doesn't balance the two halves as it does in math. What it does is actively send the resulting value of the expression on the right, to the variable on the left. This means you could have:

```
Total_Pets = Total_Pets + 2;
```

This is ridiculous in math but in programming it's fine. Let's look at it in context; imagine we'd rewritten the last part of the program to include the above statement. Here is a fragment of the program as it would appear now:

```
Total_Pets = Cats + Dogs + Ponies + Others;
Total_Pets = Total_Pets + 2;
printf("The total number of pets is: %d", Total_Pets);
```

The value of **Total_Pets** can change depending on what you do to it. By the end of the first line of the fragment, **Total_Pets** stores the value 50. Then in the second line you add 2 to that total. The final total that prints out is therefore 52.

> In arithmetic operations you always work out the right hand side of the = sign and send the result to the variable on the left hand side. This action replaces the value that had been contained in the variable.

Anything that results in a numeric value is known as an **expression.** The following are all expressions:

```
3
1+2
Total_Pets
```

After they have been evaluated they all have a single numeric value. In a moment we'll take a closer look at how an expression is made up, and the rules governing its evaluation. First though, we'll try some simple examples using the basic arithmetic operators we have at our disposal (see list below).

Action	Operator
Addition	+
Subtraction	–
Multiplication	*
Division	/
Modulus	%

These operate as you would expect, with the exception of division, which has a slight aberration from the norm as we shall see. Since we've seen addition already we'll start with subtraction.

Try It Out - Subtraction

Let's get back to programming and look at a greedy program, close to all our stomachs, which demonstrates subtraction:

```
/*Example 2.6 Calculation with cookies */
#include <stdio.h>

void main()
{
    int cookies;
    cookies = 5;


    cookies = cookies - 2;        /* Subtract 2 from the value of cookies  */

    printf("I've eaten 2 cookies.  There are %d cookies left", cookies);

    cookies = cookies - 3;        /* Subtract 3 from the value of cookies */

    printf("\nI've eaten the rest. Now there are %d cookies left", cookies);
}
```

This program produces the following output:

```
I've eaten 2 cookies.  There are 3 cookies left
I've eaten the rest.  Now there are 0 cookies left
```

How It Works

What is happening in this program?

```
int cookies;
cookies = 5;
```

An integer variable, **cookies**, is declared and given an initial value of **5**.

```
cookies = cookies - 2;        /* Subtract 2 from the value of cookies  */
```

The subtraction operator is used to subtract 2 from the value of cookies.

```
printf("I've eaten 2 cookies.  There are %d cookies left", cookies);
```

The **printf()** displays the number of cookies that are left after two have been eaten. Since 5-2 = 3, the result is 3.

```
cookies = cookies - 3;      /* Subtract 3 from the value of cookies */
```

Since the value of cookies is now only 3, when 3 is subtracted 0 are left, which is displayed in the final **printf()**,

```
printf("\nI've eaten the rest. Now there are %d cookies left", cookies);
```

Easy, isn't it? Let's finish our tour of the math you learned in school with a quick look at multiplication and division.

Try It Out - Multiplication and Division

By now you should be feeling more confident about what's going on. Multiplication and division are used in exactly the same way as you would expect. This example is therefore pretty simple but it illustrates an important concept that we have hinted at before.

Suppose we have a jar of 42 cookies and a group of 7 hungry children. We share out the cookies and work out how many each child has. Then we get 2 more cookies for each child and work out how many cookies there are now in total. This program is not that true to life though, because we assume that the children don't actually eat any of the cookies.

```
/*Example 2.7 cookies and kids   */
#include <stdio.h>

void main()
{

    int cookies, children, cookies_per_child;
    cookies = 42;
    children = 7;

    cookies_per_child = cookies / children;     /* No of cookies per child */
    printf("You have %d children and %d cookies\n", children, cookies);
    printf("Give each child %d cookies.", cookies_per_child);

    cookies_per_child = cookies_per_child + 2;  /*  Buy some more cookies  */
    printf("\nThe children want more cookies, so you buy 2 more for each.");
    printf("\nNow each child has %d cookies.", cookies_per_child);

    cookies = cookies_per_child * children;     /* Total no of cookies     */
    printf("\nThere are now %d cookies in total", cookies);

}
```

Try It Out!

When you run the program you will get the output below:

```
You have 7 children and 42 cookies.
Give each child 6 cookies.
The children want more cookies, so you buy 2 more cookies for each.
Now each child has 8 cookies.
There are now 56 cookies in total.
```

How It Works

Let's go through this step-by-step.

```
int cookies, children, cookies_per_child;
cookies = 42;
children = 7;
```

Three integer variables **cookies**, **children** and **cookies_per_child** are declared, and the first two are given initial values of **42** and **7**.

```
cookies_per_child = cookies / children;    /* No of cookies per child */
printf("You have %d children and %d cookies\n", children, cookies);
printf("Give each child %d cookies.", cookies_per_child);
```

The number of cookies is divided by the number of children using the division operator **/**. The result is stored in **cookies_per_child**. You print out a message to say what's happening.

```
cookies_per_child = cookies_per_child + 2;  /*  Buy some more cookies  */
printf("\nThe children want more cookies, so you buy 2 more for each.");
printf("\nNow each child has %d cookies.", cookies_per_child);
```

Now the value of **cookies_per_child** is increased by 2. The number of cookies that each child now has is displayed.

Notice that we are still using the same variable, **cookies_per_child**. A variable only ever stores one value. The original value has been replaced by a new value, which in this case is the old value plus 2. The variable name is the same, it is only the value that has changed. Whenever you use this variable from now on, it will always have this new value (unless of course, you do another calculation and therefore replace it with an even newer value).

```
cookies = cookies_per_child * children;   /* Total number of cookies */
printf("\nThere are now %d cookies in total", cookies);
```

The multiplication operator, *, is used to multiply the new number of cookies by the number of children to find out the new total number of cookies. This new value of **cookies** is then printed out. Here the variable **cookies** has also had a new value stored in it and the old value is lost.

Try It Out - The Modulus Operator

The final operator on our list is the modulus operator %, which is only applicable to integer values. Modulus is simply the amount that's left over after we have divided one number by another. For example, the modulus of 14/3 is 2. (14 divided by 3 is 4, with 2 remainder.)

We'll stick with our theme of cookies and children as it illustrates the modulus operator very well. Let's suppose we have 5 children and we want to divide 10 cookies and 12 apples between them. We don't want to get into a fight over who eats any leftovers.

```
/*Example 2.8 cookies, kids and apples */
#include <stdio.h>
void main()
{

    int cookies, children, apples;
    cookies =  10;
    apples = 12;
    children = 5;

    cookies = cookies % children;     /* Calculate how many cookies remain */
    printf("Distribute the cookies and apples equally between the kids.");
    printf("\nThere are %d cookies left. Great, no squabbling.", cookies);

    apples = apples % children;     /* Calculate how many apples are left */
    printf("\nThere are %d apples left.", apples);
    printf("\nBetter eat them yourself to avoid any trouble.");

}
```

This program produces the output below:

```
Distribute the cookies and apples equally between the children.
There are 0 cookies left. Great, no squabbling.
There are 2 apples left.
Better eat them yourself to avoid any trouble.
```

How It Works

We can go through what's happening.

```
int cookies, children, apples;
cookies =  10;
apples = 12;
children = 5;
```

We declare and initialize our variables.

```
cookies = cookies % children; /* Calculate how many cookies remain */
printf("Distribute the cookies and apples equally between the kids.");
printf("\nThere are %d cookies left. Great, no squabbling.", cookies);
```

The expression **cookies % children** produces just the whole number remaining, when the value in the left variable, **cookies**, is divided by the value in the right variable, **children**. If the division is exact, as it is in this case, the remainder and therefore the result is zero. We print out a suitable message.

```
apples = apples % children;   /* Calculate how many apples are left */
printf("\nThere are %d apples left.", apples);
printf("\nBetter eat them yourself to avoid any trouble.");
```

Then the modulus operator is used again, this time to work out the apple split. Here the remainder is not zero and the program advises you to eat the excess yourself to avoid trouble.

Unary Operators

The operators we have dealt with so far are binary operators. This means they need two parts to be active. For example, you can't multiply a single value, you need two, because you multiply one thing by another. However, there are some operators which are unary, meaning they only need one part or value to operate on. We will see more examples later, but we will just briefly explain the most common one here.

The Unary Minus (-) Operator

The unary minus operator is the most used unary operator. You will find it very useful in more complicated programs. It makes whatever is positive negative, and vice versa. You might not immediately realize when you would use this, but think about double-entry book keeping. You have $200 in the bank. You record what happens to this money in a book with two columns, one for costs that you pay out and one for costs people pay you. One column is your expenditure (negative) and the other is your revenue (positive).

You decide to buy a CD for $50 and a $25 book. If all goes well, when you compare the initial value in the bank and subtract the expenditure ($75) you should end up with what's left. The diagram below shows how these entries could typically be recorded in a double-entry system.

	Income	Expenditure	Bank Balance
Check received	$200		
CD		$50	$150
Book		$25	$125
Closing Balance	**$200**	**$75**	**$125**

If these numbers were stored in variables you could enter both the revenue and expenditure as positive values, and only make the number a negative when you wanted to calculate how much was left. You would do this by simply placing a minus in front of the variable name.

To find out how much you had spent you could write:

```
int expenditure = 75;
printf("Your balance has changed by %d.", (-expenditure));
```

Which would result in:

```
Your balance has changed by -75.
```

The minus will remind you that you have spent this money not gained it!

Division With Integers

Now it's time to look at division with integers. We've left this until the end because it works slightly differently from the way you would expect. When you perform division on integers, you only get a whole number as a result, and any remainder is ignored. The example on the next page will illustrate this point.

```
/*Example 2.9 dividing integer numbers */
#include <stdio.h>

void main()
{
    int x = 10;
    int y = 4;
    int z;

    z = x / y;
    printf("%d divided by %d = %d", x, y, z);
}
```

When you run this program you will get the following output:

```
10 divided by 4 = 2
```

Unless your math is really bad, you will immediately see that this is wrong. To get an accurate result we need to use a different kind of variable, a **floating point variable.** We will come on to these very shortly. First though, you need to learn just a little more about memory.

Types of Variables

So far we've only looked at integer variables without considering how much space they take up in memory. Each time you declare a variable, the computer allocates a space in memory big enough to store that type of variable. The bigger the space allocated, the more memory it takes up. Memory is an important consideration in programming as it is such a valuable part of a computer. As your programs get longer you need to be able to create programs that are efficient with their use of memory.

You saw at the beginning of this chapter how a computer's memory is organized into bytes. So, how many bytes are needed to store our integers? Well, one byte can store an integer value from -127 to +127. This is enough for the variables we've seen so far, but what if we wanted to store a count of the average number of stitches in a pair of knee length socks - one byte wouldn't be anywhere near enough. So a variable not only needs a name when we define it, it also requires us to specify the type of information it will be representing. This is where integer types come into play.

As we describe each type of variable we will show a mini table with the information. The complete table will be repeated at the end.

Types of Integer Variables

Variable	Keyword	Bytes	Values
Integer	int	2 or 4 (depending on your computer)	-32,768 to +32,767 or -2,147,438,648 to 2,147,438,647
Integer	short	2	-32,768 to +32,767
Integer	long	4	-2,147,438,648 to 2,147,438,647

So what do all these mean?

We have already seen integer variable declarations, for example:

```
int cookies, children;
```

This defines two integer variables. However, the length of the variable declared by the keyword **int** can be 2 or 4 bytes depending on what sort of computer you are using. In an IBM compatible PC **int** will usually be 2 bytes, and that's what we will assume throughout this book. You could also use the keyword **short** as an alternative to **int** and get the same 2 byte variables. The previous declaration could have been written:

```
short cookies, children;
```

Why do we have two keywords for the same thing? Well in fact they are not necessarily the same. As we've said above, if you just declare an **int** it could be 2 or 4 bytes. If **int**s are 4 bytes and you really do want to use 2 byte integers, try using the keyword **short**, as **short**s are nearly always 2 bytes. Alternatively, you could write:

```
short int cookies, children;
```

which is exactly the same as the previous statement. (When you write **short**, the **int** is implied.)

If we need integers with a bigger range, to store the number of hamburgers sold by all the MacDonalds in Chicago in one day, for instance, we can use the keyword **long**:

```
long Big_Number;
```

This defines an integer variable with a length of 4 bytes which gives a range from -2,147,438,648 to 2,147,438,647. As with **short**, you can write **long int** if you wish.

Floating Point Variables

Variable Type	Keyword	Bytes	Values
Floating Point	float	4	±1.2E-38 to ±3.4E38 (7 digits)
Floating Point	double	8	±2.2E-308 to ±1.8E308 (19 digits)

If the range provided by 4 byte integers is not enough, we can use **floating point numbers**. Floating point numbers hold values with a decimal point in them. The following are examples:

1.6
0.00008
7655.899

A floating point variable is declared like this:

```
float Radius, Diameter, Length;
double Biggest, Height;
```

Because of the way floating point numbers are represented they only hold a fixed number of decimal digits. If you need to use numbers with up to 7 digits of accuracy (a range of 10^{-38} to 10^{+38}), otherwise known as a **single precision** floating point number, then you should use **float.** This will need 4 bytes for its accommodation in memory. Don't worry if you can't remember exactly what degrees of accuracy you get. We will give you a table of them in a moment.

Using **double** will give us a **double precision** floating point, needing an 8 byte space, and giving 19 digits of accuracy (a range of 10^{-308} to 10^{+308}).

Division With Floats

Let's get back to the division problem. If we rewrite our division program using **float** variables we will get an accurate answer, as the example below illustrates:

Try It Out - Division With Floats

```
/*Example 2.10 division with floats */
#include <stdio.h>

void main()
{
    float x = 10;
    float y = 4;
    float z;

    z = x / y;
    printf("%f divided by %f = %f", x, y, z);
}
```

Which gives this output:

```
10.000000 divided by 4.000000 = 2.500000
```

Great!

How It Works

This program is identical to the integer division program except that we have used a new format specifier for float variables in the **printf()** statement.

```
printf("%f divided by %f = %f", x, y, z);
```

The format specifier **%f** displays the result as a single precision floating point number.

Try experimenting with different variable types and different format specifiers. We have included a table in the summary for you to refer to. You can get some strange results, but this is a valuable lesson. If you write a program that runs perfectly well (or seems to) and does some complicated math, the last thing you want to find is that although it gives an answer it's completely wrong.

As a rule you should only use the floating point types when you need to. If you have to use floating point variables to hold integer values, you must not rely on their values being exact. In floating point, 0.9999999 is as good as 1.0 and in most instances it will make no difference. However, if you round it down to an integer, it isn't one at all, it's zero.

Keeping Math Understandable

Now we all know that arithmetic can get a lot more complicated than just dividing a couple of numbers. In fact if that was all we were trying to do we may as well use paper and pencil. Now that we have the tools of addition, subtraction, multiplication and division at our disposal, we can really start to calculate.

When things get intricate we need to make sure it's clear what's going on.

Parentheses in Arithmetic Expressions

We can use parentheses in arithmetic expressions and they work much as you would expect. Sub-expressions within parentheses are evaluated from the innermost parentheses to the outermost, with the normal rules for operator precedence. Multiplication and division happen before addition or subtraction. Therefore, the expression:

    2*(3+3*(5+4))

comes out as 60. You start with 5+4 which is 9. Then you multiply that by 3 which gives 27. Then you add 3 to that total (giving 30) and multiply the whole lot by 2.

You can also insert spaces to separate operands from operators to make your arithmetic statements more readable. If you're not quite sure of how an expression will be evaluated according to the precedence rules, you can always put in some parentheses to make sure it produces the result you want.

Try It Out - Arithmetic in Action

We can now try another program. We can have a go at calculating the circumference and area of a circle from an input value for the radius. You may remember from elementary math the equations to calculate the area and circumference of a circle using Π or Pi, (circumference = $2\Pi r$ and area = Πr^2).

Try It Out!

61

If you don't, not to worry. This isn't a math book, so just look at how the program works.

```
/*Example 2.11 calculations on a circle */
#include <stdio.h>

void main()
{
    float radius, circumference, area;
    float Pi;

    printf("Input the radius of a circle:");
    scanf("%f", &radius);                   /* Read the radius entered     */
    Pi = 3.14159;
    circumference = 2.0*Pi*radius;          /* Calculate the circumference */
    area = Pi*radius*radius;                /* Calculate the area          */
    printf("\nThe circumference is %f", circumference);
    printf("\nThe area is %f", area);
}
```

How It Works

Up to the first **printf()** the program looks much the same as those we've seen before.

```
    float radius, circumference, area;
    float Pi;
```

The variables are defined in two separate statements for no particular reason. It could have been done in one. Then we have used a new standard function, the **scanf()** function.

```
    scanf("%f", &radius);                   /* Read the radius entered     */
```

scanf() is another function defined in **STDIO.H**, this time for input from the keyboard. In effect it takes what you type in in the form specified between the quotes (in this case **%f**, **float**) and puts it in the variable **radius**. It has two arguments in parentheses, the first being a control string similar to a **printf()** string, except that it controls input rather than output. The second is the variable **radius** where we want the input value to be stored.

You've probably noticed something new here - the **&** preceding the variable name **radius**. This is called the **address of** operator, and it is needed to make the **scanf()** function work. In fact it's not quite as simple as that, but for the moment we won't go into any more detailed explanation on the **address of** operator. If you don't quite understand, just believe it for the moment and we'll see more on this, particularly in Chapter 11. The only thing to remember is to use the **address of** operator (the **&** sign) before a variable when you are using the **scanf()** function, and not to use it when you use the **printf()** function.

If you're really curious about the **address of** operator, it's used to pass the address of the variable **radius** in the memory to the function **scanf()**. This is essential, since **scanf()** is going to store the input value there.

In the case of the **printf()** statements lower down, there is no **&** preceding the variable names, so the value the variable contains is transferred to the function. This makes sense since we want the function to simply output that value - it doesn't need their addresses.

```
Pi = 3.14159;
circumference = 2.0*Pi*radius;     /* Calculate the circumference */
area = Pi*radius*radius;           /* Calculate the area          */
```

The first of these three statements sets the variable **Pi** to its well known value. The second computes the circumference of a circle using the value that was input for the radius, and the third calculates the area.

```
printf("\nThe circumference is %f", circumference);
printf("\nThe area is %f", area);
```

These two **printf()** statements display the results of the calculation by outputting the values of the variables **circumference** and **area** using the format specifier **%f**. As we have seen previously, in both statements the format control string contains text to be displayed, as well as a format specifier for the variable to be output.

If you compile and run this program you should get output as follows:

```
Input the radius of a circle: 5
The circumference is 31.415901
The area is 78.539749
```

Try It Out - What Are You Worth?

We can look at another similar example which is more personal. Remember we talked about your salary right at the start. Let's take that a bit further and see what you're really worth.

```c
/*Example 2.12 Work out your wage */
#include <stdio.h>

void main()
{
    float salary, charge_per_hour, charge_per_second, hours;
    float weeks = 52;

    printf("Enter your annual salary: ");
    scanf("%f", &salary);

    printf("\nEnter the number of hours you usually work per week: ");
    scanf("%f", &hours);

    charge_per_hour = salary / hours / weeks;
    charge_per_second = charge_per_hour / 3600;

    printf("\nYou earn $%.2f.\nThis is $%.2f per hour and $%f per second.",
                        salary, charge_per_hour, charge_per_second);
    printf("\nAsk for a rise tomorrow!");

}
```

By now you probably know what the output from this will be, but can you guess the format of the final variables in the `printf()` statement? Here is the output:

```
Enter your annual salary: 20000
Enter the number of hours you usually work per week: 40
You earn $20000.00.
This is $9.62 per hour and $0.002671 per second.
Ask for a rise tomorrow!
```

How It Works

Look at the different ways of displaying the values. We have 20000.00, 9.62 and 0.002671. Let's look at the program.

```c
    float salary, charge_per_hour, charge_per_second, hours;
    float weeks = 52;
```

Firstly we do the usual declaring of variables. We could have typed 52 into the calculation, but instead we arbitrarily decided to make it a variable.

All the variables are declared as type **float** to enable us to display the hourly rate and rate per second as decimal values. Decimal values are unlikely to be whole integers.

```
printf("Enter your annual salary: ");
scanf("%f", &salary);

printf("\nEnter the number of hours you usually work per week: ");
scanf("%f", &hours);
```

Here we are getting the values we need from the user. They input their salary and it is stored in a variable called **salary** with the address. The user then inputs the number of hours, and that is stored in **hours** with the address.

```
charge_per_hour = salary / hours / weeks;
charge_per_second = charge_per_hour / 3600;
```

This is a simple calculation.

```
printf("\nYou earn $%.2f.\nThis is $%.2f per hour and $%f per second.",
                      salary, charge_per_hour, charge_per_second);
printf("\nAsk for a rise tomorrow!");
```

These final **printf()** statements are the interesting part. They are straightforward except that the conversion specifiers have been split by some numbers - **%.2f**. What this does is tell the computer that you are only interested in the result to 2 decimal places. For the rate per second, we need to leave it as a normal float otherwise we won't get as far as the actual figure, unless of course, you earn an obscene amount that we don't want to know about.

Defining Constants

We have taken the example of calculating the circumference and area of a circle. Although we have defined **Pi** as a variable it is really a constant.

We actually have a couple of choices when handling **Pi**. Pi is a set number - always. Therefore, we can define **Pi** as a symbol which is to be replaced in the program by its value. It isn't a variable at all, but more a sort of alias. Alternatively, we can define it as a variable having a constant value. You can use whichever method you prefer.

Try It Out - Defining a Constant

Let's look at the first alternative, treating **PI** as an alias for its value:

```
/*Example 2.13 More circles */
#include <stdio.h>
#define    PI 3.14159
void main()
{
    float radius, circumference, area;

    printf("Input the radius of a circle:");
    scanf("%f", &radius);
    circumference = 2.0*PI*radius;
    area = PI*radius*radius;
    printf("\nThe circumference is %f", circumference);
    printf("\nThe area is %f", area);
}
```

How It Works

After the comment and the **#include** statement for the header file we have the compiler directive:

```
#define    PI 3.14159
```

We have now defined **PI** by means of a compiler directive. We have used **PI** not **Pi** as it's common convention in C to write identifiers that appear in a **#define** statement in capitals. Wherever we reference **PI** within an expression in the program, the compiler will substitute the value we have specified for it in the **define** directive before compiling the program. When the program is ready to be compiled, it will no longer contain references to **PI**, as all occurrences will have been replaced by the numeric value specified in the **define** directive. This is only in the compiled version, your program will still contain the letters PI.

Try It Out - Defining Constant Variables

We can now try the constant variable approach, and at the same time add another wrinkle to shorten the program:

```
/*Example 2.14 Circles again but shorter*/

#include <stdio.h>

void main()
{
    float radius;
    const float Pi = 3.14159;                /*    Defines Pi as a constant    */

    printf("Input the radius of a circle:");
    scanf("%f", &radius);
    printf("\nThe circumference is %f", 2.0*Pi*radius);
    printf("\nThe area is %f", Pi*radius*radius);
}
```

How It Works

Following the declaration for the variable **radius**, we have the statement:

```
    const float Pi = 3.14159;                /*    Defines Pi as a constant    */
```

Pi is still a variable here, but we have given it an initial value and in this case the value cannot be changed. If you try to change it the compiler will complain. The **const** modifier achieves this effect. It can be applied to any type to fix the value of any variables defined. Therefore, you can have **const** as a modifier for **int**, **long**, **double**, **char**, **short** or **float**.

```
    printf("\nThe circumference is %f", 2.0*Pi*radius);
    printf("\nThe area is %f", Pi*radius*radius);
```

In this example we have also done away with the variables storing the circumference and area of the circle. The expressions for these now appear as arguments in the **printf()** statements where they are evaluated and their values are passed directly to the function.

In general, when passing a value to a function, the value can be the result of evaluating an expression, rather than the value of a particular variable. The compiler will actually create a temporary variable to hold the value which is subsequently discarded. This is fine, as long as we don't want to use these values elsewhere.

Try It Out!

Initializing Variables

We can supply an initial value to any variable when we declare it, even when it's not declared as **const**. In the previous example we could have initialized the **circumference** and **area** variables using the declaration:

```
float circumference = 0, area = 0;
```

Initializing variables as you declare them is a good idea in general. It avoids any doubt about what their initial values are, and if the program doesn't work as it should, it can help track down where the errors reside.

Not having spurious values for variables at the outset can also help avoid crashing your computer when things do go wrong. Until they are assigned a value, uninitialized variables have whatever value happened to be in the memory location concerned when the program was loaded. This will be whatever was left by the previous program or action. From now on we will always initialize variables in our examples, even if just to 0.

> You should always initialize the variables in your program where possible. This avoids leaving spurious values around, and makes it easier to discover what is wrong if your program doesn't work.

Choosing the Correct Type for the Job

In C you have to be careful when doing calculations as to the type of variable that you are using. If you use the wrong type then you may find that errors creep into your programs which can be hard to detect. This is best shown with an example.

Try It Out - The Right Types of Variables

This example is a good example of how things could go horribly wrong if you used the wrong type of variable:

```
/*Example 2.15 Choosing the correct type for the job  1*/
#include <stdio.h>
#define  REV_PER_150 4.5

void main()
{
   int JanSold =23500, FebSold =19300, MarSold =21600; /*Declare Variables */
   int QuarterSold = JanSold +FebSold +MarSold;
   float  RevQuarter =0;
   printf("Stock sold in\n Jan: %d\n Feb: %d\n Mar: %d\n",
                JanSold,FebSold,MarSold);              /*Print monthly sales */
   printf("Total stock sold in first quarter: %d",QuarterSold);

   RevQuarter = QuarterSold / 150 * REV_PER_150;
   printf("\nSales revenue this quarter is:$%f",RevQuarter);
}
```

These are fairly simple figures and you can see that the total stock sold in the quarter should be 64400. This is just the sum of each of the monthly totals, but if you run the program the output you get is:

```
Stock sold in
 Jan: 23500
 Feb: 19300
 Mar: 21600
Total stock sold in first quarter: -1136
Sales revenue this quarter is :$-31.500000
```

Obviously all is not right here. It doesn't take a genius or an accountant to tell you that adding 3 big numbers together shouldn't give a negative!

How It Works - The Problem

Let's consider what is happening in the program.

```
#include <stdio.h>
#define  REV_PER_150 4.5

void main()
```

We use the **include** statement to allow us to use **printf()**. We then define a constant to use when calculating the revenue. We don't actually use this until after the error has happened, so we must look further into the program.

```
int JanSold =23500, FebSold =19300, MarSold =21600;
int QuarterSold = JanSold +FebSold +MarSold;
float  RevQuarter =0;
```

Here we declare our variables and assign initial values to them. The error that has occurred is in the **QuarterSold** variable. We have declared it to be of type **int** and given it the initial value of the sum of the 3 monthly figures. We know that their sum is 64400 and that the program outputs a negative number. The error must therefore be in this assignment statement.

What has happened is that we tried to assign a number that was too large for type **int**. If you remember, the maximum value that an **int** variable can hold is 32,767. The computer cannot interpret the value of **QuarterSold** correctly and so gives a negative result. The solution to our problem is to use a **long** integer which will allow us to use much larger numbers.

Solving the Problem

Try changing the program and run it again. The new improved program is as follows:

```
/*Example 2.16 Choosing the correct type for the job  2*/
#include <stdio.h>
#define  REV_PER_150 4.5

void main()
{
   long JanSold =23500, FebSold =19300, MarSold =21600; /*Declare Variables*/
   long QuarterSold = JanSold +FebSold +MarSold;
   float  RevQuarter =0;
   printf("Stock sold in\n Jan: %ld\n Feb: %ld\n Mar: %ld\n",
                  JanSold,FebSold,MarSold);            /*print monthly sales  */
   printf("Total stock sold in first quarter: %ld",QuarterSold);

   RevQuarter = QuarterSold / 150 * REV_PER_150;
   printf("\nSales revenue this quarter is:$%f",RevQuarter);
}
```

When you run this program the resulting output is much more satisfactory:

```
Stock sold in
 Jan: 23500
 Feb: 19300
 Mar: 21600
Total stock sold in first quarter: 64400
Sales revenue this quarter is :$1930.500000
```

The stock sold in the quarter is correct and we have a reasonable result for revenue. Notice that we used **%ld** to output the result, this is to tell the compiler that it is to use a **long** conversion for the screen output. Just to check the program calculate the result of the revenue with a calculator.

The result you should get is in fact $1932.00. Somewhere we have lost a dollar and a half, not such a great amount, but try saying that to an accountant! Consider what's happening when we calculate the value for revenue in the program.

```
RevQuarter = QuarterSold / 150 * REV_PER_150;
```

Here we are assigning a value to **RevQuarter**. The value is the result of the expression on the right of the = sign. The compiler will calculate the result piece by piece according to the precedence rules you have already come across in this chapter. Here we have quite a simple expression which is calculated from left to right as division and multiplication have the same priority. Lets work this out:

QuarterSold/150 is calculated as 64400/150 which is: 429.333

This is where our problem occurs. **QuarterSold** is an integer and so the computer truncates the number, ignoring the .333. This means that when the next part of the calculation is evaluated the result will be short.

429 * REV_PER_150 is calculated as 429 * 4.5 which is: 1930.5

This is $1.5 short of what it should be. We now know where the error has occurred, but what can we do about it? We could change all of our variables to floating point types, but that would defeat the object of using integers in the first place. The numbers entered really are integers so we would like to store them as such.. Is there an easy solution to this? The answer is yes. In C you have the ability to calculate the result of an operation using any type of variable available to you. This is called **casting**.

Type Casting in Arithmetic Expressions

Let's look at the expression to calculate the quarterly revenue.

```
RevQuarter = QuarterSold / 150 * REV_PER_150;
```

We know that this has to be amended so that the expression is calculated in floating point form. To do this we place the type of the cast that we want in parentheses before the expression as:

```
RevQuarter = (float) QuarterSold / 150 * REV_PER_150;
```

We could even do this with our previous error when we had to use **long** integers. We do still need the **QuarterSold** to be a **long** integer, but we could leave the monthly variables as normal integers and cast the first of them in the expression where we sum them to **long**. We shall do this in the third version of our program below:

```
/*Example 2.17 Choosing the correct type for the job  3*/
#include <stdio.h>
#define  REV_PER_150 4.5

void main()
{
   int JanSold =23500, FebSold =19300, MarSold =21600; /*Declare Variables */
   long QuarterSold =0;
   float  RevQuarter =0;
   QuarterSold = (long) JanSold +FebSold +MarSold;

   printf("Stock sold in\n Jan: %d\n Feb: %d\n Mar: %d\n",
               JanSold,FebSold,MarSold);         /*Print monthly sales */
   printf("Total stock sold in first quarter: %ld",QuarterSold);

   RevQuarter = (float)QuarterSold / 150 * REV_PER_150;
   printf("\nSales revenue this quarter is:$%f",RevQuarter);
}
```

The output from this new improved program is:

```
Stock sold in
 Jan: 23500
 Feb: 19300
 Mar: 21600
Total stock sold in first quarter: 64400
Sales revenue this quarter is :$1932.000000
```

This is exactly what we require. We are using the right type of variables in the right place, and when we need to calculate expressions using bigger variables, then we have cast them into the right type.

Automatic Casting

Look at the result of the second version of the program again.

```
Sales revenue this quarter is :$1930.500000
```

Even without the explicit cast statement in the expression the result in the output was in floating point form already, even though it was still wrong. This is because the compiler automatically casts the variables when it is working with different types. Working with each pair it automatically casts to the "highest" type. So, referring back to the expression to calculate revenue:

QuarterSold / 150 * Rev_per_150

This was evaluated as:

64400 (**int**) / 150 (**int**) which equals 429 (**int**)
Then 429 (**int** cast to **float**) is multiplied by 4.5 (**float**) giving 1930.5 (**float**)

As we explained, casting works in pairs. The first pair of numbers evaluated are both **int**s, so the result is an **int**. The second pair are an **int** and a **float**. The **int** is therefore automatically cast to the highest, a **float**. Whenever there is a mixture of variable types in one arithmetic expression C will use certain rules to convert some of them to enable the expression to be evaluated

Conversion Rules

An arithmetic operation involving two values can only be performed if the values are of the same type. For each operation in an expression involving two different types, your compiler will promote the variable with the 'lower' type to be the same type as the other variable. The order of types in this context is **double** highest, then **float**, followed by **long**, **int**, and finally the lowest **char**.

Let's look at this in practice. If we declare three variables, **A** as **double** and **B** and **C** as **long**, we can see how the following expression is worked out.

```
A + B - C
```

Here, we first evaluate **A + B**. **A** is **double** and **B** is **long**, so **B** will be cast to **double** and the result will be **double**. To subtract **C** from this result, **C** is first cast to **double** and we end up with the final result as **double**.

Casts in Assignment Statements

You can also cause an implicit cast by assigning the value of a variable of one type to another. This can cause values to be changed. For instance, if you assign a **float** or **double** value to an **int** or a **long**, the fractional part of the **float** or **double** will be lost and just the integer part will be stored.

For example, after executing the following code fragment:

```
int number;
float decimal = 2.5f;
number = decimal;
```

the value of **number** will be 2. Because you have assigned the value of **decimal** (2.5) to an **int** variable, **number**, the .5 at the end will be lost and only the 2 will be stored. Notice how we've used a specifier **f** at the end of **2.5**. This indicates to the compiler that this variable is a single precision floating point variable. Any constant you define with a decimal point is floating point and will default to double precision floating point. If you don't want it to be double precision you need to append the **f**.

More Numeric Data Types

To complete the set, we should now examine the remaining numeric data types we haven't discussed.

The Character Type

Variable Type	Keyword	Bytes	Values
Character	char	1	-128 to +127 or 0 to 255 (unsigned)

A **char** variable can hold any single character, for example:

'P'
'p'
'C'
'?'

It can be any lower or uppercase letter, and it doesn't have to be alphanumeric. An example of a **char** variable declaration statement is:

```
char letter, first = 'A', last = 'Z';
```

Letter isn't initialized, the other two variables are. Note the way in which the initializing character value is enclosed within single quotes not double quotes. You may be wondering why we are including this as a numeric data type when it holds letters? Well, we'll show you a little more about how a **char** variable works below, and then you'll see that its quite logical as **char** can actually hold numeric values too.

An example of a **char** variable holding a numeric value is:

```
char character = 74;
```

A **char** value can have any numeric value from -128 to +127 since it occupies a single byte. It has a sort of dual personality, sometimes a character, and sometimes an integer.

A **char** variable can also be declared as **unsigned**, for example:

```
unsigned char letter;
```

In this case it can store values from 0 to 255.

Try It Out - Character Building

If you're wondering how on earth the computer knows whether it's dealing with a character or an integer, let's look at an example which should make it clear. Here you will meet the conversion specifier again, which tells the computer whether to output a character or an integer.

```
/*Example 2.18 Characters and numbers  */
#include <stdio.h>

void main()
{
    char first_example;
    char second_example;

    first_example = 'T';
    second_example = 20;

    printf("The first example as a letter looks like this - %c",
                                            first_example);
```

```
    printf("\nThe first example as a number looks like this - %d",
                                            first_example);
    printf("\nThe second example as a letter looks like this - %c",
                                            second_example);
    printf("\nThe second example as a number looks like this - %d",
                                            second_example);

}
```

The output from this program is shown following and needs some explanation.

```
The first example as a letter looks like this - T
The first example as a number looks like this - 84
The second example as a letter looks like this - ¶
The second example as a number looks like this - 20
```

How It Works

The program starts off in the usual way.

```
char first_example;
char second_example;

first_example = 'T';
second_example = 20;
```

We declare two variables of type **char**. Then we initialize them, one to a letter, one to a number.

```
printf("The first example as a letter looks like this - %c",
                                            first_example);
printf("\nThe first example as a number looks like this - %d",
                                            first_example);
printf("\nThe second example as a letter looks like this - %c",
                                            second_example);
printf("\nThe second example as a number looks like this - %d",
                                            second_example);
```

These four **printf()** statements are where the changes happen. They show how when you use an integer conversion specifier you get a different result to when you use the character conversion specifier. The numeric value is the ASCII   value.

> Not all computers use the ASCII character set, so you may get different values than those show above. If you do, don't worry, the reason C uses the notation 'character' is to get around this problem. So 'A' represents a capital A, no matter which system the program is compiled on, or the actual number it is internally stored as.

ASCII stands for American Standard Code for Information Interchange and is pronounced as-key, with a soft s. Have a look at Appendix B for the ASCII table if you are not familiar with it.

Try using different numbers and letters in the program. See what results you get.

Try It Out - Using char

We can now look at another example of how **char** might be used in practice:

```
/*Example 2.19 Using char  */
#include <stdio.h>

void main()
{
    char first = 'A', second = 'B', last = 'Z';
    char number = 40;
    char ex1, ex2, ex3;

    ex1 = first + 2;        /* Add 2 to 'A'        */
    ex2 = second - 1;       /* Subtract 1 from 'B' */
    ex3 = last +2;          /* Add 2 to 'Z'        */

    printf("Character values      %c  %c  %c", ex1, ex2, ex3);
    printf("\nNumerical equivalents %d %d %d", ex1, ex2, ex3);
    printf("\nThe number %d is the same as the character %c", number,
                                                        number);
}
```

If you run the program you should get the following output:

```
Character values      C  A  \
Numerical equivalents 67 65 92
Number 40 is the same as the character (
```

How It Works

This program shows the equivalence between numbers and ASCII characters and also demonstrates how we can happily perform arithmetic with **char** variables initialized with a character. The first statement in the body of **main()** is:

```
char first = 'A', second = 'B', last = 'Z';
```

This initializes the variables **first**, **second**, and **last**, to the character values you see. The numerical value of these variables will be the ASCII codes of the respective characters. Because we can treat them as numeric, as well as characters, we can perform arithmetic operations with them.

```
char number = 40;
```

We could equally well initialize a **char** variable with an integer value.

Of course, the initializing value must be within the range that a one byte variable can represent. The value 40 is the decimal value of the ASCII code for a left parenthesis.

```
ex1 = first + 2;        /* Add 2 to 'A'       */
ex2 = second - 1;       /* Subtract 1 from 'B' */
ex3 = last +2;          /* Add 2 to 'Z'       */
```

These statements create new values, and therefore new characters from the variables **first**, **second** and **last**, and store the results in the variables **ex1**, **ex2**, and **ex3**.

```
printf("Character values        %c  %c  %c", ex1, ex2, ex3);
printf("\nNumerical equivalents %d %d %d", ex1, ex2, ex3);
printf("\nThe number %d is the same as the character %c", number,
                                                        number);
```

We are using the **printf()** to do something slightly different here.

We have a new conversion specifier **%c** for characters. All three values in the first **printf()** are output according to the specifier **%c** as single characters. The second **printf()** outputs the same variables using the integer specifier **%d**, so the decimal numerical equivalents are displayed. The last **printf()** outputs the same variable twice, but with different format specifiers. In order to output the same variable twice, we simply put it in the argument list twice, and provide a suitable format specifier in the control string for each instance.

This ability to perform arithmetic with characters can be very useful. For instance, to convert from upper case to lower case you simply add the result of `'a'-'A'` (which is 32 for ASCII) to the upper case character, and to achieve the reverse subtract `'a'-'A'`. You can see that this works if you have a look at the decimal values of the alphabetic characters in Appendix B.

Unsigned Integers - Using Big Positive Integers

If you are sure you're dealing with just positive integers there is a way of maximizing the range of values you can use. The **unsigned** modifier can be used with the basic integer types we have covered and allows us to handle integers roughly twice as large as we otherwise might. It is used as follows:

```
unsigned char a_value;        /* Can be from 0 to +255        */
unsigned int number;          /* Can be from 0 to +65,535     */
unsigned long big_number;     /* Can be from 0 to 4,294,967,295 */
```

You have to be sure you only need positive values to use these. They cannot assume negative values.

We have now covered all the numeric data types in C, so here's the complete table we promised you:

Variable Type	Keyword	Bytes	Values
Character	char	1	-128 to +127 or 0 to 255
Unsigned Character	unsigned char	1	0 to 255
Integer	int	2 or 4	-32,768 to +32,767 or -2,147,438,648 to 2,147,438,647
Unsigned Integer	unsigned int	2 or 4	0 to 65,535 or 0 to 4,294,967,295
Integer	short	2	-32,768 to +32,767
Unsigned Integer	unsigned short	2	0 to 65,535
Integer	long	4	-2,147,438,648 to 2,147,438,647
Unsigned Integer	unsigned long	4	0 to 4,294,967,295
Floating Point	float	4	$\pm1.2E\text{-}38$ to $\pm3.4E38$ (7 digits)
Floating Point	double	8	$\pm2.2E\text{-}308$ to $\pm1.8E308$ (19 digits)

Using the op= Form of Assignment

Sometimes C provides you with shortcuts. Here we are going to discuss one such shortcut. Actually, this is only a shortcut in that it saves us having to do some typing. Let's consider the following line of code:

```
a_very_long_variable_name_that_we_might_type_wrong =
    a_very_long_variable_name_that_we_might_type_wrong + 10;
```

Obviously, if we had made a typing error, then at best we would get a compiler error, at worst a wrong answer that could take days to track down. But as we have said, C provides a shortcut for us. So consider the following line:

```
a_very_long_variable_name_that_we_might_type_wrong += 10;
```

The important bit is the **+=** symbol after the variable name. This has exactly the same effect as the original and it saves a bit of typing. It is one of a family of operators that can be expressed as the **op=** family where **op** can be any of the arithmetic operators:

```
+,  -,  *,  /,  %.
```

It can also be a few others which we haven't covered yet. These are:

```
<<,  >> &,  ^,  |
```

However, we will defer discussion of these to Chapter 3. The **op=** set of operators always work in the same way. If we have:

```
lhs op= rhs;
```

the effect is the same as:

```
lhs = lhs op rhs;
```

So just to reinforce our understanding of this, we can rewrite the following statement more concisely:

```
Another_variable *= 12;
```

is the same as:

```
Another_variable = Another_variable * 12;
```

We now have two different ways of incrementing an integer variable by 1. The following statements all achieve the same result.

```
Count = Count +1;
Count += 1;
```

We will learn about yet another way in the next chapter. This amazing level of choice tends to make it virtually impossible for indecisive individuals to write programs in C.

In the same way the statement:

```
a /= b+1;
```

is the same as:

```
a = a/(b+1);
```

This applies to all the operators. As the right hand side can always be an expression the general format is:

```
lhs op= rhs;
```

expanding to:

```
lhs = lhs op ( rhs );
```

Our computational facilities have been rather constrained so far. We have only been able to use a very basic set of arithmetic operators. We can get more power to our calculating elbow using standard library facilities. These are the functions included in the header files (remember **STDIO.H** that appears at the top of each program and enables us to use the **printf()** statement among others?). For the moment though we'll stick with what we've got. Rest assured, we will come to the others later.

Designing a Program

Now it's time for our end of chapter real-life example. It would be a good idea to try out some of our numeric types in a new program. We will take you through the whole process as if you were writing a program from scratch. This covers getting the problem, analyzing it, preparing a solution, writing the program, and of course, running it. This teaches you the real art of programming, beyond just the theory.

The Problem

The height of trees is very interesting to many people. If a tree is being cut down, knowing its height tells you how far away *safe* is. Our problem is to find out the height of a tree. For this you will need the aid of a friend, preferably a short friend. The tree you are measuring needs to be taller than both of you.

The Analysis

Let's start by naming the tall person (you) Lofty and the shorter person (your friend) Shorty. So that you can get an idea of what we are trying to do in this program, consider the following diagram.

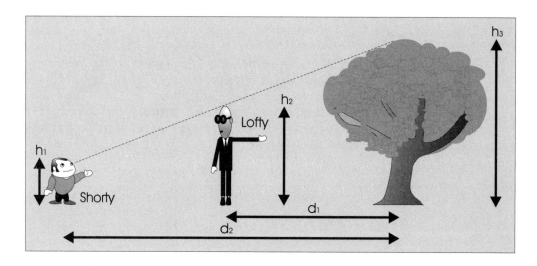

Finding the height of the tree is actually quite simple. We can use similar triangles to work out the height. This is because the ratio of the distance to the height of the two triangles is the same. For example, suppose the first (smaller) triangle has a distance1 of 2m and a height1 of 4m. The ratio between them is 1:2. If distance2 (the larger triangle) was 3m then height2 will be 6m (twice height1).

This means that we need to enter four values, the distance between Shorty and Lofty, and between Shorty and the tree. We then need the height of Lofty, and the height of Shorty, but only up to the eyes.

So our first task is to get these values into the computer. We then have to use our ratios to find out the height of the tree, and finally output the answer. So the steps are:

1 Input the values we need.

2 Use similar triangles to work out the height of the tree.

3 Display the answer.

The Solution

1 So, our first step is to get the values that we need to work out the height of the tree. This means that we have to include the **STDIO.H** header file as we need to use both **printf()** and **scanf()**. We then have to decide what variables we need to store these values in, then we use **printf()** to ask the questions and **scanf()** to get the values.

We'll first get Lofty's height as whole feet and then inches, prompting for each as we go along. We'll then convert this into just inches, as this makes Lofty's height easier to work with. We'll do the same thing for Shorty's height (but only up to their eyes), and finally the same for the distance between them. For the distance to the tree, we'll only use whole feet as this will be a bigger number, which again we'll convert to inches. So here goes with the first part of the program as shown on the next page.

83

```
/*Example 2.20  Calculating the height of trees*/
#include <stdio.h>

void main()
{
   long shorty, lofty, feet, inches, lofty_dist, tree_dist;

   printf("Enter Lofty's height, feet first: ");
   scanf("%ld", &feet);
   printf("                ...and then inches: ");
   scanf("%ld", &inches);
   lofty = feet * 12 + inches;

   printf("Enter Shorty's height up to their eyes, feet first: ");
   scanf("%ld", &feet);
   printf("                          ... and then inches: ");
   scanf("%ld", &inches);
   shorty = feet * 12 + inches;

   printf("Now enter the distance between Shorty and Lofty, feet first: ");
   scanf("%ld", &feet);
   printf("                          ... and then inches: ");
   scanf("%ld", &inches);
   lofty_dist = feet * 12 + inches;

   printf("Finally enter the distance to the tree to the nearest foot: ");
   scanf("%ld", &feet);
   tree_dist = feet * 12;
}
```

Notice how we have spaced the program to make it easier to read. You don't have to do it this way, it just means that if you decide to change the program next year, you can see by how it is laid out how the program works. Comments are also a good idea to help with this. However, you may have noticed a lack of comments in the program above. The reason for this is that comments don't always make the program any easier to read, and sometimes can make it more difficult. The program above is such a case. The text in the **printf()** statements adequately explain what is going to happen, so a comment would just clutter the program.

2   Now that we have all the data we need, lets calculate the height of the tree. As we have already said, this is done using ratios. The ratio of the difference in height between Lofty and Shorty and the distance between them is the same as the ratio of the difference in height between the tree and Shorty and the distance between them. In other words, for our two triangles;

height1 / distance1 = height2 / distance2

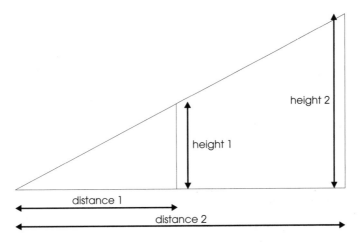

Therefore, height2 = height1 * distance2 / distance1

In code, this looks like:

```
#include <stdio.h>

void main()
{
    long shorty, lofty, feet, inches, lofty_dist, tree_dist;
    long tree;

    printf("Enter Lofty's height, feet first: ");
    scanf("%ld", &feet);
    printf("                ...and then inches: ");
    scanf("%ld", &inches);
    lofty = feet * 12 + inches;

    printf("Enter Shorty's height up to their eyes, feet first: ");
    scanf("%ld", &feet);
    printf("                        ... and then inches: ");
    scanf("%ld", &inches);
    shorty = feet * 12 + inches;

    printf("Now enter the distance between Shorty and Lofty, feet first: ");
    scanf("%ld", &feet);
    printf("                            ... and then inches: ");
    scanf("%ld", &inches);
    lofty_dist = feet * 12 + inches;

    printf("Finally enter the distance to the tree to the nearest foot: ");
    scanf("%ld", &feet);
    tree_dist = feet * 12;

    tree = (lofty - shorty) * tree_dist / lofty_dist;
    tree += shorty;
}
```

Notice the order we work out the tree height in. It is important that we multiply by the distance to the tree first, otherwise we could end up with the wrong answer. Why? Well consider the circumstance of it **tree_dist / lofty_dist** is less than 1, i.e. if **tree_dist** is 1 and **lofty_dist** equals 2, then 1 / 2 = 0.5. In this case, as we are using integers, you can't have 0.5, instead it becomes 0, and the tree height also becomes zero! When you are working with integers you should always keep things like this in mind. If you get an unexpected answer, then check the order of your calculations before anything else.

3   Finally, we need to print the answer. To do this we'll convert **tree** which is in inches back into feet and inches:

```
#include <stdio.h>

void main()
{
    long shorty, lofty, feet, inches, lofty_dist, tree_dist;
    long tree;

    printf("Enter Lofty's height, feet first: ");
    scanf("%ld", &feet);
    printf("              ...and then inches: ");
    scanf("%ld", &inches);
    lofty = feet * 12 + inches;

    printf("Enter Shorty's height up to their eyes, feet first: ");
    scanf("%ld", &feet);
    printf("                        ... and then inches: ");
    scanf("%ld", &inches);
    shorty = feet * 12 + inches;

    printf("Now enter the distance between Shorty and Lofty, feet first: ");
    scanf("%ld", &feet);
    printf("                        ... and then inches: ");
    scanf("%ld", &inches);
    lofty_dist = feet * 12 + inches;

    printf("Finally enter the distance to the tree to the nearest foot: ");
    scanf("%ld", &feet);
    tree_dist = feet * 12;

    tree = (lofty - shorty) * tree_dist / lofty_dist;
    tree += shorty;

    printf("The height of the tree is %ld feet and %ld inches.", tree / 12,
                                                       tree % 12);
}
```

And there we have it. The output from the program looks something like this:

```
Enter Lofty's height, feet first: 6
            ...and then inches: 2
Enter Shorty's height up to their eyes, feet first: 5
                    ... and then inches: 10
Now enter the distance between Shorty and Lofty, feet first: 3
                        ... and then inches: 2
Finally enter the distance to the tree to the nearest foot: 30
The height of the tree is 8 feet and 11 inches.
```

Summary

This chapter has covered a huge amount of ground. It was pretty tough, but to write good programs you need to understand the fundamentals. You won't remember it all but you can always look back over it if you need it. Armed with this knowledge we can really make use of the power of C.

By now, you know how a C program is structured and you should be fairly comfortable with any kind of arithmetic calculation. You should also be able to choose variable types to suit the job in hand. Aside from arithmetic we have added quite a bit of input and output capability to our knowledge. You are now at ease with inputting values into variables via **scanf()**. You can output text messages, and character and numeric variables to the screen.

As a final summary let's recap the variable types and the format specifiers we have used so far. You can look back at the next page to remind yourself as we continue through the book. Not bad for the first two chapters, is it? In the next chapter we shall start looking at how we can control the program by making decisions depending on the values we enter. As you can probably imagine this is key to creating interesting and professional programs.

Variable Type	Keyword	Bytes	Values
Character	char	1	-128 to +127
Unsigned Character	unsigned char	1	0 to 255
Integer	int	2 or 4	-32,768 to +32,767 or -2,147,438,648 to 2,147,438,647
Unsigned Integer	unsigned int	2 or 4	0 to 65,535 or 0 to 4,294,967,295
Integer	short	2	-32,768 to +32,767
Unsigned Integer	unsigned short	2	0 to 65,535
Integer	long	4	-2,147,438,648 to 2,147,438,647
Unsigned Integer	unsigned long	4	0 to 4,294,967,295
Floating Point	float	4	±1.2E-38 to ±3.4E38 (7 digits)
Floating Point	double	8	±2.2E-308 to ±1.8E308 (19 digits)

Format Specifier	Purpose
%c	character value
%d	signed decimal integer
%Ld	long signed decimal integer
%u	unsigned decimal integer
%f	single precision floating point number

CHAPTER
3

Making Decisions

By the end of Chapter 2 we were really starting to do interesting things. In this chapter we will take a great leap forward in the range of programs we can write and the flexibility we can build into them. We will add one of the most powerful programming tools, the ability to compare variables with other variables and constants, and based on the outcome, choose to execute one set of statements or another.

What this means is we will be able to control the flow of the program more. Up until now, once you have set your program running you can't actually control what is happening. You simply type in information and the computer displays a result. In this chapter we will change all that.

In this chapter you will:

   ◗ Make decisions based on arithmetic comparisons

   ◗ Use logical operators

   ◗ Understand more about reading characters from the keyboard

   ◗ Write a program that can be used as a calculator

The Decision-Making Process

We will start with the essentials of decision-making in a program. Decision making in a program is concerned with choosing to execute one set of program statements rather than another. In everyday life you do this kind of thing all the time. Each time you wake up you have to decide whether it's a good idea to go to work. You may go through these questions:

> Do I feel well?   If the answer is no, stay in bed.
> If the answer is yes, go to work.

You could rewrite this as:

> If I feel well I will go to work.
> Otherwise I will stay in bed.

That was a straightforward decision. Later, as you are having breakfast you notice it's raining, so you think:

If it's raining as hard as it did yesterday I will take the bus. If it's raining harder than yesterday I will drive to work. Otherwise, I will risk it and walk.

This is more complex. It's a decision based on comparing the value of the rain, and can have any of three different results.

As the day goes on you are presented with more of these decisions. Without them you would be stuck with only one course of action. Until now in this book you have had exactly this problem with your programs. All the programs will run a straight course, without making any decisions, to a defined end. This is a severe constraint, and one that we will relieve now. First let's set up some basic building blocks of knowledge to enable us to do this.

Arithmetic Comparisons

In order to make a decision, we need a mechanism for comparing things. This involves some new operators. Since we are dealing with numbers, comparing numerical values is basic to decision making. We have three fundamental operators:

```
<     is less than
==    is equal to
>     is greater than
```

The "equal to" operator has *two* successive equal signs. You will almost certainly use one equals sign on occasions by mistake. This will cause considerable confusion until you spot the problem. Look at the difference. If you type `my_weight = your_weight` it is an assignment that puts the value from the variable `your_weight` into the variable `my_weight`. If you type the expression `my_weight == your_weight` you are comparing the two values. You are asking *whether* they are exactly the same, not telling them to *be* the same.

Logical Expressions

Have a look at these examples:

```
5 < 4      1 == 2      5 > 4
```

These expressions are called logical expressions and each of them can result in just one of two values, **True** or **False**. The value **True** is represented by 1, or more generally any positive integer, and **False** is represented by 0. The first expression is **False** since 5 is patently not less than 4. The second expression is also **False** since 1 is not equal to 2. The third expression is **True** since 5 is greater than 4.

The Basic if Statement

Now we have some logical operators, we need a statement allowing us to make a decision. The simplest available to us is the **if** statement. If we wanted to compare our weights and print a different sentence depending on the result we could write the body of a program as:

```
if ( your_weight > my_weight)
 printf("You are fatter than me.\n");

if (your_weight < my_weight)
printf("I am fatter than you.\n");

if (your_weight == my_weight)
printf("We are exactly the same weight.\n");
```

The general form or **syntax** of the **if** statement is as follows:

```
if (expression)

    Statement1;

Next_statement;
```

Notice that the question part (the **if**) is enclosed in parentheses and doesn't have a semicolon at the end. The second line could be written following straight on from the first, but for clarity people tend to put it on a new line. That's why there is no need for a semicolon after the expression. Your compiler carries on reading to the end of the first statement - the end of the line. The second and last lines both end with a semicolon.

The **expression** in parentheses can be any expression giving a result **True** or **False**. If the expression has the value **True**, then **Statement1** is executed after which the program continues with **Next_statement**. If the expression is **False** then **Statement1** is skipped and execution continues immediately with **Next_statement**. This is illustrated in the following figure.

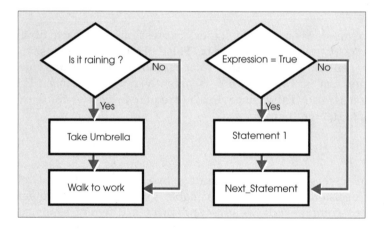

We could have used the basic **if** statement to add some rude comments in our program at the end of the previous chapter, which calculated the height of a tree. For example, we could have added the following code just after we have read in the height of the shortest person:

```
scanf(" %u", &Shorty_eye_ht);            /* Reads input for the variable */

if (Shorty_eye_ht < 36U )
   printf("\nMy, you really are on the short side, aren't you.");
......
```

Here we have used the **if** statement just to add a gratuitously offensive remark, should the input value be less than 36 inches.

Try It Out - Checking Conditions

Let's see the **if** in action. This program gets the user to enter a number between 1 and 10 and then tells them how big that number is.

```
/* Example 3.1 A simple example of the if statement*/
/*Example 3.1 Using an if */
#include <stdio.h>

void main()
{

  int number;
  printf("\nEnter a number between 1 and 10: ");
  scanf("%d",&number);

  if (number > 5)
    printf("You entered %d which is greater than 5", number);

  if (number < 6)
    printf("You entered %d which is less than 6", number);
}
```

Sample output from this program would be:

```
Enter a number between 1 and 10: 7
You entered 7 which is greater than 5
```

or

```
Enter a number between 1 and 10: 3
You entered 3 which is less than 6
```

How It Works

```
/* Example 3.1 A simple example of the if statement*/
#include <stdio.h>

void main()
{
```

As usual we include a comment to remind us what the program does. We include the **STDIO.H** header file to allow us to use the **printf()** statement. We then have the beginning of the **main()** function of the program. The function doesn't return a value so we add **void**. You're used to this part by now so we'll stop repeating it unless it changes.

93

```
int number;
printf("\nEnter a number between 1 and 10: \n");
scanf("%d",&number);
```

We declare an integer variable called **number** and then prompt the user to enter a number between 1 and 10. This number is then stored in the variable **number**.

```
if (number > 5)
   printf("You entered %d which is greater than 5", number);
```

We compare the value in **number** with the value 5. If **number** is greater than 5 then we print the next statement and go to the next part of the program. If it isn't, the **printf()** is simply skipped. We have used the **%d** conversion specifier to repeat the number the user typed in.

```
if (number < 6)
   printf("You entered %d which is less than 6", number);
}
```

Finally, we compare the value entered with 6 and if it is smaller we print the next statement. Otherwise, the **printf()** is skipped and the program ends. In all cases one or other of the lines will be printed as the number will always be less than 6 or greater than 5.

The advantage is that you can start to be selective about what input you accept and what you finally do with it. For instance, if you have a variable and you want to have its value specifically limited at some point, even though higher values may arise somehow in the program, you could write:

```
if( X > 90)
   X = 90;
```

This would mean that if anyone entered a value of x that was larger than 90 your program would automatically change it to 90. This would be invaluable if you had a program that could only specifically deal with values within a range. You could also check whether a value was higher than a given number, and if not set it to that number. In this way you could be sure the value was within the given range.

You could also use this sort of statement in the above program to detect when the user enters a value that is too high. You are asking the user to enter a number between 1 and 10 so you could add another **if** statement:

```
if( number > 10)
    printf("Your number is too big. Sorry.")
```

This would display a message if the value is too high.

Extending the if Statement - if else

The **if** statement can be extended with a small addition which gives us a lot more flexibility. Imagine it rained a little yesterday. We could write:

If the rain today is worse than the rain yesterday I will take my umbrella

Else I will take my jacket

Then I will go to work

The syntax of the **if else** statement is:

```
if (expression)
    Statement1;
else
    Statement2;
Next_statement;
```

Notice the use of parentheses and the position of the semicolons. Notice that the **else** is on its own and doesn't need an expression. This is because anything that doesn't fall into the first if will go into the else. With two **if**s even if your answer falls into the first **if**, it will still be checked by the second **if**. With an **if else**, however, it is an *either or* situation.

This works as before except that if the expression is **False**, we execute **Statement2** before executing **Next_statement**. The process would be either **Statement1** (if the expression is **True**) and then **Next_statement**, or **Statement2** (if the expression is **False**) and then **Next_statement**.

The sequence of operations involved here is shown in the next figure.

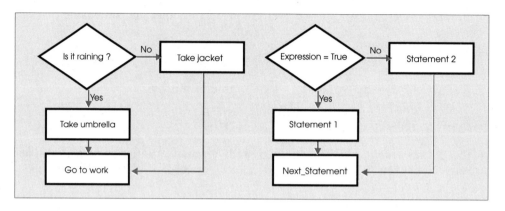

Try It Out - Using if to Analyze Numbers

We can now use our **if else** in a simple example. We can let the user enter a number and then check to see whether the number they input is odd or even. We know that all even numbers are divisible by 2 with no remainder. This means we can do this by using the modulus operator to produce the remainder after division by 2. If the result is zero, we have an even number.

```c
/* Example 3.2 Using ifs to analyze numbers            */
#include <stdio.h>

void main()
{
  long Test = 0;             /* long integer Test will have initial value 0 */

  printf("Enter an integer less than two million:");   /* Message to screen */
  scanf(" %ld", &Test);
  if ( Test % 2L == 0)                /* Check remainder against zero */
      printf("\nThe number %ld is even", Test);     /* Result is even */
  else
      printf("\nThe number %ld is odd", Test);      /* Result is odd */
}
```

Typical output from this program would be:

```
Enter an integer less than two million: 242424
The number 242424 is even


Enter an integer less than two million: 242425
The number 242425 is odd
```

How It Works

Let's look at what's going on here:

```
long Test = 0;               /* long integer Test will have initial value 0 */
```

The first bit of the program is the same as before. Inside **main()** we then declare a long variable called **Test** and initialize it to 0.

```
printf("Enter an integer less than two million:");    /* Message to screen */
    scanf(" %ld", &Test);
```

The user inputs a number and it is stored in the variable. Notice that we have used **%ld** as the specifier for reading in the value to be tested. This ensures the compiler reads it as a **long** integer.

```
    if ( Test % 2L == 0)                /* Check remainder against zero */
        printf("\nThe number %ld is even", Test);    /* Result is even */
    else
        printf("\nThe number %ld is odd", Test);    /* Result is odd */
```

This is the part we are really interested in. What is going on in the **if** expression? The logic of the expression **Test %2L == 0** is to divide the number entered by the user (stored in **Test**) by 2 and give us the remainder (this is the action of the modulus operator, **%**). The L is there to specify that it is a long integer. Notice that we are using two equals signs. Try it with one equals sign and you get an error.

Remember, you use == when you are asking *whether* two variables are exactly the same. You use = when you are telling them to *be* the same.

An even number will have no remainder and so the expression will be true. So, if the number is even then the first statement is executed and it prints the appropriate message. If it isn't even the statement after the **else** is carried out. It then prints a different, but appropriate, message. Without the **else** statement option, we would have had to use two **if** statements, one to test for even, the other to test for odd. This is what we did in the previous program. We have also made sure that the constant numbers we used (the 2L from the modulus operation **Test % 2L**) are long integers by appending **L** to the end of the number. The compiler does convert the arguments used as discussed in the rules of **casting** in Chapter 2, but by appending the letter L for **long,** we leave you in no doubt as to what is happening in our program.

Try running this with just **%d** to see the effect. It is a good pointer to a potential source of error. You will be storing the input as a short integer, but using it as though it were a long value. As you will see it produces some interesting values. For example if you input 45645, the output produced was:

```
Enter an integer less than two billion: 45645
The number -19891 is odd
```

Using Blocks of Code in if Statements

We can also replace **Statement1**, **Statement2**, or even both by a block of statements enclosed between braces {}. This means we can give many instructions to the computer after making one check of the expression simply by placing them together between braces.

This could be represented in a real life situation as below:

If the weather is sunny
I will walk to the park, eat a picnic and walk home

else
I will stay in, watch football and drink beer

The syntax for this is as follows:

```
if (expression)
{
    StatementA1;
    StatementA2;
    ...
}
else
{
    StatementB1;
    StatementB2;
    ...
}
```

Nested ifs

It is also possible to have **if**s within **if**s. For example:

if the weather is good I will sit in the garden
    and if it's cool enough I will sit in the sun
    else I will sit in the shade
else I will stay indoors
I will then drink some lemonade.

This corresponds to:

```
if (expression1)
    StatementA;
    if (expression2)
        StatementB;
    else
        StatementC;
else
    StatementD;
Statement E;
```

Here the second **if** is only checked if the first **if** is true. This is demonstrated in the following figure:

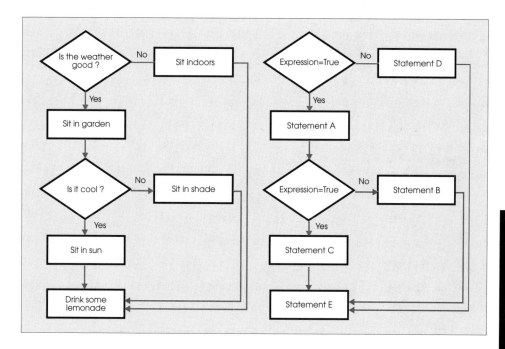

Try It Out - Analyzing Numbers Some More

We can now exercise our **if** skills with a couple more examples. Let's take our previous example a bit further. The program tests to see whether you enter an odd or even number. We could extend that and, if the number is even, test to see whether half that number is even also.

Try It Out!

```
/* Example 3.3 Using ifs to analyze numbers further - nesting      */
#include <stdio.h>

void main()
{
   long Test = 0;

   printf("Enter an integer less than two billion:");
   scanf(" %ld", &Test);
   if ( Test % 2L == 0)              /* Check remainder against zero   */
   {
       printf("\nThe number %ld is even", Test);
       if ( (Test/2L) % 2L == 0)
       {
           printf("\nHalf of %ld is also even", Test);
           printf("\nThat's interesting isn't it?");
       }
   }
   else
       printf("\nThe number %ld is odd", Test);
}
```

The output could look something like this:

```
Enter an integer less than two billion: 20
The number 20 is even
Half of 20 is also even
That's interesting isn't it?
```

Or

```
Enter an integer less than two billion: 9
The number 9 is odd
```

How It Works

This is only marginally more complicated than the previous example. Let's look at the new bits.

```
if ( Test % 2L == 0)              /* Check remainder against zero   */
{
   printf("\nThe number %ld is even", Test);
   if ( (Test/2L) % 2L == 0)
   {
       printf("\nHalf of %ld is also even", Test);
       printf("\nThat's interesting isn't it?");
   }
}
else
   printf("\nThe number %ld is odd", Test);
```

Here we have a block of two statements executed if the value entered is even. The first statement is the same as in the previous program, the second is another **if**. This prints a second comment if half the value entered is also even. This is called a nested **if**.

Notice that the first statement is an **if else**, whereas the nested **if** is a plain **if**. This is fine, but it means that if the number is even but half of that number is odd, you only display:

```
Enter an integer less than two billion: 10
The number  is even
```

Try adding a line to make the second **if** an **if else** that prints "Half of %d is odd". The answer comes just before the next heading.

> You can nest ifs anywhere inside another if, but it is not to be recommended as a technique to be applied extensively if it can be avoided. Your program is likely to end up being very hard to follow. There are a couple of extra parentheses in the nested ifs expression (Test/2L). They are not strictly necessary, but it helps to make it clear what is going on. Making programs easier to follow is the essence of good programming style.

The answer to the above question would be to insert:

```
else
    printf ("\nHalf %ld is odd") ;
```

after the second **if**'s closing brace.

Some Additional Comparison Operators

We can now add a few more numerical comparison operators that we can use in **if** statements. Three additional ones make up the set:

>   >=   is greater than or equal to
>   <=   is less than or equal to
>   !=   is not equal to

These are fairly self-explanatory, but let's consider some examples anyway starting with some arithmetic examples:

```
6 >= 5      5 <= 5      4 <= 5      4 != 5      10 != 10
```

These are all **True** except the last one which is **False**, since 10 most definitely *is* equal to 10. These also can be applied to characters, as well. If you remember, character types also have a numeric value associated with them. The ASCII table in appendix B gives a full listing of all the standard characters and their numeric equivalents. Just to remind you for the next few examples, the table below is an extract from Appendix B.

ASCII Character	Hexadecimal Number	Decimal Number
A	41	65
B	42	66
P	50	80
Q	51	81
Z	5A	90
b	62	98

A **char** value may be expressed either as an integer between -128 and 127 or as a keyboard character between quotes, such as 'A'. Here are a few examples:

```
'Z' >= 'A'      'Q' <= 'P'      'B' <= 'b'      'B' != 0x42
```

With the ASCII values of the characters in mind, the first is **True**, 'Z' (0x5A) comes after 'A' (0x41), the second is **False**, 'Q' does not come before 'P'. The third is **True**. This is because in ASCII code lower-case letters are 32 higher than their upper-case equivalents. The last is **False**. The value 0x42 *is* the ASCII hexadecimal representation of the character 'B'.

By looking at the numerical equivalents of the characters you will be able to see this result more clearly. For example, the value of `'A'` is 65 decimal and the value of `'Z'` is 90, so `'Z'` is clearly greater than `'A'`. The value of `'Q'` is one less than `'P'`. The last expression is **False** because 0x42 (the prefixed 0x tells us this is a hexadecimal number) is equivalent to `'B'`. We can use this information to write a program that will convert a capital letter to a lower case one.

Try It Out - Converting Upper-Case to Lower-Case

We are now going to prove to you that you can use the ASCII values of letters to good effect. Here we have a practical example, converting capitals to small letters.

```
/* Example 3.4 Converting upper-case to lower-case */
#include <stdio.h>

void main()
{
   char letter;

   printf("\nEnter an upper-case letter:");
   scanf("%c", &letter);
   /*we will check the input with a nested if */

   if (letter >= 'A')
     if (letter <= 'Z')
     {
     letter = letter + 'a'-'A';
     printf("\nYou entered an upper-case %c", letter);
     }
     else
       printf("\nTry using the shift key, Bud! I want a capital letter.");
}
```

Sample output from this program might be:

```
Enter an upper-case letter:G
You entered an upper-case g
```

or

```
Enter an upper-case letter:s
Try using the shift key, Bud! I want a capital letter.
```

How It Works

```
char letter;

   printf("\nEnter an upper-case letter.");
   scanf("%c", &letter);
```

First we declare a **char** variable called **letter**. We get the user to input a capital letter and store the value of what they type in.

103

```
if (letter >= 'A')
```

Here we have a simple **if** statement. It checks that the letter is greater or equal to 'A'. This verifies that the value is at least the value of 'A', or higher. If the answer is true we continue. If not the program simply skips this part and, since there is no code to execute after it, the program ends.

```
if (letter <= 'Z')
    . . .
else
printf("\nTry using the shift key, Bud! I want a capital letter.");
```

Assuming the value is at least 'A', we continue with the nested **if**. Here we begin by checking that the input is less than or equal to 'Z' to make sure the input is between 'A' and 'Z'. We need to guarantee that we have the right input before we start doing calculations. If the answer is true we continue. If it is false it goes straight to the **else** statement and prints our message.

```
if (letter <= 'Z')
{
    letter = letter + 'a'-'A';
    printf("\nYou entered an upper-case %c", letter);
}
```

If the letter is upper-case then we are happy with the input and we can convert it to lower-case. What we are doing here is taking an upper-case letter, then adding the value of a lowercase a, and then subtracting the value of an uppercase A. This converts the letter into its lower-case equivalent value. Remember, the compiler doesn't really understand what B or C are, it only understands them in terms of their ASCII (or other system) value. Since this is a number, we can increase it to display a different character. In this case adding **'a'-'A'** jumps up the character table to the upper-case characters.

We used a nested **if** statement to check for two conditions in the above example, but as you can imagine this could get very confusing when you have many criteria that you wish to check for. However, C has thought of this and allows us to use logical operators to simplify the situation.

Logical Operations

Sometimes it just isn't enough to do a single test for a decision. You may want to combine two or more checks on values, and if they are all true perform a certain action. Or you may want to perform a calculation if one or more of a set of conditions are True.

For example, you may only want to go to work if you are feeling well *and* it's a weekday. Just because you feel great doesn't mean you want to go in on a Saturday. Alternatively, you could say you will stay at home if you feel ill *or* if it's a weekend. These are exactly the sort of circumstances for which the logical operators were intended.

The AND Operator &&

We can look first at the logical AND operator, **&&**, which is a **binary operator**. A binary operator means that it is working with 2 pieces of data. The arithmetic operators are binary operators as they add and also subtract one thing from another; they are using 2 things to work upon. The expression:

```
Test1 && Test2
```

has the value **True** if both expressions **Test1** and **Test2** are **True**. If either one is **False** the overall result is **False**. Let's take an example:

```
if ( age > 12 && age < 20 )
   printf("You are officially a teenager.");
```

The **printf()** statement will only be executed if **age** has a value between 13 and 19. Naturally, you can use more than one of these logical operators in an expression:

```
if ( age > 12 && age < 20 && savings > 5000 )
   printf("You are a rich teenager.");
```

All three condition checks must be **True** for the **printf()** to be executed.

The OR Operator ||

The situation where you want to check for any one of two or more conditions being **True** is covered by the logical OR operator, ||. An example of using this operator is:

```
if ( A < 10 || B > C || C > 50 )
    printf("At least one of the conditions is True.");
```

The `printf()` will only be executed if *at least* one of the three conditions is **True**.

We can also use the logical operators in combination as in the following code fragment:

```
if ( ( age > 12 && age <20 ) || savings > 5000 )
    printf ("Either you're a teenager, or you're rich, or possibly both.");
```

The `printf()` statement will be executed if the value of **age** is between 12 and 20, or the value of **savings** is greater than 5000, or both. As you can see when you start to use more operators things can get confusing.

The NOT Operator !

Last but not least is the logical NOT operator, represented by !. Suppose we have two variables **a** and **b** with the values 5 and 2 respectively then the expression **a >b** is True. If we use our logical NOT operator, the expression **!(a>b)** is False. Thus the logical NOT operator reverses the value of a logical expression, True becomes False, and False becomes True. We recommend that you avoid using this operator as far as possible. It tends to result in code that becomes difficult to follow. As an illustration we can rewrite the previous example as:

```
if ( ( ! (age >= 12) && !( age >= 20)) || ! (savings <= 5000) )
    printf("\nYou're either not a teenager and rich ");
    printf("or not rich and a teenager,\n");
    printf("or neither not a teenager nor not rich.");
```

As you can see it becomes incredibly difficult to unravel the nots.

Try It Out - A Better Way to Convert Letters

You will remember that earlier in this chapter we had a program to enter an upper-case character. We used a nested **if** to ensure that the input was of the correct type and then the small letter equivalent, or we printed a remark when the user didn't.

We can now see that all this was completely unnecessary because we could do it this way:

```
/*    Example 3.5    Testing letters the easy way          */
#include <stdio.h>
void main()
{
   char Letter =0;

   printf("\nEnter an upper case letter");
   scanf(" %c", &Letter);

  if ((Letter >='A') && (Letter <= 'Z'))
    {
    Letter = Letter + 'a'-'A';
    printf("\nYou entered an upper-case %c.", Letter);
    }
  else
    printf("\nTry using the shift key, Bud! I want a capital letter.");
}
```

How It Works

The output is exactly the same as for the original program, but compare the two programs and you will see how much neater this is. This is the original version:

```
if (letter >= 'A')
    if (letter <= 'Z')
```

This is the new version:

```
if ((Letter >= 'A') && (letter <= 'Z'))
```

Rather than having confusing nested **if** statements, here we have checked that the character entered is greater than 'A' *and* less than 'Z' in one statement. Notice that we have put extra parentheses around the two expressions to be checked. They aren't really needed in this case, but they don't hurt and leave you or any other programmers in no doubt as to the order of execution.

The Conditional Operator

There is another way you can check data. The way this works is to raise a question (is it sunny?) and follow with two alternative courses of action depending on whether the answer is yes or no (go to the beach: stay at home). This would look like this:

Is it sunny? If yes, then go to the beach. If not, then stay at home.

This type of operator is called the **ternary operator** or **conditional operator**. This sounds as though it has some relationship with an aquatic bird, perhaps reminiscent of the old, rather cruel saying "leave no tern unstoned". It has nothing to do with this. It is sometimes called the ternary operator because it involves three arguments simultaneously. It is also strongly related to the **if** statement. Its general representation looks like:

```
condition ? result1 : result2;
```

Notice the use of punctuation. There is a question mark after the question - the condition. The two possible results are separated by a colon and the whole statement ends with a semicolon. This produces the value **result1** if **condition** has the value **True**, and **result2** if **condition** produces the value **False**. We can use this in a statement such as:

```
x = condition? result1: result 2;
```

Executing this statement will result in **x** having the value **result1** if **condition** is **True**, or the value **result2** otherwise. This is therefore a nice shorthand way of writing:

```
if( condition )
    x = result1;
else
    x = result2;
```

This enables you to express some things very economically. An expression for the minimum of two variables can be written very simply using the conditional operator. We could go back to our short example that determines whether you or I earn the most. We could now write:

```
YourSalary > MySalary ? YourSalary: MySalary
```

Try It Out - Using the Conditional Operator

This would translate into this short example:

```c
/* Example 3.6 Biggest salary  */
#include <stdio.h>

void main()
{
    int MySalary=0 , YourSalary=0;
    int most_money;

    printf("\nEnter your salary: ");
    scanf("%d", &YourSalary);

    printf("Enter my salary: ");
    scanf("%d", &MySalary);

    most_money = ( MySalary > YourSalary ? MySalary : YourSalary );
    printf ("\nThe person that earns the most earns $%d",most_money);
}
```

Typical output from the program would be:

```
Enter your salary: 10000
Enter my salary: 15000

The person that earns the most earns $15000
```

Similarly, the expression to calculate which is the lowest salary:

```
YourSalary < MySalary ? YourSalary : MySalary
```

You could also calculate it using the expression:

```
YourSalary > MySalary ? MySalary : YourSalary
```

Try It Out!

109

In spite of its odd appearance, you will see this operator crop up quite frequently in C programs. A very handy application that you will see in examples in this book, is to vary the contents of a message or prompt depending on the value of an expression. For example, if you wanted to prompt for input with the message:

```
Enter a value:
```

Then on subsequent occasions you wanted to display the prompt:

```
Enter another value:
```

Assuming you were counting the number of values entered using a variable **i**, you could use one statement to produce both messages:

```
printf("Enter a%s value: ", i > 1 ? "nother" : "" );
```

This will append the string "nother" after "a" in the message when **i** is greater than 1 (when the user has had more than one try). You can use this mechanism to vary an output message depending on the value of an expression in many different ways, for using "she" instead of "he", "wrong" instead of "right", and so on. We will see this in action later in the chapter.

Operator Precedence - Who Goes First?

With all the parentheses in some of the previous examples in this chapter, it is a good time to come back to operator precedence. This is the sequence in which operators in an expression are executed. We have **&&** and **==** and **!=** and **||**. When we have more than one, how do we know which ones are used first?

For example, suppose we are to process job applications, and we want to only accept applicants who are 25 or older, and have graduated from Harvard or Yale. The age condition we can represent by the conditional expression:

```
Age >= 25
```

and we can represent graduation by variables **Yale** and **Harvard** which may be **True** or **False**. Now we can write the condition as:

```
Age >= 25 && Harvard || Yale
```

Unfortunately, this will result in howls of protest since we will now accept Yale graduates who are under 25. In fact we accept Yale graduates of any age. Because of operator precedence, this expression is effectively:

```
( Age >= 25 && Harvard ) || Yale
```

So we take anybody at all from Yale. I'm sure those wearing a Y front sweat shirt will claim this is as it should be, but what we really meant was:

```
Age >= 25 && ( Harvard || Yale )
```

Let's have a look at a table that shows the order of precedence.

Operator (in order of precedence)	Associativity (the direction in which it works)
()	left to right
! ++ -- unary+ unary-	right to left
* / %	left to right
binary+ binary-	left to right
< <= > >=	left to right
== !=	left to right
&&	left to right
||	left to right
?: (ternary operator)	left to right
= op= (e.g. +=)	right to left

The operators we have seen up to now are shown here with the highest precedence operators (that is those to be executed first) at the top. Naturally, parentheses come at the very top since they are used to override the natural priorities defined. Operators at the same level are executed as shown in the right hand column.

As you can see, all the comparison operators are below the binary arithmetic operators, and the binary logical operators are below the comparison operators. As a result, arithmetic is done first, then comparisons, then logical combinations. Assignments come last in this list so they are only performed once everything else has been completed. The ternary operator squeezes in just above assignment operators.

Note that the ! operator is highest, apart from parentheses. As a result, the parentheses around the comparisons can be essential.

Try It Out - Using Logical Operators Without Confusion

Look at the following example. We want a program that will take applicant interviews for a large pharmaceutical corporation. The program should offer interviews to applicants who meet certain educational specifications (can you guess where the company's Chief Executive studied?).

```c
/* Example 3.7 Confused recruiting policy  */
#include <stdio.h>

void main()
{
  int age;
  int college, subject ;
  int interview=0;
  printf("\nWhat college? 1 for Harvard, 2 for Yale, 3 for other: ");
  scanf("%d",&college);
  printf("\nWhat subject? 1 for Chemistry, 2 for economics, 3 for other: ");
  scanf("%d", &subject);
  printf("\nHow old is the applicant? ");
  scanf("%d",&age);

  if ((age>25 && subject==1) && (college==3 || college==1)) interview =1;
  if (college==2 &&subject ==1) interview =1;
  if (college==1 && subject==2 && !(age>28)) interview =1;
  if (college==2 && (subject==2 || subject==3) && age>25) interview =1;

  if (interview) printf ("\n\nGive 'em an interview");
  else printf ("\n\nReject 'em");
}
```

Output from this program may be something like:

```
What college? 1 for Harvard, 2 for Yale, 3 for other: 2
What subject? 1 for Chemistry, 2 for Economics, 3 for other: 1
How old is the applicant? 24

Give 'em an interview
```

How It Works

The program works in a fairly straightforward way. The problem comes with the number of operators.

```
if ((age>25 && subject==1) && (college==3 || college==1)) interview =1;
if (college==2 &&subject ==1) interview =1;
if (college==1 && subject==2 && !(age>28)) interview =1;
if (college==2 && (subject==2 || subject==3) && age>25) interview =1;
```

As you can see we have quite a lot of testing of &&s and ||s (ands and ors) in the program which makes it fairly complicated to read. The use of the parentheses helps us along though, and without them we would have no idea and would probably end up taking on entirely the wrong person. The actual recruiting policy used to produce the program is:

1) Graduates over 25 who did chemistry and who are not from Yale
2) Graduates from Yale who did chemistry.
3) Graduates from Harvard who did economics and are not older than 28.
4) Graduates from Yale who are over 25 who didn't do chemistry.

```
if (interview) printf ("\n\nGive 'em an interview");
  else printf ("\n\nReject 'em");
```

The final **if** statement tells us whether to invite the applicant for an interview or not and uses the variable **interview**. This is initialized to zero, but if any of the criteria are met then we assigned the value 1 to it. The test **if (interview)** evaluates to false when **interview** is 0 and true when **interview** has any non-zero value.

> Rather than spend hours with your family and friends doing memory tests on the precedence table, you can just use parentheses as we have done here. They are always right since they override the precedence order anyway, and if they aren't always strictly necessary, well, they make the code that much clearer, don't they?

Multiple Choice Questions

You may be wondering how we handle the situation where you have to check a lot of different conditions. It would be very tiresome to write pages and pages of **if** statements. Well, there is a simple solution provided in the form of the **switch** statement.

The switch Statement

This last condition of testing statements, the **switch** statement, is possibly the most fun to use. While maybe not typical in programming, it is analogous to picking a winner in a horse race, or any other race for that matter. You have a fixed number of choices, and some condition which allows you to make a selection. For betting on a horse, the most common selection mechanism is a pin, but in C we have to be a little more precise.

Imagine there were 3 horses numbered 1, 2 and 3 in a race. Number 3 wins and number 2 comes second. We could use the **switch** statement as follows:

```
switch (YourChoice)
{
   case 3: printf("Congratulations! You win!");
   break;
   case 2: printf("Almost won. Better luck next time.");
   break;
   default: printf("Too bad, you lose.");
}
```

This is just a fragment of a program to get the feel for using **switch**. If we were using the above example, you type in the number of the horse you think will win. That value is stored in **YourChoice**. Then you go to the **switch** statement and if **YourChoice** matches one of the cases (in this case 3 or 2) you get the appropriate message, and the **break** jumps out of the **switch**. Otherwise, you simply get the default message. For any number of horses in the race you could leave the above code exactly as it is. Anything other than 3 or 2 will always result in the default.

The general way of describing the **switch** statement is:

```
switch (integer_expression)
{
   case constant_expression_1:    statements_1;
   break;
   ....
   case constant_expression_n:    statements_n;
   break;
   default:    statements
}
```

The test is based on the value of **integer_expression**. If that corresponds to one of the case values defined by the associated **constant_expression_n**, then the statements related to that **case** value are executed. If the value of **integer_expression** differs from all of the **case** values, then the statements following **default** are executed. You can leave out **default** and its associated statements. If none of the **case** values match then nothing happens. Notice that all of the **case** values for the associated **constant_expression** must be different. If they aren't and you try to compile it you will get an error message. The **break** jumps to the statement after the closing brace.

Notice the punctuation and formatting. There is no semicolon at the end of the first **switch** expression. The body of the statement is enclosed within braces (curly brackets). The **constant_expression** is separated from the statement with a colon and each line ends with a semicolon.

Let's look at the **switch** statement with a complete and simple example.

Try It Out - Picking a Lucky Number

This example assumes we are operating a lottery where there are three winning numbers. Participants are required to guess a winning number, and our **switch** statement is designed to end the suspense and tell them about any valuable prize they might have won:

```c
/* Example 3.8 Lucky Lotteries     */
#include <stdio.h>

void main()
{

  int choice;
  printf("Pick a number between 1 and 10 and you may win a prize! ");
  scanf("%d",&choice);

  if ((choice>10) || (choice <1)) choice = 11;


  switch( choice )
  {
    case 7: printf("Congratulations!\n");
      printf("You win the collected works of Amos Gruntfuttock.");
    break;

    case 2: printf("You win the folding thermometer-pen-watch-umbrella.");
    break;

    case 8:  printf("You win the lifetime supply of aspirin tablets.");
    break;

    case 11: printf("\nTry between 1 and 10, you wasted your guess.\n");
    default: printf("Sorry, you lose.");
  }


}
```

Typical output of this program would be:

```
Pick a number between 1 and 10 and you may win a prize! 3
Sorry, you lose.


Pick a number between 1 and 10 and you may win a prize! 7
Congratulations!
You win the collected works of Amos Gruntfuttock.


Pick a number between 1 and 10 and you may win a prize! 92
Try between 1 and 10, you just wasted your guess.
```

How It Works

```
int choice;
  printf("Pick a number between 1 and 10 and you may win a prize! ");
  scanf("%d",&choice);
```

We do the usual sort of thing to start with. We declare an integer variable **choice**. Then we ask the user to enter a number between 1 and 10 and store the value they type in **choice**.

```
if ((choice>10) || (choice <1)) choice = 11;
```

Before we do anything else we need to check they have really entered a number between 1 and 10. If the value is anything else we automatically change it to 11. We don't have to do this, but to ensure the user is advised of their mistake, we set the variable **choice** to 11 to produce the error message generated by the **printf()** for that case value.

```
switch( choice )
  {
    case 7: printf("Congratulations!\n");
      printf("You win the collected works of Amos Gruntfuttock.");
    break;
  ...
  }
```

The first part of the switch statement checks the value of choice against the value 7. If they match you get the winning message.

Notice that we have included the statement **break** after each case This simply breaks out of the switch, and stops the switch continuing down the list of cases. Once the message is printed the **break** transfers you straight to the end of the body of the switch statement (after the closing brace). In this case there is no more code there so the program simply ends. In other programs the program may continue after this statement, possibly to allow the user another guess, or to move on to a different stage of the game. We will come back to **break** later.

To see the effect more clearly, try deleting the **break** statements. You will get a whole series of messages displayed.

```
case 2: printf("You win the folding thermometer-pen-watch-umbrella.");
break;

case 8:printf("You win the lifetime supply of aspirin tablets.");
break;
```

These cases work in exactly the same way as the first case, but giving different messages.

```
case 11: printf("\nTry between 1 and 10, you wasted your guess.\n");
```

This case traps any guesses outside the allowed range. If the user's guess isn't in the range, the value of their guess is immediately converted to 11, no matter what they actually typed in (this was done at the start).

```
        default: printf("Sorry, you lose.");
}
```

This last option, when all the others have been tried and rejected, is the default. It will print if none of the others match.

Try It Out - Yes or No

To illustrate another use for this statement let us suppose we have a **char** variable **letter** which we expect to have the value **'y'** or **'Y'** for one action, and **'n'** or **'N'** for another. We can do this using the **switch** statement in the following program. On its own it may be fairly useless, but you have probably encountered many occasions when a program has asked just this

Try It Out!

117

question and then performed some action as a result (saving a file for example).

```c
/*  Example 3.9 Testing cases          */
#include <stdio.h>

void main()
{
   char letter = 0;          /* This is a zero not an o */

   printf("Enter Y or N: ");
   scanf(" %c", &letter);

   switch ( letter )
   {
      case 'y': case 'Y':
         printf("\nYou responded in the affirmative.");
         break;

      case 'n': case 'N':
         printf("\nYou responded in the negative.");
         break;

      default:
      printf("\nYou did not respond correctly...");
   }
}
```

Typical output from this would be:

```
Enter Y or N: y
You responded in the affirmative.
```

How It Works

```c
   char letter = 0;

   printf("Enter Y or N: ");
   scanf(" %c", &letter);
```

In declaring the variable **letter** as a character, we also initialize it to zero. We then ask the user to type something in and store that value as usual.

```c
   switch ( letter )
   {
      case 'y': case 'Y':
         printf("\nYou responded in the affirmative.");
         break;
```

We have avoided a common mistake with this program which demonstrates why you need to think very carefully about what a user might enter before we finish the program. Here we could have just used upper-case letters. After all that's what we asked for. However, this isn't very helpful for an uninitiated user. They could easily type a lower-case letter and we have provided for this.

We have condensed our four possible legal values for the variable **letter** (Y, y, N, n) into two by putting the upper and lower-case values together. We could do this for any number of case values. Notice the punctuation for this. The two cases are combined and are separated by a colon. The resulting statements are enclosed between braces to make sure it is clear what is happening and when.

```
    case 'n': case 'N':
        printf("\nYou responded in the negative.");
        break;

    default:
    printf("\nYou did not respond correctly...");
}
```

Note the **break** statement after the **printf()** statements for the legal case values. As before, this causes execution to break off at that point, and continue after the end of the **switch** statement. Again, without it you would get the statements for succeeding cases executed, and unless there was a preceding **break** statement, you would get the **default** statements executed as well.

The goto Statement

The **if** statement has provided us with the ability to choose one or another block of statements depending on a test. This is a powerful tool that enables us to alter the naturally sequential nature of a program. We no longer have to go from A to B to C to D. We can go to A and then decide whether to skip B and C and go straight to D.

The **goto** statement, on the other hand, is a blunt instrument. It directs the flow of statements to change unconditionally - do not pass go, do not collect $200. When your program hits a **goto** it does just that. It goes to the place you send it without checking any values or asking the user whether that was really what they wanted.

We are only going to mention the **goto** briefly because it is not as great as it might at first seem. The problem with it is that it seems too easy. This might sound perverse, but the important word is *seems*. It feels so simple that people can be tempted into using it all over the place, where it would be better to use a different statement. This can result in heavily tangled code.

To use the **goto**, the position to be moved to is defined by a statement label at that point. A statement label is defined in exactly the same way as a variable name, a sequence of letters and digits, the first of which must be a letter. Like other statements the **goto** ends with a semi-colon. The destination uses the same label but ends with a colon. The **goto** statement can be used in conjunction with an **if** statement. For example:

```
    ....
if (Dice == 6)
    goto Waldorf;
else
    goto Jail;                  /* Go to the statement labelled Jail */
Waldorf:
    Comfort = high;
    ....
Jail:                   /* The label itself. Program control is sent here */
    Comfort = low;
    ....
```

We roll the dice. If we get 6 we go to the **Waldorf**, otherwise we go to **Jail**. This might seem perfectly alright, but imagine your code was littered with **goto**s. How would you know where each one led? You might end up sending the user to **Jail** and not allowing them any means of escaping. So it's best to avoid the **goto** where possible - in theory it should always be avoidable.

Designing a Program

You have reached the end of Chapter 3 successfully, so how can we apply what we have learnt in a real example?

The Problem

The problem we are set is to write a simple calculator that can add, subtract, multiply, divide, and find the modulus of two numbers.

The Analysis

All the math involved is simple, but the program has other problems. We need to make checks on the input to make sure that the user hasn't asked the computer to do the impossible.

So the steps to writing this program are:

1   Get the user to type in the calculation they want the computer to perform.

2   Check to make sure that they have not typed in something which is impossible to work out.

3   Perform the calculation.

4   Display the result.

The Solution

1   Getting the user to type something in is quite easy. We will be using **printf()** and **scanf()** so we need the **STDIO.H** header file. The only new thing we will do is in the way we get the input. Rather than asking the user for each number individually and then the operation to perform, we'll get the user to type it in more naturally. For example:

```
34.87 + 5
```

Or

```
9 * 6.5
```

We can do this because of the way **scanf()** works, but we'll discuss that after you have seen the first part of the program.

```
/*Example 3.10 A calculator*/
#include <stdio.h>

void main()
{
    double number1, number2;
    char operation;

    printf("\nEnter the calculation\n");
    scanf("%Lf %c %Lf", &number1, &operation, &number2);
}
```

`scanf()` is fairly clever when it comes to inputting. You don't actually need to put each input on a separate line. All that is required is some white space (by pressing *Space, Tab* or *Enter*) between each bit of the input.

2   Next, we have to check to make sure that the input is correct. What checks shall we use? Well, the obvious one is that the operation to be performed in valid. We have decided that the valid operations are **+**, **-**, **/**, ***** and **%**, so we need to check that the operation is one of these.

We also need to check the second number to see if it's zero. The reason for this is that you can't divide by zero, so if the operation is either **/** or **%** and the second number is **0**, then it's invalid. Also, to find the modulus you need to check to see whether either number is negative, as this gives an undefined answer. This means that the computer may give you the wrong answer. Undefined results usually occur as a result of asking for the impossible.

We could do the above checks with a couple of **if()** statements, but there is another consideration. What we do with the two numbers depends on the operation that is typed in. So if we used **if**s we have then got to do checks for the five operations. This is not a very efficient use of our time. There is a far better way of doing the check, and that is with a **switch()...case** statement.

```
#include <stdio.h>

void main()
{
    double number1, number2;
    char operation;

    printf("\nEnter the calculation\n");
    scanf("%Lf %c %Lf", &number1, &operation, &number2);
    switch(operation)
    {
      case '+':
         break;
      case '-':
         break;
      case '*':
         break;
      case '/':
         if(number2 == 0)
```

```
            printf("\n\n\aDivision by zero error!\n");
         break;
      case '%':
         if(number2 <= 0 || number1 < 0)
            printf("\n\n\aDivision by zero error!\n");
         break;
      default:
         printf("\n\n\aIllegal operation!\n");
   }
}
```

3 and 4 So now we have checked the input, we can calculate what the answer is and display the result at the same time. We don't need to store the answer, so no extra variables are involved.

```
#include <stdio.h>

void main()
{
    double number1, number2;
    char operation;

    printf("\nEnter the calculation\n");
    scanf("%lf %c %lf",&number1, &operation, &number2);
    switch(operation)
    {
       case '+':
          printf("= %lf", number1 + number2);
          break;
       case '-':
          printf("= %lf", number1 - number2);
          break;
       case '*':
          printf("= %lf", number1 * number2);
          break;
       case '/':
          if(number2 == 0)
             printf("\n\n\aDivision by zero error!\n");
          else
             printf("=%lf", number1/number2);
          break;
       case '%':
          if(number2 <= 0 || number1 < 0)
             printf("\n\n\aDivision by zero error!\n");
          else
             printf("= %d", (long)number1 % (long)number2);
          break;
       default:
          printf("\n\n\aIllegal operation!\n");
    }
}
```

123

Notice how we cast the two numbers from **doubles** to **longs** when we calculate the modulus. This is because % only works with integers. All that's left is to try it out.

```
Enter the calculation
56*75
= 4200.000000

Enter the calculation
7 % 0

Division by zero error!
```

Summary

This chapter has ended with a really exciting program. In the first 2 chapters we really just looked at the groundwork for C programs. We could do some reasonably useful things, but we couldn't control the program once it had started. In this chapter we are starting to feel the power of the language.

You have learnt how to compare variables and then use **if**s, **if else**s and **switch**es to affect the outcome. You understand more about making decisions and taking different paths. In the next chapter you will learn how to write much more powerful programs that can repeat instructions over and over again. By the end of Chapter 4 you will think your calculator is small fry.

Loops

In the last chapter we learnt how to compare items and base our decisions on the result. We were able to choose how the computer reacted based on what was input.

We ended the chapter with a promise of even greater things. You are probably starting to get a feel for the power of C programming, but are feeling frustrated by the fact that you are still restricted in what you can do. In the lottery example in the last chapter, it would have been nice to allow the user to get another try. You could have done this with **goto**, but in this chapter we'll show you a better way.

This chapter will now show you how to get the computer to start doing things more than once (letting people have more than one guess), repeating things only if certain conditions are met (they don't press a key to quit), repeating things a set number of times (you get three guesses, then your time is up). This is called **looping**.

In this chapter you will:

- Learn about repeating code, looping
- Learn about the **for, while** and **do while** loops
- Learn about some new operators, the increment and decrement operators
- Write a program that plays a Simple Simon game

Loops

The programming mechanism for executing a series of instructions repeatedly, a given number of times, or until a particular condition is fulfilled, is called a **loop**. This is a fundamental programming tool along with the ability to compare items. Once you can compare items and repeat actions, you can do both together. For example, you can repeat an action until two items that you are comparing are the same. Once they *are* the same you can go on to perform a different action.

In the lottery example, you could give the user exactly 3 guesses (in other words let them continue to guess until **number_of_guesses** equals 3). Alternatively, you could set up a specific number (let's say 0) so that when they type it, it cancels the lottery. You could then continue letting the user guess a number until they enter 0, and give them a message to say they have hit your number.

The way a typical loop works is described in the figure below.

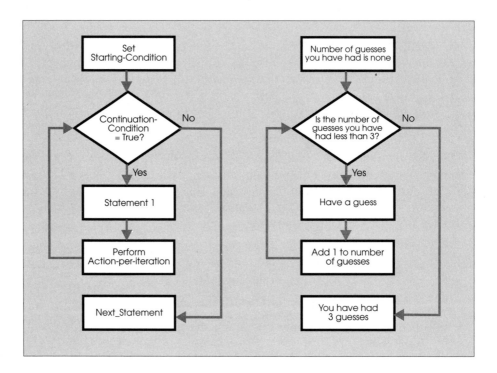

More often than not, you will find that you want to use the same calculation with different sets of data values. Without loops you would need to write out the instructions to be performed as many times as there are sets of data values to be processed. Remember the calculator program right at the end of the last chapter? What if you wanted to be able to do lots of calculations without having to re-run the program each time. You don't want to have to repeat all that code for the number of calculations required. It's not only time that would be a problem, you would also have constraints on the available memory.

Without loops you could possibly restart a program from scratch each time you wanted it to repeat, but this wouldn't even solve a problem as simple as computing the average of an arbitrary number of values. Writing a program for a repetitive calculation with a loop allows you to use the same program code for any number of sets of data to be entered.

Before we discuss the various type of loops available to us in C we will briefly mention two operators encountered frequently in C programs, the increment and decrement operators. These operators are used very often with loops which is why we will discuss them here. We are going to give you a very quick explanation of what they are. Then we will throw you straight into an example and, in explaining how the example works, we will explain them a little more.

The Increment and Decrement Operators - A Quick Tour

The increment (**++**) and decrement (**--**) operators are used to add (increment) or subtract (decrement) the value of 1 from the variable they apply to. Think of them as meaning "plus one" and "minus one" for the time being. At first they may look a bit awkward, but once you are familiar with them, they make reading code very easy. They are a real asset once you get used to them, especially when writing loops.

Let's get straight to it and look at the simplest form of loop, the **for** loop. There are other types of loop, **while** and **do while**, that are similar to the **for** loop. We will spend a longer time on the **for** loop, as once you have cracked this one the others will be easy.

The for Loop

The **for** loop used in its basic form enables you to execute a block of statements a given number of times. If we were writing a program that imitates a telephone by making a ringing noise and we want the telephone to ring 10 times and then stop. Instead of writing the code 10 times we could write it like this:

```
for (no_of_rings = 1 ; no_of_rings <= 10 ; ++no_of_rings)
    {
    printf("\aRingRing");
    }
```

The **for** loop operation is defined in the first line. It controls the starting value, the conditions under which it will continue (and therefore when it will stop), and anything that should happen each time the loop loops. The action that should occur each time is the statement or statements that immediately follow the **for** loop. This is contained in the body of the **for** loop.

To start with we set **no_of_rings = 1** so the telephone rings for the first time. The condition that must be met for the action to continue is **no_of_rings <= 10**. Once the telephone rings for the 10th time, the loop ends and control will pass to the next statement after it. Each time the loop loops we need to add 1 to the number of loops. This is where the fantastic increment operator comes into play. Look how easy it is to increment **no_of_rings** to the right amount. If we forget this, the **no_of_rings** will never reach 10 and we will loop the loop forever. The body of the program, the event that occurs each time, is a ring.

Notice the punctuation. The **for** loop parameters are contained within parentheses and don't end with a semi-colon. Each part of the loop is separated by a semi-colon. You could leave any of the parameters empty, but if you do you must still include the semi-colon. For example, you could initialize the variable **no_of_rings** to 1 when you declare it:

```
int no_of_rings = 1;
```

Then you wouldn't need to specify the first parameter and the for loop could look like this:

```
for ( ; no_of_rings <= 10 ; ++no_of_rings)
```

The body of the loop is contained within braces, although since we only have one statement here, we could leave them out.

As a silly experiment we could make this into a real program simply by adding a few lines:

```
/*Example 4.1 Phone home! */
#include <stdio.h>

void main()
{
    int no_of_rings;

    for (no_of_rings = 1 ; no_of_rings <= 10 ; ++no_of_rings)
    {
    printf("\nRingRing\a\a");
    }
    printf("\nNo one home.");
}
```

Don't try this one too many times though, or you'll get a headache. They will never be home anyway. The way the program works is shown in the following figure.

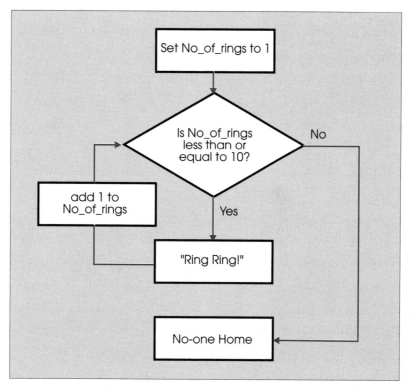

Let's try a more serious example.

Try It Out - Drawing a Box

Consider the situation where you want to draw a box on the screen. We could just use the **printf()** statement lots of times, but the typing would be exhausting. We can use a **for** loop to draw a box with much more ease. Let's try this.

```
/* Example 4.2 Drawing a box   */
#include <stdio.h>

void main()
{
   int count;

   printf("\n**************");

   for ( count=1 ; count <= 8 ; ++count )
   printf("\n*            *");

   printf("\n**************");
}
```

No prizes for guessing, but the output for this program looks like:

```
* * * * * * * * * * * *
*                    *
*                    *
*                    *
*                    *
*                    *
*                    *
*                    *
*                    *
* * * * * * * * * * * *
```

How It Works

```
/* Example 4.2 Drawing a box   */
#include <stdio.h>

void main()
{
   int count;

   printf("\n**************");
```

As usual we have included the **STDIO.H** header file to allow us to use the **printf()** statement. The program itself is really very simple. We first declare an integer called **count** which we shall use to count the number of times to loop. The first **printf()** statement is used to print the top of the box to the screen. We are using a line of 12 stars.

```
for ( count=1 ; count <= 8 ; ++count )
   printf("\n*            *");
```

The next statement is our **for** loop. This tells us that the following statement is to be repeated a number of times. In this case the statement is used to write the sides of our box. Our program has repeated this **printf()** statement 8 times. Let's look how this is done.

```
for ( count=1 ; count <= 8 ; ++count )
```

The operation of the loop is defined within the parentheses of the **for** statement. There are 3 arguments separated by semi-colons.

```
count=1
```

The first of these is an assignment of the **loop control variable**, in this case it is the integer **count** which we set to 1. We could have used other types of variables for this, but integers are convenient for the job.

```
count <= 8
```

The second argument is the **continuation condition**, we have used **count <= 8**. This is checked each time the statement following the **for** loop has finished, to see whether the computer should execute the statement again. It asks the question "does the loop continue?" For our example the answer is yes as long as our variable **count** is less than or equal to 8.

```
count++
```

The final part of the **for** loop is the action that should be taken each time the loop is executed. We have used this to increment the value of **count** by 1. This allows us to change the value of **count** so that when the **printf()** statement has done its work, the value of **count** is increased by 1. Then the new value is checked against the condition in the second statement - is it still less than or equal to 8? The process continues until **count** becomes greater than 8. As you have seen, this loop results in the computer writing vertical lines of 8 stars to the screen. These are the sides of our box.

When this has repeated 8 times the program finally passes the **for** statement and carries on with the rest of the program.

```
printf("\n***************");
}
```

Our last line prints the bottom of the box on the screen.

> Anytime you find yourself repeating something more than a couple of times it's worth considering a loop. They will usually save you time and memory.

The general pattern of the **for** loop is:

```
for (starting_condition; continuation_condition ; action_per_iteration)
{
   Statement1;
}
Next_statement;
```

The statement to be repeated is **Statement1**. In general, this could equally well be a block of statements (a group of statements) contained between a pair of braces. In this way you can get various commands to be repeated several times.

The **starting_condition** usually, but not necessarily, sets an initial value to a loop control variable. The loop control variable is typically, but not necessarily, a counter of some kind which tracks how often you go round the loop.

The **continuation_condition** is a logical expression evaluating to **True** or **False**. This determines whether the loop should continue to be executed or not. As long as this condition has the value **True** the loop continues. It typically checks the value of the loop control variable, but any logical expression can be placed here, as long as you know what you are doing.

You should note that the **continuation_condition** is tested at the beginning of the loop rather than the end. This obviously makes it possible to have a **for** loop whose statements are not executed at all if the **continuation_condition** starts out as **False**. This can be invaluable for padding out your program with useless code if you are embarrassed by the fact that your program is a little on the small side.

The `action_per_iteration` is executed each time execution of the loop is traversed and is usually, but again not necessarily, an increment of the loop control variable. At each iteration of the loop, the statement or block of statements immediately following the **for** statement is executed. The loop is terminated, and execution continues with **Next_statement** as soon as the **continuation_condition** is **False**.

The Increment and Decrement Operators

We have seen an increment operator in action here, so let's delve a little deeper and see what these operators actually do. They are both unary operators, which means they are only used with one argument, and they are used to increment (increase) or decrement (decrease) a value stored in a variable.

The Increment Operator

Let's start with the increment operator. This takes the form ++ and adds 1 to the variable it acts on. For example, assuming the variables are of type **int**, the following three statements all have exactly the same effect:

```
count = count + 1;
count += 1;
++count;
```

They each increment the variable **count** by 1. The last form is clearly the most concise. The action of this operator in an expression is to increment the value of the variable, then use the incremented value in the expression. For example if **count** has the value 5, then the statement:

```
total = ++count + 6;
```

results in the variable **total** being assigned the value 12. **count** (5) has 1 added to it (6) and then 6 added to it (12).

Similarly if we declared a variable count and initialized it to 1:

```
int count = 1;
```

and then we repeated the following statement 6 times in a loop:

```
++count;
```

by the end of the code **count** would have a value of 7. Remember, the value stored in **count** is not constant. Each time you execute **++count** you add one more. At the outset, **count** has the value 1 stored in it. After the first cycle **count** would equal 2 (1+1). Then before the second iteration starts, **count** is equal to 2, and after the second iteration it would equal 3 (2+1), and so on up to 7.

Prefixing and Postfixing

So far we have written the operator (++) in front of the variable to which it applies. This is called the **prefix form**. It can also be written *after* the variable to which it applies, as the **postfix form**, where the effect is slightly different. If you write count++, the incrementing of the variable occurs after its value has been used in context. This sounds more complicated than it is. Let's look at the earlier example:

```
total = count++ + 6;
```

With the same initial value of 5 for **count**, **total** is assigned the value 11. This is because the initial value of **count** is used to evaluate the expression (5+6). The increment of 1 (the ++) is only applied at the end of the expression. The statement above is equivalent to the two statements:

```
total = count + 6;
++count;
```

It actually isn't a good idea to use the increment operator as we have here. It would be clearer to write:

```
total = 6 + count++;
```

You still need to remember that this means you add 6 and the value of **count** (5) which gives 11. This is stored in **total** and then you add one to the **value**.

Where we have an expression such as **a++ + b**, or **a+++b**, it becomes even less obvious what is meant to happen, or what the compiler will achieve. They are actually the same, but in the second case you might really have meant **a + ++b** which is different. It evaluates to one more than the other two expressions.

For example, if **a = 10** and **b =5**

then in the statements:

```
x = a++ + b;
y = a+ ++b;
```

x will have the value 15 from (10 + 5) as **a** is incremented after the expression is evaluated. The next time you use **a**, however, it will have the value 11. In the second statement, **y** will have the value 16 (10 + 6) as **b** is incremented before the statement is evaluated.

The Decrement Operator

The decrement operator works exactly the opposite. This takes the form **--** and subtracts 1 from the variable it acts on. It is used in the same way as **++**. For example, assuming the variables are of type **int**, the following three statements all have exactly the same effect:

```
count = count - 1;
count -= 1;
--count;
```

They each decrement the variable **count** by 1. For example if **count** has the value 10, then the statement:

```
total = --count + 6;
```

results in the variable **total** being assigned the value 15. **count** (10) has 1 subtracted from it (9) and then 6 added to it (15).

Exactly the same rules as we discussed in relation to the increment operator apply to the decrement operator. For example, if **count** has the initial value 5, then the statement:

```
total = --count + 6;
```

results in **total** having the value 10 assigned, whereas:

```
total = 6 + count-- ;
```

sets the value of **total** to 11. Both operators are usually applied to integers, but we shall also see in later chapters that they can be applied to certain other data types in C.

The for Loop Revisited

Now we understand a bit more about **++** and **--** let's get on with another example.

Try It Out - Summing Numbers

This is a more useful and interesting program than drawing a box with stars (not to say that it wasn't useful and interesting). Here we are going to read in an integer value, and then use the **for** loop to sum all the integers from 1 to the value entered.

```
/*  Example 4.3 Sum the integers from 1 to a user specified number */

#include <stdio.h>

void main()
{
  long sum = 0L;
  int  i = 0, count = 0;

  printf("Enter the number of integers you want to sum: ");
  scanf(" %d", &count);
  for (i = 1 ;  i <= count  ; i++ )
  sum += i;
  printf("\nTotal of the first %d numbers is %ld", count, sum);
}
```

The typical output you should get from this program is:

```
Enter the number of integers you want to sum: 10
Total of the first 10 integers is 55
```

How It Works

```
  long sum = 0L;
  int  i = 0, count = 0;
```

We start by declaring 3 variables. We use **sum**, which we initialize to the value 0L (an integer of type **long**), to hold the final value of our calculations, **count** (initialized to 0) to hold the amount of numbers we want to sum, and **i** (initialized to 0) to control the loop.

```
printf("Enter the number of integers you want to sum: ");
scanf(" %d", &count);
```

The user enters an integer to define the sum required. This means if they entered 4, the program should add 1, 2, 3 and 4 together.

```
for (i = 1 ;  i <= count  ; i++ )
```

After reading in the integer value **count**, the loop variable **i** starts at 1. This is assigned by the starting condition in the **for** statement (**i=1**). Until the value of **i** is the greater than the value of **count** (**i <= count**), the value of **i** is to be incremented by 1 each iteration by the action per iteration (**i++**).

```
sum += i;
```

There is just one statement in the loop immediately following the **for** statement, which adds the current value of **i** to **sum**. The continuation condition for the loop is **i <= count** so the last iteration is with the value of **i** the same as **count**.

```
printf("\nTotal of the first %d numbers is %ld", count, sum);
```

As soon as **i** equals **count** the loop ends and the succeeding **printf()** is executed.

As we have hinted with the occasional "not necessarily", the **for** statement is very flexible about what you can put in the parentheses after the **for**. The example below demonstrates two things you can change in your **for** loop..

Try It Out - The Flexible for

```c
/*   Example 4.4 Summing integers - compact program  */
#include <stdio.h>

void main()
{
  long sum = 0L;
  int i = 1, count = 0;
  printf("Enter the number of integers you want to sum: ");
  scanf(" %d", &count);
  for ( ; i<= count ; sum += i++ );

  printf("\nTotal of the first %d numbers is %ld", count, sum);
}
```

Typical output would be:

```
Enter the number of integers you want to sum: 6

Total of the first 6 numbers is 21
```

How It Works

This will execute exactly the same as the previous program. Isn't that neat? The first difference is that we haven't placed anything into the starting condition part of the **for** loop statement.

```
long sum = 0L;
int i = 1, count = 0;
...
for ( ; i<= count ; sum += i++ );
```

Instead, we have set the value of **i** to 1 when we declared it. It is important that we still include the semi-colon after the opening parentheses, otherwise it wouldn't be clear that the first statement was the continuation condition, and the compiler would produce an error.

Omitting the initialization of the loop count isn't a good idea unless there are other reasons to do so. In this case we have a very short and simple program so it is easy to see what is going on. In a larger, more realistic example, it will be much less obvious how the loop count gets initialized. It also tends to encourage problems if you modify the program. If you were using **count** in different **for** loops you might forget that you needed to initialize **count** to a particular value for it to work inside one of the **for** loops.

It is very easy in a larger example to introduce changes between the initialization of the loop variable in its declaration, and where it is used in the loop. Such changes may well result in the initial value being modified. The count may then start with a value of 2 when it should be one and then the loop and program won't work properly. You may not get a compiler error but the results may be very strange.

The second difference comes at the end of the **for** statement:

```
for ( ; i<= count ; sum += i++ );
```

Just to show how flexible the **for** statement is about its parameters, we have incorporated the summation into it, and there are no loop statements after the set up statement for the **for** loop. This is indicated by the semi-colon at the end of the **for** statement.

More About the Loop Control Variable

So far we have only used the loop control variables (the counter) to count the number of times we have looped. We aren't limited to using the value of the loop control variable just in the statement itself. We can use it in the statement that is actually looped as well. Let's go straight to a simple example.

Try It Out - Using the Loop Control Variable

This example is a little shorter than the last, so less trouble on your fingers. Can you work out what's going on without looking at the output?

```
/*   Example 4.5 Using the loop control variable   */
#include <stdio.h>

void main()
{
   int j;
   for( j = 1 ; j <= 10 ; j++ )
   printf("\n j = %d", j );

}
```

The output of this program is:

```
j = 1
j = 2
j = 3
j = 4
j = 5
j = 6
j = 7
j = 8
j = 9
j = 10
```

Try It Out!

How It Works

This loop works a little differently. We use the value of the counter in the printf() statement.

```
int j;
```

We declare only one variable, **j**.

```
for( j = 1 ; j <= 10 ; j++ )
```

Next we have a simple **for** loop. The first expression defines the initial condition which is **j = 1**. The second defines the conditions under which the statement following the for statement will continue to be executed, which is as long as **j <= 10**. The last expression defines an action for each iteration, in this case to increment **j** by 1 after each iteration has been executed. Notice how there is no semi-colon at the end of this **for** loop. This indicates that the following statement (the **printf()**) is part of the loop:

```
printf("\n j = %d", j );
```

The statement to be repeated is the **printf()** following the for statement. We first move to a new line, and then print **j =** followed by the value stored in **j** at the time. We then check with the for loop how we should continue.

The **printf()** will first execute with **j** set to 1 (**j = 1**), then with **j** set to 2 (**j = 2**), and so on until **j** is set to 10. When **j** is set to 11 the loop terminates and the statement after the **printf()** is executed. So you see that in this example we have used the value of **j** in the repeated statement. In other respects this example is very similar to the previous one.

Modifying the Loop Variable

Of course we aren't limited to incrementing the loop control variable by 1. We can change it by any value, either positive or negative. We could have summed the first n integers backwards if we wished as in the following example:

```
/*  Example 4.6 Summing integers backwards    */
#include <stdio.h>
void main()
{
  long sum = 0L;
  int i = 0, count = 0;

  printf("Enter the number of integers you want to sum: ");
  scanf(" %d", &count);

  for (i = count ; i >= 1 ; sum += i-- );

  printf("\nTotal of the first %d numbers is %ld", count, sum);
}
```

Just to keep any mathematically inclined readers happy, I should mention that it is quite unnecessary to use a loop to sum the first n integers. A tidy little formula:

$$0.5*n*(n+1)$$

would do the trick much more efficiently. However, it wouldn't teach you much about loops, would it?

A for Loop with No Parameters

As we have already mentioned, we have no obligation to put any parameters in the **for** loop statement at all. The minimal **for** loop looks like this:

```
for ( ;; )
  statement;
```

Here, as previously, **statement** could be a block of statements enclosed between braces. Since the condition for continuing the loop is absent, as is the initial condition and the loop increment, the loop will continue indefinitely. As a result, unless you want your computer to be indefinitely doing nothing, **statement** must contain the means of exiting from the loop, as in the next example.

Try It Out - A Minimal for Loop

```
/*  Example 4.7 The almost indefinite loop - computing an average     */
#include <stdio.h>

void main()
{
   char Test;
   float total = 0.0, value = 0.0, count = 0.0;
   printf("This program calculates the average of any number of values.");
   for( ;; )                              /* Infinite loop        */
      {
      printf ("\nEnter a value: ");
      scanf(" %f", &value);
      total += value;                     /* Accumulate sum of values   */
      ++count;                            /* Maintain count of values   */
      printf("Do you want to enter another value? (Y or N): ");
      scanf(" %c", &Test );
      if ( Test == 'N' || Test == 'n' )       /*look for any sign of no  */
         break;
      }
   printf ("\nThe average is %f ", total/count );   /*  We finish here     */
}
```

In this example we have set up the loop to continue indefinitely by using a **for** loop that has no end condition specified. The program continues to increase the count of how many times the loop has executed by using:

```
++count;                               /* Maintain count of values    */
```

The values that are entered are added to the running total each time round the loop by the statement:

```
total += value;                        /* Accumulate sum of values    */
```

The program continues to accept input until you enter a character **'N'**, or **'n'**, to indicate you have finished entering data. The program checks the input for an 'n' or 'N' with an **if** statement and then terminates the loop by **break**ing out of the loop with the **break** statement. It then computes the average and exits. Typical output from this example might be:

```
This program calculates the average of any number of values.
Enter a value: 1
Do you want to enter another value? (Y or N): y

Enter a value: 2
Do you want to enter another value? (Y or N): y

Enter a value: 3
Do you want to enter another value? (Y or N): y

Enter a value: 4
Do you want to enter another value? (Y or N): y

Do you want to enter another value? (Y or N): n
The average is 2.500000
```

The **break** statement we used is familiar to us from the **switch** statement. Its use here is also quite similar. We have used it to exit from the loop in which it appears. The program then continues from after the closing brace of the loop.

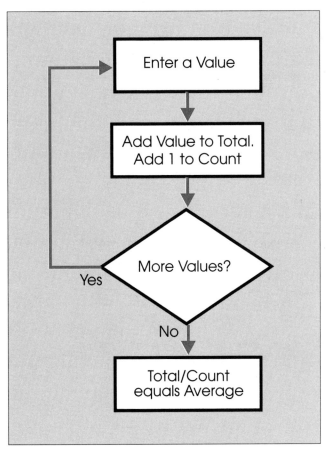

Loops in Action - Customizing Your Output

You can use a **for** loop when you are getting input from the user to allow them to input more than one thing and respond differently depending on the number of entries they have made. Let's write a guessing game.

Try It Out - A Guessing Game

This program is going to get the user to guess the number we have picked as the lucky number. It uses one **for** loop and plenty of **if** statements. We have also thrown in a conditional operator or two, just to check you haven't forgotten how to use it!

```c
/*  Example 4.8  A Guessing Game */
#include <stdio.h>

void main()
{
  int chosen = 15;
  int guess = 0;
  int count = 0;

  printf("\nThis is a guessing game.");
  printf("\n\nI have chosen a number between 1 and 20.");
  printf("\nYou have 3 tries to guess which number:  ");
  scanf("%d", &guess);
  ++count;

  for (  ; count <= 3 ; ++count )
  {
    if (guess == chosen)
    {
      printf("\nYou guessed it!");
      break;
    }
    if ( count == 3)
    {
      printf("Sorry, time's up. The number was %d.", chosen);
      break;
    }

    if ( guess > 20 )
    {
      printf("\nI said between 1 and 20. ");
    }
    printf("%so. ", guess > 20 ? " So, n" : "N");
    printf("\nYou have had %d tr%s. ", count, count == 1 ? "y" : "ies");
```

```
      printf("You have %d tr%s left.", 3 - count, count == 2 ? "y" : "ies");
      printf("\nTry again: ");
      scanf("%d", &guess);
   }
}
```

Can you work out what the program is doing?

Some sample output would be:

```
This is a guessing game.

I have chosen a number between 1 and 20.
You have 3 tries to guess which number: 12
No.
You have had 1 try. You have 2 tries left.
Try again: 45

I said between 1 and 20. So, no.
You have had 2 tries. You have 1 try left.
Try again: 3
Sorry, time's up. The number was 15.
```

This program is a bit longer than the first ones and we are using the **for** loop in a controlled way.

How It Works

As the program is quite intricate we will step through it:

```
/*  Example 4.8 A Guessing Game */
#include <stdio.h>

void main()
{
   int chosen = 15;
   int guess = 0;
   int count = 0;
```

This first bit is straightforward. We use the usual header file (we aren't using any new functions) and in **main()** we declare and initialize 3 **int** variables, **chosen**, **guess** and **count**. These are to store respectively: the number you choose to be the lucky number, the number the user guesses and the number of guesses they have had.

```
int chosen = 15;
```

Notice that we have created a variable for the chosen number. We could just have used the number 15 in the program, but doing it this way makes it much easier to alter the value of **chosen** once it has been guessed.

```
printf("\nThis is a guessing game.");
printf("\n\nI have chosen a number between 1 and 20.");
```

We give an opening message that explains what's happening.

```
printf("\nYou have 3 tries to guess which number:   ");
scanf("%d", &guess);
++count;
```

Here we are told that we have 3 guesses and we enter our first guess. This is stored in the variable **guess**, and since that is one try gone, we add 1 to the value in **count**.

Then things start to look complicated (they aren't of course).

```
void main()
{
...
    for ( count = 1 ; count <= 3 ; ++count )
    {
...
    }
}
```

Look at the braces in the program. Look at the way we have indented and grouped the statements. This is a good way of demonstrating how useful program layout can be. You can see that within the **main** function braces there is one large set of braces under the **for** loop. You can see quite clearly all the statements that are contained within the loop.

This means that the whole of the rest of the program is controlled by the **for** loop. For as long as the **for** loop repeats, each time it repeats we run through the whole set of **if**s and **else**s, checking our input. There are no other statements after the **for** loop is executed. That's what makes it so simple.

The first check in the loop is whether you have guessed correctly:

```
if (guess == chosen)
{
    printf("\nYou guessed it!");
    break;
}
```

If your guess is correct we display the message you can see, and exit the loop. Since there are no statements after the loop, the program ends.

We can only reach the next check in the loop if you didn't guess correctly:

```
if ( count == 3)
{
    printf("Sorry, time's up. The number was %d.", chosen);
    break;
}
```

Here we check whether this is your third guess. If it is, then you have exhausted your chances to guess, so we display a message and exit the loop.

The last check in the loop is executed if you failed to guess correctly and it is not your last attempt:

```
if ( guess > 20 )
{
  printf("\nI said between 1 and 20. ");
}
```

This group of statements tests whether the value you entered is within the prescribed limits. If it isn't, a message is displayed reminding you of the limits.

Finally there is the sequence of statements:

```
    printf("%sope. ", guess > 20 ? " So, n" : "N");
    printf("\nYou have had %d tr%s. ", count, count == 1 ? "y" : "ies");
    printf("You have %d tr%s left.", 3 - count, count == 2 ? "y" : "ies");
    printf("\nTry again: ");
    scanf("%d", &guess);
}
```

If we manage to reach this point we tell you how many tries you have had and how many you have left. We then go back to the beginning of the **for** loop for another try.

Look at all our conditional operators. This is so we can make the word try plural in some cases. If we didn't do this we would have a rather unprofessional program that would output:

```
You have had 1 tries.
```

Or

```
You have 1 tries left.
```

The program is designed so you can easily change the value of the variable chosen and have endless fun. Well, endless fun for a short while anyway.

The while Loop

That's enough of the **for** loop. Now that we've done several examples of **for** loops, let's look at a different kind - the **while** loop. With a **while** loop, the mechanism for repeating a set of statements allows execution to continue as long as a specified expression has the value **True**. In English this could be represented like this:

> While this condition is true
>
> > Keep on doing this;
>
> > Then do this

In other words:

> While you are hungry
>
> > Eat sandwiches
>
> > Then drink coffee

This means that you ask yourself "am I hungry?" If the answer is yes you eat a sandwich and then ask yourself "am I still hungry?" You keep eating sandwiches until the answer is no, at which point you go on to drink some coffee.

The syntax for this is:

```
while ( expression )
{
    Statement1;
}
Statement2;
```

As always, **statement1** could be a block of statements. If you were hungry you might decide to eat a sandwich and drink some lemonade, which is why we have included the braces. A diagram of the logical process of the **while** loop is shown in the next figure. Just like the **for** loop, the condition for continuation of the **while** loop is tested at the start, so that if **expression** starts out **False**, none of the loop statements will be executed. If you answer the first question "no I'm not hungry" you don't get to eat any sandwiches and you go straight to the coffee.

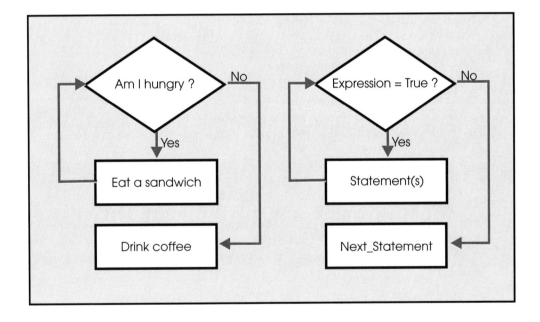

Try It Out - Using the while Loop

This looks fairly straightforward, so let's go straight into that old favorite, humming and summing integers:

```
/*  Example 4.9 While programming and summing integers    */
#include <stdio.h>

void main()
{
  long sum = 0L;
  int i = 1, count = 0;
  printf("Enter the number of integers you want to sum: ");
  scanf(" %d", &count);
  while ( i <= count )
  sum += i++;

  printf("\nTotal of the first %d numbers is %ld", count, sum);
}
```

Typical output from this program would be:

```
Enter the number of integers you want to sum: 7
Total of the first 7 numbers is 28
```

How It Works

Well really this works pretty much the same as when we used the **for** loop. The only aspect of this example worth discussing is the **while** loop.

```
  while ( i <= count )
  sum += i++;
```

It contains a single statement action accumulating **sum**, which continues to be executed with **i** values up to 10. Because we have the postfix increment operator here (the ++ comes after the variable), **i** is incremented *after* its value is used to compute **sum** on each iteration. What the statement really means is:

```
  sum += i;
  i++;
```

So the value of sum is not affected by the increment of i until the next loop.

Let's see whether we can explain in normal English. It's time to analyze what is really happening.

When you enter the while loop **i** equals 1 and count equals whatever you have typed in (let's say 3).

In the loop we first check that **i <= count** (in this case that 1 <= 3) which is true so we do the action in the loop. First the value of **i** (1) is added to the variable sum. **sum** was equal to 0, it's now equal to 1. The variable i is then incremented after we calculated the value to be stored in **sum** because we have the postfix increment operator. So **i** has the value 2 and we return to the beginning of the loop. We now check the **while** expression and see whether the value in **i** is still **<= count**. Since **i** is now 2, which is indeed less than 3 we execute the loop again.

In the second loop iteration, we add the new value of **i** (2) to the old value of **sum** (1) and store the result in **sum**. The variable **sum** now equals 3. We add 1 to **i** (**i** now equals 3) and go back to the loop expression to check. At this point **i** is equal to **count** so we can still do the action in the loop. We add the new value of **i** (3) to the old value of **sum** (3) and store the result in **sum**. **Sum** now equals 6. We add 1 to **i** (**i** now equals 4) and go back to the loop expression to check. 4 is greater than 3 so the expression **i <= count** is false and we leave the loop.

This example has used the increment operator as postfix. How could we change the program above to use **++** as a prefix? Try it yourself and see whether you can work it out. The answer is given below.

How It Works - Using ++ as a Prefix

The obvious bit of code that will change will be the **while** loop:

```
sum += ++i;
```

Try just changing this. If you run the program now you get the wrong answer:

```
Enter the number of integers you want to sum: 3
Total of the first 3 numbers is 9
```

This is because the **++** is adding 1 to the value of **i** *before* it stores the value in **sum**. **i** starts at 1 and is increased to 2. That value is stored in **sum** before we can stop it. **Sum** and **i** are both wrong from the first pass.

To fix it we would need to start **i** off as 0. This means that the first increment would make the value of **i** correct. So:

```
int i = 0, count = 0;
```

However, this still doesn't work properly because it carries on doing the calculation until the value in **i** is greater than **count**. The other change we need to make therefore is to change the expression to less than (but not equal to):

```
while ( i < count )
```

Now it will work. This example should help you really understand post and prefixing. If you study it for a moment and look at how the two options work, you won't go wrong.

Nested Loops

Sometimes you may want to place one loop inside another. The simplest way to illustrate the need for this is to look at an example.

Try It Out - Using Nested Loops

We could use a simple example based on our summing integers program to demonstrate a nested loop. The program just uses nested **for** loops. Here we produce the sums of all integers step-by-step up to the value entered. If you look at the program output it will become clearer.

```
/* Example 4.10 Sums of integers step-by-step */
#include <stdio.h>

void main()
{
  long sum = 0L;
  int i = 1, count = 1, number = 0;
  printf("Enter the number of integers you want to sum: ");
  scanf(" %d", &number);

  for( count = 1 ; count <= number ; count++ )
  {
    sum = 0L;

    for(i = 1 ; i <= count ; i++ )
      {
```

```
        sum += i;
    }

    printf("\n%d\t%ld", count, sum);
  }
}
```

You should get ouput like this:

```
Enter the number of integers you want to sum: 5

1    1
2    3
3    6
4    10
5    15
```

How It Works

The program calculates the sum for each integer value up to the value of **count** entered. The important thing to grasp about this nested loop is that the inner loop completes all its iterations on each pass through the outer loop. Thus the outer loop sets up the value **count** which determines how many times the inner loop will repeat.

```
for( count = 1 ; count <= number ; count++ )
{
    sum = 0L;
...
    printf("\n%d\t%ld", count, sum);
}
```

The outer loop starts off by setting **count** to 1, and checking whether **count** (the number of times you have looped) is greater than **number** (the number of times you want to loop). With **count** set to 1, the inner loop is executed, and the result displayed by the **printf()**. The inner loop cannot increase any further as count is still 1. We therefore return to the beginning of the outer loop where **count** is incremented and is checked against the value of **number**. If it is less than or equal to number you go through the for loop again, and then add one to count (you have looped one more time)using **count++**. Remember, you only increment **count** by one at the end of the loop, just before the next iteration.

```
for(i = 1 ; i <= count ; i++ )
  {
    sum += i;
  }
printf("\n%d\t%ld", count, sum);
```

The inner loop totals the integers from 1 to **count** in the variable **sum**, and the outer loop runs the variable **count** from 1 to **number**. Each time the inner loop finishes, control passes back to the end of the outer loop which also contains the **printf()** to output each sum as it is produced. We then go back to the beginning of the outer loop, check the expression and continue.

Look at the output again to see the action of the nested loop. The first loop simply sets the variable **sum** to zero each time round and the inner loop adds up all the numbers from 1 to the current value of **count**.

The do while Loop

There is a third type of loop, the **do while** loop. Now you may be thinking, why should we need this when we already have the **for** and the **while**? Well there is a very subtle and cunning difference. The test is at the end of the loop.

The **while** loop tests at the beginning of the loop. So before any action takes place we check the expression. Look at this fragment of code:

```
int number = 4;
while (number < 4 )
      {
          printf("\nNumber = %d", number);
          number++;
      }
```

Here you would never print anything.

The **do while** loop however, always executes at least once. If we replace the **while** loop above with a **do while** loop leaving the rest of the statements the same;

```
int number = 4;
do
{
```

```
    printf("\nNumber = %d", number);
    number++;

}
while (number < 4 );
```

then when we run through this loop we will get Number = 4 printed out. This is because you will only get a false answer to **number < 4** when you have already displayed the value of number as 4.

The general representation of this loop is as follows:

```
do
{
    Statement;
}
while (expression);
```

> Notice the semicolon after the `while` statement in a `do while` loop. There isn't one in the `while` loop.

In a **do while**, if the value of **expression** is **True** the loop continues, and as you will surely suspect if you have stayed with it so far, only exits when the value of **expression** becomes **False**. You can see how it works more clearly in the next figure.

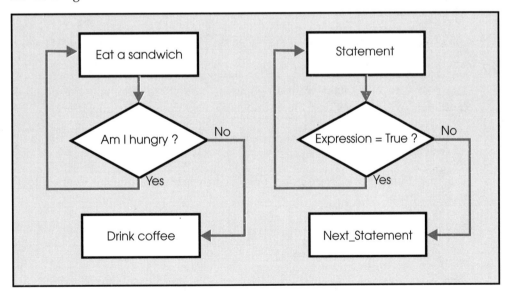

Here you can see that we eat a sandwich *before* we check whether we are hungry or not. We will always eat at least 1 sandwich.

Try It Out - Using a do while Loop

We can illustrate the **do while** loop with a little program that reverses the digits of a positive number:

```
/* Example 4.11 Reversing the digits    */
#include <stdio.h>
void main()
{
  int number = 0, rebmun = 0, temp = 0;

  printf("\nEnter a positive integer: ");
  scanf(" %d", &number);
  temp = number;
  do
  {
    rebmun = 10*rebmun + temp % 10;
    temp = temp/10;
  }
  while (temp);
  printf ("\nThe number %d reversed is  %d rebmun ehT", number, rebmun );
}
```

The following is a sample of output from this program:

```
Enter a positive integer: 43

The number 43 reversed is 34 rebmun ehT
```

How It Works

The best way to explain what is going on here is to step you through a small example. We shall assume the number 43 was entered by the user.

```
  scanf(" %d", &number);
  temp = number;
```

The first thing that the program does is to copy the value in **number** to the variable **temp**.

```
  do
  {
    rebmun = 10*rebmun + temp % 10;
    temp = temp/10;
  }
```

Now we enter the **do while** loop. We get the rightmost digit from **temp** by using the modulus operator, **%** to get the remainder after dividing by 10. We assign the value of **10*rebmun + temp%10** to **rebmun**. Initially the value of **rebmun** is zero. In the loop we store the remainder of the previous calculation, which is 3.

We have now stored the rightmost digit of our input in **rebmun** and we eliminate it from the rest of the calculation by dividing **temp** by 10. This is an integer so the fractional part (the .3) will be removed.

We now reach the bottom of the loop and the **while(temp)** which in our case evaluates to **while(4)** which is **true**. To be **false** the value would have to be zero. Therefore, we go to the top of the loop.

This time we assign to **rebmun** 10 times itself, which is 30 plus the remainder of **temp** divided by 4, so the result is that **rebmun** becomes 34. We again divide **temp** by 10 so it becomes 0. Now when we arrive at the while statement **temp** is 0, which is false so the loop finishes and we have reversed our number. You can see how this would work with numbers with more digits. An example of the program running with a longer number is:

```
Enter a positive integer: 1234

The number 1234 reversed is 4321 rebmun ehT
```

This form of loop is used, but only rarely, compared with the other two forms. Keep it in the back of your mind though, as when you need a loop that executes at least once, it delivers the goods.

Designing a Program

The Problem

The problem we are going to solve is to write a game of Simple Simon. Simple Simon is a memory-test game. The computer displays a set of numbers on the screen for a short period of time. You have to remember them and type them in exactly correctly. As time goes on, the numbers get longer and longer and harder and harder to remember.

The Analysis

Each game is played by the computer generating a stream of numbers between 0 and 9, displaying them on the screen, and the player has to type in the corresponding stream. The stream gets longer until the player gets it wrong. A score is then calculated and the player asked if they would like to play again.

In this situation, it is not always best to start at the top and work through the problem, mainly because of the loops involved. In fact for this problem, we'll start at the outer loop and work inwards.

1   Create a loop that asks if the player wants to play again.

2   Create a loop that keeps going until the player gets a stream wrong.

3   Generate a stream of numbers that grows at regular intervals, i.e. gets harder to remember.

4   Display, then erase the sequence of numbers.

5   Get the player's input and check it against the computer's stream

The Solution

1   Creating this loop is the easiest of the lot. We want the player to have had at least one game before asking whether they want another go. So the loop check must go at the end of the loop, which is a **do while()** loop!

```
/*Example 4.12 simple simon */
#include <stdio.h>

void main()
{
   char another_go;

   do
   {
       printf("\nDo you want to play again (y/n)? ");
       scanf("%c", &another_go);
   } while (another_go == 'y' || another_go == 'Y');
}
```

There is a flaw with this code. If the player types anything other than **y** or **Y** the loop terminates. Instead of trying to fix this, we'll say it is a feature.

2   Now we need another loop which terminates when the player has typed in a wrong sequence of numbers. Again, the question is when do we want to check to see if the player has got it wrong? Again the obvious place is at the end of the loop, which means another **do while()**.

```
/*Example 4.12 simple simon */
#include <stdio.h>

void main()
{
    char another_go, wrong;

    do
    {
      wrong = 'n';
      do
      {
      } while (wrong == 'n');
      printf("\nDo you want to play again (y/n)? ");
      scanf("%c", &another_go);
    } while (another_go == 'y' || another_go == 'Y');
}
```

As you can see, we have used a variable **wrong** to check to see if the player has typed in the wrong sequence. We initialize this to n before the loop starts so that if they have another go, **wrong** is reset.

A word of warning, you may have noticed that at each stage the programs are fully functional and working. This is for a good reason. As you develop your own programs, you want to make sure that they work. If you wrote the whole program in one go, then you may end up with hundreds of errors to correct, and as you correct one problem, more may appear. This can be very frustrating. By breaking the program into pieces, each one works by itself and the problems are easier to manage. This brings us back to the program above. If you run this, then your computer will be completely taken over by the program and you won't easily get it back. The reason is the inner **do while()** loop. The condition for that loop is always true, since the loop doesn't do anything to change the value of **wrong**. However, we will be writing that bit of the program shortly.

3   Now we have a difficult bit to do, generating the list of numbers. There are two problems here to be tackled. The first is to actually generate the numbers. The second is to store those numbers in the computer so that we can check the player's input against the computer's.

Generating the numbers is a problem. The reason is that the numbers have to be random. Luckily for us, C comes to the rescue and gives us a function, `rand()`, in one of the libraries that generates random numbers for us. There is a difficulty with this function though, the numbers are pseudo-random. This means that the sequence of numbers is always the same, and starts at the same number every time the program is run. However, C does have a solution, the function `srand()` which we can use to initialize the sequence at a particular number. Both of these functions are from the **STDLIB** library.

Now, let's think about this a bit more. We need the stream of numbers twice, once to display, and the second time to check against the player's input. We have a function `rand()` which can produce the same list of numbers twice, if it is started at the same number using `srand()`. This actually cures our problem of storing the sequence of numbers. We don't store them, we generate the same sequence twice. We can initialize each sequence by calling `srand()` with the same argument.

The only problem that remains is getting the number to use with `srand()`. Again, this number has to be different each time the program is run, otherwise the sequences will be the same. Yet again, C is our knight in shining armor, and actually provides us with a number which is continuously changing. This number represents the length of time the computer has been on, so you can see that it will be somewhere between difficult and impossible to get the same sequence of numbers each time you play the game. The function that returns this number is called `clock()` and is from the **TIME.H** library.

So let's write some more code now:

```
/*Example 4.12 simple simon */
#include <stdio.h>
#include <stdlib.h>
#include <time.h>

void main()
{
    char another_go, wrong;
    long now;
    int counter, sequence, list;
```

```
    do
    {
        wrong = 'n';
        counter = 0;
        sequence = 2;
        do
        {
/* Set now to be equal to how long the computer has been turned on */
            now = clock();

/* If the player has had 4 successful goes with the current */
/* length of sequence, increase the length */
            if(counter++ % 4 == 0)
                sequence++;

/* Generate a sequence of numbers and display the number*/
            srand((int)now);
            for(list = 1; list <= sequence; list++)
            {
                printf("%d ", rand() % 10);
            }
        } while (wrong == 'n');
        printf("\nDo you want to play again (y/n)? ");
        scanf("%c", &another_go);
    } while (another_go == 'y' || another_go == 'Y');
}
```

There are a couple of other things to notice about the code. First is the conversion of now from a **long** to an **int**. This is because **srand()** requires that we use **int**, but we have a **long** from **clock()**. This limits the number of starting numbers we can use, but not so much that we get repeating patterns. Secondly, we obtain a number between 0 and 9 by taking the modulus of the random number when we divide by 10. This is not the best way of obtaining random digits in the range 0 to 9, but it's a very easy way.

After setting the variable **now** to the current **clock()** value, we check how many times the game has been played using the current sequence length. If the count of the number of games played is a multiple of four, we increase the length of the sequence.

Lastly, if you do run this code as it is, then you may get repeats in the sequence, simply because the value of **clock()** does not change quickly enough. This problem will disappear once we have got the player input code done.

4   As you can see, we have already completed the part that displays the random sequence. We now have to erase the sequence. But before we do, it would be best to let the player see the sequence for a while. To do that we can use **clock()** again. All we have to do is wait until the value of clock has increased by some value above that we have already stored in **now**. But how many? Well, let's say we want the sequence on the screen for only one second. The **TIME.H** header file provides us with a variable that is the number of counts per second - convenient eh?

So let's write that bit of the code before doing the blanking:

```
/*Example 4.12 simple simon */
#include <stdio.h>
#include <stdlib.h>
#include <time.h>

void main()
{
    char another_go, wrong;
    long now;
    int counter, sequence, list;

    do
    {
        wrong = 'n';
        counter = 0;
        sequence = 2;
        do
        {
/* Set now to be equal to how long the computer has been turned on */
            now = clock();

/* If the player has had 4 successful goes with the current */
/* length of sequence, increase the length */
            if(counter++ % 4 == 0)
                sequence++;

/* Generate a sequence of numbers and display the number*/
            srand((int)now);
            for(list = 1; list <= sequence; list++)
            {
                printf("%d ", rand() % 10);
            }
            for(;clock() - now < CLOCKS_PER_SEC;);
        } while (wrong == 'n');
        printf("\nDo you want to play again (y/n)? ");
        scanf("%c", &another_go);
    } while (another_go == 'y' || another_go == 'Y');
}
```

The **for** loop continues until one second's worth of counts have passed since the time recorded in **now**.

Now how do we erase the line? Well, we have not used a **\n** at any point when we displayed the sequence, so we are still on the same line as the output. So if we go to the start of the line, and overwrite what is there with spaces, then we have it. We can go to the start of the line by doing a carriage return without a linefeed, and the **\r** does just that.

```c
/*Example 4.12 simple simon */
#include <stdio.h>
#include <stdlib.h>
#include <time.h>

void main()
{
    char another_go, wrong;
    long now;
    int counter, sequence, list;

    do
    {
        wrong = 'n';
        counter = 0;
        sequence = 2;
        do
        {
/* Set now to be equal to how long the computer has been turned on */
            now = clock();

/* If the player has had 4 successful goes with the current */
/* length of sequence, increase the length */
            if(counter++ % 4 == 0)
                sequence++;

/* Generate a sequence of numbers and display the number*/
            srand((int)now);
            for(list = 1; list <= sequence; list++)
            {
                printf("%d ", rand() % 10);
            }
            for(;clock() - now < CLOCKS_PER_SEC;);
            printf("\r");
            for(list = 1; list <= sequence; list++)
                printf("  ");
        } while (wrong == 'n');
        printf("\nDo you want to play again (y/n)? ");
        scanf("%c", &another_go);
    } while (another_go == 'y' || another_go == 'Y');
}
```

5 Now let's get the player input. We can check the input at each number of the sequence, rather than after all of them have been entered. This saves having to store the numbers typed in. If we come across a number that is wrong, we simply set wrong to **y** which terminates the inner **do while()** loop.

```c
/*Example 4.12 simple simon */
#include <stdio.h>
#include <stdlib.h>
#include <time.h>

void main()
{
    char another_go, wrong;
    long now;
    int counter, sequence, list, number;

    do
    {
        wrong = 'n';
        counter = 0;
        sequence = 2;
        do
        {
/* Set now to be equal to how long the computer has been turned on */
            now = clock();

/* If the player has had 4 secessful goes with the current */
/* length of sequence, increase the length */
            if(counter++ % 4 == 0)
                sequence++;

/* Generate a sequence of numbers and display the number*/
            srand((int)now);
            for(list = 1; list <= sequence; list++)
            {
                printf("%d ", rand() % 10);
            }
            for(;clock() - now < CLOCKS_PER_SEC;);
            printf("\r");
            for(list = 1; list <= sequence; list++)
                printf("  ");
            printf("\nNow you type in the sequence\n");
            srand((int)now);
            for(list = 1; list <= sequence; list++)
            {
                scanf("%d", &number);
                if(number != rand() % 10)
                {
                    wrong = 'y';
                    break;
                }
            }
```

```
    } while (wrong == 'n');
    printf("\nDo you want to play again (y/n)? ");
    scanf("%c", &another_go);
  } while (another_go == 'y' || another_go == 'Y');
}
```

All that remains is to generate a score to display once the player has got a sequence wrong. We will use the number of sequences completed, and how many seconds it took them. We will also display a message explaining how to play the game.

There is one remaining problem with this program that needs seeing to. If you have played the game already you may have noticed a problem. If one of the numbers typed by the player is wrong, then the loop exits, and the player is asked if they want to play again. However, if the player has typed ahead, then we could end up with the next number typed in as the answer to **Do you want to play again (y/n)?** What we need to do is remove any information that is still in the **keyboard buffer**. So there are two problems, first, how to address the keyboard buffer, and secondly, how to clean out the buffer.

> The keyboard buffer is memory that is assigned to the keyboard. What you type in is stored in the keyboard buffer. Generally, programs look in the keyboard buffer for input rather than the keyboard itself.

With standard input and output, there are actually two buffers, one for input called **stdin** and one for output, **stdout**. Now that we know what the buffer is called, how do we remove the information in it? Well, C provides us with a function for clearing out buffers, although this tends to be used for files which are covered later in the book. However, the function will work for any buffer at all, we simply tell the function which buffer. And the function's name? Well, it's called **fflush()**. So to clean out the contents of the input buffer, we simply use **fflush(stdin);** as you will see below:

```
/*Example 4.12 simple simon */
#include <stdio.h>
#include <stdlib.h>
#include <time.h>

void main()
{
  char another_go, wrong;
  long now, time_taken;
  int counter, sequence, list, number;
```

```
    printf("To play Simple Simon, ");
    printf("watch the screen for a sequence of  numbers.\n");
    printf("Watch carefully, as the numbers ");
    printf("are only displayed for a second!\n");
    printf("The computer will then prompt you ");
    printf("to type in the sequence. When you do,\n");
    printf("you must either put spaces between each number, ");
    printf("or press return\n");
    printf("after each.\n");
    printf("\nGood Luck!\nPress return to play\n");
    scanf("%c", &another_go);

 do
 {
     wrong = 'n';
     counter = 0;
     sequence = 2;
     time_taken = clock();
     do
     {
/* Set now to be equal to how long the computer has been turned on */
         now = clock();

/* If the player has had 4 secessful goes with the current */
/* length of sequence, increase the length */
         if(counter++ % 4 == 0)
             sequence++;

/* Generate a sequence of numbers and display the number*/
         srand((int)now);
         for(list = 1; list <= sequence; list++)
         {
             printf("%d ", rand() % 10);
         }
         for(;clock() - now < CLOCKS_PER_SEC;);
         printf("\r");
         for(list = 1; list <= sequence; list++)
             printf("  ");
         printf("\nNow you type in the sequence\n");
         srand((int)now);
         for(list = 1; list <= sequence; list++)
         {
```

```
            scanf("%d", &number);
            if(number != rand() % 10)
            {
               wrong = 'y';
                break;
            }
         }
      } while (wrong == 'n');
      time_taken = (clock() - time_taken) / CLOCKS_PER_SEC;
      printf("\n\n Your score is %d", --counter * 100 / time_taken);

      fflush(stdin);

      printf("\nDo you want to play again (y/n)? ");
      scanf("%c", &another_go);
   } while (another_go == 'y' || another_go == 'Y');
}
```

Now we just need to see what happens when we actually play:

```
To play Simple Simon, watch the screen for a sequence of numbers.
Watch carefully, as the numbers are only displayed for a second!
The computer will then prompt you to type in the sequence. When you do,
you must either put spaces between each number, or press return
after each.

Good Luck!
Press return to play


Now you type in the sequence
4 2 9

Now you type in the sequence
8 2 2


 Your score is 7
Do you want to play again (y/n)? n
```

Summary

In this chapter we have covered all we need to know about repeating actions using loops. With the powerful array of programming tools you have learnt up to now, you should be able to create quite complex programs of your own.

In keeping with this chapter topic we will now repeat ourselves and reiterate some of the rules and recommendations we have come across so far.

> Before you start programming, work out the logic of the process and computations you want to perform, and write it down - preferably in the form of a flow chart. Try to think of lateral approaches to a problem, there may be a better way than the obvious approach.

> Use parentheses to ensure expressions do what you want, and are readily understood.

> Comment your programs to explain all aspects of their operation and use. Assume the comments are for the benefit of someone else reading your program with a view to extending or modifying it. Explain the purpose of each variable as you declare it.

> Program with readability foremost in your mind. Go for the simple, easy to understand programming style, rather than the flashy, convoluted, and opaque use of the language facilities.

> Avoid using ! as far as you can in complicated logical expressions.

> Use indentation to visually indicate the structure of your program.

Prepared with this advice let's move on to the next chapter.

Arrays

When you write programs you often want to store lots of similar information about one thing. For example, if you are a regular basket ball player you might want to write a program to store your scores over a season's games. You could then print out your scores from the different games, or work out your on-going average. Armed with what you have learnt so far, you could write a program that does this using a different variable for each score. However, if you play a lot of games, this won't be very efficient. All your scores are really the same kind of thing. The values are different, but they are all basket ball scores. Wouldn't it be great if you could group these values together without having to declare separate variables for each one?

In this chapter we will show you how to do just that, using C to group collections of data, in particular, collections of data that are of the same type. We will then show you how useful this can be when you start to write bigger programs that process collections of information like this. These collections are called arrays.

In this chapter you will:

- Learn what arrays are
- Learn how to use them
- Understand a little more about memory
- Learn what a multi-dimensional array is
- Write a program to work out your hat size
- Write a game of tic-tac-toe

An Introduction to Arrays

The best way to show you what an array is and how powerful it can be is to go through an example where we need an array, but don't use one. What we are going to do is use an example to show what problems arise, and see how an array will solve them. Let's look at ways in which we could find the average score of the students in a college.

Programs Without Arrays

To find the average score of a class of students we'll assume that there are only 10 students in the class (mainly because we hate typing in a lot of numbers). To work out an average of a group of numbers, we add them all together and then divide by how many we have (in this case 10):

```c
/* Averaging ten numbers without storing the numbers */
#include <stdio.h>

void main()
{
    int number = 0, counter = 0;
    float average = 0.0f;
    long sum = 0L;

/* Enter in the ten numbers to be averaged */
    for(counter = 0; counter <= 9; counter ++)
    {
        printf("Enter grade: ");
        scanf("%d", &number);
        sum += number;
    }

/* Now we have the ten numbers, we can calculate the average */
    average = (float)sum / 10.0;

    printf("Average of the ten numbers entered is: %f", average);
}
```

If we are only interested in the average we don't have to remember what the previous grades were. All we are interested in is the sum of them all, which we then divide by 10. The program is simple and uses a single variable (**number**) to enter the grade within a loop. We've done this sort of thing before, so the program should be clear.

But, let's assume that this is part of a longer program, and that you will need the values you enter later. Perhaps you might want to print out each person's grade with the average grade next to it to compare them. In the above program you only have one variable. Each time you add a grade, the old value is no longer stored and you can't get it back again.

So how do you store the results? One way you can do this is by declaring ten integers to store the grades in, but then you can't use a **for** loop to enter the values. Instead you have to enter the values individually. This would work, but is quite tiresome:

```
/* Averaging ten numbers - storing the numbers the hard way */
#include <stdio.h>

void main()
{
    int number0 = 0, number1 = 0, number2 = 0, number3 = 0, number4 = 0;
    int number5 = 0, number6 = 0, number7 = 0, number8 = 0, number9 = 0;

    float average = 0.0f;
    long sum = 0L;

/* Enter in the ten numbers to be averaged */
    printf("Enter the first five numbers,\n");
    printf("use a space or RETURN between each number.\n");
    scanf("%d%d%d%d%d", &number0, &number1, &number2, &number3, &number4);
    printf("Enter the last five numbers,\n");
    printf("use a space or RETURN between each number.\n");
    scanf("%d%d%d%d%d", &number5, &number6, &number7, &number8, &number9);

/* Now we have the ten numbers, we can calculate the average */
    sum = number0 + number1+ number2 + number3 + number4;
    sum += number5 + number6 + number7 + number8 + number9;
    average = (float)sum / 10.0;

    printf("Average of the ten numbers entered is: %f", average);
}
```

This is OK for ten students, but what if your class had 30 students, or 100, or 1000? How can you do it then? Well, this is where arrays come in.

What is an Array?

An array is a collection of data elements that are all of the same type. This is an important feature of an array - the elements of individual arrays are all **int**s, **long**s or whatever. So we can have **int** arrays, **float** arrays, **long** arrays and so on. To declare a **int** array with 10 elements we write:

```
long numbers[10];
```

This is very similar to how you would declare a normal variable that contains a single value, except that we have placed a number between brackets [ ] following the name. This tells us how many elements we want to store in our array. The important feature here is that all the data stored in the array is accessed by the same name, in our case this is **numbers**.

If we only have one variable name, but are storing 10 values, how do we differentiate between them? This is where the number in the brackets comes in. Each individual value in the array is referenced and accessed by placing a different integer in the brackets. This is called an **index value**. The index values in the above array would run from 0 to 9. Therefore, the array elements would be **numbers[0]**, **numbers[1]**, **numbers[2]** … **numbers[9]**. You can see this in the following figure.

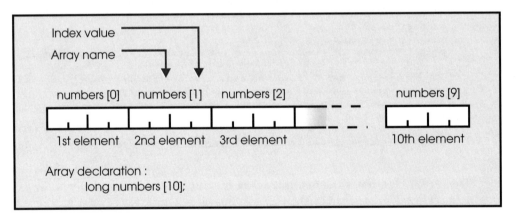

Notice that they don't start from 1, they start from 0. In a 10 element array the last element's index value is 9. This means that to access the fourth value in our array we would type **numbers[3]**.

> The individual elements of an array have index values starting at zero. This can cause confusion at first because the fifth element of an array (called `array` for example) will have an index of 4 (`array[4]`). Remember, the last element always has an index value of one less than the number of elements.

To access an individual value in the array **numbers**, we could also place an expression in the square brackets following the array name. The expression would have to result in an integer value that corresponded to one of the possible index values. For example, you could write **numbers[3-2]**. This would be a long-winded way of accessing **numbers[1]**, the second element.

To summarize, you have two ways to access an element of an array. You can use a simple number to explicitly reference which element you want to access. Alternatively, you can use an expression using integer constants and variables which are evaluated during the execution of the program.

If you try to use an index value in your program that is outside the legal range for an array, the program won't work properly. After all, who knows what number you would get if you asked for the score of the 11th student when you only had 10.

Using Arrays

That's a lot of theory, but we still haven't solved our average score problem. How can we put what we have learnt into practice?

Try It Out - Averages With Arrays

Now that we understand arrays, we can use an array to store all the scores we want to average. This means that all the values will be saved and we will be able to re-use them. We can now re-write the program to average ten scores:

```
/* Example 5.1 Averaging ten numbers - storing the numbers the easy way */
#include <stdio.h>

void main()
{
    int number[10];
    int counter = 0;
```

```
   float average = 0.0f;
   long sum = 0L;

/* Enter in the ten numbers to be averaged */
   printf("Enter the ten numbers:\n");
   for(counter = 0; counter <= 9; counter++)
   {
      printf("%2d> ", counter+1);
      scanf("%d", &number[counter]);
      sum += number[counter];
   }

/* Now we have the ten numbers, we can calculate the average */
   average = (float)sum / 10.0;

   printf("Average of the ten numbers entered is: %f", average);
}
```

The output from the program looks something like this:

```
Enter the ten numbers:
 1> 450
 2> 765
 3> 562
 4> 700
 5> 598
 6> 635
 7> 501
 8> 720
 9> 689
10> 527
Average of the ten numbers entered is: 614.700000
```

How It Works

```
/* Example 5.1 Averaging ten numbers - storing the numbers the easy way */
#include <stdio.h>
```

We start off the program with the ubiquitous **#include <stdio.h>**.

```
void main()
{
   int number[10];
   int counter = 0;

   float average = 0.0f;
   long sum = 0L;
```

Next, we declare an array of ten integers, and then the other variables we will need for this example. Notice that we have initialized **sum** to zero at the same time as we declare it. This short-cut is something that you will notice keeps cropping up in C programs, and we hope that you start using it too.

```
/* Enter in the ten numbers to be averaged */
   printf("Enter the ten numbers:\n");
```

Now we display a message asking the user to type in ten numbers.

```
for(counter = 0; counter <= 9; counter++)
   {
```

This is the start of the loop. Although we are repeating ourselves, don't forget that the loop counts from 0 to 9, rather than 1 to 10. This way we can use the loop variable to reference the members of the array.

```
      printf("%2d> ", counter+1);
```

This is just an ordinary **printf()** statement that tells the user which number they are typing in. But is it really so ordinary? Look closely at the output specifier. There is a 2 there. The 2 is a modifier for the output specifier. We are using the **%d** specifier because we are displaying an integer value and the 2 in the middle of the specifier tells the **printf()** function to use a field width of 2 characters. We are not just using single figures, the number 10 is double figures. Using the 2 means that the prompts will all line up:

```
 1>
 2>
 3>
 4>
 5>
 6>
 7>
 8>
 9>
10>
```

If we had used **%d** instead, the output would have been:

```
1>
2>
3>
4>
5>
6>
7>
8>
9>
10>
```

which, for the artistically minded, is terrible. We'll introduce you to more modifiers as we go along.

```
    scanf("%d", &number[counter]);
    sum += number[counter];
```

Next we get the value from the user, specifying the member of the array in which we want to store the input by using **number[counter]**. We then add this to **sum**. This is one reason why we have initialized **sum** to zero at the start. As we are using **sum += number[counter]**, this expands to **sum = sum + number[counter]**. If we had not initialized **sum** before we started the loop, the program wouldn't be correct because we are using an uninitialized variable. We keep going around this loop until we have ten values.

```
    average = (float)sum / 10.0;

    printf("Average of the ten numbers entered is: %f", average);
}
```

Finally, we calculate the average by dividing the sum by 10, and print the result. Again, notice how we have told the compiler to convert **sum**, which is defined as **long**, into a **float**. This is not necessary as the compiler will do this itself, but when it does, some compilers complain, and we hate complaints!

Try It Out - Proving that the Numbers are Stored

This example in itself doesn't show how useful the array is, but we can expand it a little to demonstrate the advantages. We have only made a few changes to the original program (highlighted below), but now we can print out all the values we typed in. This means that we can access those values whenever we want.

```
/* Example 5.2 Proving that the numbers are stored */
#include <stdio.h>

void main()
{
    int number[10];
    int counter = 0;

    float average = 0.0f;
    long sum = 0L;
```

```
/* Enter in the ten numbers to be averaged */
   printf("Enter the ten numbers:\n");
   for(counter = 0; counter <= 9; counter++)
   {
      printf("%2d> ", counter+1);
      scanf("%d", &number[counter]);
      sum += number[counter];
   }

/* Now we have the ten numbers, we can calculate the average */
   average = (float)sum / 10.0;

   for(counter = 0; counter <= 9; counter++)
   printf("\nGrade No %d was %d", counter + 1, number[counter]);

   printf("\nAverage of the ten numbers entered is: %f", average);
}
```

Typical output would be:

```
Enter the ten numbers:
 1> 56
 2> 64
 3> 34
 4> 51
 5> 52
 6> 78
 7> 62
 8> 51
 9> 47
10> 32

Grade No 1 was 56
Grade No 2 was 64
Grade No 3 was 34
Grade No 4 was 51
Grade No 5 was 52
Grade No 6 was 78
Grade No 7 was 62
Grade No 8 was 51
Grade No 9 was 47
Grade No 10 was 32
Average of the ten numbers entered is: 52.700001
```

How It Works

We will just quickly explain the new bits.

```
for(counter = 0; counter <= 9; counter++);
    printf("\nGrade No %d was %d", counter + 1, number[counter]);
```

We have simply added another **for** loop to repeat the values in the array. As the loop loops, we print out the number of the element and the value stored there. These numbers obviously correspond to the numbers we typed in.

```
printf("\nAverage of the ten numbers entered is: %f", average);
```

The only change here is that we have used **\n** to put this on a new line.

Before we go any further with these wonderful information containers called arrays, we need to discuss how your variables are stored in the computer memory. We also need to understand how an array is different from the variables we have seen up to now.

A Reminder About Memory

Let's quickly recap on what we told you about memory in Chapter 2.

You can think of the memory of your computer as an ordered line of boxes. Each of these boxes is one of two states, either the box is full (let's call this state 1), or the box is empty (this is state 0).

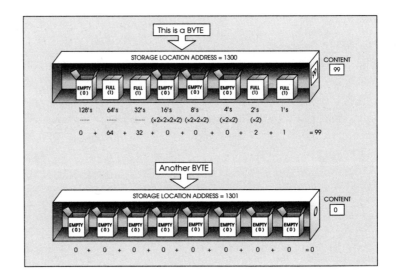

For convenience we group our boxes in sets of 8. To get to the contents we label each of the groups of 8 boxes with a number, starting from 0 and going up to whatever number of groups of boxes we have. To return to the real world situation, each of these groups of boxes is a **byte** of storage and each box a **bit**. A bit can only be either 1 or 0 and a byte can only be made up of a series of 1s and 0s.

This storage is similar to your computer's memory. The computer stores information in its Random Access Memory (or RAM) as a series of 0s and 1s. These **binary** digits (or **bits**) are grouped together in groups of 8 known as **bytes**, and each of these bytes is given a reference number or **address**.

You may recall the **address of** operator **&**, which we have been using with the **scanf()** function. We have been using this to enter data from the user into the variable. Remember how we always have to prefix the variable name with an **&**. The **address of** operator simply gives us the address of the variable and this then allows us to store information there. The best way to get a feel for the **address of** operator is to use it a bit more, so let's try.

Try It Out - Using the Address of Operator

The variables that you use in your programs all take up a certain amount of memory, measured in bytes, which is dependent on their type. Let's try finding the address of some variables of different types.

```
/* Example 5.3 Using the & operator   */
#include<stdio.h>

void main()
{
  int a =1,b =2,c =3;                    /* declare some integers */
  float d =4.0,e =5.0,f =6.0;            /* declare some floats    */

  printf("\nThe address of a is: %p,  The Address of b is: %p", &a, &b);
  printf("\nThe address of c is: %p", &c);
  printf("\nThe address of d is: %p,  The Address of e is: %p", &d, &e);
  printf("\nThe Address of f is: %p", &f);
}
```

Output from this program will be something like this:

```
The address of a is: FFF4   The address of b is: FFF2
The address of c is: FFF0
The address of d is: FFEC   The address of e is: FFE8
The address of f is: FFE4
```

How It Works

Don't be too concerned if your results are different from these, it depends on the computer that you are using.

```
int a =1,b =2,c =3;                    /* declare some integers */
float d =4.0,e =5.0,f =6.0;            /* declare some floats   */
```

We declare and initialize some variables or different types.

```
printf("\nThe address of a is: %p,  The Address of b is: %p", &a, &b);
printf("\nThe address of c is: %p", &c);
printf("\nThe address of d is: %p,  The Address of e is: %p", &d, &e);
printf("\nThe Address of f is: %p", &f);
```

We then display the addresses of those variables using the **address of** operator. This is the **&** that precedes the variables. We have also used another format specifier **%p** to print the address of the variables. This is an ANSI standard format specifer which is frequently used when dealing with addresses and which usually produces output in hexadecimal format. Each of our addresses is four hexadecimal digits.

In fact, the interesting part isn't the program itself so much as the output. Look at the addresses that print out. You can see that the value of the address gets steadily lower in a regular pattern. The address of **b** is lower than **a** by 2, and **c** is lower than **b** also by 2. There is a similar situation with the variables **d**, **e**, and **f** except that the difference is 4. What is the difference between the first 3 variables and the last 3?

The first 3 are integers and the last 3 are floating point variables. The conclusion that can be drawn from this is that **float**s take up more of your memory than **int**s. Also you can see that the variables are stored sequentially one after the other in the memory area of the computer. If you look at the next figure we can see how this works. The value of your variable is stored at an address in memory.

Once we have the address of a variable, what do we find there?

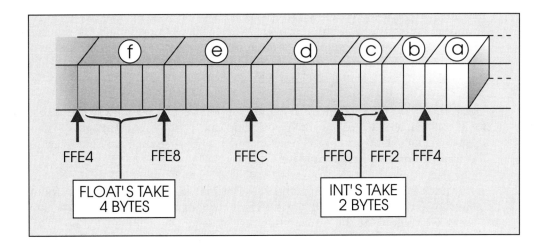

How to Remember More Than 1s and 0s

As we have seen, the computer is quite content to deal with just 1s and 0s, but for your average human there isn't a great deal that we can do with these. We need some sort of interpretation to take place so that these digits can be used in a meaningful way. This is why we declare our variables with a type.

The type tells the compiler what sort of value you are going to store in the variable, and how to interpret the information displayed as 1s and 0s. For example, when we declare an **int** variable to hold values in the range of -32,768 to +32,767, the compiler will allocate 2 bytes of memory (that is 16 binary digits). If we want to use floating point numbers, then we need to store information about the number itself (the mantissa), and the power of 10 which it is multiplied by (the exponent). This takes up more than 2 bytes. You can see this from our example, where the variables declared as **float** occupy 4 bytes.

Storing Alphabetic Information in Memory

You now have an idea about how we store numbers in memory, but what about characters and all the other alphabetic information we wish to hold as computer data? We use computers to store records about people, for example detailing their names and addresses. For this numbers alone aren't enough, so what method does the computer provide for characters?

Basically, the answer is none. However, we can store the characters by adopting the convention that each character will be represented by a number that we can store in a single byte of memory. So, to represent the letter 'A', if we are using ASCII codes, we use the decimal number 65, (or hexadecimal 0x41). For 'T' we use the decimal 84.

There is a code for each character and symbol we can use. There are also codes for the characters '0' to '9' which you shouldn't confuse with integers. Also, there are many non-printing characters such as the newline \n character and all the other format control characters.

As a quick summary of binary and hexadecimal numbers, look at the following table that compares values in the different formats. To remind you how the system works look at the figure after the table.

Decimal	Binary	Hexadecimal
0	0000	0
1	0001	1
2	0010	2
3	0011	3
4	0100	4
5	0101	5
6	0110	6
7	0111	7
8	1000	8
9	1001	9
10	1010	A
11	1011	B
12	1100	C
13	1101	D
14	1110	E
15	1111	F

DECIMAL					BINARY						HEXADECIMAL		
(10×10×10)	10×10	10	U		2×2×2×2	2×2×2	2×2	2	U		16×16	16	U
1000s	100s	10s	1s		16s	8s	4s	2s	1s		256s	16s	1s
0	0	1	6	=	1	0	0	0	0	=	0	1	0
0	0	2	3	=	1	0	1	1	1	=	0	1	7
0	0	2	8	=	1	1	1	0	0	=	0	1	C

Look at the table on the previous page. You can see that a 4 digit binary number (from 0000 to 1111) can represent values from 0 to 15 in decimal. This is the same range as for a single hexadecimal digit (0 to F). Hexadecimal is frequently used when dealing with the numeric value held in a byte of memory, because of this relationship between hexadecimal and binary. Two hexadecimal digits represent one byte.

The full set of ASCII codes can be found in Appendix B.

Arrays and Addresses

With arrays, the method of addressing is slightly different. The name of the array is not as simple to use as a normal variable because it can reference more than one item of information. If you have an array called **number**, you may have 10 values stored in it. The array name **number** gets you to the right area of memory where your data is stored and the specific location is found with the index value.

The index is a way of telling the compiler how far into the array the data you require is held. When you declare your array the computer allocates a certain area in memory for the values you will store there. You give it all the information it needs here. You tell it the type of value (which will require a certain number of bytes) and how many there will be (the number of elements). From this it can create the necessary space as a row of named, but as yet empty boxes. The address of the whole array (the array name) gets you to the first box. The index tells you how many boxes along you have to go. Once you are there you can find out what the address of this array element is.

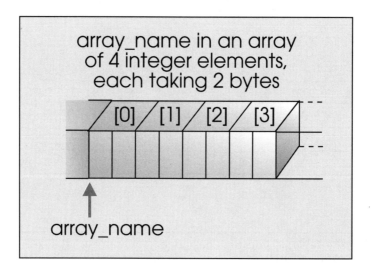

The figure represents the way that array variables are held in memory.

We can obtain the address of an array element in a similar way to the one we used for ordinary variables. For an integer variable called **number**, we would use the following statement to print its address:

```
printf("\n%p", &number);
```

To obtain the address of the third element of an array called **many**, we could write the following:

```
printf("\n%p", &many[2]);
```

Remember that we use the value 2 in the brackets to reach the third element. Here we have taken the address of the element with the **address of** operator. If you used the same line but deleted the **&**, you would print out the actual value stored in the 3rd element of the array, not its address.

Multi-dimensional Arrays

So far we have been dealing with one-dimensional arrays. You are not limited to just one index dimension for an array. You can declare arrays of two or more dimensions. If you grew carrots in a field in 25 rows of 50 plants, you could use a two-dimensional array to record how big each carrot turned out to be. If you had ten fields of carrots on your farm you could use a three-dimensional array. One dimension would be for the fields, one dimension for the row in the field, and the third for the particular carrot. Of course if you had several farms...well, you get the idea. Let's stick to two dimensions for the moment and work our way up. A two-dimensional array can be declared as:

```
float carrots[25][50];
```

This declares an array **carrots** containing 25 rows of 50 floating point elements. Similarly, we can declare another two-dimensional array of floating point numbers with the statement:

```
float numbers[3][5];
```

Like the vegetables in the field, we tend to visualize these as rectangular arrangements. They are actually stored in memory sequentially by row as shown in the figure below.

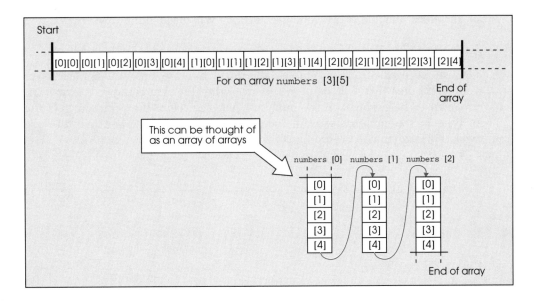

Each element of an array needs a certain number of bytes to store it. To show an array of a different size, the following figure illustrates how a **float** array **numbers[4][10]** is stored.

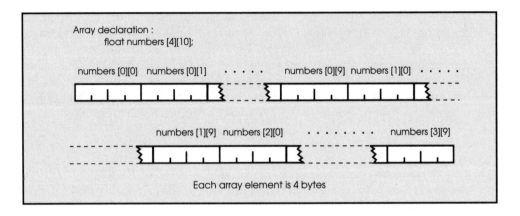

```
Array declaration :
    float numbers [4][10];

numbers [0][0]  numbers [0][1]   · · · · ·     numbers [0][9]  numbers [1][0]  · · · · ·


            numbers [1][9]  numbers [2][0]   · · · · · · · ·     numbers [3][9]


                    Each array element is 4 bytes
```

It is easy to see that the rightmost index varies first. You can also envisage a two-dimensional array as one-dimensional, where each element is itself a one-dimensional array. Let's look at the **numbers** array above. The first row of 10 **float** type numbers is held in memory at an address labeled **numbers[0]**, and the next 10 at **numbers[1]**, the next 10 at **numbers[2]** and so on. The amount of memory that is allocated to each element is of course dependent on the type of variables that the array contains. **float**s will need more than **int**s.

Try It Out - Multidimensional Arrays

Let's move away from vegetables and turn to more practical applications for your computer that will help you in everyday life. We could use arrays in a program to help you to work out your hat size. Here the program gets the user to type in the circumference of their head in inches and then tells the user what hat size that corresponds to.

Try It Out!

```
/* Example 5.4 Know your hat size - if you dare....        */
#include <stdio.h>
void main()
{
  char Size[3][12] = {
      {'6', '6', '6', '6', '7', '7', '7', '7', '7', '7', '7', '7'},
      {'1', '5', '3', '7', ' ', '1', '1', '3', '1', '5', '3', '7'},
      {'2', '8', '4', '8', ' ', '8', '4', '8', '2', '8', '4', '8'}
                      };               /* Hat sizes as characters       */
  int Headsize[12] =
      {164,166,169,172,175,178,181,184,188,191,194,197};
                                       /* Values in 1/8 inches          */
  float Cranium =0.0;                  /* Value in decimal inches       */
  int Your_Head = 0;                   /* Headsize in whole eighths     */
  int i =0;                            /* Loop counter
           */
  int hat_found = 0;                   /* Checks if a hat is found to fit */
  int too_small = 0;                   /* Used when headsize is too small */
  printf("\nEnter the circumference of your head above your eyebrows "
      "in inches as a decimal value: ");
  scanf(" %f", &Cranium);
  Your_Head = 8.0* Cranium;        /* Convert to whole eighths of an inch */

  for ( i=0 ; i< 12 ; i++ )
  {
      if (Your_Head > Headsize [i] )
        continue;
        if(( i == 0) && (Your_Head < Headsize[0] -1))
          {
          printf("\nYou are the proverbial pinhead. "
                  "No hat for you I'm afraid.");
                    too_small = 1;
      break;
          }
          if( Your_Head < Headsize[i] - 1 )
            i-=1;
          printf("\nYour hat size is %c %c%c%c",
            Size[0][i], Size[1][i], (i==4)?' ' : '/', Size[2][i]);
          hat_found =1;
          break;
  }
  if ((hat_found ==0) && (too_small == 0))
  printf("\nYou, in technical parlance, are a fathead."
                    " No hat for you, I'm afraid.");
}
```

Typical output from this program would be:

```
Enter the circumference of your head above your eyebrows in inches as a
decimal value: 22.5
Your hat size is 7 1/4

Enter the circumference of your head above your eyebrows in inches as a
decimal value: 29
You, in technical parlance, are a fathead. No hat for you I'm afraid.
```

How It Works

Before we start discussing this example, we should give a word of caution. Don't use it to assist large football players to determine their hat size unless they are known for their sense of humor. Remember the old saying - "the bigger they are, the harder they hit".

This example is here to illustrate using arrays rather than programming elegance, so it looks a bit complicated. Let's go through what's happening.

The first declaration is:

```
char Size[3][12] = {
    {'6', '6', '6', '6', '7', '7', '7', '7', '7', '7', '7', '7'},
    {'1', '5', '3', '7', ' ', '1', '1', '3', '1', '5', '3', '7'},
    {'2', '8', '4', '8', ' ', '8', '4', '8', '2', '8', '4', '8'}
};      /* Hat sizes as characters */
```

This array corresponds to twelve possible hat sizes, each of which are made up of 3 values. For each size we have stored three characters to make it more convenient to output the fractional sizes. The smallest hat size is 6 1/2, so the first three characters corresponding to the first size are in `Size[0][0]`, `Size[1][0]`, and `Size[2][0]`. They contain the characters '6', '1', and '2' representing the size 6 1/2. The biggest hat size is 7 7/8 and is stored in `Size[0][11]`, `Size[1][11]`, `Size[2][11]`.

```
int Headsize[12] =
    {164,166,169,172,175,178,181,184,188,191,194,197};
                                /* Values in 1/8 inches */
```

We then declare the array `Headsize`, which provides the reference dimensions in this declaration. The values in the array are all whole eighths of an inch. They correspond to the values in the `Size` array containing the hat sizes. This means that a head size of 164 eighths of an inch (about 20.5 inches) will give a hat size of 6 1/2.

Notice that the head sizes don't run consecutively. You could get a headsize of 171, for example, which doesn't fall into a definite hat size. We need to be aware of this later in the program so that we can decide which is the closest hat size for the head size.

```
float Cranium =0.0;          /* Value in decimal inches        */
int Your_Head = 0;           /* Headsize in whole eighths      */
int i =0;                    /* Loop counter                   */
                    */
int hat_found = 0;           /* Checks if a hat is found to fit */
int too_small = 0;           /* Used when headsize is too small */
```

After declaring our arrays, we then declare all the variables we are going to need. Notice that **Cranium** is declared as a **float**, but the rest are all **int**s. This is important later.

```
printf("\nEnter the circumference of your head above your eyebrows "
    "in inches as a decimal value: ");
scanf(" %f", &Cranium);
```

You enter your head size in inches, and the value is stored in the variable **Cranium** (remember it's a **float**, so at this stage we can store values that are not whole numbers).

```
Your_Head = 8.0* Cranium;  /* Convert to whole eighths of an inch */
```

The value of **Cranium** is converted with the above statement into eighths of an inch. These values will then correspond to the values declared in the second array.

However, this new value is stored in **Your_Head**, which is an **int** not a **float**. This means that, after the conversion to eighths of an inch, the result stored will be your head size as an integral number of whole eighths of an inch. Any fraction of an eighth will be lost. We will use this new number to find your hat size in the array **Headsize[12]**.

```
for ( i=0 ; i< 12 ; i++ )
{
  if (Your_Head > Headsize [i] )
    continue;
  . . .
}
```

Our process is a simple one, and is carried out in this **for** loop. What happens is the loop compares your head size with each value stored in the array **Headsize** to find the first value that is less than or equal to your input size. The first **if** compares the size you entered with the current **Headsize** element, and if **Your_Head** is greater, the **continue** is executed.

The **continue** is a new keyword for use in a loop. In some respects it's similar to the **break** keyword which we have used before, in that it causes the computer to skip the rest of the statements in the loop. However, unlike the **break** statement the loop isn't exited. Instead the end of loop operation is carried out, which in this case increments the variable **i** by one. The loop then carries on as normal.

So, in our example, if the value of **Your_Head** is less than the value in the current position (the **i**th position) in the **Headsize** array, then we use **continue** to move to the end of the loop. This increments **i** by 1 and then takes us back to the beginning of the loop to check against the next value in **Headsize**. Once the value in the **i**th element of **Headsize** is greater than **Your_Head**, we can find your hat size.

It's possible that someone could enter a value that was too big or too small for our hats. We first check for small heads.

```
if(( i == 0) && (Your_Head < Headsize[0] -1))
    {
    printf("\nYou are the proverbial pinhead. "
            "No hat for you I'm afraid.");
                too_small = 1;
break;
    }
```

This **if** checks whether the first time you loop (**i == 0**) the value of **Your_Head** is less than the first value in the **Headsize** array. To be precise it checks whether **Your_Head** is more than 1 eighth of an inch less (**Your_Head < Headsize[0] - 1**). If so, then we know that the value entered must be smaller than that for a size 6 1/2 (our smallest size) and we write the pinhead message. We also assign the value 1 to **too_small**. We then **break** out of the loop because there is no point in checking against all the larger sizes.

```
if( Your_Head < Headsize[i] - 1 )
    i-=1;
printf("\nYour hat size is %c %c%c%c",
    Size[0][i], Size[1][i], (i==4)?' ' : '/', Size[2][i]);
hat_found =1;
break;
```

Once we have incremented **i** the right number of times, so that the value stored in the **i**th element of the **Headsize** array is greater than the value of **Your_Head**, we can at last find out our hat size.

The first line may look a little strange. Why are we subtracting 1 from **Headsize**? We have to do this because the **Headsize** values don't run consecutively. Imagine that **Your_Head** had a value of 170. We would loop 4 times and **i** would go up to 3 (so **Headsize** would be 172) before the line **Your_Head > Headsize** was true and we got to this final part of the code.

Imagine **Your_Head** is 170 you really want a 169 **headsize** equivalent, not a 172 which is too big. If **Your_Head** is smaller than **Headsize** minus 1 (in our example, if 170 is less than 172 minus 1, which it is), we subtract 1 from **i** so that you get the previous hat size.

We now use the value of the loop counter, **i**, to print the size of the hat for the given head size.

```
printf("\nYour hat size is %c %c%c%c",
    Size[0][i], Size[1][i], (i==4)?' ' : '/', Size[2][i]);
```

As we said, the hat sizes are stored in the array **Size** as characters to simplify the outputting of fractions. Assuming a suitable size has been found, the output is performed by the above statement.

The **printf()** here uses the conditional operator to decide when to print a blank and when to print a slash (/) for the fractional output value. The fifth element of the **Headsize** array corresponds to a hat size of exactly 7. We don't want it to print **7 /** we just want **7**. Therefore we customize the **printf()** depending on whether element **i** is equal to 4 (remember this is the fifth element, starting your count from zero).

If the program falls through the end of the loop and on each loop the size of **your_head** was greater than the value in the **Headsize** array, then the value entered must have been larger than all the stored values. So we print the offensive message, checking we haven't found a hat and that **too_small** is 0.

Try leaving out the part of the **if** statement that checks the **too_small** variable and enter a small value for the size of **Your_Head**. You will see that both offensive remarks are used which isn't what we want at all. This illustrates why we used the variables **too_small** and **hat_found** to control what we output to the screen.

Remember, when using this program, if you lie about the size of your head, your hat will not fit.

Initializing Arrays

The last example showed you how to declare and initialize both a one-dimensional and a two-dimensional array. Note how the basic structure of the declaration is the same as we have seen before, except that we need to put the initial values between braces `{}`. Each set of values for a row is between braces, and where there are two or more rows, the whole lot goes between another pair of braces. The basic reason for this is that we may want to initialize only part of an array. If, in the previous example, we only wanted to put the first three values in each of the first row and the last row, and wanted to leave the second row uninitialized, we would write:

```
char Size[3][12] = {
        {'6', '6', '6'},
        {},
        {'2', '8', '4'}
     };
```

We could then initialize the values of the second row later. It's a good idea to align the braces for the initial values to make it clear which elements of the array are initialized by which values.

Designing a Program

Now that we have learnt about arrays, let's see how we can put them into a real-life problem. We have seen several serious programs in the last few chapters so let's have a go at writing a game.

The Problem

The problem we are set is to write a program to allow two people to play tic-tac-toe (or noughts and crosses) on the computer.

The Analysis

Tic-tac-toe is played on a grid of 3 by 3, and the players take it in turn to enter either Xs or Os into the grid. The player that manages to get three in a line wins. We know how the game works but how does this translate into designing our program. What we need is:

1   A way to get the two players to take turns

2   A 3 by 3 grid in which to store the turns of the two players

3   A way of displaying the grid

4   Some way of specifying where to place the mark on the grid and checking to see if it is a valid go

5   A method of finding out if one of the players has won

The Solution

1   To get the two players to take turns we will use a loop. This has an added advantage in that it can tell us when the game is over when nobody wins. The game is over when there are no spaces on the grid left. There can never be any more than 9 goes in the game, so we need a loop from 0 to 8. Let's see how the first part of the code looks.

```
/* Tic-tac-toe */
#include <stdio.h>

void main()
{
    int counter;

    for( counter = 0; counter < 9; counter ++)
    {
    }
}
```

Now we to need to declare our players and get either player 1 or player 2 to have their go. The easiest way to do this is to declare just one player and check **counter** to see if it is odd or even. If it is odd it's player 1 and if it is even it's player 2. We can do this by using the modulus operator (**%**) to take the remainder of dividing **counter** (which records the number of goes) by 2. The result will be either 0 or 1. We can then add 1 to this to get which player it is. How does this fit into what we have?

```
/* Tic-tac-toe */
#include <stdio.h>

void main()
{
    int counter, player;

    for( counter = 0; counter < 9; counter ++)
    {
        player = (counter % 2) + 1;
        printf("\nPlayer %d, please enter your go: ", player);
    }
}
```

2   Now we have to have somewhere to store the goes that each player enters, even though as yet we haven't designed the part that will allow the players to enter anything. As tic-tac-toe is played on a grid, an array is the best way to store the player's goes:

```
/* Tic-tac-toe */
#include <stdio.h>

void main()
{
    int counter, player;
    char board[3][3] = {{' ',' ',' '},
                        {' ',' ',' '},
                        {' ',' ',' '}};

    for( counter = 0; counter < 9; counter ++)
    {
        player = (counter % 2) + 1;
        printf("\nPlayer %d, please enter your go: ", player);
    }
}
```

We have used a **char** array, because when a player selects a place to put their marker, we want to store their marker either as an X or an O.

3   We now need some way of displaying the grid. We need to do this before each player's turn. We simply display what is in the array, and put a grid around it. We draw the grid by typing horizontal and vertical lines using the **printf()** function. We will use the character conversion specifier **%c** to actually fill in the contents of the grid - our Os and Xs. Initially however, it will be a blank grid as we haven't designed the player's goes yet.

```
/* Tic-tac-toe */
#include <stdio.h>

void main()
{
    int counter, player;
    char board[3][3] = {{' ',' ',' '},
                        {' ',' ',' '},
                        {' ',' ',' '}};

    for( counter = 0; counter < 9; counter ++)
    {
        printf("\n\n\n");
        printf(" %c | %c | %c\n", board[0][0], board[0][1], board[0][2]);
        printf("---+---+---\n");
        printf(" %c | %c | %c\n", board[1][0], board[1][1], board[1][2]);
        printf("---+---+---\n");
        printf(" %c | %c | %c\n", board[2][0], board[2][1], board[2][2]);

        player = (counter % 2) + 1;
        printf("\nPlayer %d, please enter your go: ", player);
    }
}
```

4 Now we can see the grid and we want to be able to enter a go, but how? We need some way of specifying where on the grid we want to place our O or X. As there are nine spaces, let's number the spaces 1 to 9. We can then get the players to enter a number between 1 and 9, telling us where they want to go:

```
/* Tic-tac-toe */
#include <stdio.h>

void main()
{
    int counter, player, go;
    char board[3][3] = {{'1','2','3'},
                        {'4','5','6'},
                        {'7','8','9'}};

    for( counter = 0; counter < 9; counter ++)
    {
        printf("\n\n\n");
        printf(" %c | %c | %c\n", board[0][0], board[0][1], board[0][2]);
        printf("---+---+---\n");
        printf(" %c | %c | %c\n", board[1][0], board[1][1], board[1][2]);
        printf("---+---+---\n");
        printf(" %c | %c | %c\n", board[2][0], board[2][1], board[2][2]);
```

```
        player = (counter % 2) + 1;
        printf("\nPlayer %d, please enter your go: ", player);
        scanf("%d", &go);
    }
}
```

We are now letting the player type in their go. As usual, when we ask
for input we need to check the value entered to make sure it complies
with what we want. If it is less than 1 or greater than 9, we can't use
the value so we need to ask them for a different number. We can do
this with a **do while** loop. We don't want a **while** loop because we
want the code to execute at least once, to get the first value.

```
/* Tic-tac-toe */
#include <stdio.h>

void main()
{
    int counter, player, go;
    char board[3][3] = {{'1','2','3'},
                        {'4','5','6'},
                        {'7','8','9'}};

    for( counter = 0; counter < 9; counter ++)
    {
        printf("\n\n\n");
        printf(" %c | %c | %c\n", board[0][0], board[0][1], board[0][2]);
        printf("---+---+---\n");
        printf(" %c | %c | %c\n", board[1][0], board[1][1], board[1][2]);
        printf("---+---+---\n");
        printf(" %c | %c | %c\n", board[2][0], board[2][1], board[2][2]);

        player = (counter % 2) + 1;
        do
        {
            printf("\nPlayer %d, please enter your go: ", player);
            scanf("%d", &go);
        }while(go < 1 || go > 9);
    }
}
```

This checks to make sure that the number is in the right range, but we
still have to make sure the space hasn't already being taken. We can
establish whether the space the player wants to fill has been filled
already by checking to see whether there is an O or X there. To do this
we need to work out the position on the grid and then check the
contents.

We can work out the position on the grid by using a value that corresponds to which column it's in and a value that corresponds to which row it's in. The player enters a number from 1 to 9 to select a square. 1, 2 and 3 on the first row; 4, 5 and 6 on the second; 7, 8 and 9 on the third. This value is stored in **go**. We could get its position by dividing the number by an integer, and the most obvious choice is 3. This should give a different result for each row, but the same result for each value in that row.

However, before we jump in and do that, let's think about it. If we subtract 1 from the value entered, then dividing each value in each row by three will give a result of 0, 1 and 2 the three rows. If we subtract 1 from all the values we end up with: 0, 1, and 2 on the first row; 3, 4 and 5 on the second; 6, 7 and 8 on the third. Now if we divide by 3 we end up with 0 for the first row, 1 for the second and 2 for the third. (Remember, we are dealing with integers. After dividing by 3 we lose any value after the decimal point.) We can now differentiate each row.

Original			Subtract 1 from each value			divide each int by 3		
1	2	3	0	1	2	0	0	0
4	5	6	3	4	5	1	1	1
7	8	9	6	7	8	2	2	2

This simple calculation has, in effect, given us the row number of the choice. To calculate the column number of the choice we use the modulus operator. We have already subtracted 1 from the value entered, so let's see what remainder we get after dividing by 3.

Our new possible values run 0 - 8. The numbers 0, 3, and 6 in the first column produce a result of 0. 1, 4, and 7 produce 1 and give us the second column. 2, 5 and 8 produce 2 and give us the third column.

			mod 3		
0	1	2	0	1	2
3	4	5	0	1	2
6	7	8	0	1	2

Using our row and column values as indices in the array, we can check whether the value there is greater than the ASCII value of 9 (which both O and X are). If it is then we know that the space has already been used and we prompt the player to try again. We also have to change the **do while** loop. Remember, to work out the row and column numbers, the variable we are testing, **go**, has decreased by 1.

```c
/* Tic-tac-toe */
#include <stdio.h>

void main()
{
    int counter, player, go, grid_x, grid_y;
    char board[3][3] = {{'1','2','3'},
                         {'4','5','6'},
                         {'7','8','9'}};

    for( counter = 0; counter < 9; counter ++)
    {
        printf("\n\n\n");
        printf(" %c | %c | %c\n", board[0][0], board[0][1], board[0][2]);
        printf("---+---+---\n");
        printf(" %c | %c | %c\n", board[1][0], board[1][1], board[1][2]);
        printf("---+---+---\n");
        printf(" %c | %c | %c\n", board[2][0], board[2][1], board[2][2]);

        player = (counter % 2) + 1;
        do
        {
            printf("\nPlayer %d, please enter your go: ", player);
            scanf("%d", &go);

            grid_x = --go / 3;
            grid_y = go % 3;
        }while(go < 0 || go > 9 || board[grid_x][grid_y] > '9');
    }
}
```

Finally for this section, we have to fill in the array space with the player's mark. This is quite a simple task. If it's player 1's turn then we place an X in the location of the choice. Otherwise, if it's player 2's go we place an O. We can use the conditional operator to do this.

```c
/* Tic-tac-toe */
#include <stdio.h>

void main()
{
```

```
     int counter, player, go, grid_x, grid_y;
     char board[3][3] = {{'1','2','3'},
                          {'4','5','6'},
                          {'7','8','9'}};

     for( counter = 0; counter < 9; counter ++)
     {
        printf("\n\n\n");
        printf(" %c | %c | %c\n", board[0][0], board[0][1], board[0][2]);
        printf("---+---+---\n");
        printf(" %c | %c | %c\n", board[1][0], board[1][1], board[1][2]);
        printf("---+---+---\n");
        printf(" %c | %c | %c\n", board[2][0], board[2][1], board[2][2]);

        player = (counter % 2) + 1;
        do
        {
           printf("\nPlayer %d, please enter your go: ", player);
           scanf("%d", &go);

           grid_x = --go / 3;
           grid_y = go % 3;
        }while(go < 0 || go > 9 || board[grid_x][grid_y] > '9');
        board[grid_x][grid_y] = (player == 1) ? 'X' : 'O';
     }
  }
```

5   All that remains is to find out which player, if any, has won. How do
we do this? We can check each row, each column and the two diagonals,
to see whether they contain all the same characters. Doing it this way
means that we are doing more checks than is necessary, but it's a lot
easier. The one thing a computer is really good at is doing is a lot of
tedious calculations.

```
/* Tic-tac-toe */
#include <stdio.h>

void main()
{
   int counter, player, go, grid_x, grid_y, line, winner = 0;
   char board[3][3] = {{'1','2','3'},
                       {'4','5','6'},
                       {'7','8','9'}};

   for( counter = 0; counter < 9; counter ++)
   {
      printf("\n\n\n");
      printf(" %c | %c | %c\n", board[0][0], board[0][1], board[0][2]);
```

```
      printf("---+---+---\n");
      printf(" %c | %c | %c\n", board[1][0], board[1][1], board[1][2]);
      printf("---+---+---\n");
      printf(" %c | %c | %c\n", board[2][0], board[2][1], board[2][2]);

      player = (counter % 2) + 1;
      do
      {
         printf("\nPlayer %d, please enter your go: ", player);
         scanf("%d", &go);

         grid_x = --go / 3;
         grid_y = go % 3;
      }while(go < 0 || go > 9 || board[grid_x][grid_y] > '9');
      board[grid_x][grid_y] = (player == 1) ? 'X' : 'O';

      for(line = 0; line <= 2; line ++)
      {
         if(board[line][0] == board[line][1] &&
            board[line][0] == board[line][2]) winner = player;
         if(board[0][line] == board[1][line] &&
            board[0][line] == board[2][line]) winner = player;
      }
      if(board[0][0] == board[1][1] &&
         board[0][0] == board[2][2]) winner = player;
      if(board[0][2] == board[1][1] &&
         board[0][2] == board[2][0]) winner = player;
   }
}
```

We have declared a new variable, **winner**, and initialized it to zero. If there is a line, we set the value of **winner** to the value of the current **player**. We don't have to worry about which counters are in the spaces as we check for a winner after each go and the only new counter is for the current player. If we find a winner, then we have to stop the game and display a message of congratulations. We can stop the game by placing another condition in the outer **for** loop that checks to see whether **winner** is zero or not.

```
/* Tic-tac-toe */
#include <stdio.h>

void main()
{
   int counter, player, go, grid_x, grid_y, line, winner = 0;
   char board[3][3] = {{'1','2','3'},
                       {'4','5','6'},
                       {'7','8','9'}};
```

```
for( counter = 0; counter < 9 && winner == 0; counter ++)
{
    printf("\n\n\n");
    printf(" %c | %c | %c\n", board[0][0], board[0][1], board[0][2]);
    printf("---+---+---\n");
    printf(" %c | %c | %c\n", board[1][0], board[1][1], board[1][2]);
    printf("---+---+---\n");
    printf(" %c | %c | %c\n", board[2][0], board[2][1], board[2][2]);

    player = (counter % 2) + 1;
    do
    {
        printf("\nPlayer %d, please enter your go: ", player);
        scanf("%d", &go);

        grid_x = --go / 3;
        grid_y = go % 3;
    }while(go < 0 || go > 9 || board[grid_x][grid_y] > '9');
    board[grid_x][grid_y] = (player == 1) ? 'X' : 'O';

    for(line = 0; line <= 2; line ++)
    {
        if(board[line][0] == board[line][1] &&
            board[line][0] == board[line][2]) winner = player;
        if(board[0][line] == board[1][line] &&
            board[0][line] == board[2][line]) winner = player;
    }
    if(board[0][0] == board[1][1] &&
        board[0][0] == board[2][2]) winner = player;
    if(board[0][2] == board[1][1] &&
        board[0][2] == board[2][0]) winner = player;
}
if(winner == 0)
    printf("\nHow boring, it is a draw");
else
    printf("\nCongratulations, player %d, YOU ARE THE WINNER!", winner);
}
```

The final task to do is to re-display the grid a final time, just to show what the winning or drawing move was. This is really just for aesthetic reasons - to finish the game cleanly:

```
/* Tic-tac-toe */
#include <stdio.h>

void main()
{
```

```c
int counter, player, go, grid_x, grid_y, line, winner = 0;
char board[3][3] = {{'1','2','3'},
                     {'4','5','6'},
                     {'7','8','9'}};

for( counter = 0; counter < 9 && winner == 0; counter ++)
{
   printf("\n\n\n");
   printf(" %c | %c | %c\n", board[0][0], board[0][1], board[0][2]);
   printf("---+---+---\n");
   printf(" %c | %c | %c\n", board[1][0], board[1][1], board[1][2]);
   printf("---+---+---\n");
   printf(" %c | %c | %c\n", board[2][0], board[2][1], board[2][2]);

   player = (counter % 2) + 1;
   do
   {
      printf("\nPlayer %d, please enter your go: ", player);
      scanf("%d", &go);

      grid_x = --go / 3;
      grid_y = go % 3;
   }while(go < 0 || go > 9 || board[grid_x][grid_y] > '9');
   board[grid_x][grid_y] = (player == 1) ? 'X' : 'O';

   for(line = 0; line <= 2; line ++)
   {
      if(board[line][0] == board[line][1] &&
         board[line][0] == board[line][2]) winner = player;
      if(board[0][line] == board[1][line] &&
         board[0][line] == board[2][line]) winner = player;
   }
   if(board[0][0] == board[1][1] &&
      board[0][0] == board[2][2]) winner = player;
   if(board[0][2] == board[1][1] &&
      board[0][2] == board[2][0]) winner = player;
}

printf("\n\n\n");
printf(" %c | %c | %c\n", board[0][0], board[0][1], board[0][2]);
printf("---+---+---\n");
printf(" %c | %c | %c\n", board[1][0], board[1][1], board[1][2]);
printf("---+---+---\n");
printf(" %c | %c | %c\n", board[2][0], board[2][1], board[2][2]);

if(winner == 0)
   printf("\nHow boring, it is a draw");
else
   printf("\nCongratulations, player %d, YOU ARE THE WINNER!", winner);
}
```

Typical output from this program and a very bad player number 2 would be:

```
1 | 2 | 3
---+---+---
4 | 5 | 6
---+---+---
7 | 8 | 9

Player 1, please enter your go: 1

X | 2 | 3
---+---+---
4 | 5 | 6
---+---+---
7 | 8 | 9

Player 2, please enter your go: 2

X | O | 3
---+---+---
4 | 5 | 6
---+---+---
7 | 8 | 9

Player 1, please enter your go: 5


X | O | 3
---+---+---
4 | X | 6
---+---+---
7 | 8 | 9

Player 2, please enter your go: 3


X | O | O
---+---+---
4 | X | 6
---+---+---
7 | 8 | 9

Player 1, please enter your go: 9

X | O | O
---+---+---
4 | X | 6
---+---+---
7 | 8 | X

Congratulations, player 1, YOU ARE THE WINNER!
```

Summary

In this chapter we have explained what arrays are and how to use them. We have covered a bit more about memory in your computer to help you understand how your computer thinks about and works with the information you give it. We have covered one-dimensional and multi-dimensional arrays and showed you how these work in real life by going through the design and implementation of a game of tic-tac-toe.

This chapter has covered some quite big and complicated programs. Once you start dealing with arrays, particularly multi-dimensional arrays, you are dealing with a lot more information. The possibilities for your programs are greatly increased, but you have to invest more time in planning and designing your programs.

Up until now we have really concentrated on numbers in all the chapters. The examples haven't really dealt with text. We are going to put that right now and in the next chapter we are, at last, going to get on to doing things with letters and words.

Applications with Strings and Text

In the last chapter we introduced the idea of arrays, and in this chapter we will extend our knowledge of arrays. So far we have just dealt with arrays of numbers, but in this chapter we are going to look at arrays of characters. An important kind of variable in computing generally is a **string**, which is a sequence of characters. As you will see, C doesn't provide us with a string data type, which you may have come across if you have ever programmed in other languages. Instead C uses an array of characters (**char**) to store the string in.

This can make life a little difficult when we want to use strings in our programs, but we will show you how another library can be of considerable help. We will also have further techniques for managing strings in the next chapter.

In this chapter you will:

- Learn about creating strings
- Learn how to join strings
- Learn how to compare strings
- Understand how to use arrays of strings
- Use library functions to handle strings
- Write a password protection program

What is a String?

We have already met examples of **string constants**, quite frequently in fact. A string constant is a sequence of characters or symbols inside quotes which the compiler interprets literally. This means it displays literally everything inside the quotes including any whitespace or tab characters. Every time we have displayed a message using **printf()**, we have defined the message as a string constant. Examples of strings are:

```
printf("This is a string.");
printf("This is quite a long string.");
printf("AAA");
```

The string constants are the letters and characters contained inside the quotes. The computer stores the characters in a string in sequence in successive bytes in memory. The problem is, how does C know where each string ends? To understand this better, let's take the first example:

```
This is a string.
```

This is typically stored in the computer as a sequence of values representing the letters, spaces and the period at the end. So in ASCII, the string above would be stored as follows:

T	h	i	s		i	s		a		s	t	r	i	n	g	.
84	104	105	115	32	105	115	32	97	32	115	116	114	105	110	103	46

But the next byte could contain absolutely anything. With what we have here, the computer has no way of knowing that the next byte is not part of the string. Obviously something extra is necessary to indicate where the end of the string is. In C a special character is added to the end of a string - a byte containing zero. This character is known as the **null character** (not to be confused with **NULL**, which we will come on to later) and we can represent this character as **\0**. With string constants in C this character is added automatically to the end of the string, so our string above is actually:

T	h	i	s		i	s		a		s	t	r	i	n	g	.	
84	104	105	115	32	105	115	32	97	32	115	116	114	105	110	103	46	0

From this you can see that strings are actually one bigger than the number of characters in them. This is important as you will see later.

Our three examples can be represented in the following figure:

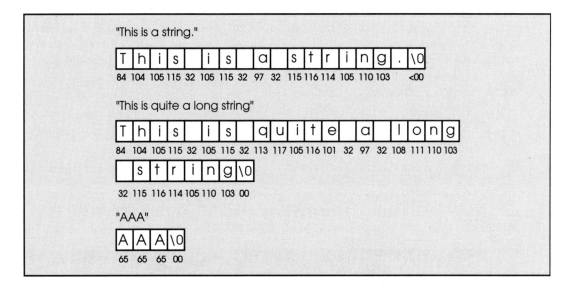

There is nothing to prevent you adding a \0 character to the end of a string yourself, but if you do, you will simply end up with two of them. We can illustrate how the null character \0 works with a simple example. Have a quick look at the following program:

```
/* Example 6.1 Displaying a string */
#include <stdio.h>

void main()
{

  printf("The character \0 is used to terminate a string");
}
```

If we run this program, then the output is:

```
The character
```

Oops! What has happened to the rest of the string? The reason why the string ends after the first two words is that **printf()** starts printing the string constant from the start, and stops when it reaches the first null character, \0. The **printf()** function thinks that the string has finished there and won't print out the remaining words. Even though there is another \0 at the end of **string**, it will never be reached.

String and Text Handling Methods

The C programming language has no specific provision within its syntax for string typed variables, or special operators for processing strings. Fortunately, with the tools we have at our disposal already, we are quite well equipped. With arrays we have the means for handling strings easily and efficiently.

Declaring String Variables

As we said earlier, we can use an array of type **char** to hold strings. This is the simplest form of string variable. We could declare a **char** array variable as:

```
char string[20];
```

This variable can hold up to 19 characters, allowing one for the termination character.

> Remember, you must declare the array one bigger than the number of characters because the computer will automatically add \0.

We could also initialize the above string variable in the declaration:

```
char string[] = "This is a string.";
```

Here we have not explicitly defined the array dimension. The compiler will assign a value to the dimension sufficient to hold the initializing string constant. In this case it will be 18, allowing an extra one for the terminating '\0'. Each element of the array will contain one character of the string. We could, of course, have put a value for the dimension ourselves, but if the compiler does it, we can be sure it will be correct.

We could also initialize just part of a string array:

```
char str[40] = "To be";
```

Here, the compiler will initialize the first five elements from **str[0]** to **str[4]** with the characters of the specified string in sequence. **str[5]** will contain the null value, '\0'. Of course, space is allocated for all 40 elements of the array, and they are all available to use in any way we want.

Initializing a **char** array and declaring it as constant is a good way of handling standard messages:

```
const char message[] = "The end of the world is nigh";
```

Here, because we have declared **message** as **const**, it's protected from being specifically modified within the program. Any attempt to do so will result in an error message from the compiler. This technique for defining standard messages is particularly useful if they are used in various places within a program. It prevents accidental modification of such constants in other parts of your program. Of course, if you do need to be able to change the message, then you don't have to specify the array as **const**.

The main disadvantage of using **char** arrays to hold variable strings, is the potentially wasted memory. Because they are, by definition, of a fixed length, you have to declare these kinds of arrays with their dimension set to accommodate the maximum string length you are likely to want to process. In most circumstances, your typical string length will be somewhat less than the maximum, so you end up wasting precious memory. Since we are normally using our arrays here to store a variable length string, getting the length of a string is important if you want to add to it. Let's look at this using an example.

Try It Out - Finding Out the Length of a String

In this example we are going to initialize two strings and then find out how many characters there are in each (not including the null character):

```
/* Example 6.2 Lengths of strings  */
#include <stdio.h>
void main()
{
  char str1[40] = "To be or not to be", str2[40] = ",that is the question";
  int count = 0;

  while (str1[ count ] != '\0') /* Increment count till we reach the string  */
  count++;                                /*  terminating character.              */
  printf("\nThe length of the string \"%s\" is %d characters.", str1, count);
  count = 0;
  while ( str2[count] != '\0' )        /* Count characters in second string  */
  count++;
  printf("\nThe length of the string \"%s\" is %d characters.", str2, count);
}
```

Try It Out!

The output you will get from this program is:

```
The length of the string "To be or not to be" is 18 characters.
The length of the string ",that is the question" is 21 characters.
```

How it Works

Make sure you follow this example. Let's go through it.

First we have the inevitable declarations:

```
char str1[40] = "To be or not to be", str2[40] = ",that is the question";
int count = 0;
```

We declare two **char** arrays, each initialized with a string with a length considerably less than the length of the array. There are other possibilities here if we don't need the extra space, as we shall see later. We also declare and initialize a counter to use in the loops in the program.

Next we have the first loop to work out the length of the first string:

```
while (str1[ count ] != '\0')  /* Increment count till we reach the string  */
count++;                       /*    terminating character.                 */
```

Using loops as we have here is very common in programming with strings. To find the length we simply use the **while** loop to keep incrementing a counter as long as we haven't reached the end of string character. You can see how the condition for the continuation of the loop is whether the terminating '\0' has been reached. At the end of the loop the variable **count** will contain the number of characters in the loop, excluding the terminating null.

It would also possible to put the incrementing of **count** in the **while** condition with a statement such as:

```
while (str1[ count++ ] != '\0'); /* Increment count till we reach the string */
```

However, we would then have to decrement **count** by 1 after the loop finished, as **count** would have been incremented one more time on the exit from the loop when the '\0' is detected. This would be fine if we wanted the length to include the termination character. However, with the loop as we have it in the example, we come out with the correct value, since **count** is incremented in the loop proper, rather than in the exit condition. It doesn't get incremented when the `'\0'` is found.

Although it didn't quite suit our purpose here, this alternative approach, where everything is done in the loop condition, crops up quite frequently in C.

Now we have the length, we display the string with the statement:

```
printf("\nThe length of the string \"%s\" is %d characters.", str1, count);
```

This also displays the count of the number of characters it contains, excluding the terminating null. Notice that we are using a new format specifier, **%s**. This outputs characters from the string until it reaches the terminating null. If there was no terminating character it would continue to output characters until it found one somewhere in memory. In some cases that can mean a lot of output. We are also using the escape character, `\"`, to include quotes in the string. If we didn't precede the quotes character with the backslash, the compiler would think it had reached the end of the string.

Finding the length of the second string and displaying the result is performed in exactly the same way as the first string.

Operations With Strings

So, now we know how to find the lengths of strings, how can we manipulate them?

Unfortunately, we can't use the assignment operator to copy a string in the way we do with **int** or **double** variables. To achieve the equivalent of an arithmetic assignment with a string, the second string has to be copied element by element to the first. In fact, performing any operation on string variables is very different from the arithmetic operations with numeric variables we have seen so far. Let's look at some common operations you might want to perform with strings and how they would be achieved.

Joining Strings Together

Adding one string to the end of another is a common requirement. For instance, we might want to assemble a single message from two or more strings. Error messages for example, might consist of a few basic text strings plus a variety of strings that are appended to make the message specific to a particular error.

Try it Out - Joining Strings

We could extend the last example to join strings:

```
/* Example 6.3 Joining strings       */
#include <stdio.h>
void main()
{
  char str1[40] = "To be or not to be", str2[40] = ",that is the question";
  int count1 = 0, count2 =0;

  /* find the length of the first string  */
  while (str1[ count1 ] != '\0') /* Increment count till we reach the string */
  count1++;                                       /* terminating character. */

  /* Find the length of the second string  */
  while ( str2[count2] != '\0' )      /* Count characters in second string  */
  count2++;

  /* Check that we have enough space for both strings  */
  if ( ( sizeof( str1 ) / sizeof( str1[0] ) ) < ( count1 + count2 + 1) )
  {
    printf("\nYou can't get a quart into a pint pot.");

  }

  else
  {
    /* Copy 2nd string to first  */
    count2 = 0;
    while ( str2[ count2 ] != '\0' )
    str1[ count1++ ] = str2[ count2++ ];
    str1[ count1 ] = '\0';                         /* Make sure we add terminator */
    printf("\n%s", str1 );
  }
}
```

Typical output from this program would be:

```
To be or not to be,that is the question
```

How it Works

This program first finds the lengths of the two strings exactly as before. It then checks that **str1** has enough elements to hold both strings and the terminating null:

```
if ( ( sizeof( str1 ) / sizeof( str1[0] ) ) <  ( count1 + count2 + 1) )
   {
   printf("\nYou can't get a quart into a pint pot.");
}
```

Notice how the **sizeof** operator is first used to get the total number of bytes in the array by just using the array name as an argument. This value is then divided by the length of an individual element, supplied by the second use of **sizeof**, to produce the total number of elements in the array. So what we have here is :

(total memory for array) / (memory for one character)
= (total characters in array)

If we discover that the array is too small to hold the contents of both strings, then we display a message and end the program. It is essential not to try and place more characters in the array than it can hold, as this could be disastrous for your program and could crash the whole system.

We reach the **else** block only if we are sure that both strings will fit in the first array. Here, we reset the variable **count2** to zero and copy the second string to the first array with the statements:

```
   count2 = 0;
   while ( str2[ count2 ] != '\0' )
     str1[ count1++ ] = str2[ count2++ ];
str1[ count1 ] = '\0';                        /* Make sure we add terminator */
```

The variable **count1** starts from the value left by the loop to determine the length of the first string. This is why we have used two variables to count the string length for the two strings. Because the array is indexed from 0, the value stored in **count1** will point to the '\0' of the first string. So, when we use **count1** to index the array **str1** we know that we are starting at the end of the message proper.

We then copy characters from **str2** to **str1** until we find the '\0' in **str2**. We still have to add a terminating '\0' to **str1**, since it isn't copied from **str2**. The end result of the operation is that we have added the contents of **string2** to the end of **string1**, overwriting the terminating null character for **string1**, and adding a terminating null to the end of the combined string.

We could have replaced the three lines of code above with a more concise alternative to copy the second string:

```
while ( (str1[count1++] = str2[ count2++ ] ) != '\0' );
```

This would replace the loop we have in the program as well as the statement to put a '\0' at the end of **str1**. This statement would copy the '\0' from **str2** to **str1**, since the copying occurs in the loop continuation condition. This works because of the precedence of the operators. Let's consider what happens at each stage.

The parentheses around the assignment ensure that this is done before the result is compared with '\0'. The parentheses have the highest order of precedence, so we carry out all the operations contained within them first. This means the sequence of events is as follows. First assign the value of **str2[count2]** to **str1[count1]**. Next, increment each of the counters by one, using the postfix form of the **++** operator. Finally, check whether the last character stored in **str1** was '\0'. The loop ends after the '\0' has been copied to **str1**. The diagram on the opposite page illustrates this process.

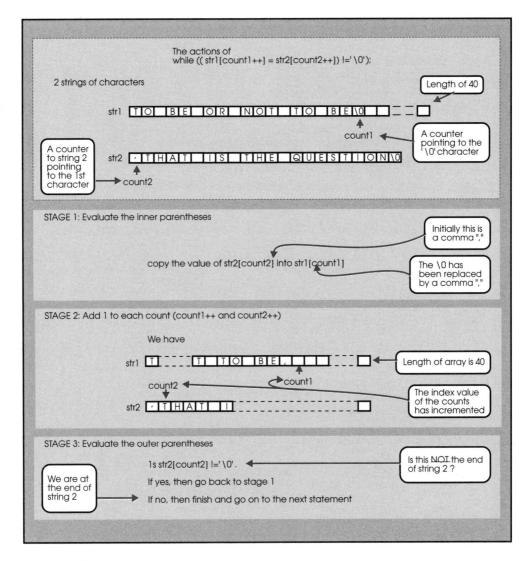

Arrays of Strings

It must have occurred to you by now that we could use a two-dimensional array, where each row is used to hold a string. In this way we could arrange to store a whole bunch of strings, and refer to them through a single variable name. We could change the last example to work in this way.

Try it Out - *Arrays of Strings*

Try It Out!

```
/* Example 6.4 Arrays of strings      */
#include <stdio.h>
void main()
{
  char str[2][40] = {
                      { "To be or not to be"},
                      {",that is the question"}
                    };
  int count1 = 0, count2 =0, too_small =0;


  /* find the length of the first string  */
  while (str[ 0 ][ count1 ] != '\0')  /* Increment count till we reach the */
  count1++;                           /*  string terminating character. */

  /* Find the length of the second string   */
  while ( str[ 1 ][count2] != '\0' )     /* Count characters in 2nd string  */
  count2++;

  /* Check that we have enough space for both strings  */
  if ( ( sizeof( str[ 0 ] ) /sizeof( str[ 0 ][ 0 ] ) )<(count1 + count2 + 1) )
    {
    printf("\nYou can't get a quart into a pint pot.");
    too_small =1;
    };

  if (too_small ==0)
  /* Copy 2nd string to first        */
  count2 = 0;
  while ( str[ 1 ][ count2 ] != '\0' )
    str[ 0 ][ count1++ ] = str[ 1 ][ count2++ ];
    str[ 0 ][ count1 ] = '\0';               /* Make sure we add terminator  */
  printf("\n%s", str[ 0 ] );
}
```

Typical output from this program would be:

```
To be or not to be,that is the question
```

How it Works

Well, you have to admit, it isn't a great improvement on the previous version. We declare just 1 two-dimensional **char** array, instead of the 2 one-dimensional arrays we had before:

```
char str[2][40] = {
    { "To be or not to be"},
    {",that is the question"}
};
```

The first initializing string is stored with the first index value as 0, and the second initializing string with the first index value as 1.

To access any particular string in the program, we have just used an index to the first array dimension, 0 for the first string and 1 for the second. Otherwise, it's the same as the previous example. We would probably come out much further ahead if we had twenty strings instead of two. And, of course, if we needed to cope with a variable number of strings, we couldn't make it in practice with naming them individually. A disadvantage of this approach, is that if our strings are significantly less than 40 characters long, we waste quite a bit of memory in the array.

String Library Functions

Now that you have struggled through the previous examples, laboriously copying strings from one variable to another, it's time to reveal that there is a standard library for string functions that can take care of all these little chores. Still, at least you will know what's going on when you use the library functions.

The string functions are in the file **STRING.H**, so you will need to put:

```
#include <string.h>
```

at the beginning of your program if you want to use them. The library actually contains quite a lot of functions, usually at least twenty, and your compiler may provide an even more extensive range of string library capabilities. We will just discuss a few of the essential functions to demonstrate the basic idea, and leave you to explore the rest on your own.

Copying Strings Using a Library Function

First, let's return to copying strings. The **while** loop mechanism we carefully forged to do this must still be fresh in your mind. Well, we can do the same thing with:

```
strcpy( string1, string2);
```

where the argument variables are **char** array names. What the function actually does is to copy **string2** to **string1**. The copy operation will include the terminating **'\0'**. It's your responsibility to ensure that the array **string1** has sufficient space to accommodate **string2**. The function **strcpy()** has no way of checking the sizes of the arrays, so if it goes wrong it's all your fault, and it's back to the **sizeof** operations again.

Determining String Length Using a Library Function

To find out the length of a string we have the function **strlen()** which returns the length of a string as an unsigned integer. In our example to do this we wrote:

```
/* Find the length of the second string      */
   while ( str2[count2] != '\0' )      /* Count characters in second string */
   count2++;
```

Instead of this rigmarole we could simply write:

```
count2 = strlen( str2 );
```

All the counting, and searching that's necessary to find the end of the string is performed by the function, so you no longer have to worry about it.. Note that it returns the length of the string *excluding* the **'/0'**, which is generally the most convenient result.

Joining Strings Using a Library Function

In our example, we also got into copying the second string onto the end of the first using the following rather complicated looking code:

```
/* Copy 2nd string to first       */
   count2 = 0;
   while ( str2[ count2 ] != '\0' )
     str1[ count1++ ] = str2[ count2++ ];
   str1[ count1 ] = '\0';                      /* Make sure we add terminator    */
```

Well, the string library gives a slight simplification here, too. We could use a function which joins one string to the end of another. We could achieve the same result as the fragment above with the following exceedingly simple statement:

```
strcat( str1, str2 );
```

This function finds the end of **str1**, and then copies **str2** to the end of **str1**. The **strcat()** function is so called because it performs **string cat**enation.

Try it Out - Using the String Library

We now have enough tools to make a good job of rewriting Example 5.2:

```
/* Example 6.5 Joining strings - revitalised          */
#include <stdio.h>
#include <string.h>
#define STR_LENGTH 40

void main()
{
  char str1[STR_LENGTH] = "To be or not to be",
    str2[STR_LENGTH] = ",that is the question";

  if( STR_LENGTH > strlen( str1 ) + strlen( str2 ) )      /* Enough space ? */
    printf("\n%s", strcat( str1, str2 ) );  /* yes, so print joined string */
  else
    printf("\nYou can't get a quart into a pint pot.");
}
```

Here we get exactly the same output as before.

How it Works

Well, what a difference a library makes. It actually makes the problem trivial, doesn't it? We simply check we have enough space in our array by means of the **if** statement:

```
if( STR_LENGTH > strlen( str1 ) + strlen( str2 ) )       /* Enough space */
  printf("\n%s", strcat( str1, str2 ) ); /* yes, so print joined string */
else
  printf("\nYou can't get a quart into a pint pot.");
```

If we do, we join the strings using the **strcat()** function within the argument to the **printf()** and display the result. If we don't we just display a message.

Comparing Strings

The string library also provides the facility for comparing strings, and deciding whether one string is greater than or less than another. It may sound a bit odd applying such terms to strings, but the result is produced quite simply. Successive corresponding characters of the two strings are compared based on the numerical value of their ASCII codes. This mechanism is illustrated graphically in the next figure, where the ASCII codes are shown as hexadecimal.

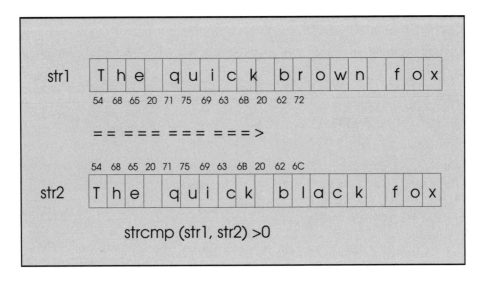

If the two strings are identical, then of course they are equal. The first pair of characters that are different, determine whether the first string is less than, or greater than the second. The function **strcmp(str1, str2)** compares the two strings. It returns an **int** value that is less than, equal to, or greater than zero, corresponding to whether **str1** is less than, equal to, or greater than **str2**.

Try it Out - Comparing Strings

We can demonstrate the use of this in an example:

```
/* Example 6.6 Comparing strings    */
#include <stdio.h>
#include <string.h>

void main()
{
    char word1[20];
    char word2[20];
```

```
   printf("\nType in two words:\n1: ");
   scanf("%s", word1);
   printf("2: ");
   scanf("%s", word2);

   if(strcmp(word1,word2) == 0)
      printf("You have entered identical words");
   else
      printf("%s comes before %s",
         (strcmp(word1, word2) < 0) ? word1 : word2,
         (strcmp(word1, word2) < 0) ? word2 : word1);
}
```

The program will read in two words and then to tell you which one is
alphabetically before the other. The output looks something like this:

```
Type in two words:
1: apple
2: banana
apple comes before banana
```

How it Works

```
/* Example 6.6 Comparing strings     */
#include <stdio.h>
#include <string.h>
```

We have started the program with the **include** statements for the header files
for the standard input and output library, and the string handling library.

```
void main()
{
   char word1[20];
   char word2[20];
```

Next we have declared two character arrays for our two words. We have set
the size of the arrays to 20. This should be enough for an example, but we
should give a word of warning. As with the **strcpy()** function it's *your*
responsibility that you allocate enough space for what the user may key in.
The function **scanf()** has no way to tell when it runs out of space, and it will
happily overwrite things it shouldn't.

```
   printf("\nType in two words:\n1: ");
   scanf("%s", word1);
   printf("2: ");          /
   scanf("%s", word2);
```

Our next task is to get some words from the user, so after a short prompt, we use **scanf()** twice to get a couple of words. Notice how in this example we haven't used an **&** before the variables. We could have, by writing instead:

```
scanf("%s", &word1[0]);
```

Therefore, **&word1[0] == word1**! This is another of those really important features of C which we will go into more detail in the next chapter.

```
if(strcmp(word1,word2) == 0)
    printf("You have entered identical words");
else
    printf("%s comes before %s",
        (strcmp(word1, word2) < 0) ? word1 : word2,
        (strcmp(word1, word2) < 0) ? word2 : word1);
```

Finally, we do the checking. We use the **strcmp()** function to compare the two words that were entered. If the value the function returns is zero, then the two strings are equal, and we display a message to inform you. If not, then we print out a message specifying which word comes before the other. We do this using the conditional operator (**?:**) to specify which word we want to print first and which second. A **switch** statement is more efficient but this looks interesting don't you think?

Searching Text

There are several string searching functions in the string library, but we will only look at two at this point. But before we get into these, we have to take a peek at the subject of the next chapter.

The Idea of a Pointer

As we shall see in detail in the next chapter, C provides a remarkably useful type of variable called a **pointer**. A pointer is a variable which contains an address, that is a reference to another location in memory which can contain a value. We have already used an address when we used the function **scanf()**. A pointer is described very simply in the next figure.

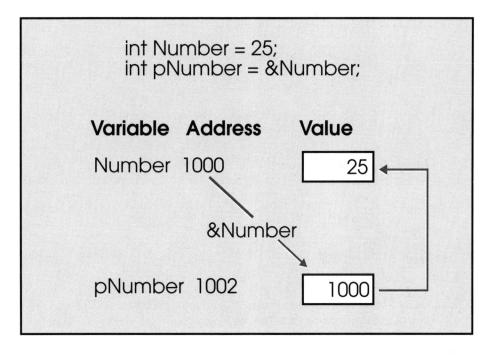

int Number = 25;
int pNumber = &Number;

We declare a variable **Number** with the value 25, and a pointer **pNumber** which contains the address of **Number**. We can now use the variable **pNumber** in the expression ***pNumber** to obtain the value contained in **Number**.

The main reason for introducing this idea early is that the functions we will now discuss return pointers, so you could be a bit confused by them. If you end up confused anyway, don't worry, hopefully all will be illuminated in the next chapter.

String Search Functions

The first function, **strchr(str,c)**, searches a given string for a specified character. The first parameter is a string (which is a **char** array name), the second parameter is an **int** variable used to store a character. The function will return a pointer to the first position in the string where the character is found, which is the address of this position. It is used as follows:

```
pGot_char = strchr(str, c );
```

The result of this is illustrated in the figure below.

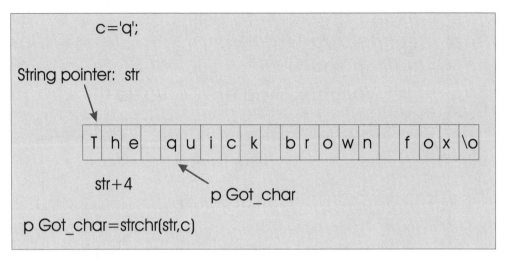

The second function , **strstr(str1, str2)**, is probably the most useful of all the searching functions in **STRING.H**. It searches one string for the first occurrence of another string, and it returns a pointer to the position in the first string where the second string is found.

If it doesn't find a match, it returns **NULL**. **NULL** is a predefined constant which is the equivalent of zero for a pointer. We shall see a lot more of **NULL** in the next chapter. So if the value returned isn't **NULL**, you can be sure that the searching function you are using has found an occurrence of what it was searching for. The function **strstr()** is used as follows:

```
pFound = strstr( str1, str2 );
```

The two arguments to the function are the string to be searched, and the string sought, respectively.

Try it Out - Searching a String

We could show what we have been talking about in action in the following example:

```
/* Example 6.7 A demonstration of seeking and finding  */
#include <stdio.h>
#include <string.h>
void main()
{
```

```
    char str1[] = "This string contains the holy grail.";
    char str2[] = "the holy grail";
    char str3[] = "the holy grill";

    if ( (strstr(str1, str2)) == NULL )
       printf("\nString not found.");
    else
       printf("\nString: %s\n was found in string: %s",str2, str1);

    if( (strstr(str1, str3)) == NULL )
       printf("\nString not found.");
    else
       printf("\nWe shouldn't get to here!");
}
```

Typical output would be:

```
String: the holy grail
 was found in string: This string contains the holy grail.
String not found.
```

How it Works

We have three strings defined, **str1**, **str2**, and **str3**.

```
    if ( (strstr(str1, str2)) == NULL )
       printf("\nString not found.");
    else
       printf("\nString: %s\n was found in string: %s",str2, str1);
```

In the above statements we use the library function **strstr()** to search for the occurrence of the second string in the first. We then display a message corresponding to the result by testing the returned value of **strstr()** against **NULL**. If the value returned is equal to **NULL**, this indicates the second string wasn't found in the first, so a message is displayed to that effect. If the second string *is* found the **else** is executed. In this case a message is displayed indicating the string was found.

We then repeat the process and check for the occurrence of the third string in the first. If we get output from the first or the last **printf()** in the program, something is seriously wrong. Note that the value for the position of the second string in the first assumes the first position is numbered zero.

Analyzing Strings

If you need to examine the internal contents of a string, there is a standard library, **CTYPE.H**, that provides you with a very flexible range of functions to help.

Function	Test	Function	Test
isalpha()	Alphabetic	isupper()	Upper-case
isdigit()	Numeric Digit	islower()	Lower-case
isxdigit()	Hexadecimal digit	isspace()	Whitespace
isalnum()	Alphabetic or digit	ispunct()	Punctuation character
isprint()	Printable character	isgraph()	Printable but not space
iscntrl()	Control character		

The argument in parentheses is the character to be tested.
Functions return *True* if the test character type is found, *False* otherwise.

The functions include character conversion facilities as well as character classification routines. The basic set of analytical functions is shown in the figure above. They each return the value True if the specified character type is found.

Try it Out - Using the CTYPE.H Library

We can demonstrate how they can be used with a simple example:

```
/* Example 6.8 Exercising ctype.h    */
#include <stdio.h>
#include <ctype.h>
void main()
{
  char  Buffer[ 80 ];                /* Input buffer   */
  int i = 0;                         /* Index value    */
  int num_letters = 0, num_digits = 0;
```

```
    printf("\nEnter an interesting string of less than 80 characters:\n");
    gets( Buffer );
    while( Buffer[i] != '\0' )
    {
      if( isalpha( Buffer[i] ) )
        num_letters++;
        if( isdigit( Buffer[i++] ) )
        num_digits++;
    }
  printf("\nYour string contained %d letters and %d digits.\n", num_letters,
num_digits);
  }
```

Typical output from this program is:

```
Enter an interesting string of less than 80 characters:
I was born on the 3rd of October 1965

Your string contained 24 letters and 5 digits.
```

How it Works

This example is quite straight forward. Input is performed by the statement:

```
    gets( Buffer );
```

The string you enter is read into the array **Buffer** using the function **gets()**. So far, we've used **scanf()** to accept input from the keyboard. The **gets()** function is another way of doing this. The function **gets()** has the advantage that it will read all the characters entered from the keyboard, including blanks, up to when you press the *Enter* key. This is then stored as a string into the area specified by its argument, which in this case is the array **Buffer**.

The interesting part is provided by the statements:

```
    while( Buffer[i] != '\0' )
    {
      if( isalpha( Buffer[i] ) )
        num_letters++;
      if( isdigit( Buffer[i++] ) )
        num_digits++;
    }
```

The input string is tested character by character in the **while** loop. Checks are made for alphabetic characters and digits in turn in the two **if** statements. As either is found, the appropriate counter is incremented. Note that we increment the index to the array **Buffer** in the second **if**. Remember, the check is made using the value of **i**, and then **i** is incremented because we are using the postfix form of the increment operator.

This is not a particularly efficient way of doing things, since we test for a digit even if we have already discovered the current character is alphabetic. You could try to improve on this if the TV is really bad one night.

Converting Characters

The conversion functions in **CTYPE.H** are:

> **toupper()** Converts from lower-case to upper-case
> **tolower()** Converts from upper-case to lower-case

The functions won't change characters that are already in the case being converted to. You can therefore convert a string using the statement:

```
while( ( Buffer[ i ] = toupper( Buffer[ i ] ) ) != '\0' ) i++;
```

assuming, of course, that the index **i** has been initialized to zero. This loop will convert the entire string to upper-case by stepping through the string one character at a time, converting lower case to upper-case, and leaving upper-case characters unchanged. The loop stops when it reaches the string termination character **'\0'**.

Try it Out - Converting Characters

We could exercise the function **toupper()** together with the **strstr()** function, to find out how many times one string occurs in another, ignoring case. Look at the following example:

```
/* Example 6.9 Finding occurrences of one string in another  */
#include <stdio.h>
#include <string.h>
#include <ctype.h>

void main()
{
   char  string1[ 100 ], string2[ 40 ]; /* Input buffers */
```

```
    int i = 0;                              /* Index value & counter */
    int str2_len = 0;                       /* Length of string2      */
    char *pstr1 = string1;                  /* Pointer to string1     */

    printf("\nEnter the string to be searched(less than 100 characters):\n");
    gets ( string1 );
    printf("\nEnter the string sought (less than 40 characters ):\n");
    gets( string2 );

/* Convert both strings to upper case. */
    while( ( string1[ i ] = toupper( string1[ i ] ) ) != '\0' ) i++;
    i = 0;
    while( ( string2[ i ] = toupper( string2[ i ] ) ) != '\0' ) i++;

    str2_len = strlen( string2 );           /* Get length of string2 */
    i=0;                                     /* set counter to 0      */

/* Loop until no string2      */
    while ( (pstr1 = strstr( pstr1, string2 ) ) != NULL )
    {
        i++;                                /* Increment counter */
        pstr1 += str2_len;              /* Set pointer at end of last found */
    }
    printf("\nThe second string was found %d times in the first.", i );
}
```

Typical operation of this example will produce:

```
Enter the string to be searched(less than 100 characters):
Smith, where Jones had had 'had had', had had 'had'. 'Had had' had had the
examiner's approval.

Enter the string sought (less than 40 characters):
had

The second string was found 11 times in the first.
```

How it Works

This program has three distinct phases, getting the input strings, converting both strings to upper-case, and searching the first string for occurrences of the second.

```
printf("\nEnter the string to be searched(less than 100 characters):\n");
    gets ( string1 );
    printf("\nEnter the string sought (less than 40 characters ):\n");
    gets( string2 );
```

First of all **printf()** displays messages to tell the user to enter two strings, and **gets()** is used to store the input in **string1** and **string2.** We use the function **gets()** because it will read in a string from the keyboard including blanks.

The conversion to upper-case is made using the statements:

```
/* Convert both strings to upper case. */
   while( ( string1[ i ] = toupper( string1[ i ] ) ) != '\0' ) i++;
   i = 0;
   while( ( string2[ i ] = toupper( string2[ i ] ) ) != '\0' ) i++;
```

This uses the **while** loop to do three things. It converts an element of **string1** to upper-case, it stores that result back in the same position in **string1**, and it checks to see whether the character is equal to '\0'. The incrementing of the index **i** is made external to the **while** condition because the condition uses **i** twice. This ensures there is no confusion as to when the incrementing of **i** takes place. The index **i** is reset to zero for use in the second loop converting **string2**.

```
str2_len = strlen( string2 );      /* Get length of string2   */
   i=0;                             /* set counter to 0        */
```

The function **strlen()** is used to find the length of **string2**. Then the index **i** is reset to zero again for use in the final **while** loop.

The search process may be a little confusing for you. If so, the mists will surely clear when you get to the next chapter. It is contained in the statements:

```
   while ( (pstr1 = strstr( pstr1, string2 ) ) != NULL )
   {
     i++;                                /* Increment counter */
     pstr1 += str2_len;           /* Set pointer at end of last found */
   }
```

The function **strstr()** is used to search the first string for occurrences of the second. We have set the pointer variable **pstr1** to point to the beginning of **string1** at the beginning of the program. We then use this as a way to refer to the string to be searched, **string1**. The **while** loop will continue searching the first string for as long as **pstr1** is not equal to **NULL**, in other words., for as long as **string2** can be found in **pstr1**. Every time the second string is found in the first, the counter **i** is incremented. At the same time, **pstr1** is set to a position following the last occurrence of **string2** that was found using the statement:

```
pstr1 += str2_len;                    /* Set pointer at end of last found */
```

The first time through the loop, **pstr1** is pointing to the beginning of the array **string1**. Since **str2_len** is the value for the length of **string2**, this statement will move **pstr1** along **string1** by the length of **string2** in the first pass through the loop. In other words it will move **pstr1** to point to the end of the first **"had"** in **string2**. So when the loop is re-entered, **strstr()** will re-start its search after the first **"had"** and start searching the remainder of the string for the next occurrence of **string2**. The loop continues until **string2** isn't found anywhere in the remainder of **string1**.

```
printf("\nThe second string was found %d times in the first.", i );
```

The program finally displays how many times the second string was found in the first. This whole process is illustrated in the figure below, where it is arbitrarily assumed **string1** is stored starting at location 1000 in memory.

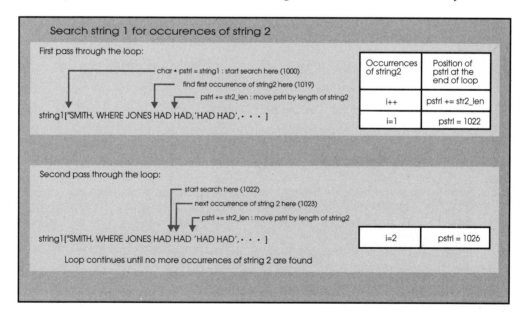

There is just one remaining statement that needs to be addressed in this program, and it occurs near the top of the program:

```
char *pstr1 = string1;              /* Pointer to string1     */
```

This is the declaration for the pointer **pstr1**, which is a pointer to **char** type variables. The declaration ensures that **pstr1** is initialized with the *address* of the array **string1**. Don't worry about the details of this. We will cover it all in the next chapter.

In the analysis above you have seen how this variable **pstr1** is used to move the point from which you start searching the string each time. If we didn't do this, then **strstr()** would always search from the start of the string, would always find the first and only the first occurrence, and would repeat this process indefinitely. So, by increasing the value of **pstr1** each time we find an occurrence, we are able to search for all the instances of **string2** in **string1**.

Therefore, the first time through the loop, the string we are searching is:

```
Smith, where Jones had had 'had had', had had 'had'. 'Had had' had had the
examiner's approval.
```

While the second time it is:

```
had 'had had', had had 'had'. 'Had had' had had the examiner's approval.
```

And so on, until we arrive at the string:

```
the  examiner's  approval.
```

At this point the contents of **string2** isn't found and the search process stops.

> The routines in the library CTYPE.H work fine with the basic ASCII characters we have been using here. If you use them with strings containing characters in the upper half of the ASCII table they can cause problems, so if you intend to do this check the details in your library documentation.

Designing a Program

We have almost come to the end of this chapter. It just remains for us to go through a program to use some of what we have learnt here.

The Problem

The program we are going to write is one which will lock your computer until someone types in a password.

The Analysis

We are not going to store the password as a normal string, as it would be possible to find out the password by looking at the program. Instead we are going to write this program in two distinct parts, the first to generate an encrypted password, which we will then use in the final version.

Therefore, the steps are as follows:

1 Develop an encryption scheme, and use this to encrypt the password to be used in the program.

2 Use the above program as a base for the final protection program. This works by:

- Getting the password from the user.

- Encrypting it.

- Comparing it to the previously encrypted password.

The Solution

1 The most difficult part of this program is designing the encryption scheme. What we will do is set the length of the password to twenty characters. When we actually encrypt the password, we will apply it to all twenty characters. This way, no-one will know the true length of the password.

But, what is the encryption going to be? Let's make another assumption. We want the final encrypted word just to contain alphabetic characters. This will allow us to use **strcmp()** later and also means we won't have any problems printing it out. So what we'll do is take each character in turn, encrypt it, then use the result to encrypt the next character.

Of course, we don't have a previously encrypted character for the first character. What we can do here is take the sum of all the characters, calculate the remainder after dividing by 52, and use that as the starting point.

We are now left with designing the actual encryption process. For that we'll take the values of the two characters (unencrypted and encrypted ones), multiply them together and then take the remainder after dividing by 52. This produces a value from 0 to 52 which we will use to select from A to Z and a to z. The following diagram helps to explain this more clearly.

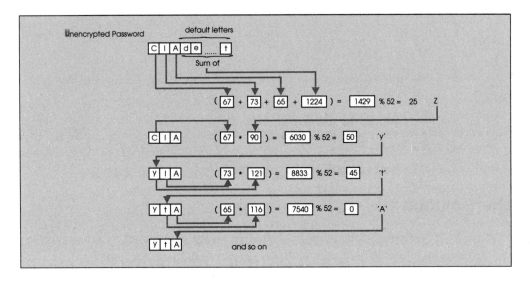

Let's put this into action. First we need to set up the variables our program is going to use and get the password from the user.

```c
#include <stdio.h>

void main()
{
    char unencrypted[] = "abcdefghijklmnopqrst";
    char encrypted[21], password[21];
```

```
    scanf("%s", password);
}
```

We have set the unencrypted password to **abcdefghijklmnopqrst** so that regular patterns at the end of the password don't appear. Now we need to copy **password** into **unencrypted**, missing off the terminating **'\0'** on the end of the typed in password.

```
#include <stdio.h>

void main()
{
    char unencrypted[] = "abcdefghijklmnopqrst";
    char encrypted[21], password[21];
    int counter;

    scanf("%s", password);
    for(counter = 0; counter < 20 && password[counter] !=  '\0'; counter++)
        unencrypted[counter] = password[counter];
}
```

Now lets encrypt the password and print it out.

```
#include <stdio.h>

void main()
{
    char unencrypted[] = "abcdefghijklmnopqrst";
    char encrypted[21], password[21];
    int counter;
    long code;

    scanf("%s", password);
    for(counter = 0; counter < 20 && password[counter] !=  '\0'; counter++)
        unencrypted[counter] = password[counter];

    code = 0;
    for (counter = 0; counter  < 20; code += unencrypted[counter++]);
    code = code % 52;
    code += (code < 26) ? 'A' : 'a' - 26;
    for (counter = 0; counter < 20; counter++)
    {
        code *= unencrypted[counter];
        code = code % 52;
        code += (code < 26) ? 'A' : 'a' - 26;
        encrypted[counter] = (char)code;
    }
    encrypted[counter] = '\0';

    printf("\nEncrypted password is: %s", encrypted);
}
```

2   Now we have our encrypted version, we can change this code into the checking program. It will loop through entering and checking the password until the encrypted password matches the saved version. It's important that when you type in your own encrypted word you get it right, otherwise, you will never get control of your computer back!!

Actually, this isn't entirely true as we have no way of disabling the *Break* key. This means that anyone can break your program using *Break* and gain access to the computer. Another flaw you need to be aware of is that the password attempt appears on the screen as you type, and remains there. There are ways around both of these problems, but it's dependent on the computer you are using, so we won't go into them in this book.

```c
#include <stdio.h>
#include <string.h>

void main()
{
/* Enter your own encrypted password here. */
/* If you want to use this one the password is wroxpress */
    char encrypted[] = "ZQvQYGvyfwtwXIrcHsRw";
    char password[21], unencrypted[21];

    int counter;
    long code;

    do
    {
        strcpy(unencrypted, "abcdefghijklmnopqrst");
        scanf("%s", password);
        for(counter = 0; counter < 20 && password[counter] != '\0'; counter++)
            unencrypted[counter] = password[counter];

        code = 0;
        for (counter = 0; counter < 20; code += unencrypted[counter++]);
        code = code % 52;
        code += (code < 26) ? 'A' : 'a' - 26;
        for (counter = 0; counter < 20; counter++)
        {
            code *= unencrypted[counter];
            code = code % 52;
            code += (code < 26) ? 'A' : 'a' - 26;
            password[counter] = (char)code;
        }
        password[counter] = '\0';
    } while (strcmp(password, encrypted) != 0);
}
```

As you can probably imagine, it's hard to present output from this program, so we won't try.

Summary

In this chapter we have applied the techniques acquired in earlier chapters to the general problem of dealing with character strings. Strings present a different, and perhaps more difficult problem than the numeric data types.

We have introduced you to two new libraries, **STRING.H** and **CTYPE.H**, which add considerable capability when working with strings and individual characters is necessary, and they make programmers' lives a lot easier by providing virtually all the basic functions you are likely to need. With the resources provided by the libraries in C, developing applications which use strings becomes much simpler.

Most of the chapter has been about handling strings using arrays, but we have also mentioned pointers. These will provide you with even more flexibility in dealing with strings, and many other things besides, as you will discover as soon as you turn the page and get on to the next chapter.

CHAPTER 7

Pointers

In the last chapter we gave you a glimpse of pointers, and just a small hint at what they can be used for. Here we will delve a lot deeper into the subject of pointers and show you just what you can do with them. They are one of the most useful tools in C and at the same time, have the potential to appear difficult.

You may find it useful to go through the whole of this chapter and then start at the beginning again. This means that you will be able to read the text and programs the second time with some idea of where we are going. We cover a lot of new concepts here, so you may need to repeat some things a few times. It's a long chapter, so spend some time on it, playing around with our examples. Remember that the basic ideas are very simple, but they can be applied to complicated problems. By the end of this chapter you will be equipped with an essential element for effective C programming.

In this chapter we will:

- Learn about pointers
- Understand the relationship between pointers and arrays
- See how to use pointers with strings
- Learn about arrays of pointers
- Write an improved calculator program

A First Look at Pointers

We now come to one of the most extraordinarily powerful tools in the C language. It is also potentially the most confusing, so it's important you get the ideas clear in your mind at the outset, and maintain a clear idea of what's happening as we dig deeper.

Back in Chapters 2 and 5 we talked about memory. We talked about how when you declare a variable your computer allocates an area of memory for it. You refer to this area in memory using the variable name in your program, but once your program is compiled and run, your computer references it by the address in memory. This is the number that the computer has assigned to the 'box' in which the value of the variable will be stored.

Look at the following code fragment:

```
int number = 5;
```

Here we have allocated an area of memory for an integer and called it **number**. We have stored the value 5 in this area. The computer references the area using an address. The address is specific to your computer, whereas the variable name is specific to your program.

In C there is a type of variable that is designed to hold an address. These variables are called **pointers**, and the address held in a pointer is usually that of another variable. This is illustrated in the following figure. We have a pointer **P** which contains the address of another variable **number**, which is an integer containing the value 5.

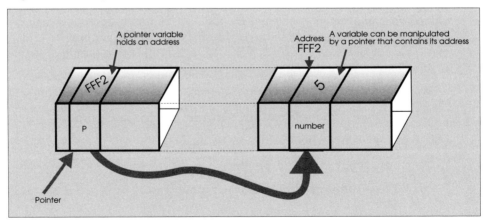

The first thing that is important to appreciate, is that it's not enough to know that a particular variable, such as **p**, is a pointer. You, and more importantly, the compiler, must know the type of variable to which it points. Without this information it's virtually impossible to know how to handle the contents of the memory to which it points. A pointer to a value of type **char** is pointing to a value occupying one byte, whereas a pointer to a value of type **long** is pointing to a value occupying four bytes. This means that every pointer will be associated with a specific variable type, and can only be used to point to variables of that type. **int** pointers can only point to **int** variables, **float** pointers to **float** variables and so on.

Declaring Pointers

So much for the theory. Let's look at a small program to highlight the capabilities of this special variable. When you have written a few programs like the one below you should at least feel comfortable with what is actually going on when you use a pointer.

Try It Out - Declaring Pointers

In this example we are simply going to declare a variable and a pointer. We will then show how we can output their addresses and values:

```
/* Example 7.1 A simple program using pointers */

#include <stdio.h>

void main()
{
    int number;
    int *pointer;

    number = 10;
    printf("\nnumber's address: %p", &number);
    printf("\nnumber's value: %d\n\n", number);

    pointer = &number;
    printf("pointer's address: %p", &pointer);
    printf("\npointer's value: %p", pointer);
    printf("\nvalue pointed to: %d", *pointer);
}
```

Try It Out!

The output from the program will look something like this. Remember, the actual address will be different on different machines.

```
number's address: 33BE
number's value: 10

pointer's address: 33C0
pointer's value: 33BE
value pointed to: 10
```

How It Works

Let's see what's happening here.

```
int number;
int *pointer;

number = 10;
```

We declare a variable and a pointer, both of type **int**. Pointers need to be declared just like any other variable. To declare the pointer **pointer** we put an asterisk (*) in front of the variable name in the declaration. The asterisk defines **pointer** as a pointer, and the type, **int**, fixes it as a pointer to integer variables. There is nothing special about this declaration. We can declare regular variables and pointers in the same statement. For example, the statement:

```
double value, *pVal, fnum;
```

declares two double precision floating point variables, **value** and **fnum**, and a pointer to **double** variables, **pVal**.

So how do we get a pointer to point to a variable? For that we need the help of the address of operator **&**. In the above example we wrote:

```
pointer = &number;
```

This statement obtains the address of the variable **number** and stores that address in **pointer**.

So what does our program actually do?

```
printf("\nnumber's address: %p", &number);
printf("\nnumber's value: %d\n\n", number);
```

Well it first prints out the address (using **&number**) of the variable **number**, and then its value. To output its address we have used the output specifier **%p**. This outputs the value as a memory address, usually using a hexadecimal format. We used this when we discussed the **address of** operator.

```
pointer = &number;
```

As we have seen already, here we are assigning the address of **number** to **pointer**. We have initialized **number** to 10. Here we are initializing the pointer **pointer** with the address of **number**. We are storing the address value there in the same way as we normally store ordinary numeric values.

```
printf("pointer's address: %p", &pointer);
printf("\npointer's value: %p", pointer);
printf("\nvalue pointed to: %d", *pointer);
```

Let's go through this line by line.

```
printf("pointer's address: %p", &pointer);
```

Here we are printing the address of the pointer. Remember the pointer itself has an address, just like any other variable. We use **%p** as the conversion specifier to display an address and use the **&** (**address of**) operator.

```
printf("\npointer's value: %p", pointer);
```

Here we get the actual value stored in **pointer**, which is the address of **number**. This is an address so we use **%p** to display it, but we just use the normal variable name to access the value.

```
printf("\nvalue pointed to: %d", *pointer);
```

Here we see the really important part. We are now using the pointer to point to the actual value stored in **number**. We use **%d** because we know it is an integer value. **pointer** stores the address of **number**, so using that address we can actually find the value stored in **number**.

The addresses shown will be different on different computers, and sometimes different at different times on the same computer, but you can see what is going on with the pointers. The addresses of **number** and **pointer** are where in the computer the variables are stored. Their values are what is stored at that address. For **number**, it is an actual integer value (**10**), but for the **pointer**, it is the address of **number**. Using ***pointer** actually gives us access to the value of **number**. We are pointing at the variable.

Now I can hear the muttering. You thought * was multiply didn't you? And so it is. The compiler tells the difference between these symbols from the context in which the symbol appears. There is no risk of confusion for the compiler. Depending on where the asterisk appears the compiler will understand whether it should interpret it as a pointer or as a multiplication sign. You are going to have to be able to recognize the difference too.

The figure below illustrates using a pointer.

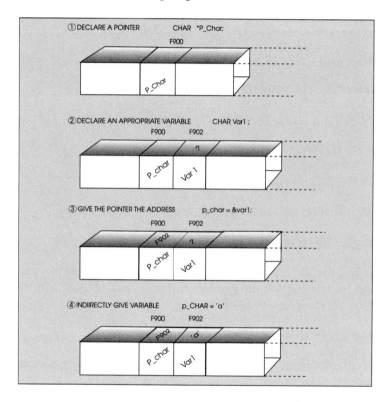

Using Pointers

Well, now we have **pointer** pointing at **number** what can we do with it? You are probably wondering what use it is to be able to point to something. If we can access the contents of **number** through the pointer **pointer** then the statement:

```
*pointer = *pointer +25;
```

increments the value of **number** by 25. The * indicates we are accessing the contents of whatever **pointer** is pointing to, that is, the contents of **number**. The unary operator * is called the **dereferencing** operator, or sometimes the **indirection** operator since the access mechanism is indirect. We are changing the value of **number** indirectly.

pointer can point to any variable of type **int**. This means we can change the variable that **pointer** points to by a statement such as:

```
pointer = &AnotherNumber;
```

The same statement as we used previously:

```
*pointer = *pointer + 25;
```

is now operating with the new variable, **AnotherNumber**. This means a pointer can assume the guise of any variable of the same type, so we can use one pointer variable to change the values of many other variables, as long as they are of the same type as the pointer.

Try It Out - Using Pointers

Let's exercise this new found facility in an example. Here we will use pointers to increase values stored in variables.

```
/* Example 7.2  What's the pointer     */
#include <stdio.h>
void main()
{
   long num1 = 0, num2 = 0, *pnum;
   pnum = &num1;                          /* Get address of num1 */
   *pnum = 2;                             /* setting num1 to 2    */
   ++num2;                                /* Incrementing num2    */
   num2 += *pnum;                         /* Adding num1 to num2  */
   pnum = &num2;                          /* Get address of num2  */
   ++*pnum;                  /* Incrementing num2 via the pointer */
   printf ("\nnum1 = %ld    num2 = %ld    *pnum = %ld    *pnum + num2 = %ld",
      num1, num2, *pnum, *pnum + num2);
}
```

When you run this program, you should get the output:

```
num1 = 2    num2 = 4    *pnum = 4    *pnum + num2 = 8
```

Try It Out!

How It Works

The comments should make the program easy to follow up to the **printf()**. Our first statement in the body of **main()** is the declaration:

```
long num1 = 0, num2 = 0, *pnum;
```

This ensures we set out with initial values for the two variables **num1** and **num2** at zero. It also declares an integer pointer **pnum**.

The next statement is an assignment:

```
pnum = &num1;                          /* Get address of num1    */
```

The pointer **pnum** is set to point to **num1** here, since we take the address of **num1** using the **address of** operator, and store it in **pnum**.

Another assignment statement:

```
*pnum = 2;                        /* Setting num1 to 2      */
++num2;                           /* Incrementing num2      */
```

exploits our new found power of the pointer, and we set **num1** to 2 indirectly. The variable **num2** then gets incremented by 1 in the normal way using the increment operator.

The statement:

```
num2 += *pnum;                    /* Adding num1 to num2      */
```

adds the contents of the variable pointed to by **pnum**, to **num2**. Since **pnum** still points to **num1**, **num2** is being increased by the value of **num1**.

The next two statements are:

```
pnum = &num2;                        /* Get address of num2    */
++*pnum;                     /* Incrementing num2 via the pointer */
```

First the pointer is reassigned to point to **num2**. The variable **num2** is then incremented indirectly through the pointer. You can see that the expression **++*pnum** increments the value pointed to by **pnum** without any problem However, if we wanted to use the postfix form, we would have to write **(*pnum)++.** The parentheses are essential assuming we want to increment the value not the address. If we omit them, the increment would apply to the address contained in **pnum**. This is because the operators **++** and unary ***** (and also unary **&** for that matter) share the same precedence level and are evaluated right to left. The compiler would apply the **++** to **pnum** first, incrementing the address and only then dereference to get the value. This is a common source of error when incrementing values through pointers, so it's probably a good idea to use parentheses in any event.

Finally, the last statement is the **printf()**:

```
printf ("\nnum1 = %ld    num2 = %ld    *pnum = %ld    *pnum + num2 = %ld",
        num1, num2, *pnum, *pnum + num2);
```

This displays the values of **num1**, **num2**, and **num2** incremented by 1 through **pnum**, and lastly **num2** in the guise of **pnum**, with the value of **num2** added.

Go through the program again slowly. Pointers can get confusing when you are just starting. You can work with addresses or values, pointers or variables and sometimes it is hard to work out what exactly is going on. The best thing is to keep writing short programs that use the things we have described, getting values using pointers, changing values, printing addresses and so on. This is the only way to really get confident about what is happening.

Try It Out - Using a Pointer With scanf()

Until now, when we have used **scanf()** to input values, we have used the **&** operator to obtain the address to be transferred to the function. Where we have a pointer which already contains an address, we just need to put the pointer name as a parameter as illustrated in the following simple example:

```
/* Example 7.3  Pointer argument to scanf      */
#include <stdio.h>
void main()
{
   int    value = 0, *pvalue = NULL;
   pvalue = &value;
   printf ("Input an integer: ");
   scanf(" %d", pvalue);
   printf("\nYou entered %d", value);
}
```

This program will just echo what you enter. How unimaginative can you get? It could be used as a parrot simulator though. Typical output should be:

```
Input an integer: 10
You entered 10
```

How It Works

Everything should be pretty clear up to `scanf()`.

```
scanf(" %d", pvalue);
```

We normally store the value entered by the user at the address of the variable. Is this case we could have used `&value`. Here the pointer, `pvalue`, is used to hand over the address of `value` to `scanf()`. We have already linked the address of `value` with the value stored in `pvalue` (`pvalue = &value`). `pvalue` and `&value` are the same, so we can use either.

```
printf("\nYou entered %d", value);
```

Then we just display `value`.

Although this is a rather pointless example, it illustrates how pointers and variables can work together. There is one thing we haven't explained and that is the use of `NULL` in the pointer declaration.

The Null Constant

The variable declaration in the last example is:

```
int    value = 0, *pvalue = NULL;
```

In the declaration for `pvalue`, we initialize it with the value `NULL`. `NULL` is a special constant in C and for pointers is roughly the equivalent of zero with ordinary numbers.

This is because pointers are *not* integers, they are used as addresses. Therefore to avoid confusion, `NULL` is used as the value for a pointer that doesn't point to anything. The value `NULL` is guaranteed not to be the same as any real address value that might occur.

Some people write code assuming `NULL` is zero. This provides some slight economy in the amount of keying, as if you want to test whether the pointer `pvalue` is `NULL` or not, you can write:

```
if( pvalue )
{...}
```

rather than the statement:

```
if( pvalue == NULL )
{...}
```

To be on the safe side, I prefer to program as though it isn't, and always test values against **NULL**. This also makes the program much clearer.

Naming Pointers

We have already started to write some big programs. As you can imagine when your programs get even bigger it is going to get even harder to remember which variables are normal variables and which are pointers. Therefore, it's quite a good idea to reserve names beginning with p for use as pointer names. If you follow this religiously, you will never be any doubt as to which variables are pointers and which are not.

> It is possible to assign specific values to pointers using numeric constants which are usually specified in hexadecimal notation. This means you can access memory locations anywhere in the computer which may hold values of interest. It becomes very hazardous once you introduce the possibility of storing values in such specifically defined addresses. Unless you are absolutely sure what you are doing, the practice is best avoided. You can even cause damage to computer in this way.

Arrays and Pointers

You will need a clear head for this bit, with or without a hat. Let's recap for a moment as they say, and recall what an array is and what a pointer is:

▶ An array is a collection of objects of the same type which we can refer to using a single name. For example, an array called **scores[50]** could contain all our basket ball scores for a 50-game season. We different index values for each particular element in the array. **scores[0]** is our first score and **scores[49]** is our last. If we had 10 games each month we could use a multi-dimensional array, **scores[12][10]**. If we play start in January, the third game in June would be referenced by **scores[5][2]**.

A pointer is a variable which has as its value the address of another variable or constant of a given type. We can use a pointer to access different variables at different times as long as they are all of the same type.

Actually, arrays and pointers are very closely tied together, in fact they can sometimes be used interchangeably. Let's consider strings. A string is just an array of type **char**. If we wanted to input a single character with **scanf()**, we would use:

```
char single;
scanf("%c", &single);
```

Here we need the address of operator for **scanf()** to work. However, if we are reading in a string:

```
char multiple[10];
scanf("%s", multiple);
```

we don't use the **&**. We are using the array name just like a pointer. If we use the array name in this way without an index value it refers to the address of the first element in the array. However, there is an important difference. Arrays are *not* pointers. You can change the address contained in a pointer, but you cannot change the address referenced by an array name.

Arrays and Pointers in Practice

What we are going to do here is go through a few examples to show you how arrays and pointers work together. The following examples all link together as a progression. We don't get to the real nitty-gritty of **How It Works** until nearer the end, so bear with us.

Try It Out - Arrays and Pointers

Just to further illustrate the point, try running the following program on your own computer:

```
/* Example 7.4  Arrays and pointers - A simple program*/
#include <stdio.h>

void main()
{
   char multiple[] = "I am a string";

   printf("Using address of operator: %p\n", &multiple[0]);
   printf("     Without the operator: %p", multiple);
}
```

Try It Out!

On our computer, the output is:

```
Using address of operator: 3396
      Without the operator: 3396
```

How It Works

Ha! So `&multiple[0] = multiple`.

So let's take this a bit further, if `multiple` refers to the same thing as `&multiple[0]`, what does `multiple + 1` equal? Let's try the following example.

Try It Out - Arrays and Pointers Taken Further

```
/* Example 7.5 Arrays and pointers taken further */

#include <stdio.h>

void main()
{
   char multiple[] = "another string";

   printf("         value of second element: %c\n", multiple[1]);
   printf("value of multiple after adding 1: %c", *(multiple + 1));
}
```

The output is:

```
         value of second element: n
value of multiple after adding 1: n
```

How It Works

So you can see that `multiple[1]` is the same as `*(multiple + 1)`. We can further confirm this if we display the addresses rather than the values:

```
/* Example 7.5 Arrays and pointers taken further */

#include <stdio.h>

void main()
{
   char multiple[] = "another string";

   printf("         address of second element: %p\n", &multiple[1]);
   printf("address of multiple after adding 1: %p", multiple + 1);
}
```

we would get:

```
        address of second element: 33A3
 address of multiple after adding 1: 33A3
```

Nothing unusual there, nor is there anything unusual if we display the addresses of the first, second and third element of the array:

```c
#include <stdio.h>

void main()
{
   char multiple[] = "another string";

   printf(" first element: %p\n", multiple);
   printf("second element: %p\n", multiple + 1);
   printf(" third element: %p", multiple + 2);
}
```

```
  first element: 33A2
 second element: 33A3
  third element: 33A4
```

Try It Out - Different Types of Arrays

Great, but we already knew that the computer can add numbers together without much problem, but let's change to a different type of array, and see what happens:

```c
/* Example 7.6 Different types of arrays */

#include <stdio.h>

void main()
{
   int multiple[] = {1, 2, 3};

   printf(" first element address: %p value: %d\n", multiple, *multiple);
   printf("second element address: %p value: %d\n", multiple + 1,
       *(multiple + 1));
   printf(" third element address: %p value: %d", multiple + 2,
       *(multiple + 2));
}
```

If we compile and run this program, we get an entirely different story:

```
  first element address: 33C4 value: 1
 second element address: 33C6 value: 2
  third element address: 33C8 value: 3
```

How It Works

Look at the output. Now, with this example, **multiple** (**33C4**) **+ 1** = **33C6**! You can see that **33C6** is 2 bigger than **33C4** although we only added **1**. This isn't a mistake. C realizes that when you add 1 to an address value, what you actually want to do is access the next variable of that type. This is why, when you declare a pointer, you have to specify the *type* of variable pointed at. Remember that **char** data is stored in one byte, and that variables declared as **int** needed 2 or 4 bytes. As you can see, on our computer variables declared as **int** are 2 bytes. Remember, although when we use an array name in this way it behaves like a pointer, it is still different, it is still an array at a fixed address.

Multi-Dimensional Arrays

So far we have looked at one-dimensional arrays, but is it the same story with multi-dimensional arrays? Well, to some extent it is. However, a gap starts to appear between pointers and array names. Let's consider the array we used for the tic-tac-toe program at the end of Chapter 5. We declared the array as:

```
char board[3][3] = {{'1','2','3'},
                     {'4','5','6'},
                     {'7','8','9'}};
```

We can use this for the examples in this section.

Try It Out - Using Two-Dimensional Arrays

We can first have a look at some addresses related to our array **board** using the example:

```
/* Example 7.7 Two-Dimensional arrays */

#include <stdio.h>

void main()
{
   char board[3][3] = {{'1','2','3'},
                        {'4','5','6'},
                        {'7','8','9'}};

   printf("address of board      : %p\n", board);
   printf("address of board[0][0]: %p\n", &board[0][0]);
   printf("but whats in board[0] : %p\n", board[0]);
}
```

Try It Out!

The output might come as a bit of a surprise to you:

```
address of board      : 33A2
address of board[0][0]: 33A2
but whats in board[0] : 33A2
```

How It Works

Look at the output. As you can see they are all the same, so what can we deduce from this? The answer is quite simple. When you declare a one dimensional array, placing **[number1]** after the array name tells the compiler that it is an array of size **number1**. So placing another **[number2]** actually says make an array of size **number1**, where each element is an array of size **number2**. We create an array of sub-arrays. So using the array name with a single index value references the address of one of the sub-arrays, and using the array name by itself references the address of the beginning of the whole array of arrays, which is the same as the address of the beginning of the first sub-array.

To say this another way,

```
board = board[0] = &board[0][0]
```

This also means that **board[1]** actually contains the address of **board[1][0]**. This should be reasonably easy to understand. The problems start when we use pointer notation to get to the values within the array. We still have to use the dereference operator, but we must be careful. If we change the above program to display the value of the first element, you'll see why:

```
/* Example 7.7 Two-Dimensional arrays */

#include <stdio.h>t

void main()
{
    char board[3][3] = {{'1','2','3'},
                        {'4','5','6'},
                        {'7','8','9'}};

    printf("value of board[0][0]: %c\n", board[0][0]);
    printf("value of board[0]   : %c\n", *board[0]);
    printf("value of board      : %p\n", *board);
}
```

As you can see, if we use **board** as a means of obtaining the value of the first element, then we need to use two dereference operators to get it, in other words ****board.** We were able to use just one ***** in the previous program because we were dealing with a one dimensional array. If we only used the one, we would get the address of the first element of the array of arrays, which is the address referenced by **board[0]**.

The relationship between the arrays is shown in the following diagram:

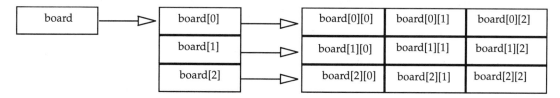

So, can we use **board** to get to all the values of the array? The answer is yes. We do this in the following example.

Try It Out - Getting All the Values in a Two-Dimensional Array

This example takes our previous example a bit further using a **for** loop.

```
/* Example 7.8  Getting the values in a two-dimensional array */

#include <stdio.h>

void main()
{
   int counter;
   char board[3][3] = {{'1','2','3'},
                       {'4','5','6'},
                       {'7','8','9'}};

   for(counter = 0; counter < 9; counter++)
     printf(" board: %c\n", *(*board + counter));
}
```

The output from the program is:

```
board: 1
board: 2
board: 3
board: 4
board: 5
board: 6
board: 7
board: 8
board: 9
```

Try It Out!

How It Works

The thing to notice about this program is the way we dereference **board**.

```
printf(" board: %c\n", *(*board + counter));
```

As you can see, we used the equation ***(*board + counter)**. It is important that the brackets are included. Leaving them out would have given us the value pointed to by **board**, that is the value stored in the location referenced by the address stored in **board**, with the value of **counter** added to this value. So if **counter** had the value 2, we would simply increase the value of the first element of the array by 2. What we actually want to do, is to add the value of **counter** to the address contained in **board**, and then dereference this new address to obtain a value.

Try changing the initial values for the array so that the characters go from '9' to '1'. If you leave out the brackets you should get output that looks something like:

```
board: 9
board: :
board: ;
board: <
board: =
board: >
board: ?
board: @
board: A
```

This is because you are adding the value of **counter** to the contents of the first element of the array **board**. The characters you get come from the ASCII table, starting at 9 and continuing to A.

Also if you used ****(board + counter)**, this too would have given erroneous results. In this case, ****(board + 0)** points to **board[0][0]**, ****(board + 1)** points to **board[1][0]**, and ****(board + 2)** points to **board[2][0]**. If we use higher increments, we would be accessing memory locations outside the array because there isn't a fourth element of the array of arrays.

Multi-Dimensional Arrays and Pointers

So now we have used the array name using pointer notation for referencing a two-dimensional array, what about using a declared pointer. As we have said, this is where there is a difference. If we declare a pointer and assign the address of the array to it, then we can use the pointer to access the members of the array.

Try It Out - Multi-Dimensional Arrays and Pointers

We can see this in action in this next example:

```
/* Example 7.9  Multi-dimensional arrays and pointers*/

#include <stdio.h>

void main()
{
   int counter;
   char *pointer;
   char board[3][3] = {{'1','2','3'},
                       {'4','5','6'},
                       {'7','8','9'}};

   pointer = *board;
   for(counter = 0; counter < 9; counter++)
      printf(" board: %c\n", *(pointer + counter));
}
```

Here you get the same output as before:

```
board: 1
board: 2
board: 3
board: 4
board: 5
board: 6
board: 7
board: 8
board: 9
```

How It Works

Here we have initialized **pointer** to the first element of the array, then just used normal pointer arithmetic to move through the array.

```
pointer = *board;
for(counter = 0; counter < 9; counter++)
    printf(" board: %c\n", *(pointer + counter));
```

We could have initialized **pointer** by using:

```
pointer = &board[0][0];
```

It doesn't make any difference. There is one final way of initializing **pointer** and that is:

```
pointer = board;
```

Strictly speaking this isn't legal, since **pointer** and **board** have different levels of indirection. What this means is that **pointer** needs one * to get to the value, and **board** needs two. Most compilers will allow you to do this, just giving a warning about what you have done. However, it's bad practice, so we don't advise you to do it.

Using What We Have Learnt

Now we know that for a two-dimensional array we have several ways of accessing the information in that array. For our array **board**, the table below lists them all for you.

board	0	1	2
0	board[0][0]	board[0][1]	board[0][2]
	*board[0]	*(board[0]+1)	*(board[0]+2)
	**board	*(*board+1)	*(*board+2)
1	board[1][0]	board[1][1]	board[1][2]
	*(board[0]+3)	*(board[0]+4)	*(board[0]+5)
	*board[1]	*(board[1]+1)	*(board[1]+2)
	*(*board+3)	*(*board+4)	*(*board+5)

Continued

board	0	1	2
2	`board[2][0]`	`board[2][1]`	`board[2][2]`
	`*(board[0]+6)`	`*(board[0]+7)`	`*(board[0]+8)`
	`*(board[1]+3)`	`*(board[1]+4)`	`*(board[1]+5)`
	`*board[2]`	`*(board[2]+1)`	`*(board[2]+2)`
	`*(*board+6)`	`*(*board+7)`	`*(*board+8)`

Let's see what we can do with the information we have learnt so far. Remember the example that works out your hat size in Chapter 5. We can now see how we could have done things a little differently.

Try It Out - Know Your Hat Size Revisited

We could rewrite the hat sizes example using pointer notation just for fun:

```
/* Example 7.10  Understand pointers to your hat size  - if you dare....  */
#include <stdio.h>
void main()
{
   char Size[3][12] =   {
     {'6', '6', '6', '6', '7', '7', '7', '7', '7', '7', '7', '7'},
     {'1', '5', '3', '7', ' ', '1', '1', '3', '1', '5', '3', '7'},
     {'2', '8', '4', '8', ' ', '8', '4', '8', '2', '8', '4', '8'}
                      };                        /* Hat sizes as characters   */
   int Headsize[12] =
   {164,166,169,172,175,178,181,184,188,191,194,197}; /*Values in 1/8 inches*/
   float Cranium =0.0;                         /*Value in decimal inches*/
   int Your_Head = 0;                          /*Headsize in whole eighths*/
   int i;
   int hat_found=0, too_small=0;

   printf("Enter the circumference of your head above your eyebrows "
                 "in inches as a decimal value: ");
   scanf(" %f", &Cranium);
   Your_Head = 8.0* Cranium;

   for ( i=0 ; i< 12 ; i++ )
   {
      if (Your_Head > *(Headsize +i) )
```

```
    continue;
    if(( i == 0) && (Your_Head < (*Headsize) -1))
    {
      printf("\nYou are the proverbial pinhead.");
      printf(" No hat for you I'm afraid.");
      too_small =1;
      break;
    }
    if( Your_Head < (*Headsize+i) - 1 )
      i-=1;
    printf("\nYour hat size is %c %c%c%c",
        *(*Size + i), *(Size[1] + i), (i==4)?'  ' : '/', *(*Size+24+i));
    hat_found=1;
    break;
  }
  if ((hat_found==0) && (too_small==0))
  {
  printf("\nYou, in technical parlance, are a fathead.");
  printf(" No hat for you I'm afraid.");
  }
}
```

The output here is the same as in Chapter 5, it is the code that is interesting.

How It Works

With fun like this, who needs their teeth drilled? The example speaks for itself if you were following the previous paragraphs. It operates essentially the same way as the example from Chapter 5. If you examine the **printf()** in the middle, you will see we mixed the notation a bit, just to show we can handle it.

If you are confused about what we have covered so far in this chapter, don't be disgruntled, everyone finds it hard. If you feel a bit lost try going through the first half of the chapter again and try playing about with the programs to see what happens.

You will find in practice you can just use pointers instead of messing around with dereferencing array names, and after you have played with pointers for a while you will feel quite gruntled again, as they aren't so difficult when you get used to them.

Using Memory As You Go

Pointers are an extremely flexible and powerful tool for programming over a wide range of applications. The majority of programs in C use pointers to some extent. C also has a further facility which enhances the power of pointers, in that it permits memory to be allocated dynamically.

Think back to our program that averages student's scores (from Chapter 5). At the moment it only works for 10 students. Suppose we wanted to write the program so that it would work without knowing the number of students in the class in advance, and wouldn't use any more memory than necessary for the number of student scores specified. Dynamic memory allocation allows us to do just that. We can produce arrays large enough to hold the right amount of data for the task we require.

Dynamic Memory Allocation - The malloc Function

The function to allocate memory as you go along is called **malloc()** and its definition is in the **STDLIB.H** header file which we will need to include when we use it. When you use the **malloc()** function the number of bytes of memory needs to be specified as a parameter, and the function returns the address of the first byte of memory allocated in response to your request. Since we get an address returned, a pointer is a useful place to put it.

A typical example of dynamic memory allocation might be:

```
int *pNumber;
pNumber = (int*) malloc(100);
```

Here we have requested one hundred bytes of memory, and assigned the address of this memory block to **pNumber**. Any time we use the variable **pNumber**, assuming we haven't modified it, it will point to the first **int** location at the beginning of the one hundred bytes allocated. This whole block can hold 50 **int** values, assuming the typical **int** takes 2 bytes.

> Notice the cast that we have used to make the function use a pointer of type **int** (**int***). We have done this because **malloc()** is a general purpose function that is used to give pointers for all types of variables and so it actually returns a **void** pointer. The type **void** can best be described as an absence of type. Some compilers automatically cast to the appropriate type, but it doesn't hurt to be specific.

We could request any number of bytes we need, subject only to the amount of free memory on the computer and the limit on **malloc()** imposed by a particular implementation. If it can't be allocated for any reason, **malloc()** returns a pointer with the value **NULL**. Remember that this is the equivalent of zero for pointers. It's always a good idea to check any dynamic memory request immediately, using an **if** to make sure the memory is actually there before you try to use it. As with money, using memory you haven't got is generally catastrophic. Writing:

```
if(pNumber == NULL)
    ......;
```

with a suitable action if the pointer is **NULL** is good enough. For example, you could display a message ("not enough memory") and terminate the program. In some instances though, you may be able to free up a bit of memory you have been using elsewhere, which might give you enough memory to continue.

Using the sizeof Operator

The previous example is all very well but we don't usually deal in bytes, we deal in **int**s or **double**s and such like. It would be useful to allocate memory for 75 **int**s for example. We can do this with the following statement:

```
pNumber = (int*) malloc( 75*sizeof( int ) );
```

As we have seen already, **sizeof** may look at first sight like a function, but it is actually an operator. It is part of the C language. It returns an unsigned integer which is the count of the number of bytes required to store its argument. It will accept a type keyword such as **int** or **float** as an argument, and it will also accept a variable or an array name. With an array name as an argument it returns the number of bytes required to store the whole array. In the example above we have asked for enough memory to store 75 **int**s.

Try It Out - Dynamic Memory Allocation

We can put this into practice by using pointers to help calculate prime numbers. If you've forgotten, prime numbers are integers that are only divisible (with no remainder) by 1, themselves and nothing else. We will write this program using pointers and dynamic memory allocation:

```
/* Example 7.11  A dynamic prime example        */
#include <stdio.h>
#include <stdlib.h>
int main()
{
   long *primes = NULL, *start =NULL, *open = NULL, trial = 0;
   int  i = 0, found = 0, total = 0;
```

Try It Out!

```
    printf("How many primes would you like?  ");
    scanf("%d", &total);             /* Total is how many we need to find   */
    primes = (long *)malloc(total * sizeof( long ));
    if (primes == NULL)
    {
        printf("\nNot enough memory. Hasta la Vista, baby.");
        return 0;
    }

    /* We know the first three so let's give the program a start. */
    *primes = 2,  *(primes+1) =3,   *(primes+2) = 5;
    open = primes + 3;                       /* Get address of next free slot */
    trial = 5;
    do
    {
        trial += 2;                          /* Next value for checking     */
        start = primes;                      /* Set at beginning of primes   */
        found = 0;
        for (i = 0 ; i < open-primes ; i++ )
        if (found = (trial % *start++) == 0 ) break;
        if (found == 0 )                                     /* we got one    */
            *open++ = trial;
    }
    while (open-primes<=total );

    for (i = 0 ; i < 5*(total/5) ; i += 5 )          /* Display primes 5-up   */
        printf ("\n%121d%121d%121d%121d%121d",
        *(primes+i),*(primes+i+1),*(primes+i+2),*(primes+i+3),*(primes+i+4));
    printf("\n");                            /* Newline for any stragglers    */
    for (i = total-(total%5); i<total ; i++)
        printf("%12d",*(primes+i));                      /* Display any left   */
}
```

The output from this program looks something like this:

```
How many primes would you like?  25

        2           3           5           7          11
       13          17          19          23          29
       31          37          41          43          47
       53          59          61          67          71
       73          79          83          89          97
```

How It Works

With this example, you can enter how many prime numbers you want computed.

After you have input a value, the program requests some memory to be allocated in the statements:

```
primes = (long *)malloc(total * sizeof( long ));
if (primes == NULL)
{
    printf("\nNot enough memory. Hasta la Vista, baby.");
    return 0;
}
```

The maximum you can specify depends on two things: the memory available on your computer, and the amount that `malloc()` can allocate at one time with your compiler. The latter is probably the major constraint. The ANSI C specification provides for a maximum of at least 32,767 bytes, but some compilers will have a `malloc()` function supporting considerably more.

The primes are stored in the memory area supplied by the `malloc()` function. The variable `primes` is a pointer to `long` integers. Notice that we included a check to see whether a `NULL` pointer is returned. As we have already said, this is important, since there is no other indication that the memory you requested can't be allocated. If you don't check, sooner or later you will be trying to work with memory you haven't got. If the `malloc()`function does return a `NULL` pointer then we execute the statement `return`. This causes the program to exit the function in which the statement occurs. In this case, the function is `main()` and exiting `main()` stops the program. This means if our check on the `malloc()` function gives us a `NULL` we exit the program and display an appropriate message.

We have a couple of extra pointers declared for convenience:

```
long *primes = NULL, *start =NULL, *open = NULL, trial = 0;
```

One points to the beginning of the `primes` memory block, and is used to step through the known primes to check for exact division into the value under test in `trial`. The other pointer, `open`, keeps track of the next available `long` integer space in the block of memory allocated. Of course we initialize all our pointers to `NULL`, just to be on the safe side.

The loop control is specified by:

```
while (open-primes<=total );
```

We can take the difference between pointers **open** and **primes** to check when we should stop the **do while** loop. The value of the expression **open - primes** is equal to the total stored since **open** points to the next available slot. So as soon as this value exceeds the value of **total**, the computation stops and the results are displayed.

```
for (i = 0 ; i < 5*(total/5) ; i += 5 )          /* Display primes 5-up */
   printf ("\n%12ld%12ld%12ld%12ld%12ld",
   *(primes+i),*(primes+i+1), *(primes+i+2), *(primes+i+3), *(primes+i+4));
printf("\n");                              /* Newline for any stragglers */
for (i = total-(total%5); i<total ; i++)
   printf("%12d",*(primes+i));                      /*Display any left*/
```

These statements produce the output from the program.

We had to allow for displaying a number of results that might not be a multiple of 5, so we display the maximum multiple of five that is less than or equal to **total**, with the first **for** loop. We then display separately any that are left in the second **for** loop. If you don't have a newline character in the output format string, **printf()** just continues output on the same line, so the stragglers all appear on the last line.

Pointers to Strings

As well as **char** array variables, we can also use a pointer to **char** as a string variable. This will give us quite a lot of flexibility as we shall see. We can declare a pointer to **char** with a statement such as:

```
char *pString = NULL;
```

At this point it is worth remembering what a pointer is. Remember it's a variable containing the address of another memory location. So far we have only created the pointer, not a place to store a string. We can declare a block of memory that we intend to use to store string data, and then use pointers to keep track of where we have stored the strings.

Try It Out - Pointers to Strings

We can try this in the following example:

```c
/* Example 7.12  Managing memory and storing strings      */
#include <stdio.h>
#define BUFFER_LEN 240
void main()
{
    char Buffer[BUFFER_LEN];                              /* store strings */
    char *pS1 = NULL, *pS2 = NULL, *pS3 = NULL;          /* String pointers */
    char *pBuffer = Buffer;                               /* Pointer to Buffer */

    printf("\nEnter a message\n");
    pS1 = pBuffer; /* Save start of first string */
    while ( (*pBuffer++ = getchar() ) != '\n');/*Get input until Enter pressed*/
    *(pBuffer - 1) = '\0'; /* add terminator */

    printf("\nEnter another message\n");
    pS2 = pBuffer;  /* Keep start of next string */
    while ( (*pBuffer++ = getchar() ) != '\n'); /*Get input till Enter pressed*/
    *(pBuffer - 1) = '\0';                                /* add terminator    */

    printf("\nEnter another message\n");
    pS3 = pBuffer; /* Keep start of next string */
    while ( (*pBuffer++ = getchar() ) != '\n');/*Get input till Enter pressed*/
    *(pBuffer - 1) = '\0';                                /* add terminator    */

    printf("\nThe strings you entered are:\n\n%s\n%s\n%s",
            pS1, pS2, pS3);
    printf("\nThe buffer has %d characters unused.",
                    &Buffer[ BUFFER_LEN - 1 ] - pBuffer + 1);
}
```

Typical output from this would be:

```
Enter a message
Hello World!

Enter another message
Today is a great day for learning about pointers.

Enter another message
That's all.

The strings you entered are:
Hello World!
Today is a great day for learning about pointers.
That's all.
The buffer has 165 characters unused.
```

How It Works

The first thing of note in this example is that we use the value **Buffer_len**, specified in the **#define** pre-processor directive, as the dimension for the array **Buffer**:

```
#define BUFFER_LEN 240
```

The **#define** directive defines a value to be substituted for the name **BUFFER_LEN** wherever it is used. This is a common technique where you want to be able to change values in a program easily. By changing the value assigned to **BUFFER_LEN** in the define statement, you change the value at every point in the program where the dimension is used.

The initial declarations for the program are:

```
char Buffer[BUFFER_LEN];                    /* space to store strings  */
char *pS1 = NULL, *pS2 = NULL, *pS3 = NULL; /* String pointers         */
char *pBuffer = Buffer;                     /* Pointer to Buffer        */
```

Here we declare the string storage space as the array **Buffer** with the length determined by the **define** directive. We declare three pointers to keep track of where we put the strings, and a pointer, **pBuffer**, to keep track of the current position in **Buffer** when working through it.

The basic operation of the program is to store messages as they are entered in the array **Buffer**. They are stored contiguously from the start of the array, the end of each string being marked by the usual `'\0'`. The pointers **pS1**, **pS2**, and **pS3** keep track of the addresses of the beginning of each of the messages entered.

```
pS1 = pBuffer;                              /* Save start of first string  */
while ( (*pBuffer++ = getchar() ) != '\n');/* Get input until Enter pressed*/
*(pBuffer - 1) = '\0';                      /* add terminator              */
```

After outputting a prompt to the screen, input is managed by the above statements. The pointer **pS1** is set to the current value of **pBuffer** which is still at its initial value here, which is the address of the first element of the **Buffer** array. The input mechanism using **getchar()**, uses a pointer to the **Buffer** array to step through the array as characters are entered. The process continues until the *Enter* key is pressed when the **\n** will be detected. We couldn't use the name of the array here as, although we could use it as a pointer to access elements of the array, we couldn't change its value as an address. Attempting to do so would cause an error.

Notice how we can compute the address on the left hand side of an assignment using the pointer **pBuffer** in an expression, **(pbuffer -1)**. This expression results in the address in which we want to store the **\0** at the end of each string. We can only use an expression on the left-hand side of an assignment statement when it results in an address.

The subsequent strings are input using exactly the same process as for the first. Of course the value of **pBuffer** will have changed so that it points to the next free element in the array **Buffer**.

In the last **printf()**:

```
printf("\nThe buffer has %d characters unused.",
                    &Buffer[ Buffer_len - 1 ] - pBuffer + 1);
```

we output the number of characters left in the string. The computation is illustrated graphically in the figure below.

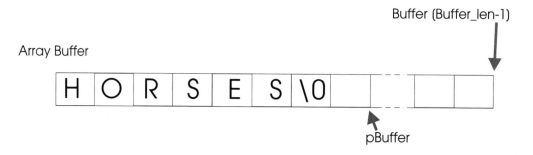

Remember the last index value of the array is **Buffer_len - 1**, as in the arithmetic expression, since array indexing starts from zero. It is a very common error, particularly when using named constants, to put **Buffer_len** as the last index value, rather than **Buffer_len - 1**.

At the outset, we initialized our pointers to **NULL**. We can also initialize a pointer with the address of a constant string:

```
char *pS = "To be or not to be";
```

This statement allocates sufficient memory for the string, places the constant string in the memory allocated, and after allocating space for it, sets the value of the pointer **pS** as the address of the first byte of the string. Contrast this with the declaration we had in Example 6.2 where we wrote:

```
char str1[ 40 ] = "To be or not to be";
```

These two statements are quite different in their effect, in spite of the apparent similarities. The first initializes the pointer to the address of a string constant. This constant can't be changed, but the pointer can be set to point to something else. The second initializes the array with the character string as an initial value. This isn't a constant, and we can change the contents of the array whenever we wish. However, as we pointed out before, the address referenced by using the array name **str1** can't be altered.

Arrays of Pointers

That last example was a bit repetitive. We used the same code repeated for each string entered. If we could set up the pointers to the strings entered as an array of pointers, we could maybe shorten the program quite a bit. The question is how.

Try It Out - Arrays of Pointers

The following example is a rewrite of the previous one and demonstrates how we could use arrays of pointers:

```
/* Example 7.13 Arrays of Pointers to Strings       */
#include <stdio.h>
#define BUFFER_LEN 240
void main()
{
   char Buffer[BUFFER_LEN];              /* space to store strings   */
   char *pS[ 3 ] = { NULL };             /* Array of string pointers */
   char *pBuffer = Buffer;               /* Pointer to Buffer        */
   int i = 0;                            /* loop counter             */

   for (i=0; i<3 ; i++)
   {
     printf("\nEnter %s message\n", i>0? "another" : "a" );
     *(pS + i) = pBuffer;                     /* Save start of  string   */
     while ( (*pBuffer++ = getchar() ) != '\n');
                                 /* Get input till Enter pressed */
     *(pBuffer - 1) = '\0';            /* add terminator             */
```

```
        }
        printf("\nIn reverse order, the strings you entered are:\n\n%s\n%s\n%s",
                              *(pS + 2), *(pS + 1), *pS );
        printf("\nThe buffer has %d characters unused.",
                              &Buffer[ BUFFER_LEN - 1 ] - pBuffer + 1);
}
```

The output from this program is the same as from the previous one, so we won't repeat it.

How It Works

This is much neater isn't it? The declarations at the beginning are now:

```
    char Buffer[BUFFER_LEN];        /* space to store strings   */
    char *pS[ 3 ] = { NULL };       /* Array of string pointers */
    char *pBuffer = Buffer;         /* Pointer to Buffer        */
    int i = 0;                      /* loop counter             */
```

The difference here is that we now have an array of three pointers to **char**, **pS**, each of which is initialized with **NULL**. We also have an extra integer variable **i** declared, which we need as an index in the **for** loop.

```
    printf("\nEnter %s message\n", i>0? "another" : "a" );
```

Here we use our snappy way to alter the prompt in the **printf()** suitably after the first iteration of the **for** loop using our old friend the conditional operator: This outputs "a" on the first iteration, and "another" on all subsequent iterations.

We now input all three strings in the **for** loop, and so only have to write the statements to do it once. Look at the statement where we save the current address of the beginning of the string from **pBuffer**:

```
    *(pS + i)  = pBuffer;           /* Save start of  string    */
```

The expression on the left hand side of the assignment, *(pS +i), is equivalent to pS[i], and is a pointer since we have an array of pointers. This assignment statement is therefore storing the address stored in the pointer **pBuffer**, in an element of the **pS** pointer array. If the left side didn't have the *, it would be referring to the address of one of the elements of **pS**, which isn't the same thing at all.

In fact, if you try leaving out the de-reference operator the program won't compile. The most likely message from the compiler is that an **lvalue** is required. This sounds a bit obscure, but an **lvalue** is just somewhere where you can store a result.

The **printf()** statement:

```
printf("\nIn reverse order, the strings you entered are:\n\n%s\n%s\n%s",
       *(pS + 2), *(pS + 1), *pS );
```

displays the strings in reverse order. It defines the address of each string to be output using pointer notation in the form shown. These correspond to ***pS[2]**, ***pS[1]**, and ***pS[0]** respectively, in array notation. In each case the result of the expression is the address of the first character of one of the strings. This is compatible with the format specifier **%s**, which, as we noted previously, expects to process an array of characters terminated by **\0**.

If we developed this example just a little further, we would be able to allow input of an arbitrary number of messages, only limited by the number of string pointers provided for in the array.

Try It Out - Generalizing String Input

Let's try rewriting the example to generalize string input:

```
/* Example 7.14 Generalizing string input */
#include <stdio.h>
#include <stdlib.h>

#define BUFFER_LEN 240
#define NUM_P 10
int main()
{
  char Buffer[BUFFER_LEN];              /* space to store input string   */
  char *pS[NUM_P] = { NULL };           /* Array of string pointers      */
  char *pBuffer = Buffer;               /* Pointer to Buffer             */
  int i = 0, j = 0;                     /* loop counters                 */

  for (i=0; i < NUM_P; i++)
  {
    pBuffer = Buffer ;                  /* Set pointer to beginning       */
```

```
      printf("\nEnter %s message, or press Enter to end\n",
                              i>0? "another" : "a");
   while ( (*pBuffer++ = getchar() ) != '\n');
   if ( (pBuffer - Buffer) < 2 )                    /* check for empty line */
      break;
   *(pBuffer - 1) = '\0';                           /* add terminator */
   pS[i] = (char* ) malloc( pBuffer - Buffer ); /* Get memory for string */
   if ( pS[i] == NULL )                        /* Check we actually got some */
   {
      printf("\nOut of memory - bye folks.");
      return 0;                                     /* Exit if we didn't */
   }
   j = 0;                                           /* Copy from Buffer */
   while( (*(pS[i] + j) = Buffer[ j ]) != '\0')     /* to new memory */
      j++;
}
printf("\nIn reverse order, the strings you entered are:\n");
while (--i >= 0 )
{
   printf("\n%s", *(pS + i) );            /* Display strings last to first */
   free( *(pS + i) );                        /* Release memory we got */
   *(pS + i) = NULL;                    /* Set pointer back to NULL for safety */
}
}
```

The output is very similar to the previous two examples:

```
Enter a message, or press Enter to end
Hello

Enter another message, or press Enter to end
World!

In reverse order, the strings you entered are:
World!
Hello
```

How It Works

This has expanded a little bit, but we have included quite a few extras compared to our original attempt at this. We now handle as many strings as we provide pointers for, in the array **pS**. The dimension of this array is defined at the beginning to make it easy to change:

```
#define NUM_P 10
```

If you want to alter the number of strings the program will handle, changing the value of **Num_p** in this statement will get you your required number of pointers.

The declarations:

```
    char Buffer[BUFFER_LEN];          /* space to store input string */
    char *pS[ NUM_P ] = { NULL };     /* Array of string pointers    */
    char *pBuffer = Buffer;           /* Pointer to Buffer           */
    int i = 0, j = 0;                 /* loop counters               */
```

declare the initial data areas we need. The array **Buffer** is now just an input buffer. Therefore, the **define** for **BUFFER_LEN** now defines the maximum length of string we can accept. We then have the declaration for our pointer array of length **NUM_P**, and our pointer for working within **Buffer**. Finally we have a couple of loop index variables.

The loop control:

```
    for (i=0; i< NUM_P; i++)
```

ensures that input can only occur for a number of strings up to the number of pointers we have declared. Once you have entered the maximum number of strings, the loop ends and you fall through to the output section of the program.

Within the loop, a string is entered using a similar mechanism with **getchar()** to what we have seen before:

```
    while ( (*pBuffer++ = getchar() ) != '\n');
```

The whole process takes place in the condition for the continuation of the **while** loop. A character obtained by **getchar()** is stored at the address pointed to by **pBuffer** which starts out as the address of **Buffer**, **pBuffer** is incremented to point to the next available space, and the character stored as a result of the assignment is compared with **\n**. If it is **\n** the loop terminates.

Note that a weakness here is the absence of any check to ensure that the size of **Buffer** isn't exceeded. If you enter more characters than the array **Buffer** has capacity for, the program will continue quite happily, overwriting who knows what.

The input process is followed by the check in the statement:

```
if ( (pBuffer - Buffer) < 2 )              /* check for empty line    */
    break;
```

This detects an empty line since, if you just press the *Enter* key, only one character will be entered - the **\n**. In this case the break immediately exits the **for** loop, and begins the output process.

The next statement is:

```
*(pBuffer - 1) = '\0';              /* add terminator              */
```

This places the **\0** in the position occupied by the **\n** character, since **pBuffer** was left pointing to the first free element in the array **Buffer**.

Once a string has been entered, sufficient memory is requested using **malloc()** to hold the string exactly:

```
pS[i] = (char* ) malloc( pBuffer - Buffer );  /*Get memory for string*/
if ( pS[i] == NULL )                    /* Check we actually got some    */
{
    printf("\nOut of memory - bye folks.");
    return 0;                          /* Exit if we didn't    */
}
```

The number of bytes required is the difference between the address currently pointed to by **pBuffer**, which is the first vacant element in **Buffer**, and the address of the first element of **Buffer**. The pointer returned from **malloc()** is stored in the current element of the **pS** array, after casting it to type **char**. After checking we didn't get a **NULL** pointer back, the contents of **Buffer** are copied to the new memory we have just obtained.

Look at the **while** loop copy mechanism. It continues as long as the result of the assignment:

```
(*(pS[i] + j) = Buffer[j])
```

is not **\0**. We get the address to store the character from **Buffer[j]** by adding **j** to the address in **pS[i]**. The dereference operator indicates we are modifying the contents of the location referenced by this address..

Once we exit the loop, either because we entered an empty string, or we used all the pointers, we generate the output:

```
while (--i >= 0 )
{
    printf("\n%s", *(pS + i) );      /* Display strings last to first */
    free( *(pS + i) );                       /* Release memory we got */
    *(pS + i) = NULL;                /* Set pointer back to NULL for safety */
}
```

The index **i** will have a value one greater than the number of strings entered. So after the first loop condition check, we can use it to index the last string. The loop continues counting down from this value, and the last iteration will be with **i** at zero, which will index the first string. The expression ***(pS + i)** is equivalent to **pS[i]** in array notation. Using pointer notation on the array of pointers here is just for exercise.

You can see we use a new function **free()** after the last **printf()**. This function is complementary to **malloc()**, and it releases memory previously allocated by **malloc()**. It only requires the pointer to the memory allocated as a parameter. Although memory will be freed at the end of the program automatically, it's good practice to free memory as soon as you no longer need it.

You should also take care to free memory you have obtained through **malloc()** before your pointer goes out of scope. Remember, as soon as a variable goes out of scope, it can no longer be accessed. This means that, obviously, you won't be able to free the memory pointed to by an out of scope pointer. It's also a good idea to make sure pointers that aren't set to a valid address are set to **NULL**, as we have done here.

> Errors with pointers can produce catastrophic results. If an uninitialized pointer is used to store a value before it has been assigned an address value, the address used will be whatever happens to be stored in the pointer location. This could overwrite virtually anywhere in memory.

The only other thing required to make this example solid, is to check that some idiot doesn't try to enter more characters than we can hold in **Buffer**. There are various ways in which this can be done, and if you have been keeping up, you should find it a piece of cake.

Try It Out - Sorting Strings Using Pointers

Using the string library, we can demonstrate the effectiveness of using pointers by an example showing a simple method of sorting:

```c
/* Example 7.15 Sorting strings   */
#include <stdio.h>

#include <stdlib.h>
#include <string.h>
#define BUFFER_LEN 80
#define NUM_P 10
void main()
{
  char Buffer[BUFFER_LEN];              /* space to store input string */
  char *pS[NUM_P] = { NULL };           /* Array of string pointers    */
  char *pTemp = NULL;                   /* Temporary pointer           */
  int i = 0, j = 0;                     /* loop counters               */
  int last_string = 0;                  /* Index of last string input  */

  printf("\nEnter successive lines, pressing Enter at the end of each line. \
    Just press Enter to end.\n\n");
  while(  ( *( gets( Buffer ) ) != '\0' ) && ( i < NUM_P)  )
    {
      pS[ i ] = ( char *) malloc ( strlen( Buffer )  + 1);
      strcpy( pS[ i ], Buffer );
      i++;
    }
  last_string = i;                            /*  Save last string index   */
  while( j == 0 )
  {
    j = 1;
    for ( i = 0 ; i < last_string - 1 ; i++ )
      if( strcmp( pS[ i ], pS[ i + 1 ] ) > 0 )
        {
          j = 0;                    /* indicator that we were out of order */
          pTemp= pS[ i ];           /* Swap pointers pS[ i ]               */
          pS[ i ] = pS[ i + 1 ];    /*  and pS[ i + 1 }                    */
          pS[ i + 1 ]  = pTemp;
        }

  }
  printf("\nYour input sorted in order is:\n\n");
  for ( i = 0 ; i < last_string ; i++ )
    {
      printf("%s\n", pS[ i ] );
      free( pS[ i ] );
    }
}
```

Assuming you enter the same input data, the output from this program is:

```
Enter successive lines, pressing Enter at the end of each line.
Just press Enter to end.

Many a mickle makes a muckle.
A fool and your money are soon partners.
Every dog has his day.
Do unto others before they does it to you.
A nod is as good as a wink to a blind horse.


Your input sorted in order is:

A fool and your money are soon partners.
A nod is as good as a wink to a blind horse.
Do unto others before they does it to you.
Every dog has his day.
Many a mickle makes a muckle.
```

How It Works

This is quite an interesting example. It really will sort the wheat from the chaff. To simplify things a bit we are using the input function **gets()** which reads a complete string up to the point you press *Enter*, and then adds '/0' to the end. Its only parameter is a pointer to the memory area where you want the string to be stored. Its return value is either the address where the input string is stored, that is **str**, or **NULL** if an error occurs. The overall operation of this program is quite simple, and involves three distinct activities:

- First, read in all the input strings,

- Second, sort them in order,

- Third and last, display them in alphabetical order.

After the initial prompt lines are displayed, the input process is handled by the statements:

```
while(  ( *( gets( Buffer ) ) != '\0' ) && ( i < NUM_P)  )
  {
    pS[ i ] = ( char *) malloc ( strlen( Buffer )  + 1);
    strcpy( pS[ i ], Buffer );
    i++;
  }
```

The input process continues until an empty line is entered, or until you run out of space in the pointer array. Each line is read into **Buffer** using the **gets()** function. This is inside the **while** loop condition, which allows the loop to continue as long as **gets()** does not read a string containing just '\0', and the total number of lines entered does not exceed the pointer array dimension. The empty string with just '\0' will be a result of you pressing *Enter* without entering any text. We use the * to get at the contents of the pointer address return by **gets()**. This is the same as **Buffer** of course.

As soon as we collect each input line in **Buffer**, we allocate the correct amount of memory using **malloc()**. We should really check for a **NULL** return from **malloc()**, but it was omitted for simplicity. We get the count of the bytes we need using the **strlen()** function to provide a count of the number of characters, and adding 1 for the '/0' at the end.

Once we have all our strings safely stowed away, we sort them using the simplest, and probably the most inefficient sort going - but it's easy to follow. This is in the statements:

```
while( j == 0 )
{
  j = 1;
  for ( i = 0 ; i < last_string - 1 ; i++ )
    if( strcmp( pS[ i ], pS[ i + 1 ] ) > 0 )
      {
      j = 0;                    /* indicator that we were out of order */
      pTemp= pS[ i ];           /* Swap pointers pS[ i ]               */
      pS[ i ] = pS[ i + 1 ]; /*  and pS[ i + 1 }               */
      pS[ i + 1 ]  = pTemp;
    }

  j = 0;
}
```

The sort takes place inside the **while** loop which continues as long as **j** is zero. The sort proceeds by comparing successive pairs of strings using the **strcmp()** function inside the **for** loop. If the first is greater than the second we swap pointer values. Using pointers as we have here, is a very economical way of changing the order. The strings themselves remain undisturbed exactly where they were, it's just the sequence of their addresses that changes in the pointer array **pS**. This mechanism is illustrated in the following figure. The time to swap pointers is obviously a fraction of the time that would be required to move all the strings around.

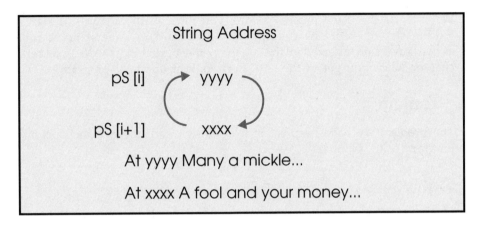

The swapping continues through all the string pointers. If we had to interchange any during a pass through all the strings, we repeat the whole thing. It we repeat the whole thing without interchanging any, they are in order and we have finished the sort. We track the status of this with the integer variable **j**. This gets set to 0 if any interchange occurs, but gets set back to one each cycle through. If we exit a cycle with **j** still one, no interchanges occurred so everything must be in order and we will exit from the **while** loop.

The reason this sort is none too good, is that each pass through all the items being sorted only moves a value by one position in the list. In the worst case when we have the first entry in the last position, the number of times we have to repeat the process is one less than the number of entries in the list.

Handling strings and other kinds of data in this way is an extremely powerful mechanism in C. You can throw the basic data, the strings in this case, into a bucket of memory in any old order, and you can process them in any sequence you like without moving the data at all. You just change the pointers. You could use ideas from this example as a base for programs for sorting any text. You would do well to sort out a better sort of sort though.

Designing a Program

Congratulations! You have got through a really tough part of the C language, and now we can show you an application using some of what you have learnt. We will use the usual process, taking you through the analysis, design and writing step-by-step. The concepts are quite hard to understand at times, but, as we have said already in this chapter, the best thing to do is to reread the chapter when you get to the end. Let's look at our final program.

The Problem

The problem we have been set is to re-design and improve the calculator program using pointers.

The Analysis

The main improvement we want to make is to allow the user to type in more than one calculation and also to enter more complex calculations. We can't use different variables for each number, as we don't know in advance how many numbers are going to be used. Instead, we are going to have to get a complete string from the user, and then analyze this to see what the numbers and operators are. The technical term for this is **parsing**.

We aren't going to extend the calculator that much. The extensions are in the following table:

Extension	Meaning
^	multiply the first number by itself, uses the second number to indicate how many times to do it.
=	simply displays the result so far.

We are also going to cheat a little by not taking into consideration the precedence of the operators, but simply calculate from the first to the last.

The steps are:

1   Loop until the string entered by the user is **quit**.

2   Loop through again, executing each operator in turn.

3   Display the result.

The Solution

1   This is not as easy as it first appears. We need to be able to enter a whole string including the spaces that the user uses. **scanf()** doesn't allow us to do this as it stops at the first white space character. However, we can use another function from the **STDIO.H** library that will do what we want, and you have seen it used for this reason already. This is the **gets()** function. We can actually combine the input and the overall program loop together as follows:

```
#include <stdio.h>
#include <string.h>

void main()
{
    char input[256];                              /* Input string storage */

    while(strcmp(gets(input), "quit") != 0)
    {
    }
}
```

We can do this because the function **strcmp()** expects to get a pointer to the string, and the function **gets()** actually returns a pointer to the string the user has typed in, **&input[0]** in this case. We can then compare this with **quit**.

We have set the input string to a length of 256. This should be enough as most computers keyboard buffers are 255 characters. (This refers to the maximum number of characters that you can type in before having to press *Enter*.)

2   Once we have our string, it is time to perform the calculations. We do this by going through the string and selecting the contiguous sequence of characters that make up a number. We convert these to a numeric value which we store in the variable **number**, except for the first value we obtain, which we store in **result** ready for use with the number following the first operator. We combine **result** with the following value stored in **number** using the operator we found immediately preceding **number**. The actual calculation bit we have borrowed from the previous version of the calculator, with just a few modifications.

```c
#include <stdio.h>
#include <string.h>
#include <stdlib.h>

void main()
{
    char input[256];                        /* Input string storage          */
    char number_string[30];   /* Store numeric strings here one at a time    */
    char operator;                      /* Store for operator when found     */
    double result = 0;                      /* Store result of calculation   */
    double number;                 /* Store converted numeric character string */
    unsigned int counter;               /* Position in the input string      */
    unsigned int input_length;              /* Total length of input string  */
    unsigned int number_counter; /*Tracks length of numeric character string*/

    while(strcmp(gets(input), "quit") != 0)
    {
        input_length = strlen(input);

/* Skip any leading spaces on the input string */
        for(counter = 0; counter < input_length; counter++)
            if(*(input+counter) != ' ') break;

/* Everything up to the next space is assumed to be the number */
        number_counter = 0;
        while((*(number_string+number_counter++) = *(input+counter++) ) != ' ');
        *(number_string+number_counter) = '\0';

/* Convert to a double so we can use it in the calculation */
        result = atof(number_string);

/* Now process the rest of the string */
        for(;counter < input_length;)
        {
/* Skip any spaces first non-blank is operator */
            while(( operator = *(input + counter++)) == ' ');

/* Skip any spaces */
            for( ;*(input + counter) == ' '; counter++);

/* Everything upto the next space is assumed to be the number */
            for(number_counter = 0; *(input+counter) != ' '
```

```
                  && counter < input_length; number_counter++)
*(number_string+number_counter++) = *(input+counter++);
   *(number_string+number_counter) = '\0';

/* Convert to a double so we can use it in the calculation */
         number = atof(number_string);
      }
   }
}
```

3 Now we can add the modified code from Chapter 3, and add some
instructions at the start:

```
#include <stdio.h>
#include <string.h>
#include <stdlib.h>
#include <math.h>

void main()
{
   char input[256];
   char number_string[30], operator;
   double result = 0, number;
   unsigned int counter, input_length, number_counter;

   printf("\nTo use this calculator, enter an expression using spaces");
   printf("\nbetween the numbers and operators.");
   printf("\n   Use = to see an intermediate result of the calculation.");
   printf("\n   Use quit by itself to stop calculator.\n\n");

   while(strcmp(gets(input), "quit") != 0)
   {
      input_length = strlen(input);

/* Skip any leading spaces on the input string */
      for(counter = 0; counter < input_length; counter++)
         if(*(input+counter) != ' ') break;

/* Everything up to the next space is assumed to be the number */
      number_counter = 0;
       while( (*(number_string+number_counter++) = *(input+counter++) ) != '');
      number_string[number_counter] = '\0';

/* Convert to a double so we can use it in the calculation */
      result = atof(number_string); /* Store fisrt number as result */

/* Now process the rest of the string */
      for(;counter < input_length;)
      {
/* Skip any spaces first non-blank is operator */
while(( operator = *(input + counter++)) == ' ');
```

```
/* If the operator is = then print result so far and continue the loop */
        if(operator == '=')
        {
            printf("= %f\n", result);
            continue;
        }

/* Skip any spaces */
        for(;*(input+counter) == ' '; counter++);

/* Everything upto the next space is assumed to be the number */
        for(number_counter = 0; *(input+counter) != ' '
            && counter < input_length; number_counter++)
        *(number_string+number_counter++) = *(input+counter++);
    *(number_string+number_counter) = '\0';

/* Convert to a double so we can use it in the calculation */
        number = atof(number_string);
/* switch copied and modified from old calculator program */
        switch(operator)
        {
            case '+':
                result += number;
                break;
            case '-':
                result -= number;
                break;
            case '*':
                result *= number;
                break;
            case '/':
                if(number == 0)
                    printf("\n\n\aDivision by zero error!\n");
                else
                    result /= number;
                break;
            case '%':
                if(number <= 0 || result < 0)
                    printf("\n\n\aDivision by zero error!\n");
                else
                    result = (double)((long)result % (long)number);
                break;
            case '^':
                result = pow(result, number);
                break;
            default:
                printf("\n\n\aIllegal operation!\n");
        }
    }
    printf("= %f\n", result);
}
}
```

The output looks something like:

```
To use this calculator, enter an expression using spaces
between the numbers and operators.
    Use = to see an intermediate result of the calculation.
    Use quit by itself to stop calculator.

8 * 2
= 16.000000
8 * 2 = + 4
= 16.000000
= 20.000000
quit
```

And there we have it!

Summary

In this chapter we have covered a lot of ground. We have explained pointers in detail. We have shown the relationship between pointers and arrays (both one dimensional and multi-dimensional arrays) and demonstrated their uses. We have introduced another function - the `malloc()` function for dynamically allocating memory, which provides the potential for your programs to use just enough memory for the data being processed in each run. We also introduced the `sizeof` operator which tells you the number of bytes required to store its argument. We have described how to use pointers with strings and finally how to use arrays of pointers.

The topics covered in this chapter are fundamental to a lot of what follows in the rest of the book, and of course to writing C programs effectively.. It may not be completely clear yet, because it takes time and experience to feel really confident with pointers. As we said at the start, probably the best thing to do now is to go back to the beginning and go through hell all over again. It will be a lot clearer.

Once you feel reasonably happy with what this chapter is describing, you will be ready to go on to the next chapter and get on with structuring your programs.

CHAPTER 8

Structuring Your Programs

We mentioned in Chapter 1 that breaking a program up into reasonably self-contained units is basic to the development of any program of a practical nature. When confronted with a big job, the most sensible thing to do is to break it up into manageable chunks. You can then do each small chunk fairly easily and be sure that you have done it properly.

Implicit in the basic idea of the C language is this segmentation of a program into functions. Even with the relatively short examples we have seen so far, which we have written as a single function **main()**, we have used a variety of standard library functions for input and output, for mathematical operations, and for handling strings.

In this chapter you will learn how to make your programs more effective as well as easier to develop, by introducing more functions of your own.

In this chapter you will:

- Understand more about functions
- Define your own functions
- Learn how to return results from your functions
- See how pointers can be used with functions

Simplifying Program Development

Do you remember the omelet analogy, and the figure of producing a meal from Chapter 1, shown below?

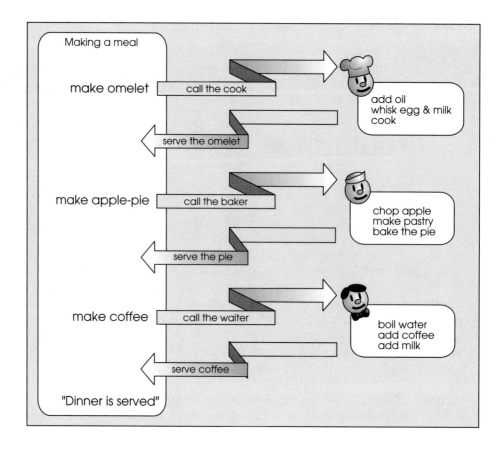

We can compare this to the next figure where you can see an idealized representation of a C program structured as five functions. It doesn't show details of the statements involved, it just shows the sequence of execution.

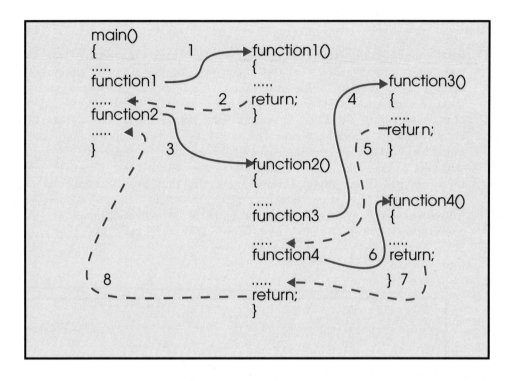

As you can see the sequence in which the instructions are executed is broken at each point where a call to a function occurs. The instructions are executed, starting at the first executable statement of the called function, until a **return** statement is reached. When it finds a **return** statement, execution goes back to the point immediately following the original function call.

The program steps through the instructions in the normal way until it comes across a call to a particular function. At this point, execution moves to the start of that function. The program continues through the function until it hits a return statement. This signals that execution should go back to the point just after where the function was originally called. Before we look in more detail at what functions really do, we need to look at a particular aspect of the way variables behave that we have glossed over so far.

Variable Scope

In all our examples up to now, we have declared the variables for the program at the beginning of the block defining the body of the function **main()**. We can also define variables at the beginning of any block. Does this make a difference? It most certainly does, as Ollie would have said. Variables only exist within the block in which they are defined. This also includes blocks that are inside a block. The variables declared at the beginning of an inner block also exist in the outer block, as long as there are no variables with the same name in the outer block, as we shall see. Variables such as these are called automatic variables, because they are automatically created and destroyed The extent within a program where a given variable exists is called the variable's scope. When you use a variable within its scope, everything is OK. If you try to reference it outside its scope, you will get an error during the compilation phase. The general idea is illustrated in the figure below.

```
{
 int a;
/* Reference to a is OK                */
/* Reference to b is an error here     */
   {
    int b;
     /* Reference to a + b OK here */


   }
/* Reference to b is an error here     */
/* Reference to a is OK                */


}
```

Try It Out - Understanding Scope

We can take a simple example:

```
/* Example 8.1 A microscopic program about scope        */
#include <stdio.h>
void main()
{
  int count1 = 0;
  do
  {
    int count2 = 0;
    ++count2;
    printf("\ncount1 = %d      count2 = %d", count1,count2);
  }
  while( ++count1 <= 8 );
  printf("\ncount1 = %d", count1);
}
```

Try running this program. You will get the output:

```
count1 = 1      count2 = 1
count1 = 2      count2 = 1
count1 = 3      count2 = 1
count1 = 4      count2 = 1
count1 = 5      count2 = 1
count1 = 6      count2 = 1
count1 = 7      count2 = 1
count1 = 8      count2 = 1
count1 = 9
```

How It Works

We declare and define **count2** inside the loop block:

```
do
{
  int count2 = 0;
  ++count2;
  printf("\ncount1 = %d      count2 = %d", count1,count2);
}
```

As a result its value is never more than 1. During each iteration of the loop the variable **count2** is created, initialized, incremented, and forgotten. The variable **count1** on the other hand exists at the **main()** block level. It continues to exist while it is incremented, so the last **printf()** produces the value 9.

Try modifying the program to make the last **printf()** output the value of
count2. It won't compile. You get an error because at the point where the
last **printf()** is, **count2** no longer exists. From this you may guess correctly
that failing to initialize automatic variables can cause untold chaos, as the
memory they use may be reallocated to something else at the end of their
existence. As a consequence, next time around, your uninitialized variables
may contain anything but what you expect.

Try It Out - More About Scope

Let's try a slight modification of the preceding example:

```
/* Example 8.2 More scope in this one    */
#include <stdio.h>
void main()
{
  int count = 0;
  do
  {
    int count = 0;
    ++count;
    printf("\ncount = %d ", count);
  }
  while( ++count <= 8 );
  printf("\ncount = %d", count);
}
```

Now we have used the same variable name **count** at the **main()** block level
and in the loop block. See what happens when you compile and run this.

```
count = 1
count = 1
count = 1
count = 1
count = 1
count = 1
count = 1
count = 1
count = 9
```

How It Works

The output is boring, but interesting at the same time. We actually have two
variables called **count**, but inside the loop block the local variable hides the
version of **count** that exists at the **main** block level. Inside the loop only the

local version of **count** can be reached. The **printf()** inside the loop block displays the local **count** value which is always 1 for the reasons given previously. As soon as we exit from the loop, the other **count** variable becomes visible, and the last **printf()** displays its exit value from the loop as 9. Clearly the variable controlling the loop is the one declared at the beginning of **main()**. This little example demonstrates why it is not a good idea to use the same variable name for two different variables in a function, even though it is legal. At best it is most confusing. At worst you will be thinking 'that's another fine mess I've got myself into'.

Variable Scope and Functions

The last point to note before we get into the detail of creating functions is that every function is a block (which may contain other blocks of course). As a result, the variables declared within a function are local to the function and do not exist elsewhere. Therefore the variables declared within one function are quite independent of those declared in another function. There is nothing to prevent you from using the same name for variables in different functions, and they will remain quite separate.

This becomes more significant when you are dealing with large programs where the problem of ensuring unique variables could become intolerable if this were not so. Obviously it is still a good idea to avoid unnecessary or misleading overlapping of variable names in various functions, and of course you should try to use names that are meaningful to make your programs easy to follow. We will see more about this as we get deeper into functions in C.

Functions

In our programs so far, we have used in-built functions such as **printf()** or **strcpy()**. Here you have seen how they are executed when we reference them by name with suitable arguments within the executable portion of our program. We transferred information to a function using arguments in parentheses following the function name. For example, with the **printf()** function the first argument is usually a text string in quotes, and the succeeding arguments (of which there may be none) are a series of variables or expressions whose values are to be displayed.

We then received information back from a function in two ways. One way was through one of its arguments in parentheses. We provided an address of a variable through an argument to a function, and the function placed a value in that variable. For example, when we use **scanf()** to read data from the keyboard, the input is stored in an address we supply as an argument. The other way is as a return value. For example, with the **log()** function, the value which is the logarithm of the argument we supply appears in the program code in the position where the function call is made. Where a function returns a value of a given type, the function call can appear as part of any expression where a variable of the same type could be used. The functions you will write and use can provide exactly the same range of options for transferring information, and since you have already written the function **main()** in all your programs already, you already have the basic knowledge of how a function is constructed.

Defining a Function

To create a function you need to specify a function header as the first line of the function definition, followed by the executable part which is the function body enclosed between braces, **{}**. The function header defines the name of the function, its parameters, and its return value type. The function body determines what calculations the function performs. The general form is essentially the same as you have been using for **main()**, and looks like this:

```
Return_type  Function_name( Parameters - separated by commas )
{
    Statements;
}
```

The statements in the function body can be absent, but the braces must be present. In this case the return type must be **void** and the function will have no effect. Although it may not be immediately apparent, presenting a function with a content-free body is often useful during the testing phase of a complicated program. This allows you to run the program with only selected functions actually doing something, and add bodies gradually until the whole thing works.

Naturally, the statements in the body of a function can also contain nested blocks of statements. However, a function can't be defined inside the body of another function.

Naming a Function

The function name, specified in the first line of our general representation of a function, can be any legal name in C that isn't a reserved word such as **int** or **double** or **sizeof**, and isn't the same as the name of another function or the name of a variable. In particular, you should take care not to use the same names as the standard library functions, since it will prevent you from using the library function of the same name, and it's confusing.

One way of differentiating your function names is to start them with a capital letter, although some programmers find this rather too restricting. A legal name has the same form as that of a variable - a sequence of letters and digits, the first of which is a letter. As with variable names, the underline character counts as a letter. Other than that, the name of a function can be anything you like, but ideally should give some clue as to what the function does. Examples of valid function names that you might choose are:

```
cube_root   FindLast   Explosion Back2Front
```

You will often want to define function names (and variable names come to that), which consist of more than one word. There are two basic approaches you can adopt, epitomized by the first two examples. You can choose to separate words with an underline character, or you can capitalize the first letter of each word. Which you choose is a matter of taste, but it is a good idea to pick an approach and stick to it. You can of course use one approach for functions and the other for variables. Within the book, both have been sprinkled around to give you a feel for how they look. By the time you reach the last page you should be ready to choose.

Function Parameters

Function parameters are defined in the function header. The parameters are a list of variable names and their types, with successive parameters separated by commas. The whole thing is enclosed between parentheses following the function name. They provide the means to get information *from* the calling program *into* the function. The term **parameter** is used to mean the variable name used in the function definition to reference values to be supplied by the calling function. The parameter names are local to the function. The values supplied when the function is called are referred to as **arguments**. The computation in the body of the function is written using the parameter names appearing in the function header.

A typical function header is:

```
int SendMessage( char* Text )
```

This function has one parameter, **Text**, which is of type pointer to **char**, and returns a value of type **int**.

A function is called by just using the function name followed by the arguments to the function in parentheses. When you actually call the function by referencing it in some part of your program, the arguments you specify in the call, will be substituted for the parameters in the function. As a result, when the function executes, the computation will proceed using the values supplied as arguments. The arguments you specify when you call a function need to agree in type, number and sequence with the parameters specified in the function header. The relationship and information passing between the calling and called function is illustrated in the figure below.

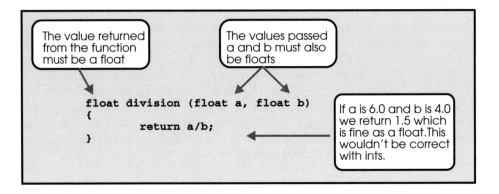

Return Value Type Specification

The **Return_type** specifies the type of the value returned by the function. If the function is used in an expression, or as the right hand side of an assignment statement, the return value supplied by the function will effectively be substituted for the function in its position. The type of value to be returned by a function can be specified as any of the legal types in C, or pointers to those types. The type can also be specified as **void**, meaning no value is returned. A function with a **void** return type can't be used in an expression, or anywhere in an assignment statement.

The return type can also be a pointer to **void**, which is a pointer value but with no specified type. This latter type is used when you want the flexibility to be able to return a pointer that may be used for a variety of purposes, as in the case of the **malloc()** function for allocating memory. Legitimate return types are show in the following table.

Type	Meaning	Type	Meaning
int	integer - 2 or 4 bytes	int *	int * pointer to int
short	Integer - 2 bytes	short *	pointer to short
long	integer - 4 bytes	long *	pointer to long
char	character - 1 byte	char *	pointer to char
float	floating point - 4 bytes	float *	pointer to float
double	floating point - 8 bytes	double *	pointer to double
void	no value	void *	pointer to undefined type

The return Statement

The **return** statement provides the means of exiting from a function and resuming execution of the calling function at the point from which the call occurred. It its simplest form the return statement is just:

```
return;
```

In this form it is used in a function with the return type declared as **void**. It doesn't return any value. The more general form of the return statement is:

```
return expression;
```

This form of **return** statement must be used when the return value type has been declared as other than **void**.

You will get an error if you compile a program containing a function declared with a `void` return type that tries to return a value. Likewise you will get an error if you use a bare `return` in a function with the return type declared other than `void`.

The return **expression** can be any expression, and should result in a value with the same type as that declared for the return value in the function header. If it isn't, the compiler will cast the type to that required, if possible. The modifier **signed** or **unsigned** may be used with any variety of **int** or with **char.**

There can be more than one **return** statement in a function, but each **return** statement must supply a value with the same type as that specified for the return value. The calling function doesn't have to recognize or process the value returned from a called function. We had the example of the string function **strcpy()** in the previous chapter which returned the address of the first string argument, and it was your choice as to whether you chose to use this address or not.

Try It Out - Using Functions

It is always easier to understand with an example, so let's start with a trivial illustration of a program comprising two functions. We will write a function to compute the average of two floating point variables which will be called from **main()**. This is to illustrate the mechanism rather than to present a practical use of functions:

```
/* Example 8.3 Average of two float values    */
#include <stdio.h>

/* Definition of the function to calculate an average */
float average( float x, float y )
{
    return (x + y) / 2.0;
}

/* main program - execution always starts here    */
void main()
{
    float average( float, float );

    float value1 = 0.0F, value2 = 0.0F, value3 = 0.0F;

    printf("Enter two floating point values separated by blanks: ");
    scanf("%f %f",&value1, &value2);
    value3 = average( value1, value2 );
    printf("\nThe average is: %f",  value3 );
}
```

Try It Out!

Typical output of this program would be:

```
Enter two floating point values separated by blanks: 2.34 4.567

The average is: 3.453500
```

How It Works

We shall go through this step-by-step. Look at the following figure. It describes the order of execution in our example.

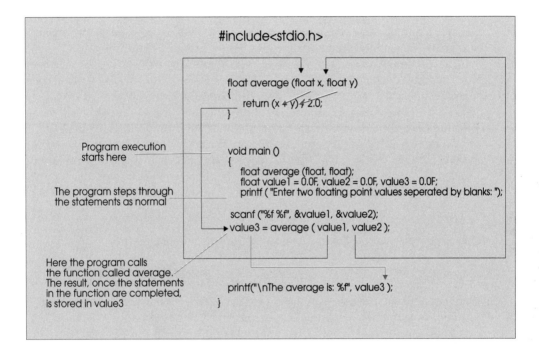

As we already know, execution begins at the first executable statement of our function **main()**. The first statement in the body of **main()** is:

```
float average( float , float );
```

This is not an executable statement. All we are doing is declaring the function. The purpose is to tell the compiler the essential specifications of the function. It includes specifications for the return type (**float**) and the parameter types (**float** and **float**) in addition to the name of the function, **average()**. Note that it requires a semi-colon at the end just as a variable declaration does. Compare this with the function header in the function definition which doesn't have a semicolon and includes sample parameters **x** and **y**:

```
float average( float x, float y )
```

The compiler is able to ensure that when we use the function, we provide arguments of the appropriate type, and that the return value is handled properly in any expression in which it is used. The variables x and y are local to the function **average()** and we are free to use the same variable names in the calling function, or any other function for that matter.

The function declaration is not strictly necessary in this case. If you delete it you will see that the program will still compile and run. This is because the definition of the function **average()** precedes its use in **main()**, so the compiler already knows all about it. If the definition followed **main()**, it would be essential to include the function declaration. It's good practice to always include declarations for all of the functions in a program. Function declarations do not typically appear in the position shown in the example above. They usually appear at the beginning of a program file, preceding **main()** and the other functions in the program.

Our first executable statement actually doing something is:

```
printf("Enter two floating point values separated by blanks: ");
```

There is nothing new here; this is simply a call to the function **printf()** with one argument, a string. The actual value transferred to **printf()** will be a pointer containing the address of the beginning of the string. The function will display the string we have supplied as an argument.

Our next statement is also a familiar one:

```
scanf("%f %f",&value1, &value2);
```

This is a call to the input function **scanf()**. This has three arguments: a string, which is therefore effectively a pointer as in our previous statement, and the addresses of two variables - again effectively pointers. As we have discussed, **scanf()** must have the addresses for the last two arguments, as we want the input data stored in them.

Once we have read in the two values, the assignment statement is executed:

```
value3 = average( value1, value2 );
```

This calls our function **average()** which expects two **float** type values as arguments, and we have correctly supplied **value1** and **value2** which are both of type **float**.

There is a very important point here, illustrated in the next figure.

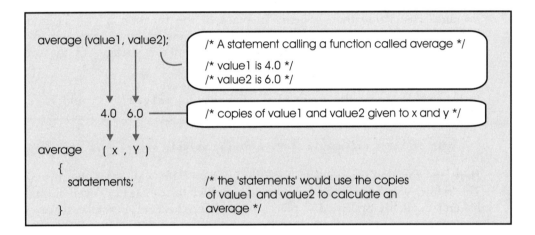

The values received by **average** are referenced as **x** and **y** and are distinct copies of the original values stored in **value1** and **value2**.

Copies of the values of **value1** and **value2** are transferred to our function, *not the variables themselves*. The function can't change **value1** or **value2**. For instance, if we input the values 4.0 and 6.0 for the two variables, the compiler will create separate copies of these two values to transfer to the function **average()** when it is called. This mechanism is how all argument transfers to functions take place in C, and it is termed a **call-by-value** mechanism.

The only way a function can change something in the program from which it is called, is if it has an address of a variable as an argument when it is called, and the corresponding parameter in the function header is specified as a pointer. Even when you pass an address, a copy of the address is actually passed, not the original. We will come back to this point later in the chapter.

Now our function is executed with the values from **value1** and **value2** substituted for the parameter names in the function which are **x** and **y** respectively. The function is defined by the statements:

```
float average( float x, float y )
{
    return (x + y) / 2.0;
}
```

The function only has one statement, the **return** statement. The **return** contains an expression for the value to be returned which works out the average. This value then appears in place of the function in the assignment statement back in **main()**. From the point of view of any expression in which it appears, a function that returns a value acts like a variable of the same type as the return value.

Instead of assigning the result of the function to **value3**, we could have written the last **printf()** statement as:

```
printf("\nThe average is: %f", average( value1, value2 ) );
```

Here, the function **average()** receives copies of the values of the argument. The return value from the function is supplied to **printf()**, even though we haven't explicitly specified a place to store it. The compiler takes care of assigning some memory to store the value returned from **average()**. It will also take the trouble to make a copy to hand over to the function **printf()** as an argument. Of course, once the **printf()** has been executed, we have no means of accessing the value returned from the function.

A further possible option is to use explicit values in a function call. What happens then? Let's stretch our **printf()** out of context now and take, for example:

```
printf("\nThe average is: %f", average( 4.0, 6.0 ) );
```

In this case, the compiler will create a memory location to store each of the constant arguments to **average()**, and then supply copies of those values to the function exactly as before. A copy of the result returned from the function **average()** will then be passed to **printf()**.

The next figure illustrates calling the function **useful()** from **main()** and getting a value returned. The arrows in the figure show how values correspond between **main()** and the function called. The value returned is finally stored in the variable **x** in **main()**.

```
void main()
{

.....
  x = useful ( y , z );
....

}

              long useful( int a , int b )
              {
                long c; /* A local variable we are using to hold a result */
                .....          /* In here would be useful statements */
                return c;
              }
```

Function Declarations

As we have seen in the previous example, the function declaration defines the essential characteristics of a function, its name, its return value type, and the type of each of its parameters. You can actually write it exactly the same as the function header plus a semi-colon at the end if you want. A function declaration is also called a **function prototype** because it models how you use the function. It enables the compiler to generate the appropriate instructions at each point where we use the function, and to check that we use it correctly in each case.

In a variation on our example, we first define the function **main()**, and then the function **average()**:

```c
#include <stdio.h>

void main()
{
    float average( float, float );
...
}
```

Then we put the declaration at the beginning of the body of **main()**, since **main()** uses the function.

```c
float average( float x, float y )
{
    return (x + y) / 2.0;
}
```

The declaration here is local to **main()** since its scope is defined by the limits of the body of **main()**. If we wanted to use the function **average()** in several different functions, we could put the same declaration in the body of each.

There is also another possibility. We could put the declaration of **average()** at the beginning of the file along with our **#include** statements. It would then be external to all of our functions in the file, and its scope would extend to the end of the file, thus allowing any of our functions to use it, without further need to declare it. This is the typical position for a function declaration, and we shall show this approach in our next example.

Pointers and Functions

We have already seen that it's possible to pass a pointer as an argument to a function. More than that, we have seen that it's necessary if a function is to modify the value of a variable defined in a calling program. In fact this is the only way it can be done. Let's see how this works out in practice.

Try It Out - Functions Using Ordinary Variables

Let's first take an elementary example that doesn't use a pointer argument. Here we are going to try to change the contents of a variable by sending it as an argument to a function, changing it and then returning it. We will print its value both within the function and back in **main()** to see what the effect is:

```
/* Example 8.4 The change that doesn't   */
#include <stdio.h>

int change( int  );                            /* Function prototype   */

void main()
{
    int number = 10;                           /* Starting Value   */
    int result = 0;                  /* Place to put the returned value   */

    result = change( number );
    printf("\nIn main, result = %d\tnumber = %d", result, number );
}

/* Definition of the function change() */
int change( int number )
{
    number = 2 * number;
    printf("\nIn function change, number = %d", number );
    return number;
}
```

The output from this program is:

```
In function change, number = 20
In main, result = 20     number = 10
```

How It Works

This example demonstrates that we can't change the world without pointers. We can only change the values locally in the function.

```c
#include <stdio.h>

int change( int  );                              /* Function prototype   */

void main()
{
```

The first thing of note about this example, is that we have put the prototype for the function **change()** outside of **main()** along with our **#include** statement. This makes it global, and if we had other functions in the example they would all be able to use this function.

```c
    int number = 10;                          /* Starting Value    */
    int result = 0;          /* Place to put the returned value    */
```

In **main()** we have set up an integer variable, **number,** with an initial value of 10. We also have a second variable **result**, which we will use to store the value we get back from the function **change()**.

```c
    result = change( number );
```

We then call the function **change()** and send the value of the argument **number**.

```c
int change( int number )
{
    number = 2 * number;
    printf("\nIn function change, number = %d", number );
    return number;
}
```

This is the called function. Within the function **change()** the first statement doubles the value stored in the argument that has been passed to it from **main()**. We even use the same variable name in the function that we have used in **main()**, to reinforce the idea that we want to change the original value. The function **change()** displays the new value of **number** before it sends it back to **main()** by means of the **return** statement.

```
printf("\nIn main, result = %d\tnumber = %d", result, number );
}
```

In **main()** we also display what we got back from **change()**, and the value of **number**.

Look at the output though. It demonstrates how vain and pathetic our attempt to change a variable value by passing it to a function has been. Clearly the variable **number** in **change()** has the value 20 on return from the function. It is displayed both in the function and as a returned value in **main()**. In spite of our transparent subterfuge of giving them the same name, the variables called number in **main()** and **change()** are evidently quite separate, so modifying one has no effect on the other.

Try It Out - Using Pointers in Functions

We can now modify the last example to use pointers, and with a following wind, we should succeed in modifying the value of a variable in **main()**.

```
/* Example 8.5 The change that does   */
#include <stdio.h>

int change( int*  );                          /* Function prototype   */

void main()
{
   int number = 10;                        /* Starting Value           */
   int* pnumber = &number;              /* Pointer to starting value  */
   int result = 0;                       /* Place to put the returned value   */

   result = change( pnumber );
   printf("\nIn main, result = %d\tnumber = %d", result, number );
}

/* Definition of the function change() */
int change( int* pnumber )
{
   *pnumber *= 2;
   printf("\nIn function change, *pnumber = %d", *pnumber );
   return *pnumber;
}
```

The output from this program looks like this:

```
In function change, *pnumber = 20
In main, result = 20     number = 20
```

How It Works

There are relatively few changes to the last example.

```
int* pnumber = &number;                 /* Pointer to starting value     */
```

We have defined a pointer in **main()**, **pnumber**, which is initialized to the address of our starting value, **number**.

```
int change( int* );                             /* Function prototype    */
...
int change( int* pnumber )
{
   *pnumber *= 2;
   printf("\nIn function change, *pnumber = %d", *pnumber );
   return *pnumber;
}
```

The function **change()** and its prototype have been modified to use a pointer, which we have again referred to by the same name as in **main()**, although this is of no consequence to the way the program works. We could call it anything we like, as long as it is a pointer of the correct type. Within the function **change()**, the arithmetic statement has been changed to:

```
   *pnumber *= 2;
```

This isn't strictly necessary, but it makes it a lot less confusing, providing you can remember what **op=** does at this point. It is exactly the same as:

```
*pnumber = 2*( *pnumber );
```

The output now demonstrates that the pointer mechanism is working correctly and the function **change()** is indeed modifying the value of **number** in **main()**. Of course, when we submit a pointer as an argument, it's still passed by value. Therefore, the compiler does not pass the original pointer, but makes a copy of the pointer to hand over to the function. Since the copy will contain the same address as the original, it still refers to the variable **number**, so everything works OK.

If you are unconvinced of this, you can demonstrate it for yourself quite easily, by adding a statement to the function **change()** that modifies the pointer **pnumber**. You could set it to **NULL** for instance. You can then check in **main()** that **pnumber** still points to **number**. Of course you will have to alter the **return** statement in **change()** to get the correct result.

Try It Out - Passing Data Using Pointers

We could exercise this method of passing data to a function using pointers in a slightly more practical way, with a revised version of our function for sorting strings from Chapter 7:

```
/* Example 8.6 The functional approach to string sorting*/
#include <stdio.h>
#include <stdlib.h>
#include <string.h>

int str_in( char ** );               /* Function prototype for str_in    */
void str_sort( char *[], int );      /* Function prototype for str_sort  */
void str_out( char *[], int );       /* Function prototype for str_out   */

#define BUFFER_LEN 80
#define NUM_P 10

/* Function main - execution starts here           */
void main()
{
   char *pS[ NUM_P ];                 /* Array of string pointers    */
   int i = 0;                         /* loop counters               */
   int last_string = 0;              /* Index of last string input  */

   printf("\nEnter successive lines, pressing Enter at the end of each line.
         "Just press Enter to end.\n");
   for( i=0; i < NUM_P ; i++ )        /* Max of NUM_P strings       */
   {
     if(str_in( &pS[ i ] ) == 0 ) break;     /* Stop input on 0 return */
   }

   last_string = i;                   /* Save last string index      */
   str_sort( pS, last_string );       /* Sort strings                */
   str_out(  pS, last_string );       /* Output strings              */
}
```

```
/****************************************************/
/*      String input routine                        */
/*         returns 0 for empty string, 1 otherwise  */
/*                                                  */
/****************************************************/
int str_in( char **P )
{
   char Buffer[BUFFER_LEN];                  /* space to store input string */

   if( *gets( Buffer ) == NULL )
      return 0;

   *P = ( char *) malloc ( strlen( Buffer )  + 1);

   if( *P == NULL )
   {
      printf("\nOut of memory.");

      return 0;
   }

   strcpy( *P, Buffer );
   return 1;
}

/****************************************************/
/*      String sort routine                         */
/*                                                  */
/****************************************************/
void str_sort( char *P[], int N )
{
   char *pTemp;                        /* Temporary pointer                 */
   int i = 0, j = 0;                   /* Loop counters                     */

   while( j == 0 )                     /* Loop until there are no swaps     */
   {
      j = 1;                           /* Initialize to indicate no swaps   */
      for ( i = 0 ; i < N - 1 ; i++ )
         if( strcmp( P[ i ], P[ i + 1 ] ) > 0 )
         {
            j = 0;                     /* indicator that we were out of order */
            pTemp= P[ i ];             /* Swap pointers P[ i ]              */
            P[ i ] = P[ i + 1 ];       /*  and P[ i + 1 }                   */
            P[ i + 1 ]  = pTemp;
         }

   }

}
```

```
/******************************************************/
/*        String output routine                       */
/*                                                    */
/******************************************************/
void str_out( char *P[] , int M )
{
   int i;                                          /* Loop counter    */

   printf("\nYour input sorted in order is:\n\n");

   for ( i = 0 ; i < M ; i++ )
   {
      printf("%s\n", P[ i ] );                     /* Display a string */
      free( P[ i ] );           /* Free memory for last string displayed */
   }

   return;
}
```

Typical output would be:

```
Enter successive lines, pressing Enter at the end of each line. Just press
Enter to end.
Mike
Adam
Mary
Steve


Your input sorted in order is:

Adam
Mary
Mike
Steve
```

How It Works

This example works in a similar way to the sorting example in Chapter 7. It looks a lot of code, but we have added quite a few comment lines in fancy boxes which occupies space. This is good practice for longer programs which use several functions. You can then be sure you know what each section does.

The whole set of statements for all the functions makes up our source file. At the beginning of the program source file, before we define **main()**, we have our **#include** statements for the libraries we are using, our constant definitions and our function prototypes. Each of these are effective from the point of their occurrence to the end of our file, since they are defined outside of all of the functions. They therefore are effective in all of our functions.

The program consists of three functions in addition to our function **main()**.

The prototypes of the functions we have defined, in addition to **main()**, are:

```
int str_in( char ** );          /* Function prototype for str_in */
void str_sort( char *[], int ); /* Function prototype for str_sort */
void str_out( char *[], int );  /* Function prototype for str_out */
```

Here we have a function to read in all the strings **str_in()**, a function to sort the strings **str_sort()**, and a function to output the sorted strings in their new sequence. Each of the function prototypes declare the types of the parameters and the return value type. Our first declaration is for **str_in()** and it declares the parameter as **char ****, which is a 'pointer to pointer to char'. Let's see what we are doing here.

In **main()**, the argument to this function is **&pS[i]**. This is the address of **pS[i]**, or in other words a pointer to **pS[i]**. And what is **pS[i]**? It is a pointer to **char**. Put these together and we have the type as declared. We have to declare it this way because we want to modify the contents of the **pS** array inside the function **str_in**. This is the only way the function can get access to this. If we only used one ***** in the parameter type definition, and used **pS[i]** as the argument, the function would receive whatever was contained in **pS[i]**, which is not what we want at all. This mechanism is illustrated in the next figure.

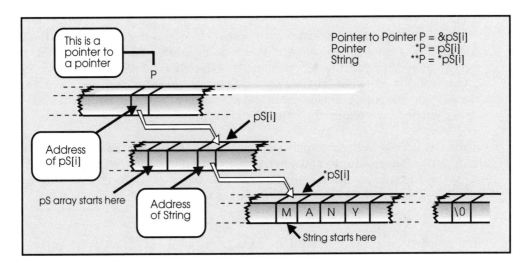

We can now take a look at the internal working of the function.

The str_in Function

First, note our fancy comment at the beginning. This is a good way of starting out a function and highlighting its basic purpose. The function definition consists of:

```
int str_in( char **P )
{
   char Buffer[BUFFER_LEN];              /* space to store input string    */

   if( *gets( Buffer ) == '\0' )
      return 0;

   *P = ( char *) malloc ( strlen( Buffer )  + 1);

   if( *P == NULL )
   {
      printf("\nOut of memory.");

      return 0;
   }

   strcpy( *P, Buffer );
   return 1;
}
```

The function **str_in()** receives from **main()** the address of **pS[i]**, the current free pointer array element which is to receive the address of the next string entered. Within the function this is referred to as the parameter **P**. The input string is stored in **Buffer** by the function **gets()**, and we check the first character in the string obtained by **gets()** against '\0'. If we get an empty string entered, we return the value 0 to **main()**.

Once we have a string, we allocate space for it using the **malloc()** function and put its address in **P**, and after checking that we did get some memory, we copy the contents of **Buffer** to the memory allocated. If **malloc()** fails to allocate memory, we simply display a message and return the value 0 to **main()**.

The function **str_in()** is called in **main()** in the loop:

```
for( i=0; i < NUM_P ; i++ )          /* Max of NUM_P strings          */
   {
      if(str_in( &pS[ i ] ) == 0 ) break; /* Stop input on 0 return */
   }
```

Since all the work is done in the function **str_in()**, all that's necessary here is to continue the loop until we get a zero returned from the function, whereupon the break is executed, or we fill up the pointer array **pS** which is indicated by **i** reaching the value **NUM_P-1** which will end the loop. The loop also counts how many strings are entered in **i**.

Having got all the strings safely stored, **main()** then calls the function **str_sort()** to sort the strings with the statement:

```
str_sort( pS, last_string );        /* Sort strings              */
```

The first argument is the array name, **pS**, so the address of the first location of the array is transferred to the function. The second argument is the index value of the last string entered, so the function can know how many strings there are to work with.

The str_sort() Function

The function **str_sort()** is defined by the statements:

```
void str_sort( char *P[], int N )
{
   char *pTemp;                      /* Temporary pointer               */
   int i = 0, j = 0;                 /* Loop counters                   */

   while( j == 0 )                   /* Loop until there are no swaps   */
   {
      j = 1;                         /* Initialize to indicate no swaps */
      for ( i = 0 ; i < N - 1 ; i++ )
        if( strcmp( P[ i ], P[ i + 1 ] ) > 0 )
          {
             j = 0;                  /* indicator that we were out of order */
             pTemp= P[ i ];          /* Swap pointers P[ i ]                */
             P[ i ] = P[ i + 1 ];    /*  and P[ i + 1 }                     */
             P[ i + 1 ]  = pTemp;
          }

   }

}
```

Within the function, the parameter variable **P**, which has been defined as an array of pointers, is used, and is substituted by the transferred address value for **pS**. We have not specified the dimension for **P**. This is not necessary since it is one dimensional and only the address is passed anyway. If the array had two or more dimensions, we would have had to specify all dimensions except the first. This would be necessary for the compiler to know the shape of the array. Of course, you can put the dimension if you wish, but in general you are likely to want the function to handle arrays of various lengths anyway.

The second parameter **N** in the function **str_sort()**, is declared as **int**, and is substituted by the argument value **last_string**. We declare two loop counters **i** and **j** for use within the function. Remember that all the variables declared within the function body are local to that function. This means that the variable **i** in the function, for instance, isn't the same variable as the variable **i** in **main()**.

The strings are sorted in the **while** loop. The process involved is shown in the figure below. In this illustration we have used the input data we saw above, and the input is completely sorted in one pass. If you try this process on paper with a more disordered sequence of the same input strings, you will see that it is not always the case.

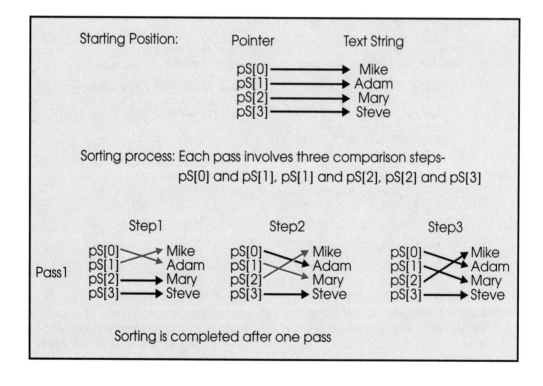

The str_out() Function

The last function called by **main()** is **str_out()**, which displays the sorted strings. In this function, the parameter **M** receives the value of **last_string** and the strings are displayed using **M** as the count of the number of strings. The process for displaying the sorted strings is the same as in the example we saw in Chapter 7.

Returning Pointer Values From a Function

We have seen how we can return numeric values from a function. We have just now learnt how to use pointers as arguments. We can also return pointers from a function. Let's look first at a very simple example.

Try It Out - Returning Values From a Function

We can use increasing your salary as the basis for the example, as it is such a popular topic.

```
/* Example 8.7 A function to increase your salary    */
#include <stdio.h>

long *IncomePlus( long* );            /* Prototype for increase function */

void main()
{
  long Your_Pay = 30000;                      /* Starting salary       */
  long *pOld_Pay = &Your_Pay;                 /* Pointer to pay value   */
  long *pNew_Pay = NULL;              /* Pointer to hold return value   */

  pNew_Pay = IncomePlus( pOld_Pay );
  printf("\nOld pay = $%ld\tNew pay = $%ld", *pOld_Pay, *pNew_Pay );
}

/* Definition of function to increment pay */
long *IncomePlus( long *pPay )
{
  *pPay += 10000;
  return pPay;
}
```

When you run the program, you will get the output:

```
Old pay = $40000       New pay = $40000
```

How It Works

```
long Your_Pay = 30000;      /* Starting salary        */
long *pOld_Pay = &Your_Pay;  /* Pointer to pay value    */
long *pNew_Pay = NULL;      /* Pointer to hold return value  */
```

In **main()** we have set up an initial value in the variable **Your_Pay**, and defined two pointers for use with the function **IncomePlus()** which is going to increase **Your_Pay**. One pointer is initialized with the address of **Your_Pay** while the other is initialized to **NULL** since it will receive the address returned by the function **IncomePlus()**.

Look at the output. It looks like a satisfactory result except that it's slightly misleading. If you overlook what you start with, it looks as though you didn't get any increase. Since the function **IncomePlus()** modifies the value of **Your_Pay** through the pointer **Old_Pay**, the original value has been changed. Clearly both our pointers, **pOld_Pay** and **pNew_Pay**, refer to the same location - **Your_Pay**. This is a result of the statement in the function **IncomePlus()**:

```
return pPay;
```

which returned the pointer value the function received when it was called, which is the address contained in **pOld_Pay**.

Try It Out - Using Local Storage

Let's look at what happens if we use local storage in the function **IncomePlus()**. After a small modification our example becomes:

```
/* Example 8.8 A function to increase your salary that doesn't   */
#include <stdio.h>

long * IncomePlus( long* );          /* Prototype for increase function */

void main()
{
   long Your_Pay = 30000;                    /* Starting salary        */
   long *pOld_Pay = &Your_Pay;               /* Pointer to pay value    */
   long *pNew_Pay = NULL;               /* Pointer to hold return value  */

   pNew_Pay = IncomePlus( pOld_Pay );
   printf("\nOld pay = $%ld", *pOld_Pay );
   printf("\tNew pay = $%ld", *pNew_Pay );
}

/* Definition of function to increment pay */
```

```
long* IncomePlus( long *pPay )
{
    long pay = 0;                      /* Local variable to hold the result   */

    pay = *pPay + 10000;
    return &pay;
}
```

How It Works

We now get the following result (it may vary depending on your machine):

```
Old pay = $30000     New pay = $27467656
```

Numbers like **$27467656** with the word pay in the same sentence, tend to be a bit startling. As we said, you may get different results on your PC. You should get a warning from your compiler with this version of the program. Using a Borland compiler, we get the message, 'Suspicious pointer conversion'. This is because we are returning the address of the variable **pay**, which goes out of scope on exiting the function **IncomePlus()**. This is the cause of the remarkable value for the new value of pay - it's junk, just a spurious value left around by something. This is an easy mistake to make, but can be a hard one to find.

Try combining the two **printf()** statements in **main()** into one.

```
printf("\nOld pay = $%ld\tNew pay = $%ld", *pOld_Pay, *pNew_Pay );
```

On our computer it produces the output:

```
Old pay = $30000     New pay = $40000
```

This actually looks right, in spite of the fact that we know there is a serious error in the program. In this case, although the variable **pay** is out of scope and therefore no longer exists, the memory it occupied hasn't been re-used yet. In the example, evidently something uses the memory previously used by the variable **pay**, and produces the enormous output value.

Don't return the address of a local variable in a function.

We could turn to the more practical application of returning pointers by modifying Example 8.6. We could have written the routine **str_in()** in this example as:

```
char *str_in( void )
{
   char Buffer[Buffer_len];              /* space to store input string */
   char *P;

   gets( Buffer );
   P = ( char *) malloc ( strlen( Buffer )  + 1);

   if( P == NULL )
   {
      printf("\nOut of memory.");
      abort();
   }

   return strcpy( P, Buffer );
}
```

Of course we would also have to modify the function prototype to:

```
char *str_in( void );
```

Now there are no parameters since we have declared them as **void**, and the return value is now a pointer to a character string rather than an integer.

We would also need to modify the **for** loop in **main()** which invokes the function to:

```
for( i=0; i < NUM_P ; i++ )                 /* Max of NUM_P strings      */
   {
      if(str_in( &pS[ i ] ) == '\0' ) break;  /* Stop input on '\0' return */
   }
```

We now compare the contents pointed to by the return value with **\0** as this would indicate that an empty string had been entered. The example would still work exactly as before, but the internal mechanism for input is a little different. Now the function returns the address of the allocated memory block into which the string has been copied. You might imagine that you could use the address of **Buffer** instead, but remember **Buffer** is local to the function, so it goes out of scope on return from the function. You could try it if you like to see what happens.

If **malloc()** returns a **NULL** pointer, indicating memory can't be allocated, we execute some statements where we have introduced a variation in that the function **abort()** is called. This function, which is found in **STDLIB.H**, terminates the program immediately.

Choosing one version of the function **str_in()** or the other is to some extent a matter of taste, but on balance this latter version is probably better because it involves using a simpler definition of the parameter, which makes it easier to understand.

Incrementing Pointers in a Function

When we use an array name as an argument to a function, a *copy* of the address of the beginning of the array is transferred to the function. As a result we have the possibility of treating the value received as a pointer in the fullest sense, incrementing or decrementing the address as we wish. For example, we could rewrite the **str_out()** function in Example 8.6 as:

```
void str_out( char *P[] , int M )
{
   int i;                                  /* Loop counter */

   printf("\nYour input sorted in order is:\n\n");

   for ( i = 0 ; i < M ; i++ )
   {
      printf("%s\n", *P );
      free( *P++ );
   }

   return;
}
```

We have replaced the array notation with pointer notation in the **printf()** and **free()** function calls, and in the latter, we increment the address. We wouldn't be able to do this with an array declared within the function scope, but since we have a copy of the original array address, it's possible here. We can treat it just like a regular pointer. Because the address we have at this point is a copy of the original in **main()**, this doesn't interfere with the original array address **pS** in any way. There is little to choose between this version of the function and the original. We prefer the latter because using the pointer notation looks a little cleaner.

Summary

This has been quite a long chapter, and it's a big topic. The next chapter also covers further aspects of using functions. So let's pause for a moment and summarize the key points you need to keep in mind when creating and using functions:

- A C program consists of one or more functions, one of which is called `main()`. The function `main()` is where execution always starts and is called by the operating system through a user command.

- A function is a self-contained named block of code in a program. The name of a function is a unique sequence of letters and digits, the first of which is a letter (an underline counts as a letter).

- A function definition consists of a header and a body. The header defines the name of the function, the type of the value returned from the function, and the type of all parameters to the function. The body contains the executable statements for the function, what you want the function to actually do. An example of a simple function is:

```
int product(int a, int b)
{
  return a*b;
}
```

- All the variables declared in a function are local to the function, including the parameter names. In the example above, the variables **a** and **b** that appear in the function, do not exist outside it.

- To use a function you need a function declaration that defines the return type, the parameter types for the function, and the function name. The function declaration must have a semi-colon at the end. The function declaration must be placed before any function in which it is used. An example of a function declaration is:

```
int product( int, int );
```

- Arguments to the function must be of the same type as the parameters specified in the header. If you specify a parameter to be of type **int,** you can't then pass an argument of type **float**. The function won't work.

▶ A function that returns a value can be used in an expression as though it was a value of the same type as the return value. For example, with the function **product()** defined as above, and assuming our variables are of type **int**, we can write:

```
total_stock = loose_stock + product( num_boxes, num_per_box );
```

▶ A function (other than **main()**) can be called as often is you need by using its name in a program. For example:

```
void main()
{
    int num1 = 5, num2 = 2;
    num1 = 3 + product( num1, num1 + 6 );
    printf("\nresult = %d", num1 - product( num2, num2 );
}
```

▶ Copies of the argument values are transferred to a function, not the original variables. If you want a function to modify a variable in a calling program, the address of the variable needs to be transferred as an argument. This address can then be used in the function as a pointer.

That covers the essentials of creating your own functions. In the next chapter we will add a few techniques for using functions to what we have covered here, and we will also add a more substantial example of applying functions in a loosely practical context.

CHAPTER 9

More on Functions

Now that you have completed Chapter 8, you have a good grounding in the essentials of creating and using functions. In this chapter you will build on this by extending your knowledge of how functions can be used and manipulated, in particular accessing a function through a pointer. You will also get to grips with some more flexible methods of communicating between functions.

The topics we will grapple with in this chapter include:

- Understanding pointers to functions
- Using static variables in functions
- Sharing variables between functions
- Understanding how functions can call themselves
- Write an Othello-type game (or reversi)

Pointers to Functions

Up to now, we have considered pointers as an exceptionally useful device for manipulating data and variables that contain data. It's a bit like handling things with a pair of tongs. We can manipulate a whole range of hot items with one pair of tongs. Similarly we can use pointers to handle functions at a distance. Since a function has an address in memory at which its execution starts, the basic information to be stored in a pointer to a function is the starting address of the function.

If you think about it, though, this isn't going to be enough. If a function is going to be called through a pointer, information also has to be available about the number and type of the arguments to be supplied, and the type of return value that is to be expected. The compiler couldn't deduce these just from the address of the function.

Declaring a Pointer to a Function

The declaration for a pointer to a function looks a little strange, and can be confusing, so let's start with a simple example:

```
int (*pfunction) ( int );
```

This declares a pointer to a function. The pointer's name is **pfunction**, and it's intended to point to functions with one argument of type **int**, that return an **int** value to the calling program. The components of this declaration are illustrated in the following figure. We can only use it for pointing to functions with these characteristics. If we want a pointer to functions which accept a **long** argument, we need to declare another pointer with the required characteristics.

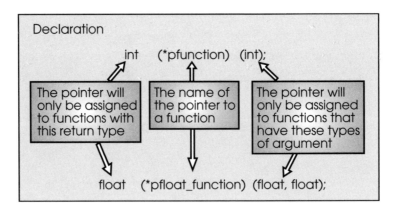

There are a lot of parentheses here. The ***pfunction** part of the declaration must be between parentheses. If you omit them, then you will have a declaration for a function called **pfunction** that returns a value that is a pointer to **int**, which isn't really what you want. Try it and see. With pointer to function declarations you must always put the ***** plus the pointer name within parentheses. The second pair of parentheses just enclose the parameter list as they do with a function declaration.

Try It Out - Using Pointers to Functions

Let's try a simple example and see how it works:

```
/* Example 9.1 Pointing to functions   */
#include <stdio.h>

/* Function prototypes   */
int sum( int, int );
int product( int, int );
int difference( int, int );

void main()
{
   int a = 10, b = 5;                       /* Starting values            */
   int result = 0;                          /* Storage for results        */
   int ( *pfun ) (int, int );               /* Function pointer declaration */

   pfun = sum;
   result = pfun( a , b );
   printf("\npfun = sum\tresult = %d", result );

   pfun = product;
    result = pfun( a , b );
   printf("\npfun = product\tresult = %d", result );

   pfun = difference;
   result = pfun( a , b );
   printf("\npfun = difference\tresult = %d", result );
}

/* Definition of the function sum   */
 int sum( int x, int y )
 {
   return x + y;
 }

  /* Definition of the function product   */
 int product( int x, int y )
 {
   return x * y;
 }
```

```
/* Definition of the function difference    */
int difference( int x, int y )
{
   return x - y;
}
```

The output from this program looks like this:

```
pfun = sum result = 15
pfun = product result = 50
pfun = difference result = 5
```

How It Works

We have declared and defined three different functions to return the sum, the product and the difference between two integer arguments. We declare a pointer to a function with the statement:

```
int ( *pfun ) (int, int );    /* Function pointer declaration    */
```

This pointer can be assigned to point to any function which accepts two **int** arguments, and also returns an **int** value. Notice the way we assign a value to the pointer:

```
pfun = sum;
```

We just use a regular assignment statement which has the name of the function, completely unadorned, on the right hand side. We don't need to put the parameter list or anything. If we did, it would be wrong, since it would then be a function call, not an address, and the compiler will produce a rude message. A function is very much like an array in its usage here. If you want the address, you just use the name by itself.

In **main()**, we assign the address of each function in turn to the function pointer **pfun**. We then call each function using the pointer, and display the result. You can see that to call a function using the pointer in the statement:

```
result = pfun( a , b );
```

you just use the name of the pointer as though it were a function name, followed by the argument list between parentheses. You are using the pointer to function variable name as though it were the original function name, so the argument list must correspond with the parameters in the function header for the function you are calling. This is illustrated graphically in the following figure.

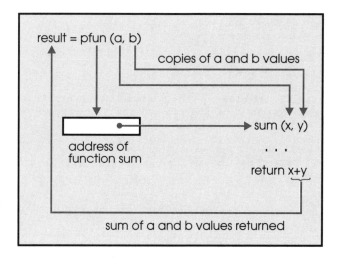

Arrays of Pointers to Functions

Of course, a function pointer is a variable like any other. We can therefore create an array of pointers to functions. Let's see how this would work in practice.

Try It Out - Arrays of Pointers to Functions

We can demonstrate this with a variation on the last example:

```
/* Example 9.2 Arrays of Pointers to functions    */
#include <stdio.h>

/* Function prototypes    */
int sum( int, int );
int product( int, int );
int difference( int, int );

void main()
{
   int i = 0;                       /* Loop counter                        */
   int a = 10, b = 5;               /* Starting values                     */
   int result = 0;                  /* Storage for results                 */
   int ( *pfun[ 3 ] ) (int, int );  /* Function pointer array declaration   */

/* Initialize pointers */
   pfun[0] = sum;
   pfun[1] = product;
   pfun[2] = difference;
```

```
/* Execute each function pointed to */
   for( i = 0 ; i < 3 ; i++ )
   {
      result = pfun[i]( a , b );
      printf("\nresult = %d", result );
   }
   result = pfun[1]( pfun[0]( a , b ), pfun[2]( a , b ) );
   printf("\n\nThe product of the sum and the difference = %d", result );

}

/* Definition of the function sum    */
 int sum( int x, int y )
 {
   return x + y;
 }

  /* Definition of the function product    */
 int product( int x, int y )
 {
   return x * y;
 }

  /* Definition of the function difference    */
 int difference( int x, int y )
 {
   return x - y;
 }
```

The output from this program is:

```
result = 15
result = 50
result = 5

The product of the sum and the difference = 75
```

How It Works

The major difference to the last example is our pointer array declared as:

```
int ( *pfun[ 3 ] ) (int, int );   /* Function pointer array declaration   */
```

This is the same as the previous declaration for a single pointer variable with the addition of the array dimension in square brackets. If we wanted a two-dimensional array, two sets of square brackets would have to appear here, analogous with declarations for ordinary array types. We still enclose the parameter list between parentheses as we did in the declaration of a single pointer. Again, paralleling what happens with ordinary arrays, all the elements of our array of pointers to functions are of the same type and will only accept the argument list specified. So in our example they can all only point to functions which take two arguments of type **int**, and return an **int** value.

When we want to assign a value to a pointer within the array, we write it in the same way as an element of any other array:

```
pfun[0] = sum;
```

Apart from the function name on the right of the equals sign, this could be a normal data array. It is used in exactly the same way. When it comes to calling the function an array element points to, we write it as:

```
result = pfun[i]( a , b );
```

This again is very like our previous example, with just the addition of the index value in square brackets, following the pointer name. We index it with the loop variable **i**, as we have done many times before with ordinary data arrays.

Look at the output. The first three lines are generated in the **for** loop, where the functions **sum()**, **product()**, and **difference()**, are each called in turn through the corresponding element of the pointer array. This last line is produced using the value **result** from the statement:

```
result = pfun[1]( pfun[0]( a , b ), pfun[2]( a , b ) );
```

This statement shows that we can incorporate function calls through pointers into expressions, in the same way as we might use a normal function call. Here we have called two of the functions through pointers, and the results are used as arguments to a third function called through a pointer. Because the elements of the array correspond to the functions **sum()**, **product()**, and **difference()** in sequence, this statement is equivalent to:

```
result = product( sum( a, b ), difference( a, b ) );
```

The sequence of events in this statement is:

1   Execute **sum(a,b)** and save the return value.

2   Execute **difference(a, b)** and save the return value.

3   Execute the function **product()** with the returned values from step 1 and step 2 as arguments, and save the value returned.

4   Store the value obtained in step 3 in the variable **result**.

Pointers to Functions as Arguments

We can also pass a pointer to a function as an argument. This allows a different function to be called, depending on which function is addressed by the pointer that is passed.

Try It Out - Pointers to Functions as Arguments

We could produce a variant of the last example using this technique, as follows:

```
/* Example 9.3 Passing a Pointer to a function   */
#include <stdio.h>

/* Function prototypes   */
int sum( int, int );
int product( int, int );
int difference( int, int );
int any_function( int( *pfun )( int, int ), int x, int y );

void main()
{
    int a = 10, b = 5;                  /* Starting values      */
    int result = 0;                     /* Storage for results  */
    int (*pf ) ( int, int ) = sum;      /* Pointer to function   */

    result = any_function( pf, a, b ); /* Passing a pointer to a function */
    printf("\nresult = %d", result );

    result = any_function( product, a, b ); /* Passing the address of function */
    printf("\nresult = %d", result );

    printf("\nresult = %d", any_function( difference, a, b ) );
}
```

```
/* Definition of a function to call a function */
int any_function( int( *pfun )( int, int ), int x, int y )
{
   return pfun( x, y );
}

/* Definition of the function sum   */
 int sum( int x, int y )
 {
   return x + y;
 }

  /* Definition of the function product   */
 int product( int x, int y )
 {
   return x * y;
 }

  /* Definition of the function difference   */
 int difference( int x, int y )
 {
   return x - y;
 }
```

The output looks like this:

```
result = 15
result = 50
result = 5
```

How It Works

The function which will accept a pointer to a function as an argument is
any_function(). It is declared in the statement:

```
int any_function( int( *pfun )( int, int ), int x, int y );
```

The function has three parameters. The first parameter type is a pointer to a
function which accepts two integer arguments and returns an integer. The last
two parameters are integers which will be used in the call of the function
specified by the first parameter. The function **any_function()** returns an
integer value which will be the value obtained by calling the function indicated
by the first argument.

Within the definition of the function, the function specified by the pointer argument is called in the **return** statement:

```
int any_function( int( *pfun )( int, int ), int x, int y )
{
   return pfun( x, y );
}
```

The name of the pointer **pfun** is used, followed by the other two parameters, as arguments to the function to be called. The value of **pfun**, and the values of the other two parameters **x** and **y** which are to be passed to the function to be called through **pfun**, all originate in **main()**.

Notice how we initialize the function pointer **pf** we have declared in **main()**:

```
int (*pf ) ( int, int ) = sum;       /* Pointer to function      */
```

We have placed the name of the function **sum()** as the initializer after the equals sign. In this way we can initialize function pointers to the addresses of specific functions just by putting the function name as an initializing value.

The first call of **any_function()** passes the value of the pointer **pf** and the values of the variables **a** and **b** to the function:

```
result = any_function( pf, a, b );   /* Passing a pointer to a function   */
```

The pointer is used as an argument in the usual way, and the value returned by **any_function()** is stored in the variable result. Because of the initial value of **pf**, the function **sum()** will be called in **any_function()**, so the returned value will be the sum of the values of **a** and **b**.

The next call to **any_function()** is in the statement:

```
result = any_function( product, a, b ); /* Passing the address of a function
*/
```

Here we have explicitly entered the name of a function, **product**, as the first argument, so within **any_function(),** the function **product** will be called with the values of **a** and **b** as arguments. In this case we are effectively persuading the compiler to create an internal pointer to the function **product**, and passing it to **any_function()**.

The final call of **any_function()** takes place in the argument to the **printf()** call:

```
printf("\nresult = %d", any_function( difference, a, b ) );
```

In this case we are also explicitly specifying the name of a function, **difference**, as an argument to **any_function()**. The compiler knows from the prototype of **any_function()** that the first argument should be a pointer to a function. Since we have specified the function name, **difference**, explicitly as an argument, the compiler will generate a pointer to this function for us, and pass that to the function **any_function()**. Finally the value returned by **any_function()** is passed as an argument to the function **printf()**. When all this unwinds, we will eventually get the difference between the values of **a** and **b** displayed.

Take care not to confuse the idea of passing an address of a function to a function, such as in the expression:

```
any_function( product, a, b )
```

and passing a value returned from a function, as in the statement:

```
printf("\n%d", product( a, b ) );
```

In the latter case we are calling the function **product()** before we call **printf()**, and passing the result obtained to **printf()**. In the former case, we are passing the address of the function **product()** as an argument, and if and when it gets called depends on what goes on inside the body of the function **any_function()**.

Variables in Functions

The structuring of a program into functions, not only simplifies the process of developing the program, but also extends the power of the language to solve problems. The power of the language is further enhanced by the properties of variables within a function, and some extra capability that C provides in declaring variables.

Static Variables - Keeping Track Within a Function

So far, all the variables we have used have gone out of scope at the end of the block in which they were defined, and their memory is free for reallocation. These are called automatic variables because they are automatically created at the point of entry to their scope, and automatically destroyed on leaving. This is a very efficient way of using memory. Memory containing data in a function is only retained for as long as you are executing statements within the function in which the variable was declared.

However, there are many circumstances in which you might want to retain information from one call to the next within a program. You may wish to maintain a count of something, such as the number of times the function has been called, or the number of lines output to a printer, and with automatic variables, you have no way of doing this within a function.

C does provide a way to do this with variables that are called **static**. We could declare a **static** counter, for example, with the declaration:

```
static int count = 0;
```

The word **static** in this statement is a keyword in C. The variable declared in this statement differs from an automatic variable in two ways. First of all, in spite of the fact that it may be defined within the scope of a function, it does not get destroyed when execution leaves the function when a return occurs. Second, whereas an automatic variable is initialized each time its scope is entered, the initialization of a variable declared as **static** occurs only once, essentially right at the beginning of the program.

Try It Out - Using Static Variables

We can demonstrate this with a very elementary example as follows:

```
/* Example 9.4 Static versus automatic variables    */
#include <stdio.h>

/* Function prototypes    */
void test1( void );
void test2( void );

void main()
{
    int i = 0;
```

```
   for( i = 0; i < 5; i++ )
   {
      test1();
      test2();
   }

}

/* Function test1 with an automatic variable   */
void test1(void)
{
   int count = 0;
   printf("\ntest1   count = %d ", ++count );
}

/* Function test2 with an automatic variable   */
void test2(void)
{
   static int count = 0;
   printf("\ntest2   count = %d ", ++count );
}
```

This produces the output:

```
test1 count = 1
test2 count = 1
test1 count = 1
test2 count = 2
test1 count = 1
test2 count = 3
test1 count = 1
test2 count = 4
test1 count = 1
test2 count = 5
```

How It Works

As you can see, the two variables called **count** are quite separate. The changes in the values of each show clearly that they are independent of one another. The **static** variable **count** is declared in the function **test2()**:

```
static int count = 0;
```

This counts the number of times the function is called. This is initialized on the first entry to the function, but its current value when the function is exited is maintained, and it is not re-initialized on subsequent calls to the function. Because it has been declared as **static**, the compiler arranges things so that it will only be initialized the first time the function is called.

The automatic variable **count** in the function **test1()** is declared as:

```
int count = 0;
```

This gets re-initialized to zero at each entry to the function and it is discarded on exit from **test1()**, so it never gets a value that is higher than 1. We saw in Example 8.8 how the memory occupied by an automatic variable in a function can get re-used almost immediately.

We can make any type of variable **static**, and although it persists as long as the program is running, it has local scope, and is only visible within the scope in which it was declared.

Sharing Variables Between Functions

We also have a way of sharing variables between all our functions. In the same way that we can declare constants at the beginning of a program file, outside the scope of the functions making up the program, we can also declare variables that will be available to all. These are called **global variables** as they are accessible anywhere, and are declared in the normal way.

Try It Out - Using Global Variables

By way of a demonstration we can modify our previous example to share **count** between functions:

```
/* Example 9.5 Global variables      */
#include <stdio.h>

int count = 0;

/* Function prototypes    */
void test1( void );
void test2( void );

void main()
{
   int count = 0;

   for( ; count < 5; count++ )
   {
      test1();
      test2();
   }

}
```

```
/* Function test1 with an automatic variable   */
void test1(void)
{
     printf("\ntest1   count = %d ", ++count );
}

/* Function test2 with an automatic variable   */
void test2(void)
{
   static int count = 0;
   printf("\ntest2   count = %d ", ++count );
}
```

The output will be:

```
test1 count = 1
test2 count = 1
test1 count = 2
test2 count = 2
test1 count = 3
test2 count = 3
test1 count = 4
test2 count = 4
test1 count = 5
test2 count = 5
```

How It Works

In this example, we now have three separate variables called **count**, believe it or not.

```
#include <stdio.h>

int count = 0;
```

The first is the global variable **count** declared at the beginning of the file.

```
void main()
{
   int count = 0;
```

The second is an automatic variable **count** declared in **main()**.

```
   static int count = 0;
```

The third is a static variable **count** declared in the function **test2()**.

The function **test1()** works using the global **count**. The functions **main()** and **test2()** use their local versions of **count** as the local declaration hides the global variable of the same name.

Clearly the **count** variable in **main()** is varying from 0 to 4 since we have 5 calls to each of the functions **test1()** and **test2()**. This has to be different from the **count** variables in either of the functions called, otherwise they could not have the values 1 to 5 as displayed in the output.

You can further demonstrate this is the case by simply removing the declaration for **count** in **test2()** as a **static** variable. You will then have made **test1()** and **test2()** share the global **count**, and the values displayed will run from 1 to 10. If you then put a declaration back in **test2()** for **count** as an initialized automatic variable with the statement:

```
int count = 0;
```

the output from **test1()** will run from 1 to 5, and the output from **test2()** will remain at 1, since the variable is now automatic and is re-initialized on each entry to the function.

Global variables can replace the need for function arguments and return values. They look very tempting as the complete alternative to automatic variables. However, you should use global variables sparingly. They can be a major asset in simplifying and shortening some programs, but if you use them excessively, it will make your programs prone to errors. It's very easy to modify a global variable and forget what consequences it might have throughout your program. The bigger the program, the more difficult it becomes to avoid erroneous references to global variables. The use of local variables provides very effective insulation for each function against the possibility of interference from the activities of the others.

As a rule it is unwise to use the same names in C for local and global variables. There is no particular advantage to be gained other than to demonstrate the effect, as we have done with our example. Using local and global variables with the same name also makes programs more error prone, and certainly makes them harder to follow.

Functions That Call Themselves - Recursion

It is possible for a function to call itself. This is termed **recursion**. You are unlikely to come across a need for this very often, so we won't dwell on it. There are also a variety of jokes based on the notion of recursion, but we won't dwell on those either.

Try It Out - Recursion

The primary use of recursion is to simply demonstrate that it's possible. For this we'll follow the crowd and use the standard illustration - the calculation of the factorial of an integer. A factorial of any integer is the product of all the integers from 1 up to the integer, so here we go:

```c
/* Example 9.6 Calculating factorials using recursion    */
#include <stdio.h>

long factorial( long );

void main()
{
   long number = 0;
   printf("\nEnter an integer value: ");
   scanf(" %ld", &number );
   printf("\nThe factorial of %ld is %ld", number, factorial( number ) );
}

/* Our recursive factorial function    */
long factorial( long N )
{
   if ( N == 1 )
      return N;
   else
      return N * factorial( N - 1);
}
```

Typical output from the program would look like this:

```
Enter an integer value: 4

The factorial of 4 is 24
```

Try It Out!

How It Works

This is very simple once you get your mind round what's happening. We could go through a simple example of how it works. Assume you enter the value 4. The sequence of events is shown in the following figure.

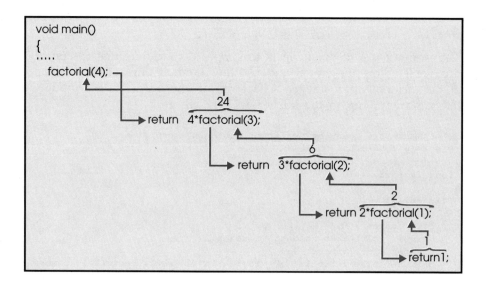

Within the statement:

```
printf("\nThe factorial of %ld is %ld", number, factorial( number ) );
```

the function **factorial()** gets called from **main()** with **number** having the value 4 as the argument.

In the function, since the argument is greater than 1, the statement executed is:

```
return N * factorial( N - 1);
```

This is the second **return** statement in the function, and it calls **factorial()** again with the argument value 3 from within the arithmetic expression. This expression cannot be evaluated and the return can't occur until the value is returned from this call to the function **factorial()** with the argument 3.

This continues as shown in the above figure until the argument in the last call is 1. In this case the first return statement:

```
return N;
```

is executed and the value 1 is returned to the previous call point. This is in fact inside the second return in the **factorial()** function which can now calculate 2*1 and return to the previous call.

In this way the whole process unwinds, ending up with the value required being returned to **main()** where it is displayed. So for any given number **n**, we will have **n** calls to the function **factorial()**. For each call, a copy of the argument is created, and the location to be returned to is stored. This can get expensive on memory with a lot of levels of recursion. A loop to do the same thing would be cheaper and faster. If you do need to use recursion, the most important thing to remember is that there has to be a way to get back. In other words there must be a mechanism for *not* repeating the recursive call. In our example we use a check for the argument supplied being 1.

Notice how factorial values grow very quickly. With quite modest input values, you will exceed the capacity of a **long** integer and start getting the wrong results.

Libraries of Functions - Header Files

We have already mentioned that your compiler comes with a wide range of standard functions declared in **header files**, sometimes called **include files**. These represent a rich source of help for you when you are developing your own applications. We have already met some of these since header files are such a fundamental component of programming in C. So far we have used functions from the following header files:

STDIO.H	Input/Output Functions
MATH.H	Mathematical Floating Point Functions
STDLIB.H	Memory Allocation Functions
STRING.H	String Handling Functions
CTYPE.H	Character Conversion Functions

All of the above contain declarations for a range of functions as well as various constant definitions. They are all ANSI standard libraries so all ANSI conforming compilers will support them and provide at least the basic set of functions, but typically they will supply much more. To comprehensively discuss the contents of even the ANSI standard library header files and functions could double the size of this book, so we'll just mention the most important aspects of the ANSI header files, and leave you to browse the documentation that came with your compiler.

The header file **STDIO.H** contains declarations for quite a range of high-level input/output functions so we will be devoting the whole of Chapter 10 to looking into many of these.

As well as memory allocation functions, **STDLIB.H** provides facilities for converting character strings to their numerical equivalents from the ASCII table. There are also functions for sorting and searching. Functions that generate random numbers are also available through **STDLIB.H**.

We described and used the **STRING.H** file in Chapter 6. With some compilers, this header file also declares functions for managing buffers, as there is a strong affinity between these functions and the general process of handling strings. They generally compare, copy, and move fixed length blocks of memory, whereas the functions we discussed in Chapter 6 we oriented towards variable length strings.

A header file providing a very useful range of functions also related to string processing is **CTYPE.H** that we saw in Chapter 6. It includes functions to convert characters from upper to lower-case, and vice versa, and a number of functions checking for alphabetic characters, numeric digits, and so on. These provide an extensive toolkit for you to do your own detailed analysis of the contents of a string, particularly on input.

By spending a little time understanding the contents of the header files supplied with your compiler, you will greatly increase the ease with which you can develop applications in C. Each header file provides the necessary declarations for all the functions it includes, so you do not have to write declarations yourself for functions that you use from a library.

Designing a Program

At this point you have finished with functions, and you are more than half way through the capabilities of C, so a practical example of reasonable complexity would not come amiss. In this program we are going to use a number of the things we have learnt so far in this book, including some of the things from this chapter.

The Problem

The problem we are going to solve is to write another game. There are several reasons for choosing to write a game, rather than anything else. Firstly, games tend to be just as complex, if not more so, than other types of programs. And, secondly, games are more fun! The game is in the same vain as Othello, or for those of you who are reading this that remember Microsoft Windows 3.0, also known as Reversi. We will use a small grid, and the computer won't play as well as the Microsoft's version of the game, but you will have written and understood this game yourself.

The Analysis

The analysis of this problem is a little different from that we have used up to now. The whole point of this chapter is to introduce the concept of structured programming, in other words breaking a problem into small pieces.

A good way to start is with a diagram. We will start with a single box, which represents the whole program, or the **main()** function if you like. From this, on the next level down, we'll show the functions that have to be directly called by the **main()** function, indicating what these functions have to do. Below that we show the functions that those functions have to use. You don't have to show the actual functions, you can just show the tasks that need to be accomplished. However, these tasks tend to be functions, so this is a good way of designing our program. Let's see what our diagram looks like:

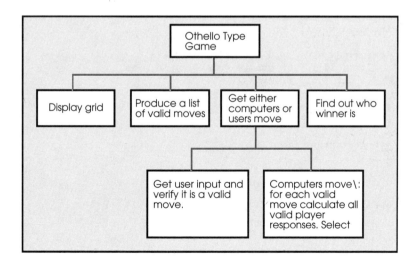

This is a good general picture of what we are trying to do. It is not absolutely fixed, of course. We are still in the process of analyzing the problem. This sort of diagram should make you more aware of the pitfalls and traps so that you don't get caught out yourself.

The Solution

1   The solution is more difficult than the analysis for this particular problem. We will leave out the majority of what occurs in **main()** until the end, and only include what is required to test our functions.

The first thing to do is to set up and display the initial grid. We are going to use a smaller than normal grid, as it makes the games shorter. You could always make the changes to the size at a later stage. To facilitate that change, we'll use a **#define** directive to specify the size of the grid.

So lets declare, initialize and display the grid:

```
#include <stdio.h>

#define GRID 6

void display(char grid[][GRID]);

void main()
{
    char grid [GRID][GRID];
    int grid_x, grid_y;

    for(grid_x = 0; grid_x < GRID; grid_x++)
       for(grid_y = 0; grid_y < GRID; grid_y++)
          grid[grid_x][grid_y] = ' ';

    grid[GRID / 2 - 1][GRID / 2 - 1] = grid[GRID / 2][GRID / 2] = 'O';
    grid[GRID / 2 - 1][GRID / 2] = grid[GRID / 2][GRID / 2 - 1] = '@';

    display(grid);
}

void display(char grid[][GRID])
{
    int grid_y;
```

```
   printf("    a   b   c   d   e   f\n");
   for(grid_y = 0; grid_y < GRID; grid_y++)
   {
      printf("  +---+---+---+---+---+---+\n");
      printf("%2d| %c | %c | %c | %c | %c | %c |\n",
         grid_y + 1,
         grid[0][grid_y],
         grid[1][grid_y],
         grid[2][grid_y],
         grid[3][grid_y],
         grid[4][grid_y],
         grid[5][grid_y]);
   }
   printf("  +---+---+---+---+---+---+\n");
}
```

Notice how we have passed the array **grid** as a parameter to the function **display()**, rather than making **grid** a global variable. This is to prevent other functions from modifying the contents of **grid** accidentally.

2   Next, we need a function to generate a list of possible moves that can be made. This is where life gets a lot more interesting. The first task is to decide how we are to represent and store this list of moves.

So what information do we need to store, and what options do we have? Well we have defined the grid such that any cell can be referenced by a number and a letter. So we could store moves as a string consisting of a number and a letter. But how many would we need? Well the maximum number would be **GRID * GRID**, or in our case 36.

There is another option. We could create a second grid to contain the valid moves. This sound fairly simple so this is what we will do. The type of the array is important at this stage. When we get to working out the computers move, we will need to assign a score to each possible move so that we decide which is the best move. To facilitate this, the new grid should contain integers. We'll initialize the grid to 0's and assign 1's to all the cells which are valid moves. In the code that follows we won't include the **display()** function, we'll just use ellipses (**...**) to indicate where it should appear..

345

```c
#include <stdio.h>

#define GRID 6

void display(char grid[][GRID] );
int valid_moves(char grid[][GRID], int moves[][GRID], char player);

void main()
{
    char grid [GRID][GRID];
    int moves[GRID][GRID];
    int grid_x, grid_y;

    for(grid_x = 0; grid_x < GRID; grid_x++)
       for(grid_y = 0; grid_y < GRID; grid_y++)
          grid[grid_x][grid_y] = ' ';

    grid[GRID / 2 - 1][GRID / 2 - 1] = grid[GRID / 2][GRID / 2] = 'O';
    grid[GRID / 2 - 1][GRID / 2] = grid[GRID / 2][GRID / 2 - 1] = '@';

    display(grid);
    valid_moves(grid, moves, 'O');
}

    ...

int valid_moves(char grid[][GRID], int moves[][GRID], char player)
{
    int dx, dy, grid_x, grid_y, x , y, no_of_moves = 0;
    char opponent;

    opponent = (player == 'O')? '@' : 'O';

    for(grid_x = 0; grid_x < GRID; grid_x++)
       for(grid_y = 0; grid_y < GRID; grid_y++)
          moves[grid_x][grid_y] = 0;

    for(grid_x = 0; grid_x < GRID; grid_x++)
    {
       for(grid_y = 0; grid_y < GRID; grid_y++)
       {
          if(grid[grid_x][grid_y] != player)continue;

/* Check all the squares around this square to see if there is the */
/* opponents counter                                               */

          for(dx = -1; dx <= 1; dx++)
          {
             for(dy = -1; dy <= 1; dy++)
             {
/* First check to make sure we are not checking outside the array */
```

```
                if(grid_x + dx < 0 || grid_x + dx >= GRID ||
                   grid_y + dy < 0 || grid_y + dy >= GRID)continue;
/* Now check the cell */
                if(grid[grid_x + dx][grid_y + dy] == opponent)
                {
/* If we find the opponent, move across the grid until the edge or a blank */
/* cell is reached                                                          */
                    x = grid_x + dx;
                    y = grid_y + dy;
                    while(1)
                    {
                        x += dx;
                        y += dy;
/* Check to make sure we are not checking outside the array or of the */
/* cell contains players counter. In which case not a valid move.     */
                        if(x < 0 || x >= GRID || y < 0 || y >= GRID)break;
                        if(grid[x][y] == player)break;
/* Now check to see the this cell contains a blank. If it does then this */
/* is a valid move, so set the moves array to 1, increase the number of  */
/* moves by 1 and move to next cell                                      */
                        if(grid[x][y] == ' ')
                        {
                            moves[x][y] = 1;
                            no_of_moves++;
                            break;
                        }
                    }
                }
            }
        }
    }
    return no_of_moves;
}
```

3   So now we have an array that contains all the valid moves. Based on our diagram, the next task is to read in the player's move and check to see if it is valid. This is very easy to do, so we will leave this to one side for the moment. A more complex task is to find out the best move for the computer.

We need a scheme to measure the effectiveness of a move. Since we are going to keep this simple, the computer will end up being a rather weak player. To calculate which move to make, we need to do several things. First, we must make copies of the two arrays, **moves** and **grid**, so that we don't accidentally change the originals at this stage. For each of the possible valid moves, we will pretend to make that move, and then we use the new grid to make moves on behalf of the opponent. We then total up the number of counters for each player, and use the difference as a score which measures how good our original trial move was. Obviously, for every move the computer could make, the opponent has a choice of several moves. This means that we can use the best move the player could make for each move the computer could make as the score. We can then choose the move that results in the least effective move of the player.

This actually means we need to write two functions not one. One function is to work out the computer's move, and the other is to actually make a move which will be also used by the first function for trial moves in the temporary grid. We will write the function to make a move first. This will need to insert the players counter, and flip all the relevant counters. We can add this function to what we have so far, as follows:

```c
#include <stdio.h>

#define GRID 6

void display(char grid[][GRID]);
int valid_moves(char grid[][GRID], int moves[][GRID], char player);
int make_move(char grid[][GRID], int moves[][GRID], int grid_x, int grid_y,
char player);

void main()
{
   char grid [GRID][GRID];
   int moves[GRID][GRID];
   int grid_x, grid_y;

   for(grid_x = 0; grid_x < GRID; grid_x++)
      for(grid_y = 0; grid_y < GRID; grid_y++)
         grid[grid_x][grid_y] = ' ';

   grid[GRID / 2 - 1][GRID / 2 - 1] = grid[GRID / 2][GRID / 2] = 'O';
   grid[GRID / 2 - 1][GRID / 2] = grid[GRID / 2][GRID / 2 - 1] = '@';

   display(grid);
   valid_moves(grid, moves, 'O');
}

...

int make_move(char grid[][GRID], int moves[][GRID],
   int grid_x, int grid_y, char player)
{
   int dx, dy, x, y;
   char opponent;
```

```
   opponent = (player == 'O')? '@' : 'O';

/* Make sure move is valid */
   if(moves[grid_x][grid_y] == 0) return -1;

   grid[grid_x][grid_y] = player;

/* Check all the squares around this square to see if there is the */
/* opponents counter                                               */

   for(dx = -1; dx <= 1; dx++)
   {
      for(dy = -1; dy <= 1; dy++)
      {
/* First check to make sure we are not checking outside the array */
         if(grid_x + dx < 0 || grid_x + dx >= GRID ||
            grid_y + dy < 0 || grid_y + dy >= GRID)continue;
/* Now check the cell */
         if(grid[grid_x + dx][grid_y + dy] == opponent)
         {
/* If we find the opponent, move across the grid until the edge or a blank */
/* cell is reached                                                         */
            x = grid_x + dx;
            y = grid_y + dy;
            while(1)
            {
               x += dx;
               y += dy;
/* Check to make sure we are not checking outside the array or of the */
/* cell is blank. In which case not a valid move.                     */
               if(x < 0 || x >= GRID || y < 0 || y >= GRID)break;
               if(grid[x][y] == ' ')break;
/* If the cell contains the player counter, then go backwards from here to */
/* where we started checking, changing the counters                        */
               if(grid[x][y] == player)
               {
                  x -= dx;
                  y -= dy;
                  do
                  {
                     grid[x][y] = player;
                     x -= dx;
                     y -= dy;
                  }while(grid[x][y] != player);
                  break;
               }
            }
         }
      }
   }
   return 1;
}
```

This function also checks to make sure the move is valid, and returns -1 to the calling function if it isn't. For a valid move, it changes all the opponent's counters that need changing, then returns 1 to indicate that there hasn't been an error.

Now we have this function, we could actually make a game out of this code. The computer can't play yet, but we'll fix that now by adding the function to determine the computer's move:

```
#include <stdio.h>

#define GRID 6

void display(char grid[][GRID]);
int valid_moves(char grid[][GRID], int moves[][GRID], char player);
int make_move(char grid[][GRID], int moves[][GRID], int grid_x, int grid_y,
char player);
int comp_move_AI(char grid[][GRID], int moves[][GRID], char player, inttest);

void main()
{
    char grid [GRID][GRID];
    int moves[GRID][GRID];
    int grid_x, grid_y;

    for(grid_x = 0; grid_x < GRID; grid_x++)
       for(grid_y = 0; grid_y < GRID; grid_y++)
          grid[grid_x][grid_y] = ' ';

    grid[GRID / 2 - 1][GRID / 2 - 1] = grid[GRID / 2][GRID / 2] = 'O';
    grid[GRID / 2 - 1][GRID / 2] = grid[GRID / 2][GRID / 2 - 1] = '@';

    display(grid);
    valid_moves(grid, moves, 'O');
}

...

int comp_move_AI(char grid[][GRID], int moves[][GRID], char player, int test)
{
    int grid_x, grid_y, x, y, temp_score, score = 0;
    char temp_grid[GRID][GRID];
    int temp_moves[GRID][GRID];
    char opponent;

    opponent = (player == 'O')? '@' : 'O';

/* Go through all valid moves */
    for(grid_x = 0; grid_x < GRID; grid_x++)
```

```
        for(grid_y = 0; grid_y < GRID; grid_y++)
        {
            if(moves[grid_x][grid_y] == 0)continue;

/* First make cpies of the two arrays */
            for(x = 0; x < GRID; x++)
                for(y = 0; y < GRID; y++)
                {
                    temp_grid[x][y] = grid[x][y];
                    temp_moves[x][y} = moves[x][y];
                }

/* Now make this move on the temporary grid array */
            make_move(temp_grid, temp_moves, grid_x, grid_y, player);
            valid_moves(temp_grid, temp_moves, opponent);

/* Now recall this function with test set to 1 if test is not 1 already*/
            if(test == 0)
                moves[grid_x][grid_y] +=
                    comp_move_AI(temp_grid, temp_moves, opponent, 1);
            else
/* count up the number of counters for each player and compare with score */
            {
                temp_score = 0;
                for(x = 0; x < GRID; x++)
                    for(y = 0; y < GRID; y++)
                    {
                        temp_score += (temp_grid[x][y] == opponent)? 1: 0;
                        temp_score -= (temp_grid[x][y] == player)? 1: 0;
                    }
                score = (score <= temp_score)? temp_score : score;
            }
        }

/* Now, if test is 1 then return score, else search moves for the highest */
/* number, and this is the compters move                                  */

    if(test == 1) return score;

    for(grid_x = 0; grid_x < GRID; grid_x++)
        for(grid_y = 0; grid_y < GRID; grid_y++)
        {
            if(moves[grid_x][grid_y] >= score)
            {
                score = moves[grid_x][grid_y];
                x = grid_x;
                y = grid_y;
            }
        }
    make_move(grid, moves, x, y, player);
}
```

4   Now we have all the major components of the game, all we have to do is combine them into a real game. All of this work happens in the **main()** function which we can now modify as follows:.

```c
#include <stdio.h>

#define GRID 6

void display(char grid[][GRID]);
int valid_moves(char grid[][GRID], int moves[][GRID], char player);
int make_move(char grid[][GRID], int moves[][GRID], int grid_x, int grid_y,
char player);
int comp_move_AI(char grid[][GRID], int moves[][GRID], char player, int
test);

void main()
{
  char grid [GRID][GRID];
  int moves[GRID][GRID];
  int grid_x, grid_y;
  int no_of_games = 1, no_of_moves, comp_score, user_score, y;
  char again, x;

  printf("REVERSAL\n\n");
  printf("We will take it in turns to go first, you will be white (O)\n");
  printf("and I'll be black (@).\n\n");
  printf("Enter your move by typing a letter, then a number with a space\n");
  printf("in between.Make sure the letter is lower case!\n\n");
  printf("Good luck!\nPress return to start\n");
  scanf("%c", &again);

  do
    {
/* Initialize no_of_moves so that the players take turns in starting */
      no_of_moves = (no_of_games % 2 == 0)? 2 : 1;
      for(grid_x = 0; grid_x < GRID; grid_x++)
         for(grid_y = 0; grid_y < GRID; grid_y++)
             grid[grid_x][grid_y] = ' ';

      grid[GRID / 2 - 1][GRID / 2 - 1] = grid[GRID / 2][GRID / 2] = 'O';
      grid[GRID / 2 - 1][GRID / 2] = grid[GRID / 2][GRID / 2 - 1] = '@';

      do
        {
          display(grid);
/* Check to see if it is the computers turn, if it is, then make a move */
          if(no_of_moves % 2 == 0)
            {
              if(valid_moves(grid, moves, '@') == 0)
                 printf("\nI have to pass, your go\n");
              else
```

```
                    comp_move_AI(grid, moves, '@', 0);
            }
/* otherwise, it's the players turn */
        else
        {
            if(valid_moves(grid, moves, 'O') == 0)
            {
                fflush(stdin);
                printf("\nYou have to pass, press return");
                scanf("%c", &again);
            }
            else
            {
/* keep getting moves until a valid move is entered */
                do
                {
                    fflush(stdin);
                    printf("Please enter your move: ");
                    scanf("%c%d", &x, &y);
                }while(make_move(grid, moves, (int)(x - 'a'), y - 1, 'O') == -1);
            }
        }

/* Get scores */
        comp_score = user_score = 0;
        for(grid_x = 0; grid_x < GRID; grid_x++)
            for(grid_y = 0; grid_y < GRID; grid_y++)
            {
                comp_score += (grid[grid_x][grid_y] == '@')?1:0;
                user_score += (grid[grid_x][grid_y] == 'O')?1:0;
            }
        no_of_moves++;
    }while(comp_score + user_score < GRID*GRID);

/* Display the final score */
    printf("The final score is:\n");
    printf("Computer %d\n    User %d\n\n", comp_score, user_score);

    fflush(stdin);
    again = 'n';
    printf("Do you want to play again (y/n): ");
    scanf("%c", again);
    no_of_games++;
  }while(again == 'y');

  printf("\nGoodbye\n");
/* valid_moves(grid, moves, 'O'); */
}
```

...

The games starts something like this:

```
REVERSAL

We will take it in turns to go first, you will be white (O)
and I'll be black (@).

Enter your move by typing a letter, then a number with a space
in between.Make sure the letter is lower case!

Good luck!
Press return to start

       a   b   c   d   e   f
     +---+---+---+---+---+---+
   1|   |   |   |   |   |   |
     +---+---+---+---+---+---+
   2|   |   |   |   |   |   |
     +---+---+---+---+---+---+
   3|   |   | O | @ |   |   |
     +---+---+---+---+---+---+
   4|   |   | @ | O |   |   |
     +---+---+---+---+---+---+
   5|   |   |   |   |   |   |
     +---+---+---+---+---+---+
   6|   |   |   |   |   |   |
     +---+---+---+---+---+---+
Please enter your move: e 3
       a   b   c   d   e   f
     +---+---+---+---+---+---+
   1|   |   |   |   |   |   |
     +---+---+---+---+---+---+
   2|   |   |   |   |   |   |
     +---+---+---+---+---+---+
   3|   |   | O | O | O |   |
     +---+---+---+---+---+---+
   4|   |   | @ | O |   |   |
     +---+---+---+---+---+---+
   5|   |   |   |   |   |   |
     +---+---+---+---+---+---+
   6|   |   |   |   |   |   |
     +---+---+---+---+---+---+
```

We should say before leaving this chapter, that Reversal doesn't play too well. The computer only looks ahead one move, and doesn't have any favoritism for edge and corner cells. Also the grid is only 6 by 6. If you want to change the grid size, then change the **GRID** macro, and then modify the **display()** function. You could use a version of the display function which automatically adapts depending on the value of **GRID**:

```
void display(char grid[][GRID])
{
  int grid_x = 0, grid_y = 0;
  char letter = 'a';

  printf("\n ");

  /* Display column reference letters    */
  for (grid_x = 0 ; grid_x < GRID ; grid_x++ )
    printf("   %c", letter++);
  printf("\n");

  /* Loop to display rows*/
  for(grid_y = 0; grid_y < GRID; grid_y++)
  {

    /* Display spacing row  */
    printf("   +");                                        /* start row */
    for (grid_x = 0 ; grid_x < GRID ; grid_x++ )
        printf("---+");                      /* One of these for each column */
      printf("\n");                          /* End spacing row */

    /* Display row of positions */
    printf("%2d|", grid_y + 1 );                           /* Display row number  */
    for (grid_x = 0 ; grid_x < GRID ; grid_x++ )
        printf(" %c |", grid[grid_x][grid_y] );        /* One per column */
      printf("\n");                          /* End row of positions */
  }

    /* Display last row */
    printf("   +");                                        /* start row */
    for (grid_x = 0 ; grid_x < GRID ; grid_x++ )
        printf("---+");                      /* One of these for each column */
      printf("\n");                          /* End spacing row */
}
```

With this version you only need to change the value of **GRID** and the whole game will adapt to the new size automatically. We didn't include this version in the original because the other version is much simpler, and shorter. We will leave it to you to figure out how this works.

Summary

If you have arrived at this point without too much trouble, you are well on the way to being a competent C programmer. This chapter and the previous one have included all you really need to write properly structured C programs. A functional structure is inherent to the C language and you should keep your functions short with a well-defined purpose. This is the essence of good C code.

You should now be able to approach your own programming problems with a functional structure in mind, right from the outset. But don't forget that pointers provide power to the perspicacious programmer. They can greatly simplify many programming problems, and you should frequently find yourself using them as function arguments and return values. After a while, it will be a natural inclination. The real teacher is experience, so going over the programs in this chapter again will be extremely useful if you don't feel completely confident. And once you feel confident with what's in this book, you should be raring to have a go at some problems of your own.

There is only one major new piece of language territory in C which will introduce really new ideas and we'll deal with this in Chapter 11. But before that we need to cover input/output in rather more detail, so that's next.

CHAPTER 10

Essential Input and Output Operations

In this chapter we are going to look in more detail at input from the keyboard, output to the screen, and output to a printer. This can get a bit tedious, as it consists of a litany of various codes. However, it is necessary if you are to have real competence in using C. On the positive side it's all fairly easy, in spite of being something of a memory test. Treat it as a breather from the last two chapters.

The C language has no input or output capability within the language. All operations of this kind are provided by functions from standard libraries. We have been using many of these functions to provide input from the keyboard, and output to the screen in all the preceding chapters.

This chapter will drag all the pieces together into some semblance of order, and round it out with the aspects we haven't explained so far. We'll also add a bit about printing since it is usually a fairly essential facility for a program. We don't have a final program with this chapter as we don't really cover anything that applies.

In this chapter you will:

- Learn how to get keyboard input
- Learn how to create and format output on the screen
- Understand how to deal with character output
- Understand more about printing output

Input and Output Streams

So far in the chapters we have used **scanf()** for keyboard input and **printf()** for output to the screen. There has been nothing in particular in their usage which specified where the input came from, or where the output went to. The information that **scanf()** received could have come from anywhere as long as it was a suitable stream of characters, and similarly, the output from **printf()** could have been going anywhere that could accept a stream of characters. This is no accident. The standard input/output functions in C have been designed to be device independent, so that the transfer of data to or from a specific device isn't the concern of the programmer. The C library functions and the operating system deal with the problem of making sure that operations with a specific device are executed correctly.

Each input source and output destination in C is called a **stream**. A stream is independent of the physical piece of equipment involved such as the display, or the keyboard. Each device that a program uses will usually have one or more streams associated with it depending on whether is it simply an input or an output device, such as a printer or a keyboard, or a device that can have both input and output operations. This is illustrated in the next figure.

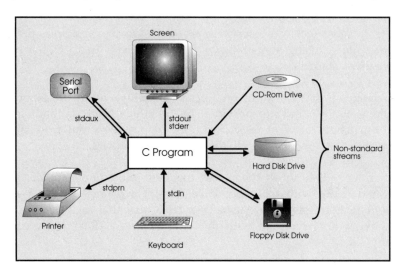

A disk drive can have multiple input and output streams, since it can contain multiple files, each of which can be an input stream or an output stream or both. A CD-ROM drive which is typically read only may represent multiple input streams since it usually contains multiple files.

There are two kinds of streams: character streams and binary streams. The main difference between them is that data transferred to or from character streams are modified by the library routine concerned according to a format specification, whereas binary streams are not. We will discuss binary streams in Chapter 12 when we discuss disk file input/output.

Standard Streams

C has three predefined standard streams which are automatically available in any program, provided, of course, you have included the necessary header file declaring the functions. These are **stdin**, **stdout**, and **stderr**. There are two others which are supported by many systems, **stdprn** and **stdaux**. There is no initialization or preparation necessary to use them. You just have to apply the appropriate library function that sends data to them. They are each pre-assigned to a specific physical device as follows:

stdin	Keyboard
stdout	Display Screen
stderr	Display Screen
stdprn	Printer
stdaux	Serial Port

We shall concentrate on the standard input stream **stdin**, the standard output stream **stdout**, and the printer stream **stdprn**. The stream **stderr**, is simply the stream to which error messages from the C library are sent, and you can direct your own error messages to **stderr** if you wish. We shan't discuss this, other than to say it points to the display screen and can't be redirected to another device. Output to the stream **stdaux** is directed to the serial port and is outside the scope of this book, for reasons of space rather than complexity.

Both **stdin** and **stdout** can be re-assigned using operating system commands to files instead of the default keyboard and screen. When this is done, error conditions can arise which don't normally arise with the default devices, so this is a good reason not to do it.

Input From The Keyboard

There are two forms of input from the keyboard on **stdin** which we have already seen in previous chapters. There is formatted input, which is provided principally by **scanf()**, and unformatted input, where we receive the raw character data with a function such as **getchar()**. There is rather more to both of these possibilities, so let's look at them in detail.

Formatted Keyboard input

As we have seen, the function **scanf()** reads characters from the stream **stdin**, and converts them to one or more internal variable values according to the format specifiers in a format control string. The general form of the function **scanf()** is:

```
int scanf(char *format, pointer_1, pointer_2,...,pointer_n )
```

The format control string parameter is actually a **char *** type - a pointer to a character string, as shown above. However, this usually appears as an explicit argument in the function call, such as in:

```
scanf("%lf", &variable);
```

although there is nothing to prevent you writing:

```
char str[] = "%lf";
scanf( str , &variable );
```

The format control string is basically a coded description, or recipe, for how **scanf()** should convert the incoming character stream to the values required. Following the format control string, we can have one or more arguments, each of which is an address where a corresponding converted input value is to be stored. As we have seen, this implies that the arguments must be the variable name preceded by **&**, to define the address of the variable rather than its value. Of course, pointer variables and array names usually appear as arguments without the **&**.

The function **scanf()** reads from **stdin** until it comes to the end of the format control string, or until an error condition stops the input process. This is usually because the input does not correspond to what is expected with the current format specifier, as we shall see. The value returned by the function is the count of the number of input values read.

Input Format Control Strings

The format control string used with **scanf()** is not precisely the same as that used with **printf()**. For one thing, blanks and tab characters are ignored. These are also called whitespace characters. You can use spaces and tabs to separate the format specifiers and so make the control string more readable. There are other differences too, as we shall see when we get to discuss formatted output a bit later in this chapter.

The most general form of a format specifier is shown in the next figure.

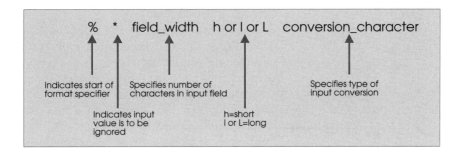

Let's take a look at the various parts of this in sequence.

- The `%` sign simply indicates the start of the format specifier.

- The next `*` is optional. If it's included, it indicates the next input value is to be ignored. This isn't normally used with input from the keyboard. It's useful when the keyboard input has been re-assigned to a file using an operating system command and you don't want to process all the values that appear in the file in your program.

- The field width is optional and is an integer specifying the number of characters `scanf()` that should assume makes up the current value being input. This allows you to input a sequence of values without spaces between them. This also frequently has application when reading files.

- The next character is also optional, and can be `h`, `L` or `l` (small 'ell'). If it's `h`, it can only be included with an integer conversion specifier (`d`, `I`, `o`, `u` or `x`) and indicates the input is to be converted as `short`. If it's `l` or `L` it indicates `long` when preceding an `int` conversion specifier, and `double` when preceding a `float` conversion specifier.

- The conversion character specifies the type of conversion to be carried out on the input stream. The possible characters and their meaning are shown in the following table.

Conversion Character	Meaning
d	Convert input to **int**
i	Convert input to **int**. If preceded by 0 assume octal digits input, if preceded by 0x or 0X, assume hexadecimal digits input.
o	Convert input to **int** and assume all digits are octal.
u	Convert input to unsigned **int**.
x	Convert to **int** and assume all digits are hexadecimal.
c	Input the next character as **char** (including blank)
s	Input the string of non-whitespace characters, starting with the next non-whitespace character.
e, f, or g	Convert input to **float**. A decimal point and an exponent in the input are optional.

Try It Out - Exercising Formatted Input

We can now exercise some of these with practical examples:

```
/* Example 10.1 Exercising formatted input         */
#include <stdio.h>

void main()
{
  int i = 0, j = 0, k = 0;
  float fp1 = 0.0;

  k = scanf(" %f %d %d ", &fp1, &i , &j);
  printf("\nReturn value = %d\n", k);
  printf("\nfp1 = %f\ti = %d\tj = %d\n", fp1, i, j);
}
```

How It Works

Execute this program and key the input as:

3.141597 8

You should get the output:

```
Return value = 3

fp1 = 3.141590i = 7j = 8
```

The value of **k** is the count of the number of values processed. The remaining variables are what you might expect. The **\t** in the **printf()** statement is the tab character.

It isn't essential that all the data is entered on a single line. If you key the first two values and press *Enter*, the **scanf()** function will wait for you to enter the next value on the next line.

Now let's change the program a little bit by altering one statement. Replace the input statement by:

```
k = scanf("%3f %2d %2d", &fp1, &i, &j);
```

Now run the program with exactly the same input line as before. You should get the output:

```
Return value = 3

fp1 = 3.10000 i = 41 j = 59
```

It should be obvious what happened here. Because we specified a field width of 3 for the floating point value, the first three characters are taken as defining the value of our first input variable. The following two integer values to be input have a field width definition of 2, so they have values defined by the successive pairs of characters from what was our first input value in the previous example. In consequence **i** has the value 41, and **j** has the value 59.

Let's try another simple variation. Change the input statement to:

```
k = scanf("%6f %2d %2d", &fp1, &i, &j);
```

With exactly the same input line as before, you should now get the output:

```
Return value = 3

fp1 = 3.141500i = 9j = 7
```

So what can we conclude from this case? The first floating point value has clearly been defined by the first six characters of input. The next two values result in integers 9 and 7. This shows that in spite of the fact that we specified a field width of 2 in each case, it appears to have been overridden. This is a consequence of the blank following each of the two digits involved, terminating the input scanning for the value being read. So whatever value we put as a field width, the scanning of the input line for a given value stops as soon as we meet the first blank. We could change the specifiers for the integer values to %12d and the result would still be the same for the given input.

We could demonstrate one further aspect to numerical input processing by running the last version of the previous example with the input line:

```
3.1415A7 8
```

You should now get the output:

```
Return value = 1

fp1 = 3.141500 i = 0 j = 0
```

The count of the number of input values is **1**, corresponding to a value for the variable **fp1** being input. The **A** in the input stream is invalid in numerical input, and so the whole process stops dead. No values for variables **i** and **j** are processed. This demonstrates how unforgiving **scanf()** is. A single invalid character in the input stream will stop your program in its tracks. If you want to be able to recover the situation when invalid input is entered, you can use the return value from **scanf()** as a measure of whether all the necessary input has been processed correctly, and include some code to retrieve the situation when necessary.

The simplest approach would perhaps be to print an irritable message and then demand the whole input be repeated. But beware of errors in your code getting you into a permanent loop in this circumstance. You need to think through all of the possible ways things might go wrong if you are to produce a robust program.

Characters in the Input Format String

You can include a character string that isn't a format conversion specifier within the input format string. If you do this you are indicating that you expect the same characters to appear in the input. These have to be matched exactly, character for character by the data in the input stream. Any variation terminates the input scanning process in **scanf()**.

Try It Out - Characters in the Input Format String

We can illustrate this by modifying the previous example to the following:

```
/* Example 10.2 Characters in the format control string        */
#include <stdio.h>

void main()
{
  int i = 0, j = 0, k = 0;
  float fp1 = 0.0;

  k = scanf("fp1 = %f i = %d %d", &fp1, &i , &j);
  printf("\nReturn value = %d\n", k);
  printf("\nfp1 = %f\ti = %d\tj = %d\n", fp1, i, j);
}
```

Program Analysis

If you enter the input string:

```
fp1=3.14159  i = 7 8
```

you will get the output:

```
Return value = 3

fp1 = 3.141590 i = 7 j = 8
```

It doesn't matter whether the blanks before and after the = are included in the input or not. They are whitespace characters and are therefore ignored. The important thing is to include the same characters that appear in the format control string, in the correct sequence and at the correct place in the input. Try the input line:

```
fp1 = 3.14159 i = 7 j = 8
```

You will get the output:

```
Return value = 2

fp1 = 3.141590 i = 7 j = 0
```

since the character **j** in the input stops processing immediately, and no value is received by the variable **j**. The input processing of characters by **scanf()** is also case-sensitive. If you input **Fp1=** instead of **fp1=**, no values will be processed at all, as the mismatch with the capital F will stop scanning before any values are entered.

Floating Point Input

The next aspect of formatted input using **scanf()** that we should look at, is the variety of forms of possible input for floating point values.

Try It Out - Floating Point Input

We can go straight to a simple example:

```
/* Example 10.3 Floating Point Input */
#include <stdio.h>

void main()
{
   float fp1 = 0.0, fp2 = 0.0, fp3 = 0.0;

printf("\nReturn value = %d\n", scanf("%f %f %f", &fp1, &fp2, &fp3) );
printf("\nfp1 = %f\tfp2 = %f\tfp3 = %f", fp1, fp2, fp3);
}
```

How It Works

In this example, we have put the **scanf()** call as the argument to the first **printf()** just to show it can be done. This makes the code rather inelegant as well as harder to follow, so it's not to be recommended.

You could run this program with the input:

```
3.14  .314E1  .0314e+02
```

And, assuming you have keyed correctly you will get the output:

```
Return value = 3

fp1 = 3.140000 fp2 = 3.140000 fp3 = 3.140000
```

We have demonstrated three different ways of entering the same value. The first is a straightforward decimal value, the second has an exponent value defined by the E1 indicating the value is to be multiplied by 10, and the third has an exponent value of e+02 and is to be multiplied by 10^2. We have the option of either including an exponent or not. If we do include an exponent, we can define it beginning with either an e or an E. You can also include a sign for the exponent value if you want. There are countless variations possible here. You can experiment with various possibilities, particularly with field width specifiers added, similar to those we used for reading integers.

Reading Hexadecimal and Octal Values

You can read hexadecimal values from the input stream using the format specifier **%x**. For octal values you should use **%o**.

Try It Out - Reading Hexadecimal and Octal Values

Try the following example:

```
/* Example 10.4 Reading hexadecimal and octal values */
#include <stdio.h>

void main()
{
  int i = 0, j = 0, k = 0, m = 0;

  m = scanf(" %d %x %o", &i , &j, &k );
  printf("\n%d values read.\n", m);
  printf("\ni = %d\tj = %d\tk = %d\n", i, j, k );
}
```

How It Works

If you enter the values:

```
12  12  12
```

you will get the output:

```
12  18  10
```

We read the three values 12, first with a decimal format specifier **%d**, second using a hexadecimal format specifier **%x**, and last using an octal format specifier **%o**. The output shows that 12_{16} is 18 in decimal notation, and 12_8 is 10 in decimal notation.

Hexadecimal data entry can be useful when you want to enter bit patterns as they are easier to specify in hexadecimal than in decimal. Each hexadecimal digit corresponds to four bits so you can specify a 16-bit word as four hexadecimal digits. Octal is hardly ever used, and appears here mainly for historical reasons.

Reading Characters Using scanf()

You can read a single character using the format specifier **%c**. For a string of characters you use the specifier **%s**.

Try It Out - Reading Characters Using scanf()

We can show this in operation with the following example:

```
/* Example 10.5 Reading characters with scanf() */
#include <stdio.h>

void main()
{
  char initial, name[80];

  printf("\nEnter your first initial: ");
  scanf("%c", &initial );
  printf("\nEnter your name:" );
  scanf("%s", name );
  if ( initial != name[0] )
    printf("\n%s,you got your initial wrong.",name);
  else
    printf("\nHi, %s. Your initial is correct. Well done!", name );
}
```

How It Works

This program expects you to enter your first initial and then your first name. It checks that the first letter of your name is the same as the initial you entered. If you try a couple of variations on the input, you can see the limitations of **scanf()** here. Try entering a space, then your initial. The program will treat the blank as the value for initial, and the single character you entered as your name. The first character you enter when using the `%c` specifier is taken to be the character, whatever it is.

You could also try entering a valid initial, but enter your full name, including surname. You will find that only your first name is recognized. The blank between your first and second name will signal the end of the input with the `%s` specifier. Therefore, you can't read strings containing blanks with `scanf()`. You have to use the function we discuss in the next section, `gets()`.

Pitfalls With scanf()

There are two very common mistakes that are made when using `scanf()` that you should keep in mind:

> Don't forget the arguments must be pointers. Perhaps the most common error is to forget the ampersand when specifying arguments to `scanf()`, particularly since you don't need them with `printf()`. Of course it isn't necessary if the argument is an array name, or a pointer variable.

> When inputting a string using `%s`, remember to ensure there is enough space for the string to be read in, *plus* the terminating `'\0'`. If you don't remember to do this, you will overwrite some data, possibly even some of your program code.

String Input From the Keyboard

As we have seen previously, we have a function in `STDIO.H` that will read a complete line of text as a string. The general syntax of the function is:

```
char *gets(char *str);
```

The function reads characters into the memory pointed to by `str` until you press the *Enter* key. It appends the terminating null, `'\0'`, in place of the newline character generated when you press *Enter*. The return value is identical to the argument, which is the address where the string has been stored.

Try It Out - Reading a String With gets()

We could modify the previous example to use **gets()** instead of **scanf()**:

```
/* Example 10.6 Reading a string with gets() */
#include <stdio.h>

void main()
{
  char initial[2], name[80];

  printf("\nEnter your first initial: ");
  gets( initial );
  printf("\nEnter your name: " );
  gets( name );
  if ( initial[0] != name[0] )
    printf("\n%s,you got your initial wrong,", name);
else
    printf("\nHi, %s. Your initial is correct. Well done!", name );
}
```

How It Works

As you can see, all we needed to do to produce this example was to replace the two calls of **scanf()** in the last example with two calls of **gets()**, after changing the variable **initial** to an array with two elements. This last change is necessary because the function **gets()** will append **'\0'** even if only one character is read. Typical output from the program is:

```
Enter your first initial: M

Enter your name: Mephistopheles

Hi, Mephistopheles. Your initial is correct. Well done!
```

It works extremely simply as there is no format specification involved. Since **gets()** will read characters until you press *Enter*, you can now enter your full name if you wish. For string input, using **gets()** is usually the preferred approach. However, it isn't quite so useful when you only want one character, as we do for reading an initial. Also, if you enter a space before you enter your initial, you will overwrite some memory, as more space will be required than we have allocated in the array **initial**.

Unformatted Input from the Keyboard

Another function we have already seen is **getchar()**, which allows us to read from **stdin** character by character. This is also defined in **STDIO.H**. Its general syntax is:

```
int getchar(void)
```

It requires no arguments and returns the character read from the input stream. Note that it is returned as **int**. The character read is displayed on the screen.

With many systems, a header file **CONIO.H** is often provided. This usually provides additional functions for character input and output. One of the most useful of these is **getch()** which will read a character from the keyboard without displaying it on the screen. This is particularly useful when you need to prevent others being able to see what is being keyed, such as when entering a password.

Output To The Screen

Output to the screen is much easier than input from the keyboard.. You know what data you are outputting, whereas with input you have all the vagaries of possible mis-keying. The primary function for formatted output to **stdout** is **printf()**.

Fortunately, or unfortunately, depending how you view the chore of getting into this stuff, **printf()** provides a myriad of variations in the possible output you can obtain - much more than that associated with **scanf()**. We have already used it extensively in previous chapters; we won't dwell on the features we have met previously, but will concentrate on those we haven't met yet. However, we will still include a mention of all the bits we are familiar with just for the sake of completeness.

Formatted Output To The Screen - Using printf()

This function is defined in the header file **STDIO.H**. The general form of the function **printf()** is:

```
int printf(char *format, argument_1, argument_2,...,argument_n)
```

The first parameter is the format control string, which can be a pointer to a string specified elsewhere. This is apparent from the representation on the previous page. Usually, though, it's entered as an explicit argument as we have seen in previous examples. The succeeding parameters are the values to be output in sequence. The arguments must be specified to correspond with the format conversion specifiers appearing in the first argument. Of course, as we have also seen in examples, if the output is simply text appearing in the control string, there are no additional arguments after the first. Where there are argument values to be output, there must be at least as many arguments as there are format specifiers. If not, the results are unpredictable. If there are more arguments than specifiers, the excess is ignored. This is because the function uses the format string as the determinant of how many arguments follow, and what type they have. This is also the reason that you get the wrong result with a **%d** specifier combined with a **long** argument.

The format conversion specifiers for **printf()** are a little more complicated than those used for input with **scanf()**. The general form of the format specifier appears in this figure.

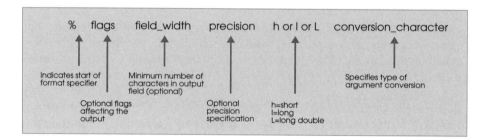

Let's take a quick pass through the bits of the general format specifier:

> The % sign indicates the start of the specifier, as it does for output.

> The optional flag characters are +, -, #, and blank. These affect the output as follows:

Character	Use
+	Used for ensuring that for signed output values, there is always a sign preceding the output value, either a plus or a minus sign.
-	Specifies that the output value is to be left-justified in the output field, and padded with blanks on the right. The default positioning of the output is right-justified.
#	Specifies that **0** is to precede an octal output value, **0x** or **0X** is to precede a hexadecimal output value, and that a floating point output value will contain a decimal point. For **g** or **G** floating point conversion characters, trailing zeroes will also be omitted
blank	Specifies that positive or zero output values will be preceded by a blank rather than a plus sign.

▶ The optional **field_width** specifies the minimum number of characters for the output value. If the value requires more characters, the field is simply expanded. If it requires less than the minimum specified it is padded with blanks, unless the field width is specified, with a leading zero, as in 09 for example, in which case it is filled on the left with zeroes.

▶ The precision specifier is also optional and is usually used with floating point output values. A specifier of .n indicates that n decimal places are to be output. If the value to be output has more than n significant digits, it is rounded or truncated.

▶ The h, l ('ell'), or L specification is necessary to specify whether the output conversion is being applied to short, long or long double values respectively.

▶ The conversion character defines how the output is to be converted for a particular type of value to be output. Conversion characters are defined in the table on the next page.

Conversion Character	Output Produced
Applicable to integers:	
d	Signed decimal integer value
o	Unsigned octal integer value
u	Unsigned decimal integer value
x	Unsigned hexadecimal integer value with a, b, c, d, e, f digits
X	As x with digits A, B, C, D, E, F
Applicable to floating point:	
f	Signed decimal value
e	Signed decimal value with exponent
E	As e but with E for exponent instead of e
g	As e or f depending on size of value and precision
G	As g but with E for exponent values
Applicable to characters:	
c	Single character
s	Outputs characters until '\0' is reached or precision characters have been output.

Believe it or not, these specifications for output options are just the most important ones. If you consult the documentation accompanying your compiler, you will find a few more. However, those we have identified will cover by far the majority of requirements. We will take a look at some of the variations we haven't tried so far. Those with field width and precision specifiers are probably the most interesting.

Escape Sequences

We can also include whitespace characters in the format control string for **printf()**. The characters referred to as whitespace embrace newline, carriage return and formfeed characters, as well as blank and tab. Some of these are represented by escape sequences which begin with \. The most common escape sequences consist of the following:

\a	Bell - sound a beep on your PC
\b	Backspace
\f	Formfeed or page eject
\n	Newline
\r	Carriage return (for printers)
\t	Horizontal tab

The escape sequence \\ is used in format control strings when the actual character \ is required to be output. This is necessary as otherwise it would be impossible to output a backslash. It would always be assumed to be the start of an escape sequence.

Different Output

Let's look at some examples of the different ways of outputting information.

Try It Out - Outputting Integers

We can try a sample of integer output formats first:

```
/* Example 10.7 Integer output variations     */
#include <stdio.h>

void main()
{
  int i = 15, j = 345, k = 4567;
  long li = 56789, lj = 678912, lk = 23456789;

  printf("\ni = %d\tj = %d\tk = %d\ti = %6.3d\tj = %6.3d\tk = %6.3d\n",
                     i ,j, k, i, j, k);
  printf("\ni = %-d\tj = %+d\tk = %-d\ti = %-6.3d\tj = %-6.3d\tk = %-6.3d\n",
                     i ,j, k, i, j, k);
  printf("\nli = %d\tlj = %d\tlk = %d\n", li, lj, lk);
  printf("\nli = %ld\tlj = %ld\tlk = %ld\n", li, lj, lk);
}
```

How It Works

When you execute the example above, you should get something like:

```
i = 15     j = 345     k = 4567     i =     015  j =      345  k =     4567

i = 15     j = +345    k = 4567   · i = 015     j = 345      k = 4567

li = -8747 lj = 0      lk = 23552

li = 56789 lj = 678912 lk = 23456789
```

Try It Out!

This example illustrates a miscellany of options for integer output. You can see by comparing the first two lines produced by the statements:

```
   printf("\ni = %d\tj = %d\tk = %d\ti = %6.3d\tj = %6.3d\tk = %6.3d\n",i ,j,
k, i, j, k);
   printf("\ni = %-d\tj = %+d\tk = %-d\ti = %-6.3d\tj = %-6.3d\tk = %-6.3d\n",i
,j, k, i, j, k);
```

that the effects of the `minus` flag cause the output to be left-justified. The effect of the field width specifier is also apparent from the spacing of the last three outputs in each group of six. Note that the default width provides just enough output positions to accommodate the number of digits to be output, so the - flag has no effect. We get a leading plus in the output of `j` on the second line because of the flag modifier. You can use more than one flag modifier if you want. With the second output of the value of `i`, we have a leading zero inserted due to the minimum precision being specified as 3. We could also have obtained leading zeroes by preceding the minimum width value with a zero in the format specification.

The third output line is produced by:

```
   printf("\nli = %d\tlj = %d\tlk = %d\n", li, lj, lk);
```

Here you can see an effect we have seen already. Failure to insert the `l` (small letter L) modifier when outputting long integers results in apparent garbage, due to the output value being assumed to be a two byte integer.

We get the correct values from the statement:

```
   printf("\nli = %ld\tlj = %ld\tlk = %ld\n", li, lj, lk);
```

It is unwise to specify inadequate values for the width and the precision for the values to be displayed. Weird and wonderful results can be produced if you do. You could play around with this example to see how much variation you can get.

Try It Out - Variations On a Single Integer

We could try one more integer example to run the gamut of possibilities with a single integer value:

```
/* Example 10.8 Variations on a single integer    */
#include <stdio.h>
void main()
{
  int k = 678;

  printf("\n%%d\t%%o\t%%x\t%%X");              /* Display format as heading */

  printf("\n%d\t%o\t%x\t%X", k, k, k, k );           /* Display values */
  /* Display format as heading */
  printf("\n\n%%8d        %%-8d        %%+8d        %%08d        %%-+8d");
  printf("\n%8d   %-8d   %-+8d   %08d   %-+8d", k, k, k, k, k );
}
```

How It Works

This program may look a little confusing at first, since the first of each pair of **printf()** statements displays the format used to output the number appearing immediately below. The **%%** specifier simply outputs the **%** character. When you execute this example you should get:

```
%d %o %x %X
678 1246  2a6 2A6

%8d %-8d %+8d %08d
     678 678       +678 00000678
```

The first row of outputs are produced by the statement:

```
    printf("\n%d\t%o\t%x\t%X", k, k, k, k );
```

The outputs are decimal, octal, and two varieties of hexadecimal for the value 678, with default width specification. The corresponding format appears above each value on your display.

The next row of output values is produced by:

```
    printf("\n%8d   %-8d   %-+8d   %08d   %-+8d", k, k, k, k, k );
```

This statement includes some varieties of flag settings with a width specification of 8. The first is normal right justification in the field. The second is left-justified because of the - flag. The third has a sign because of the + flag. The fourth has leading zeroes because the width is specified as 08 instead of 8, and also has a sign because of the + flag. The last output value uses a specifier with all the trimmings, **%-+8d**, so the output is left-justified in the field, and also has a leading sign.

377

When you are outputting multiple rows of values on the screen, using a width specification, possibly with tabs, will enable you to line them up in columns.

Outputting Floating Point Values

If plowing through the integer options hasn't got you nodding off, we can now take a quick look at the floating point output options.

Try It Out - Outputting Floating Point Values

Look at the following example:

```
/* Example 10.9 Outputting floating point values    */
 #include <stdio.h>

void main()
{
   float fp1 = 345.678, fp2 = 1.234E6;
   double  fp3 = 234567898, fp4 = 11.22334455e-6;

   printf("\n%f\t%+f\t%-10.4f\t%6.4f\n", fp1, fp2, fp1, fp2);
   printf("\n%e\t%+E\n", fp1, fp2);
   printf("\n%f\t%g\t%#+f\t%8.4f\t%10.4g\n", fp3,fp3, fp3, fp3, fp4);
}
```

How It Works

With my compiler we get the output:

```
345.678009 +1234000.000000 345.6780 1234000.0000

3.456780e+02 +1.234000E+06

234567898.00000 2.34568e+08  +234567898.000000 234567898.0000    1.22e-05
```

It's possible you may not get exactly the same output, but overall it should be close. Most of the output is a straightforward demonstration of the effects of the format conversion specifiers we have discussed, but a few points are worthy of note.

The value of the first output for **fp1** differs slightly from the value we assigned to the variable. This is typical of the kind of small difference that can creep in when floating point numbers are converted from decimal to binary.

Try It Out!

With fractional decimal values there is not always an exact equivalent in binary floating point.

In the output from the statement:

```
printf("\n%f\t%+f\t%-10.4f\t%6.4f\n", fp1, fp2, fp1, fp2);
```

the second output value for **fp1** shows how the number of decimal places after the point can be constrained, and the output is left-justified in the field. The second output of **fp2** has a field width specified that is too small for the number of decimal places required, and is therefore overridden.

The second **printf()** is:

```
printf("\n%e\t%+E\n", fp1, fp2);
```

This outputs the same values in floating point format with an exponent. Whether you get a capital **E** or a small **e** for the exponent indicator depends on how you write the format specifier.

In the last line you can see how the **g** specified output of **fp3** is rounded up compared to the **f** specified output.

There are innumerable possible variations of the output obtainable with **printf()**. It would be very educational for you to play around with the options, trying various ways of outputting the same information. On the other hand, perhaps you would prefer to wait until you are pressed into looking at them through circumstance, and in the meantime get on to the next topic a bit quicker.

Character Output

Now that we have looked at the various possibilities of outputting numbers let's look at outputting characters.

Outputting Strings

In addition to the string output capabilities of **printf()** we have the function **puts()** in **STDIO.H** which complements the **gets()** function. Its general form is:

```
int puts( char *string )
```

The function accepts a pointer to a string as an argument and displays **string** on **stdout**. The string must be terminated by **'\0'**. It returns a positive value if no errors occur on output. It's very useful for outputting single line messages as in:

```
puts("Is there no end to input and output?");
```

This will output the line appearing as an argument, then move the cursor to the next line. The function **printf()** requires an explicit **'\n'** to be included at the end of the string. The function **puts()** will, of course, also process embedded **'\n'** characters to generate new lines.

Unformatted Output to the Screen

Also included in **STDIO.H**, and complementing the function **getchar()**, is the function **putchar()**. This has the general form:

```
int putchar( int c )
```

This function outputs a single character, **c**, to **stdout** and returns the character displayed. This allows you to output a message one character at a time, which can make your programs a bit bigger. For example, you could write:

```
char string[] = "Jabberwocky!\n";
puts(string);
```

or you could write:

```
char string[] = "Jabberwocky!\n";
int i = 0;
while( string[i] )
  putchar( string[i++];
```

Both of these will output the same thought provoking message. Of course the real purpose of these functions is to give you complete control of input and output operations if you need it. With **putchar()** for instance, you could choose to output a selected sequence of characters from the middle of a string. With **puts()** of course, you can't do this.

Sending Output to the Printer

You might imagine that you were now due for another slew of miscellaneous codes to remember. After all, printing is a whole new ball game. Well, if you did you would be wrong. We just have to use a more generalized form of the **printf()** function, **fprintf()**. This is actually designed to send formatted output to any stream, but here we will stick to printing. For this purpose, its general form is:

```
int fprintf( stdprn, format_string, argument_1, argument_2,..,argument_n )
```

With the exception of the first parameter, and the extra **f** in the function name, it looks exactly like **printf()**. And so it is. If you don't have **stdprn** defined with your compiler and library, you will need to consult your documentation to see how to handle printing, but most systems support **stdprn**. You can use the same format string with the same set of specifiers to output data to your printer, in the same way that you used to display results with **printf()**. However there are a couple of minor variations you need to be aware of that we can illustrate with a simple example.

Try It Out - Printing On a Printer

This program shows the how we can get programs to output to a printer.

```
/* Example 10.10  Printing on a printer - where else?     */
#include <stdio.h>
void main()
{
  fprintf( stdprn, "The barber shaves all those who do not shave themselves." );
  fprintf( stdprn, "\n\rQuestion: Who shaves the barber?\n\r" );
  fprintf( stdprn, "\n\rAnswer: She doesn't need to shave.\f" );
}
```

Try It Out!

How It Works

The only oddities here are the new escape sequences `\r` and `\f`. The sequence `\n\r` is equivalent to new line/carriage return on a printer, and the `\f` is form feed, which produces a page-eject on printers where this is required.

Summary

As we said at the outset, input and output is a messy business. Although the various codes involved have been chosen with the idea of being as meaningful as possible, consistent with the need for providing code which is reasonably concise, there are a lot of them and they are very diverse. The only way you are going to become comfortable with them is with practice. This generally needs to be in a practical context. Exercising the various codes for understanding is fine, but they will probably only become familiar after quite a lot of practical usage in real programs. In the meantime, you can always look them up in this chapter.

CHAPTER 11

Structuring Your Data

So far we have learnt how to declare and define variables that can hold various types of data, including integers, floating point values and characters. We also have the means to create arrays of any of these types, as well as pointers to memory locations containing data of the types available to us. While these have proved very useful, there are many applications where you need even more flexibility.

For instance, suppose you wanted to write a program that processed data about breeding horses. You would need information about each horse such as its name, its date of birth, its coloring, its height, its parentage and so on. Some items are strings and some are numeric. Clearly you could set up arrays for each data type, and store them quite easily. However, this has its limitations. It doesn't allow you to refer to Dobbin's date of birth, or Trigger's height particularly easily. You would need to synchronize your arrays by relating data items through a common index. Amazingly, C provides us with a better way of and that's what we are going to discuss next.

In this chapter you will:

> Understand how to declare and define data structures

> Use structures, and pointers to structures

> Learn about pointers as structure members

> Learn how to share memory between variables

> Learn how to define your own data types

> Write a program that produces bar charts of your data

Data Structures

The keyword **struct** enables us to define a collection of variables of various types that we can treat as a unit. This will be clearer if we go straight to a simple example of a declaration of a structure:

```
struct horse
   {
        int age;
        int height;
   } Silver;
```

We have declared a **structure** type called **horse**. This isn't a variable name, it's essentially a new type. This type name is usually referred to as a **structure tag,** or a **tag name**. The naming of the structure tag follows the same rules as that of a variable name, which you should be familiar with by now. It is actually legal to use the same name for a structure tag name and another variable. It isn't generally recommended that you do so, since it introduces a significant potential for confusion in your program.

The variable names within the structure, **age**, **height** are called **structure members**. They are both of type **int** in this case. The members of the structure appear between the braces following the **struct** tag name, **horse**. An instance of the structure called **Silver** is also declared, at the same time the structure is defined. Whenever we use the variable name **Silver**, it includes both members of the structure, the member **age**, and the member **height**.

Let's look at the declaration of a slightly more complicated version of a structure type **horse**:

```
struct horse
   {
        int age;
        int height;
        char name[20];
        char father[20];
        char mother[20];
   } Dobbin =    {
            24, 17, "Dobbin", "Trigger", "Flossie"
         };
```

Any kind of variable can appear as a member of a structure, including arrays. As you see, there are five members to this structure, the integer members **age** and **height**, and the arrays **name, father,** and **mother**. Each member declaration is essentially the same as a normal variable declaration, with the type followed by the name and terminated by a semicolon. Note that initial values cannot be placed here as we are not declaring variables - we are defining members of a type called **horse**. This is a sort of specification or blueprint that can then be used to define variables. Initial values can be assigned when we define instances of the type **horse**.

Following the closing brace of the structure definition, we have a declaration of an instance of the structure **horse**, as the variable **Dobbin**. Initial values are also assigned to the member variables, in a manner similar to that used to initialize arrays, so this also defines the variable **Dobbin**. The values appearing between the final pair of braces apply in sequence, so for the structure variable **Dobbin**, member variable **age** is 24, **height** is 17, **name** is "Dobbin", **father** is the string "Trigger", and **mother** is the string "Flossie". The statement is finally terminated with a semicolon. The variable **Dobbin** now refers to the complete collection of members included in the structure. The memory occupied by the structure **Dobbin** is shown in the following figure. You can always find out the amount of memory occupied by a structure using the operator **sizeof**.

Separating Structure Definition and Structure Variable Declaration

We could have separated the declaration of the structure from the declaration of the structure variable. Instead of the statements above, we could have written:

```
struct horse
    {
        int age;
        int height;

        char name[20];
        char father[20];
        char mother[20];
    };

struct horse Dobbin =
        {
            24, 17,"Dobbin", "Trigger", "Flossie"
        };
```

We now have two separate statements, the definition of the structure tag **horse**, and the declaration of one variable of that type, **Dobbin**. Both the structure declaration and the structure variable definition statements end with a semi-colon. Notice that we have spread the definition of the variable **Dobbin** across several lines for readability.

We could also add a third statement to our previous two examples to define another variable of type **horse**:

```
struct horse Trigger =
    {
      30, 15, "Trigger", "Smith", "Wesson"
    };
```

Now we have a variable **Trigger** holding the details of the father of **Dobbin**, where it's clear that the ancestors of **Trigger** are Smith and Wesson. Of course we can also declare multiple structure variables in a single statement. This is almost as easy as declaring variables of one of the standard C types. For example:

```
struct horse Piebald, Bandy;
```

The only additional item in the declaration compared with standard types is the keyword **struct**. We haven't initialized the values to keep it simple.

Accessing Structure Members

Now we know how to define a structure and declare structure variables, we need to be able to refer to the members of a structure. A structure variable name is *not* a pointer. We need a special method to access the members. This is done by writing the structure variable name, followed by a period, followed by the member variable name. For example, if we found that Dobbin had lied about his age, and was actually much younger than the initializing value would suggest, we could amend the value by writing:

```
Dobbin.age = 12;
```

Try It Out - Using Structures

We could try out what we have covered so far about structures in a simple example designed to appeal to the horse enthusiast:

```
/*    Example 11.1    Exercising the horse    */
#include <stdio.h>

void main()
{
   struct horse          /* Structure declaration     */
      {
            int age;
            int height;
            char name[20];
            char father[20];
            char mother[20];
      };

   struct horse My_first_horse;              /* Structure variable declaration */

   printf("\nEnter the name of the horse: " );
   scanf("%s", My_first_horse.name );     /* Read the horse's name      */

   printf("\nHow old is %s? ", My_first_horse.name );
   scanf("%d", &My_first_horse.age );     /* Read the horse's age       */

   printf("\nHow high is %s ( in hands )? ", My_first_horse.name );
   scanf("%d", &My_first_horse.height ); /* Read the horse's height     */

   printf("\nWho is %s's father? ", My_first_horse.name );
   scanf("%s", My_first_horse.father );  /* Get the father's name       */

   printf("\nWho is %s's mother? ", My_first_horse.name );
   scanf("%s", My_first_horse.mother );  /* Get the mother's name       */
```

Try It Out!

387

```
/* Now tell them what we know.   */
printf("\n\n%s is %d years old, %d hands high,",
        My_first_horse.name, My_first_horse.age, My_first_horse.height);
printf(" and has %s and %s as parents.",
                    My_first_horse.father, My_first_horse.mother );
}
```

Depending on what data you key in, you should get output approximating to:

```
Enter the name of the horse: Neddy

How old is Neddy? 12

How high is Neddy ( in hands )? 14

Who is Neddy's father? Bertie

Who is Neddy's mother? Nellie


Neddy is 12 years old, 14 hands high, and has Bertie and Nellie as parents.
```

How It Works

The means of referencing members of a structure makes it very easy to follow what's going on in this example. The structure **horse** is declared by:

```
struct horse   {               /* Structure declaration    */
        int age;
        int height;
        char name[20];
        char father[20];
        char mother[20];
    };
```

The structure has two integer members, **age** and **height**, and three **char** array members, **name**, **father**, and **mother**. Since we have just a semi-colon following the closing brace, no variables of type **horse** are declared here.

After declaring the structure **horse,** we have the statement:

```
struct horse My_first_horse;        /* Structure variable declaration    */
```

This declares one variable of type **horse**, which is **My_first_horse**. This variable has no initial values assigned in the definition.

We then read in the data for the **name** member with the statement:

```
scanf("%s", My_first_horse.name );          /* Read the horse's name    */
```

No **address of** operator (**&**) is necessary here because the member name is an array, so we implicitly transfer the address of the first array element to the function **scanf()**. We reference the member by writing the structure name, **My_first_horse**, followed by a period, followed by the member name, **name**. Other than the notation used to access it, using a structure member is the same as using any other variable.

The following statements read the data for each of the other members of the structure in exactly the same manner, prompting in each case for the input. Once input is complete, the values read are output to the display as a single line using the statement:

```
printf("\n\n%s is %d years old, %d hands high,",
          My_first_horse.name, My_first_horse.age, My_first_horse.height);
  printf(" and has %s and %s as parents.",
                        My_first_horse.father, My_first_horse.mother );
```

The long names tend to make this statement appear complicated, but it's very straightforward. Following the standard sort of format control string, there is the name of each of the five member variables.

Unnamed Structures

You don't have to give a structure a tag name. Where you can declare the structure and any instances of the structure you need in a single statement, you can omit it. In the last example, instead of the structure declaration for type **horse**, followed by the instance declaration for **My_first_horse**, we could have written the statement:

```
struct    {            /* Structure declaration                   */
      int age;
      int height;
      char name[20];
      char father[20];
      char mother[20];
   } My_first_horse;        /* and structure variable declaration combined   */
```

A disadvantage with this approach is that we can no longer define further instances of the structure in another statement. All the variables of this structure type that you require in your program must be defined in the one statement.

Arrays of Structures

Our basic approach to keeping horse data is fine as far as it goes. It will probably begin to be a bit cumbersome by the time we have accumulated 50 or 100 horses. We need a more stable method for handling a lot of horses. It's exactly the same problem that we had with variables, which we solved using an array. We can do the same here. We can declare a **horse** array.

Try It Out - Using Arrays of Structures

Let's saddle up and extend the previous example to handle several horses:

```
/*    Example 11.2    Exercising the horse    */
#include <stdio.h>
void main()
{
   struct horse   {                         /* Structure declaration      */
           int age;
           int height;
           char name[20];
           char father[20];
           char mother[20];
        };

   struct horse My_horses[50];      /* Structure array declaration    */
   int hcount = 0;                  /* Count of the number of horses  */
   int i = 0;
   char test = '\0';                /* Test value for ending          */


   for(hcount = 0; hcount < 50 ; hcount++ )
   {
      printf("\nDo you want to enter details of a%s horse (Y or N)? "
                   , hcount?"nother " : "" );
      scanf(" %c", &test );
      if(test == 'N' || test == 'n')
         break;
      printf("\nEnter the name of the horse: " );
      scanf("%s", My_horses[hcount].name );        /* Read the horse's name  */
```

Try It Out!

```
      printf("\nHow old is %s? ", My_horses[hcount].name );
      scanf("%d", &My_horses[hcount].age );          /* Read the horse's age     */

      printf("\nHow high is %s ( in hands )? ", My_horses[hcount].name );
      scanf("%d", &My_horses[hcount].height );   /* Read the horse's height*/

      printf("\nWho is %s's father? ", My_horses[hcount].name );
      scanf("%s", My_horses[hcount].father );     /* Get the father's name    */

      printf("\nWho is %s's mother? ", My_horses[hcount].name );
      scanf("%s", My_horses[hcount].mother );     /* Get the mother's name    */
   }

  /* Now tell them what we know.   */
  for (i = 0 ; i < hcount ; i++ )
  {
     printf("\n\n%s is %d years old, %d hands high,",
         My_horses[ i ].name, My_horses[ i ].age, My_horses[ i ].height);
     printf(" and has %s and %s as parents.",
                     My_horses[ i ].father, My_horses[ i ].mother );
  }
}
```

How It Works

In this version of equine data processing, we first declare the **horse** structure, and this is followed by the declaration:

```
struct horse My_horses[50];          /* Structure array declaration     */
```

This declares the variable **My_horses**, which is an array of fifty such structures. Apart from the keyword **struct**, it's just like any other array declaration.

We then have a **for** loop controlled by:

```
for(hcount = 0; hcount < 50 ; hcount++ )
```

providing for the possibility of reading data on up to 50 horses. The loop control variable, **hcount**, is used to accumulate the total number of **horse** structures entered. The first action in the loop is in the statements:

```
printf("\nDo you want to enter details of a%s horse (Y or N)? "
               , hcount?"nother " : "" );
scanf(" %c", &test );
if(test == 'N' || test == 'n')
   break;
```

On each iteration, you are prompted to indicate by entering 'Y' or 'N', whether or not you want to enter data for another horse. The `printf()` statement for this uses the conditional operator to insert "nother" into the output on every iteration after the first. After reading the character you enter using `scanf()`, the `if` statement executes a `break` which immediately exits from the loop if you respond negatively.

The succeeding sequence of `printf()` and `scanf()` statements are much the same as before, but there are two points of note in these. Look at the statement:

```
    scanf("%s", My_horses[hcount].name );        /* Read the horse's name   */
```

You can see the method for referencing the member of one element of an array of structures is easier to write than to say. The structure array name has an index in square brackets, to which a period and the member name are appended. If you wanted to reference the third element, for example, of the `name` array for the fourth structure element, you would write:

```
    My_horses[3].name[2]
```

Of course, the index values start from zero, as with arrays of other types of value, so the fourth element of the structure array has the index value 3, and the third element of the member array is accessed by the index value 2.

Now look at the statement:

```
    scanf("%d", &My_horses[hcount].age );        /* Read the horse's age   */
```

The arguments to `scanf()` don't need the `&` for the string array variables such as `My_horses[hcount].name`, but do require them for the integer arguments `My_horses[hcount].age` and `My_horses[hcount].height`. It's very easy to forget the `address of` operator when reading values for variables like these.

The output from this last program example is little different to the previous example we saw dealing with a single horse. The main addition is the prompt for each horse data input. Once all data has been entered or, if you have the stamina, data on 50 horses have been entered, the program outputs a summary of all the data entered, one line per horse. The whole mechanism works very well in the mane, almost an unbridled success you might say.

You should not be misled at this point, and think the techniques are limited to equine applications. They can also be applied to porcine problems with equanimity.

Structures in Expressions

A member of a structure that is one of the built-in types can be used as any other variable in an expression. Using the structure from Example 11.2, we could write the rather meaningless computation:

```
My_horses[1].height = ( My_horses[2].height + My_horses[3].height )/2;
```

We can think of no good reason why the height of one horse should be the average of two other horses' heights unless there's some Frankenstein-like assembly going on, but it is a legal statement.

We can also use a complete structure element in an assignment statement:

```
My_horses[1] = My_horses[2];
```

This statement causes all the members of the structure `My_horses[2]` to be copied to the structure `My_horses[1]`, resulting in the two structures becoming identical. The only other operation that's possible with a whole structure is to take its address using the `&` operator. You can't add, compare, or perform any other operations with a structure. However, if you can attach meaning to these kinds of operations, you can always write your own functions to perform them.

Pointers to Structures

The ability to obtain the address of a structure raises the question of whether we can have pointers to structures. Since we can take the address of a structure, the possibility of declaring a pointer to a structure naturally follows. We use the notation we have already seen used with other types of variables:

```
struct horse *phorse;
```

This declares a pointer, `phorse`, to a structure of type `horse`. We can now set this to have the value of the address of a particular structure using exactly the same kind of statement that we have been using for other types of pointer. For example:

```
phorse = &My_horses[1];
```

Now `phorse` points to the structure `My_horses[1]`. We can immediately reference elements of this structure through our pointer. If we wanted to display the name member of this structure we could write:

```
printf("\nThe name is %s.", (*phorse).name );
```

The parentheses around the dereferenced pointer are essential because the precedence of the member selection operator, `.`, is higher than that of the pointer dereferencing operator, `*`. There is also a new way of expressing the operation of selecting a member of a structure through a pointer that is much more readable and intuitive. We could write the previous statement as:

```
printf("\nThe name is %s.", phorse -> name );
```

So we don't need parentheses or an asterisk. In case it is not obvious, you construct the operator `->` from a minus sign immediately followed by the symbol for greater than. This notation is almost invariably used in preference to the usual pointer dereferencing notation we used first, because it makes your programs so much easier to read.

Dynamic Memory Allocation For Structures

We have virtually all the tools to rewrite Example 11.2 with much more economical use of memory. In the original version we allocated the memory for an array of 50 `horse` structures, even when in practice we might not need anything like this amount. The only missing tool is an array of pointers to structures, which is declared very easily as in the statement:

```
struct horse *phorse[50];
```

This declares an array of 50 pointers to structures of type `horse`. As with previous pointer examples, only memory for the pointers has been allocated by this statement. You must still allocate the memory necessary to store the members of each structure that you need.

Try It Out - Using Pointers With Structures

This works as demonstrated in the following example:

```
/*    Example 11.3    Pointing out the horses    */
#include <stdio.h>
#include <stdlib.h>

void main()
{
   struct horse   {              /* Structure declaration               */
           int age;
           int height;
           char name[20];
           char father[20];
           char mother[20];
        };

   struct horse *phorse[50];  /* pointer to structure array declaration */
   int hcount = 0;             /* Count of the number of horses          */
   int i = 0;
   char test = '\0';           /* Test value for ending input            */


   for(hcount = 0; hcount < 50 ; hcount++ )
   {
      printf("\nDo you want to enter details of a%s horse (Y or N)? "
                  , hcount?"nother " : "" );
      scanf(" %c", &test );
      if(test == 'N' || test == 'n')
         break;

      /* allocate memory to hold a structure    */
      phorse[hcount] = ( struct horse * ) malloc( sizeof( struct horse ) );

      printf("\nEnter the name of the horse: " );
      scanf("%s", phorse[hcount] -> name );    /* Read the horse's name    */

      printf("\nHow old is %s? ", phorse[hcount] -> name );
      scanf("%d", &phorse[hcount] -> age );    /* Read the horse's age     */

      printf("\nHow high is %s ( in hands )? ", phorse[hcount] -> name );
      scanf("%d", &phorse[hcount] -> height );/* Read the horse's height   */

      printf("\nWho is %s's father? ", phorse[hcount] -> name );
      scanf("%s", phorse[hcount] -> father ); /* Get the father's name     */

      printf("\nWho is %s's mother? ", phorse[hcount] -> name );
      scanf("%s", phorse[hcount] -> mother ); /* Get the mother's name     */
   }
```

```
/* Now tell them what we know.   */
for (i = 0 ; i < hcount ; i++ )
{
   printf("\n\n%s is %d years old, %d hands high," ,
          phorse[i] -> name, phorse[i] -> age, phorse[i] -> height);
   printf (" and has %s and %s as parents.",
          phorse[i] -> father, phorse[i] -> mother );
}
}
```

The output should be exactly the same as that from Example 11.2, given the same input.

How It Works

This looks very similar to the previous version but operates rather differently. Initially, we don't have any memory allocated to any structures. The declaration:

```
struct horse *phorse[50];     /* pointer to structure array declaration  */
```

only defines 50 pointers to structures of type **horse**. We still have to find somewhere to put the structures to which we are going to point.

```
phorse[hcount] = ( struct horse * ) malloc( sizeof( struct horse ) );
```

In this statement we allocate the space for each structure as it is required. Let's have a quick reminder about how the **malloc()** function works. The **malloc()** function allocates the number of bytes specified by its argument and returns the address of the block of memory allocated as a pointer to type **void**. In our case we use the **sizeof** operator to provide the value required.

It's very important to use **sizeof** when you need the number of bytes occupied by a structure. It doesn't necessarily correspond to the sum of the bytes occupied by each of its individual members so you are likely to get it wrong if you work it out yourself. As you may already know, variables other than type **char** are stored beginning on an address which is a multiple of 2 for two byte variables, a multiple of 4 for four byte variables and so on. This can result in unused bytes occurring between member variables of different types, depending on their sequence. These have to be accounted for in the number of bytes allocated for a structure. An illustration of how this can occur is in the following figure.

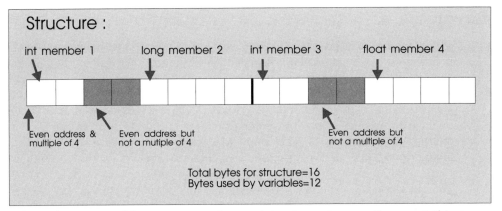

As the value returned by `malloc()` is a pointer to **void**, we then cast this to the type we require with the expression (**struct horse ***). This enables the pointer to be incremented or decremented correctly, if required.

```
scanf("%s", phorse[hcount] -> name );   /* Read the horse's name   */
```

In this statement you can see we use the new notation we discussed in the previous section for selecting members of a structure through a pointer. It's much clearer than `(*phorse[hcount]).name`, isn't it? All subsequent references to member of a specific **horse** structure use the new notation.

Finally in the program, we display a summary of all the data entered for each horse, and free the memory as we go along.

More on Structure Members

So far, we have seen that any of the basic types, including arrays, can be members of a structure. But there's more. You can also make a structure a member of a structure. Furthermore, not only can pointers be members of a structure, but a pointer to a structure can also be a member.

This opens up a whole new range of possibilities in programming using structures, and at the same time increases the potential levels of confusion for the beginner. Lets look at each of these possibilities in sequence, and see what they have to offer. Maybe it won't be a can of worms after all.

Structures as Members of a Structure

When we introduced this chapter, we talked about the needs of horse breeders and, in particular, the need to manage a variety of details about each horse, including name, height, date of birth and so on. We then went on to look at Example 11.1 which carefully avoided date of birth, and substituted age instead. This was partly because dates are messy things to deal with, as they are represented by three numbers, not to mention having all the complications of leap years to cope with. It was also to show how elegantly we can use a structure as a member of a structure in this context.

We can define a structure type designed to hold dates (and here we are not talking about the fruit of the palm tree). We can specify a suitable structure with the tag name **Date**, by the statement:

```
struct Date   {
        int day;
        int month;
        int year;
    };
```

We could now define our structure **horse**, including a date of birth variable, using the statement:

```
struct horse    {
        struct Date dob;
        int height;
        char name[20];
        char father[20];
        char mother[20];
    };
```

Now we have a single variable member within the structure representing the date of birth of a horse, that is itself a structure. Now if we define an instance of the structure **horse** with the usual statement:

```
struct horse Dobbin;
```

We can define the value of the member **height** with the sort of statement we have seen:

```
Dobbin.height = 14;
```

If we want to set the date of birth in a series of assignment statements we use the logical extension of this notation:

```
Dobbin.dob.day = 5;
Dobbin.dob.month = 12;
Dobbin.dob.year = 1962;
```

and we have a very old horse. The expression **Dobbin.dob.day** is referencing an **int** variable, so we can happily use this in arithmetic or comparative expressions.. If we were to write the expression **Dobbin.dob** we would be referring to a **struct** variable of type **Date**. Since this is clearly not a basic type but is a structure, we can only use it in an assignment such as:

```
Trigger.dob = Dobbin.dob;
```

which could mean they are twins, but doesn't guarantee it.

If you can find a good reason to do it, you can extend the notion of structures that are members of a structure, to a structure that is a member of a structure that is a member of a structure. If fact, if you can make sense of it you can continue with further levels of structure. ANSI C provides for up to 15 levels. If you reach this depth of structure nesting, you are likely to be in for a bout of repetitive strain injury just typing the references to members.

Declaring a Structure Within a Structure Declaration

We could have declared the **Date** structure within the horse structure definition, as in the statement:

```
struct horse
    {
        struct Date
            {
                int day;
                int month;
                int year;
            } dob;

        int height;
        char name[20];
        char father[20];
        char mother[20];
    };
```

This has an interesting effect. Because the declaration is enclosed within the scope of the **horse** structure definition, it doesn't exist outside it, and it now becomes impossible to declare a **Date** variable external to the **horse** structure. Of course, each instance of a **horse** type variable would contain the **Date** type member, **dob**. But any statement such as:

```
struct Date my_date;
```

will cause a compiler error. The message generated will say that the structure type **Date** is undefined. If you need to use it outside the structure **horse**, its definition must be placed outside too.

Pointers to Structures as Structure Members

Any pointer can be a member of a structure. This includes pointers which point to structures. A pointer structure member that points to the same type of structure is also permitted. For example, our **horse** type structure could contain a pointer to a **horse** type structure. Interesting, but is it of any use? Well, as it happens, it is.

Try It Out - Pointers to Structures as Structure Members

We can demonstrate this with a modification of the last example:

```
/*    Example 11.4    Daisy chaining the horses   */
#include <stdio.h>
#include <stdlib.h>

void main()
{
   struct horse   {                         /* Structure declaration     */
           int age;
           int height;
           char name[20];
           char father[20];
           char mother[20];
           struct horse *next;             /* Pointer to next structure  */
       };

   struct horse    *first = NULL,            /* Pointer to first horse    */
           *current = NULL,          /* Pointer to current horse  */
           *previous = NULL;         /* Pointer to previous horse */

   char test = '\0';                        /* Test value for ending input */

   for( ; ; )
```

```
   {
      printf("\nDo you want to enter details of a%s horse (Y or N)? "
                  , first != NULL?"nother " : "" );
      scanf(" %c", &test );
      if(test == 'N' || test == 'n')
         break;

      /* Allocate memory for a structure */
      current = ( struct horse * ) malloc( sizeof( struct horse ) );

      if( first == NULL )
         first = current;                     /* Set pointer to first horse   */

      if( previous != NULL )
         previous -> next = current; /* Set next value for previous horse */

      printf("\nEnter the name of the horse: " );
      scanf("%s", current -> name );          /* Read the horse's name        */

      printf("\nHow old is %s? ", current -> name );
      scanf("%d", &current -> age );          /* Read the horse's age         */

      printf("\nHow high is %s ( in hands )? ", current -> name );
      scanf("%d", &current -> height );      /* Read the horse's height       */

      printf("\nWho is %s's father? ", current -> name );
      scanf("%s", current -> father );        /* Get the father's name        */

      printf("\nWho is %s's mother? ", current -> name );
      scanf("%s", current -> mother );        /* Get the mother's name        */

      current -> next = NULL;                 /* In case its the last...       */
      previous = current;                     /* Save address of last horse    */
   }

   /* Now tell them what we know.   */
   current = first;

   while ( current != NULL )
   {
      printf("\n\n%s is %d years old, %d hands high,",
                  current -> name, current -> age, current -> height);
      printf(" and has %s and %s as parents.",
                  current -> father, current -> mother );
      previous = current;
      current = current -> next;
      free( previous );
   }
}
```

This example should produce the same output as Example 9.3, given the same input, but here we have yet another mode of operation.

How It Works

This time, not only do we have no space for structures allocated, but we have only three pointers defined initially. These are declared and defined in the statement:

```
struct horse    *first = NULL,      /* Pointer to first horse       */
          *current = NULL,    /* Pointer to current horse     */
          *previous = NULL;   /* Pointer to previous horse    */
```

Each of the pointers has been defined as a pointer to a **horse** structure. The pointer **first** is used solely to store the address of the first structure. The second and third pointers are working storage to hold the address of the current **horse** structure we are working with, and to keep track of the address of the previous structure that was processed.

We have added a member to our structure **horse**, with the name **next**, which is a pointer to a **horse** type structure. This will be used to link all the horses we have together, where each **horse** structure will have a pointer containing the address of the next. The last one is an exception of course. Its **next** pointer will be **NULL**. The structure is otherwise exactly as we had previously. It is shown in the following figure:

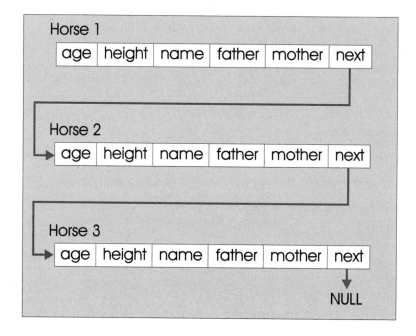

Our input loop is controlled by:

```
for( ; ; )
```

Our input loop is now an indefinite loop since we don't have an array to worry about. We don't need to mess about with indexes. It's also unnecessary to keep count of how many sets of data are read in, so we don't need the variable **hcount** or the loop variable **i**. Since we allocate memory for each horse, we can just take them as they come.

The initial statements in the loop are:

```
    printf("\nDo you want to enter details of a%s horse (Y or N)? "
                     , first != NULL?"nother " : "" );
    scanf(" %c", &test );
    if(test == 'N' || test == 'n')
       break;
```

After the prompt, we exit from the loop if the response 'N' or 'n' is detected. Otherwise we expect another set of structure members to be entered. We use the pointer **first** to get a slightly different prompt on the second and subsequent iterations, since the only time it will be **NULL** is on the first loop iteration.

Assuming we get past the initial question in the loop, we execute the statements:

```
    current = ( struct horse * ) malloc( sizeof( struct horse ) );

    if( first == NULL )
       first = current;                  /* Set pointer to first horse       */

    if( previous != NULL )
       previous -> next = current;  /* Set next value for previous horse */
```

On each iteration, we allocate the memory necessary for the current structure. To keep things short, we don't check for a **NULL** return from **malloc()**, although really you ought to do this in practice. If the pointer **first** is **NULL**, we must be on the first loop iteration, and this must be the first structure about to be entered. Consequently, we set the pointer **first** to the pointer value we have just obtained from **malloc()**, which is stored in the variable **current**. The address in **first** is our key to accessing the first horse in the chain. We can get to any of the others by starting with the address in **first**, then, by looking in the member pointer **next**, obtain the address of the next, and so on.

The **next** pointer needs to point to the next structure, but the address of the next structure can only be determined once we have the next structure. Therefore, on the second and subsequent iterations we store the address of the current structure in the member **next** of the previous structure, whose address we will have saved in **previous**. On the first iteration, the pointer **previous** will be **NULL** at this point, so of course we do nothing. This second **if** could have been replaced by an **else** clause for the first **if**, since the pointer **previous** is not **NULL** when the pointer **first** is not **NULL**.

At the end of the loop, following all the input statements, we have the statements:

```
current -> next = NULL;          /* In case its the last...   */
previous = current;              /* Save address of last horse   */
```

The pointer **next** in the structure pointed to by **current** that we are presently working with, is set to **NULL**, in case this is the last structure and there is no next structure. If there is a next structure, this pointer **next** will be filled in on the next iteration. The pointer **previous** is set to **current**, ready for the next iteration, because by then, it will be.

The strategy of the program is to generate a daisy chain of **horse** structures, where the **next** member of each structure points to the next structure in the chain. The last is an exception since there is no next **horse**, so the **next** pointer contains **NULL**. The jargon name for this arrangement is a **linked list**, which is what we showed in the last figure, repeated here.

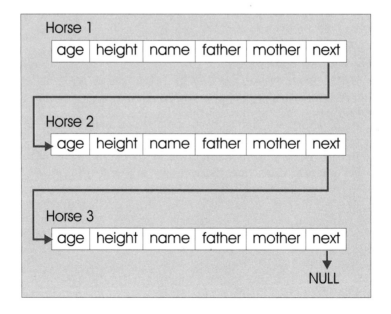

Once we have our `horse` data in a linked list, we process it by starting with the first, then getting the next through the pointer member `next`. When the pointer `next` is `NULL`, we know we have reached the end of the list. This is how we generate the output list of all the input.

Some programmers seem to go through life regarding a linked list as some kind of curiosity. In applications where you must arrange to process an unknown number of structures such as we have here, it's invaluable. The main advantages of a linked list are with memory usage and ease of handling. We only occupy the minimum memory necessary to store and process the list. Even though the memory used may be fragmented, we have no problem progressing from one structure to the next. As a consequence, in a practical situation where you may need to deal with several different types of objects simultaneously, each can be handled using its own linked list, with the result that memory use is optimized. There is a small cloud associated with this, as there is with any silver lining - you pay a penalty in slower access to the data.

The output process shows how a linked list is accessed, as it steps through the linked list we have created with the statements:

```
current = first;

while ( current != NULL )
{
    printf("\n\n%s is %d years old, %d hands high,",
                current -> name, current -> age, current -> height);
    printf(" and has %s and %s as parents.",
                current -> father, current -> mother );
    previous = current;
    current = current -> next;
    free( previous );
}
```

The pointer `current` controls the output loop, and it is set to `first` at the outset. Remember that the pointer `first` contains the first structure in the list. The loop steps through the list, and as the members of each structure are displayed, the address stored in the member `next`, which points to the next structure, is assigned to `current`.

The memory for the structure just displayed, is then freed. It's obviously fairly essential that you only free the memory for a structure once you have no further need to reference it. It's easy to fall into the trap of putting the call of the function `free()` just after you have output all the values, which would create a little confusion.

For the last structure in the linked list, the pointer `next` will contain `NULL` and the loop will terminate.

Doubly Linked Lists

A disadvantage of the linked list is that you can only go forwards. A small modification of the idea gives us the doubly linked list, which will allow us to go through a list in either direction. The trick is to include an extra pointer in each structure to record the address of the previous structure.

Try It Out - Doubly Linked Lists

You can see this in a modified version of Example 11.4:

```
/*   Example 11.5   Daisy chaining the horses both ways   */
#include <stdio.h>
#include <stdlib.h>

void main()
{
    struct horse                /* Structure declaration        */
       {
             int age;
             int height;
             char name[20];
             char father[20];
             char mother[20];
             struct horse    *next,    /* Pointer to next structure     */
                     *previous;        /* Pointer to previous structure */
       };

    struct horse    *first = NULL,     /* Pointer to first horse        */
          *current = NULL,             /* Pointer to current horse      */
          *last = NULL;                /* Pointer to previous horse     */

    char test = '\0';                  /* Test value for ending input   */

    for( ; ; )
    {
       printf("\nDo you want to enter details of a%s horse (Y or N)? "
                   , first == NULL?"nother " : "" );
       scanf(" %c", &test );
       if(test == 'N' || test == 'n')
          break;

       /* Allocate memory for each new horse structure */
       current = ( struct horse * ) malloc( sizeof( struct horse ) );
```

Try It Out!

```
      if( first == NULL )
      {
         first = current;                  /* Set pointer to first horse   */
         current -> previous = NULL;
      }
      else
      {
         last ->next = current;   /* Set next address for previous horse   */
         current -> previous = last; /* Previous address for current horse */
      }

      printf("\nEnter the name of the horse: " );
      scanf("%s", current -> name );        /* Read the horse's name       */

      printf("\nHow old is %s? ", current -> name );
      scanf("%d", &current -> age );        /* Read the horse's age        */

      printf("\nHow high is %s ( in hands )? ", current -> name );
      scanf("%d", &current -> height );     /* Read the horse's height      */

      printf("\nWho is %s's father? ", current -> name );
      scanf("%s", current -> father );      /* Get the father's name       */

      printf("\nWho is %s's mother? ", current -> name );
      scanf("%s", current -> mother );      /* Get the mother's name       */

      current -> next = NULL;               /* In case its the last horse...*/
      last = current;                       /* Save address of last horse   */
   }

   /* Now tell them what we know.    */
   while ( current != NULL )         /* Output horse data in reverse order   */
   {
      printf("\n\n%s is %d years old, %d hands high,",
                current -> name, current -> age, current -> height);
      printf(" and has %s and %s as parents.",
                current -> father, current -> mother );
      last = current;      /* Save pointer to enable memory to be freed      */
      current = current -> previous; /* current points to previous in list */
      free( last);     /* Free memory for the horse we output */
   }
}
```

For the same input, this program should produce the same output as before, except that the data on horses entered is displayed in reverse order to that of entry, just to show we can do it.

How It Works

Our initial pointer declarations are now:

```
struct horse    *first = NULL,      /* Pointer to first horse      */
      *current = NULL,              /* Pointer to current horse    */
      *last = NULL;                 /* Pointer to previous horse   */
```

We have changed the name of the pointer recording the `horse` structure entered on the previous iteration of the loop to `last`. The name change is not strictly necessary, but it helps to avoid confusion with the structure member `previous` we have added to the structure `horse`.

The structure `horse` is declared as:

```
struct horse                  /* Structure declaration           */
   {
         int age;
         int height;
         char name[20];
         char father[20];
         char mother[20];
         struct horse    *next,    /* Pointer to next structure       */
                 *previous;        /* Pointer to previous structure   */
   };
```

The structure `horse` now contains two pointers, one to point forwards in the list called `next`, the other to point backwards called `previous`. This allows the list to be traversed in either direction, as is demonstrated by the fact that we output the data at the end of the program in reverse order.

Aside from the output, the only changes to the program are to add the statements to take care of the entries for the pointer structure member `previous`. In the beginning of the input loop we have:

```
if( first == NULL )
{
   first = current;                 /* Set pointer to first horse      */
   current -> previous = NULL;
}
else
{
   last ->next = current;     /* Set next address for previous horse */
   current -> previous = last; /* Previous address for current horse */
}
```

Here we have taken the option of writing one **if** with an **else**, rather than the two **if**s we had in the previous version. The only material difference is setting the value of the structure member **previous**. For the first structure it is set to **NULL**, and for all subsequent structures it is set to the pointer **last**, whose value was saved on the preceding iteration.

The other change is at the end of the input loop:

```
last = current;              /* Save address of last horse   */
```

This statement is added to allow the pointer **previous** in the next structure to be set to the appropriate value which we are recording in the variable **last**. The address of the structure we have just processed is the value required to be inserted in the pointer member **previous** for the structure to be entered on the next iteration.

The output process is virtually the same as in the previous example, except that we start from the last structure in the list, and work back to the first.

Bit-Fields in a Structure

Bit-fields provide a mechanism that allows you to define variables that are each one or more binary bits within a single integer word, that you can nevertheless refer to explicitly with an individual member name for each. These are used when memory is at a premium, and you need to use it as sparingly as possible. However, they will slow your program down appreciably compared to using standard variable types. An example of declaring a bit-field is shown here:

```
struct   {
      unsigned int   flag1 : 1;
      unsigned int   flag2 : 1;
      unsigned int   flag3 : 2;
      unsigned int   flag4 : 3;
   } indicators;
```

This defines an instance of a structure with the name `indicators` which contains four bit fields with the names `flag1` through `flag4`. These will all be stored in a single word, as illustrated in the following figure.

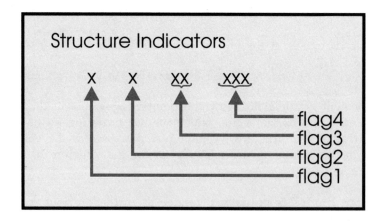

The first two of these, being a single bit specified by the 1 in their definition, can only assume the values 0 or 1. The third, `flag3`, has 2 bits and so can have a value from 0 to 3. The last, `flag4` can have values from 0 to 7 since it has 3 bits. They are referenced in the same manner as other structure members. For example:

```
indicators.flag4 = 5;
indicators.flag3 = indicators.flag1 = 1;
```

You will rarely if ever, have a need for this facility. We have included them here for completeness.

Structures and Functions

Since structures represent such a powerful feature of the C language, their use with functions is very important. We will now look at how we can pass structures as arguments to a function, and how we can return a structure from a function.

Structures as Arguments to Functions

There is nothing unusual in the method for passing a structure as an argument to a function. It is exactly the same as passing any other variable. Analogous to our **horse** structure, we could construct the structure:

```
struct family
   {
         char name[20];
         int age;
         char father[ 20 ];
         char mother[ 20];
   };
```

We could then construct a function to test whether two members of the type **family** were siblings:

```
char siblings(struct family member1, struct family member2)
{
    if( strcmp( member1.mother, member2.mother ) == 0 )
      return 1;
    else
      return 0;
}
```

This function has two arguments, each of which is a structure. It simply compares the strings corresponding to the member **mother** for each structure. If they are the same, they are siblings and 1 is returned. Otherwise they can't be siblings so 0 is returned. We are ignoring the effects of divorce, in vitro fertilization, and any other possibilities which may make this test inadequate.

Pointers to Structures as Function Arguments

Remember that a copy of the value of an argument is transferred to a function when it's called. If the argument is a large structure, this can take quite a time, as well as occupying whatever memory a copy of the structure takes. Under these circumstances you should use a pointer to a structure as an argument. This avoids the memory consumption and copying time, as now only a copy of the pointer is made. The function will access the original structure directly through the pointer. More often than not, structures are passed to a function using a pointer, just for efficiency.

Of course, there is a downside to this. The pass by value mechanism provides good protection against accidental modification of values in a calling function, by a called function. However, if you don't need to modify the values pointed to by a pointer argument, and you just want to access and use them, there is a technique for getting a degree of protection even though you are passing pointers to a function. Have a look at the last function `siblings()`. It doesn't need to modify the structures passed to it, it only needs to compare members. We could therefore rewrite its prototype (and correspondingly alter the function header) as:

```
char siblings( const struct family member1, const struct family member2);
```

You will recall the `const` modifier from earlier in the book, where we used it to make a variable effectively a constant. This function declaration specifies the parameters as constants. This implies that the arguments transferred to the function will be treated as constants within the function. Any attempt to change them will cause an error message during compilation. Of course, this doesn't affect their status as variables in the calling program. The `const` keyword only applies to the values while the function is executing. So there is no restriction on calling the function with different arguments at different times.

Returning a Structure as a Function Return Value

There is nothing unusual about returning a structure from a function either. The function prototype merely has to reflect the fact in the normal way. For example:

```
struct horse my_fun(void);
```

This is a prototype for a function taking no arguments, but returning a structure of type `horse`. While you can return a structure from a function, it is often more convenient to return a pointer to a structure.

Try It Out - Returning a Pointer to a Structure

To demonstrate how this works, let's rewrite our previous `horse` example in terms of humans, and perform the input in a separate function:

```
/*    Example 11.6    Basics of a family tree    */
#include <stdio.h>
#include <stdlib.h>

   struct Family *get_person(void);      /* Prototype for input function   */

   struct Date
      {
            int day;
            int month;
            int year;
      };

   struct Family                         /* Family structure declaration   */
      {
            struct Date dob;
            char name[20];
            char father[20];
            char mother[20];
            struct Family    *next,      /* Pointer to next structure      */
            *previous;                   /* Pointer to previous structure  */
      };

void main()
{
   struct Family    *first = NULL,       /* Pointer to first person        */
            *current = NULL,             /* Pointer to current person      */
            *last = NULL;                /* Pointer to previous person     */

   char more = '\0';                     /* Test value for ending input    */

   for( ; ; )
   {
      printf("\nDo you want to enter details of a%s person (Y or N)? "
                  , first != NULL?"nother " : "" );
      scanf(" %c", &more );
      if(more == 'N' || more == 'n')
         break;

      current = get_person();

      if( first == NULL )
      {
         first = current;                       /* Set pointer to first Family   */
         last = current;                        /* Remember for next iteration   */
      }
      else
      {
         last ->next = current;     /* Set next address for previous Family */
         current -> previous = last;/* Set previous address for current    */
         last = current;            /* Remember for next iteration          */
```

```
            }
        }

        /* Now tell them what we know.       */
        while ( current  != NULL )       /* Output Family data in reverse order   */
        {
           printf("\n%s was born %d/%d/%d, and has %s and %s as parents.",
              current -> name, current -> dob.day, current -> dob.month,
              current -> dob. year, current -> father, current -> mother );
           last = current;               /* Save pointer to enable memory to be freed*/
           current = current -> previous;  /* current points to previous list   */
           free( last);                  /* Free memory for the Family we output     */
        }
    }

    /*   Function to input data on Family members   */
    struct Family *get_person( void )
    {
        struct Family *temp;             /* Define temporary structure pointer*/

    /* Allocate memory for a structure */
        temp = ( struct Family * ) malloc( sizeof( struct Family ) );

        printf("\nEnter the name of the person: " );
        scanf("%s", temp -> name );          /* Read the Family's name               */

        printf("\nEnter %s's date of birth (day month year); ", temp -> name  );
        scanf("%d %d %d",
               &temp -> dob.day, &temp -> dob.month, &temp -> dob.year );

        printf("\nWho is %s's father? ", temp -> name );
        scanf("%s", temp -> father );        /* Get the father's name                */

        printf("\nWho is %s's mother? ", temp -> name );
        scanf("%s", temp -> mother );        /* Get the mother's name                */

        temp -> next = temp -> previous = NULL;      /* Set pointers to NULL     */

        return temp;                         /* Return address of Family structure   */
    }
```

How It Works

Although it looks like a lot of code, you should find this example quite straightforward. It operates very similarly to the previous example, but organized as two functions instead of just one.

The structure declaration:

```
struct Date
    {
            int day;
            int month;
            int year;
    };
```

defines a structure type **Date** with three members, **day**, **month**, and **year**, which are all declared as integers. No instances of the structure are declared at this point.

The declaration:

```
struct Family               /* Family structure declaration    */
    {
            struct Date dob;
            char name[20];
            char father[20];
            char mother[20];
            struct Family    *next,   /* Pointer to next structure       */
            *previous;                /* Pointer to previous structure   */
    };
```

defines a structure type **Family**, which has a **Date** type structure as its first member. It then has three conventional **char** arrays as members. The last two members are pointers to structures. They are intended to allow a doubly linked list to be constructed, being pointers to the next and previous structures in the list respectively.

Both structure declarations are external to all the functions, and are therefore available globally. This is necessary because we want to define **Family** structure variables in both the functions **main()** and **get_person()**. Of course, only the specification of the structure type is accessible globally. All the variables of type **Family** declared within each function are local in scope to the function in which they are declared.

The function **get_person()** has the prototype:

```
    struct Family *get_person(void);        /* Prototype for input function    */
```

This indicates that it accepts no arguments, but returns a pointer to a **Family** structure. The definition of the pointer as a return type is virtually identical in its appearance to a declaration for a pointer variable.

The process parallels the operation of Example 11.5, with the difference that we have global structure type declarations, and we input a structure within a separate function. After verifying that you want to enter data by checking your response in **more**, the function **main()** calls the function **get_person()**. Within the function **get_person()**, we declare the pointer:

```
struct Family *temp;          /* Define temporary structure pointer*/
```

This is a pointer to a **Family** type structure, and has local scope. The fact that the declaration of the structure type is global has no bearing on the scope of instances of the structure. The scope of each instance declared, will depend on where the declaration is placed in the program.

The first action within the function **get_person()** is:

```
temp = ( struct Family * ) malloc( sizeof( struct Family ) );
```

This obtains sufficient memory through **malloc()** to store a **Family** type structure, and store the address returned in the pointer variable **temp**. Although **temp** is local, and will go out of scope at the end of the function **get_person()**, the memory allocated by **malloc()** is not. It remains until you free it yourself, or you exit from the program completely.

The function **get_person()** then reads in all the basic data for a person, and stores it into the structure pointed to by **temp**.

The last statement in the function **get_person()** is:

```
return temp;                  /* Return address of Family structure   */
```

This finally returns a copy of the pointer to the structure it has created. Even though **temp** will no longer exist after the return, the address it contained pointing to the memory block obtained from **malloc()** is still valid.

Back in `main()` the returned pointer is stored in the variable `current`, and is also saved in the variable `first` if this is the first iteration. This is done because we don't want to lose track of the first structure in the list. We also remember the pointer `current` in the variable `last`, so that on the next iteration we can fill in the backward pointer member, `previous` for the current person whose data has just been obtained. After all the input data has been read, the program outputs a summary to the screen in reverse order, in a similar fashion to previous examples.

An Exercise in Program Modification

Perhaps we ought to produce an example combining both the use of pointers to structures as arguments, and the use of pointers to structures as return values. We can declare some additional pointers, `p_to_pa` and `p_to_ma`, in the structure type `Family` by changing it to:

```
struct Family          /* Family structure declaration    */
   {
        struct Date dob;
        char name[20];
        char father[20];
        char mother[20];
        struct Family    *next,      /* Pointer to next structure     */
                         *previous,   /* Pointer to previous structure */
                         *p_to_pa,    /* Pointer to father structure   */
                         *p_to_ma;    /* Pointer to mother structure   */
   };
```

This allows us to note the addresses of related structures in pointer members `p_to_pa` and `p_to_ma`. We will need to set them to `NULL` in `get_person()`. by adding the statement:

```
temp -> p_to_pa = temp -> p_to_ma = NULL;      /* Set pointers to NULL  */
```

just before the `return` statement.

We can now augment our program with some additional functions which will fill these in, once data for everybody has been entered. This might be coded as shown on the next page.

417

```
char test( struct Family *member1, struct Family *member2 )
{
  if( strcmp(member1 -> father, member2 -> name ) == 0 )
  {
    member1 -> p_to_pa = member2;
    return 1;
  }

  if( strcmp(member1 -> mother, member2 -> name ) == 0 )
  {
    member1 -> p_to_ma = member2;
    return 1;
  }
  else
  return 0;
}
```

```
/* Fill in pointers for mother or father relationships   */
char related (struct Family *member1, struct Family *member2 )
{
  if(test( member1, member2 ) )    return 1;
  if(test( member2, member1 ) )    return 1;
  return 0;
}
```

The function `test()` accepts pointers to `Family` structures as arguments, and checks whether `member2` is the father or mother of `member1`. If it is, the appropriate pointer is updated to reflect this, and 1 is returned, otherwise 0 is returned.

The function `related()` calls `test()` twice to test all possibilities of relationship. The return value can be used by the calling program to determine whether a pointer has been filled in or not. We now need to add some code to `main()` to use the function `related()` to fill in all the pointers in all the structures where valid addresses can be found. The following code should be inserted after the loop which inputs all the initial data:

```
current = first;

while ( current -> next != NULL ) /* Check for relation for each person in */
{                                 /*  the list up to second to last        */
   int parents = 0;          /* Declare parent count local to this block   */
   last = current;

   while( last -> next != NULL )  /* This loop tests current person        */
   {                             /*  against all the remainder in the list */
      if( related( current, last -> next ) )
```

```
        if( ++parents == 2 ) break;   /* Exit inner loop if parents found  */

    last = last -> next;
  }

  current = current -> next;
}
```

This is a relatively self-contained block of code to fill in the parent pointers where possible. Starting with the first structure, a check is made with each of the succeeding structures to see if a parent relationship exists. The checking stops for a given structure if two parents have been found, which would have filled in both pointers, or the end of the list is reached. Of necessity, some structures will have pointers where the values can't be updated. Since we don't have an infinite list, and barring some very strange family history, there will always be someone whose parent records are not included.

Of course we also need to insert prototypes for our functions `related()` and `test()` at the beginning, immediately after the prototype for the function `get_person()`. These would look like:

```
    char related( struct Family *, struct Family * );
    char test( struct Family *, struct Family * );
```

In addition, don't forget the `include` statement for the header file `STRING.H`.

To show that the pointers have been successfully inserted, we could extend the final output to display information about the parents of each person, by adding immediately after the last `printf()`, the statements:

```
if( current -> p_to_pa != NULL )
   printf("\n\t%s's birth date is %d/%d/%d  ",
          current -> father, current -> p_to_pa -> dob.day,
          current -> p_to_pa -> dob.month, current -> p_to_pa -> dob.year);
if( current -> p_to_ma != NULL )
   printf("and %s's birth date is %d/%d/%d.\n  ",
          current -> mother, current -> p_to_ma -> dob.day,
          current -> p_to_ma -> dob.month, current -> p_to_ma -> dob.year );
```

You can also amend the output loop to start from `first` in a similar manner to that employed in Example 11.4. This should then produce the dates of birth of both parents for each person using the pointers to the parents' structures, but only if the pointers have been set to valid addresses. If you have assembled all the pieces into a new example, you should have a sizable new program to play with. You could try to modify the program to output everybody in chronological order, or possibly work out how many offspring each person has.

Sharing Memory

We have already seen how economies in the use of memory can be made with the use of bit-fields, which are typically applied to handling logical variables. C has a further capability which allows you to place several variables in the same memory area. This can be applied much more widely than bit-fields when memory is short, since circumstances frequently arise in practice where you are working with several variables, but only one of them holds a valid value at any given moment.

Another instance which arises where you can share memory between a number of variables to advantage, is when your program processes a number of different kinds of data record, but only one kind at one time, the kind to be processed being determined at execution time. A third possibility is that you want to access the same data at different times, and assume it's of a different type on different occasions, although it's hard to come up with realistic contexts where this might be the case.

Unions

The facility in C which allows the same memory area to be shared by a number of different variables is called a `union`. The syntax for declaring a `union` is similar to that used for structures, and it is usually given a tag name in the same way. For example, the following statement declares a union to be shared by three variables:

```
union u_example
    {
        float decval;
        int *pnum;
        double my_value;
    } U1;
```

This statement declares a union with the tag name `u_example`, which shares memory between a floating point value `decval`, a pointer to an integer `pnum`, and a double precision floating point variable `my_value`. The statement also defines one instance of the union with the variable name `U1`. We can declare further instances of this union with a statement such as:

```
union u_example U2, U3;
```

Members of a union are accessed in exactly the same way as members of a structure. For example, to assign values to members of **U1** and **U2**, we can write:

```
U1.decval = 2.5;
U2.decval = 3.5 * U1.decval;
```

Try It Out - Using Unions

Look at the following example:

```
/* Example 11.7 The operation of a union    */
#include <stdio.h>

void main()
{
   union u_example
      {
            float decval;
            int pnum;
            double my_value;
      } U1;

   U1.my_value = 125.5;
   U1.pnum = 10;
   U1.decval = 1000.5;
   printf("\ndecval = %f\tpnum = %d\tmy_value = %lf",
                           U1.decval, U1.pnum, U1.my_value );

   printf("\nU1 size = %d\ndecval size = %d\tpnum size = %d\tmy_value size = %d",
         sizeof U1, sizeof U1.decval, sizeof U1.pnum, sizeof U1.my_value );
}
```

How It Works

This example is intended to demonstrate the structure and operation of a union. We declare our union **U1** as:

```
union u_example
   {
         float decval;
         int pnum;
         double my_value;
   } U1;
```

The three members are each of different types, and they each require a different amount of storage.

```
U1.my_value = 125.5;
U1.pnum = 10;
U1.decval = 1000.5;
```

With these assignment statements we assign a value to each of the members of the union instance **U1** in turn. Referencing each member is done in the same way as for members of a structure. The next statement outputs each of the three member values. The last **printf()** outputs the size of the union **U1**, and the size of each of its members. We get the output:

```
decval = 1000.500000 pnum = 8192 my_value = 125.50016
U1 size = 8
decval size = 4 pnum size = 2 my_value size = 8
```

The first thing to note is the last variable that was assigned a value is correct, and the other two have been corrupted. This is to be expected since they all share the same memory space. The second thing to notice is how little the member **my_value** has been corrupted. This is because only the least significant part of **my_value** is being modified. In a practical situation, such a small error could easily be overlooked, but the ultimate consequences could be dire. You need to take great care when using unions that you are not using invalid data.

The output of the size of the union and its members, shows that the size of the union is the same as the size of the largest member.

Pointers to Unions

You can also define a pointer to a union with a statement such as:

```
union u_example *pU;
```

Once the pointer has been defined, you can modify members of the union via the pointer with the statements:

```
pU = &U2;
U1.decval = pU -> decval;
```

The expression on the right of the second assignment is equivalent to **U2.decval**.

Initializing Unions

If you wish to initialize an instance of a union, you can only initialize it with a constant with the same type as the first variable in the union. The union we have just declared, **u_example**, can only be initialized with a **float** constant, as in:

```
union u_example U4 = 3.14;
```

Obviously you can always rearrange the sequence of members in a definition of a union so that the member that you want to initialize occurs first. The sequence of members has no other significance since all members overlap in the same memory area.

Structures as Union Members

Structures and arrays can be members of a union. It is also possible for a union to be a member of a structure. To illustrate this we could write:

```
struct my_structure
   {
        int num1;
        float num2;
        union
            {
                int *pnum;
                float *pfnum;
            } my_U;
   }   samples[ 5 ];
```

Here we have declared a structure type **my_structure** that contains a union without a tag name, so instances of the union can only exist within instances of the structure. We have also defined an array of 5 instances of the structure, referenced by the variable **samples**. The union within the structure shares memory between two pointers. To reference members of the union, you use the same notation that we used for nested structures. As an example, to access the pointer to **int** in the third element of the structure array, you would use the expression appearing on the left in the following statement:

```
samples[ 2 ].my_U.pnum = &my_num;
```

Here, the variable **my_num** is assumed to have been declared as **int**.

It's important to realize that when using a value stored in a union, you always retrieve the last value assigned. This may seem obvious, but in practice it's all too easy to use a value as `float`, which has most recently been stored as an integer, and sometimes the error can be quite subtle as is shown by Example 11.6. Naturally, you tend to end up with garbage if you do this.

Defining Your Own Data Types

With structures we have come pretty close to defining our own data types. It doesn't look quite right because we must use the keyword `struct` in our declarations of structure variables. Declaration of a variable for a built-in type is simpler. However, there is a feature of the C language which permits you to get over this and make the declaration of variables of types you have defined follow exactly the same syntax as for the built-in types. We have already seen this in Chapter 4, but here, with structures, it really comes into its own.

Structures and the typedef Facility

Suppose we have a structure for geometric points we declare with:

```
struct pts    {
            int x;
            int y;
            int z;
        } ;
```

We could then define an alternative name for declaring such structures with the statement:

```
typedef struct pts Point;
```

When we now want to declare some instances of the structure `pts`, we can use a statement such as:

```
Point start_pt, end_pt;
```

in which we declare the two structure variables, `start_pt` and `end_pt`. A `struct` keyword isn't necessary, and we have a very natural way of declaring structure variables. The appearance of the statement is exactly the same form as a declaration for a `float` or an `int`. We could actually have combined the `typedef` and the structure declaration as:

```
typedef struct pts
      {
            int x;
            int y;
            int z;
      } Point;
```

Don't confuse this with the basic **struct** declaration. Here **Point** isn't a structure variable name, but a type name we are defining. When we need to declare structure variables, as we have just seen, we have to use a statement such as:

```
Point my_pt;
```

You can have more than one type defined pertaining to a structure. Suppose we had occasion to frequently define pointers to the structure **pts**. We could define a type to do this for us with the statement:

```
typedef struct pts *pPoint;
```

Now when we want to declare some pointers we just write:

```
pPoint p_first, p_last;
```

The two variables declared are both pointers to **pts** structures.

Simplifying Code Using typedef

In Chapter 9, we discussed pointers to functions, which are declared with a somewhat complicated notation. In one of our examples we had the pointer declaration:

```
int ( *pfun ) (int, int );    /* Function pointer declaration   */
```

If we were using several pointers to functions of this kind, we could use **typedef** to declare a generic type for such declarations with the statement:

```
typedef int ( *pFN ) (int, int );    /* Function pointer declaration   */
```

This declares **pFN** as a type which is a pointer to function, so we could replace our original declaration of **pfun**, with the statement:

```
pFN pfun;
```

which is much simpler than what we started with. The benefit in simplicity is even more marked if we have several such pointers to declare, since we can declare three pointers to functions with the statement:

```
pFN pfun1, pfun2, pfun3;
```

Of course we can also initialize them, so if we assume we have the functions **sum()**, **product()**, and **difference()**, we can declare and initialize our pointers with:

```
pFN pfun1 = sum, pfun2 = difference, pfun3 = product;
```

The type we have defined naturally only applies to pointers to functions with the arguments and return type specified in the **typedef** statement. If we want something different we can define another type.

Designing a Program

We have reached the end of another long chapter and it's time to see how we can put what we have learnt into practice.

The Problem

The problem we are trying to solve is to write a program that produces a vertical bar-chart of data that is typed in.

The Analysis

We won't be making any assumptions about the size of the 'page' that we are going to output to, or the number of columns, or even the scale of the chart. Instead, we will just write a function that accepts all of these to produce the final bar-chart. This will make the function usable in virtually any situation.

We will have to make some assumptions, particularly about the order in which the bars appear. We are going to assume that the order is going to be the same as the order they were typed in, and we won't need to sort them at all.

The steps required are then:

1 Write a `main()` function to test the bar-chart function once it has been written.

2 Write the bar-chart function.

The Solution

1 At this stage, we need to decide several things about the function we are going to write later. The most important of these is how are we going to pass the information to the function? As we don't know in advance how many bars are on the chart, or rather how much information the user is going to enter, we have to use dynamic allocation when we get the information. We could then produce a **NULL** terminated linked list, and just pass a pointer to the start of that list.

The first stage is to design our structure that will be used throughout the program. We'll use a **typedef** so that we don't have to keep re-using **struct**:

```
#include <stdio.h>

typedef struct barTAG
{
    double value;
    struct barTAG * nextbar;
}bar;

void main()
{
}
```

Notice how we have defined the pointer in the structure to the next structure. You may have thought that the **typedef** statement would mean you wouldn't have to use **struct barTAG** in this case. But, in the declaration of the structure, you must use the later form when you reference the structure itself, because the compiler hasn't finished the **typedef** yet. In other words, the structure **barTAG** is declared first, and then the **typedef** is performed.

Now we can declare the variables we'll need in **main()** and the code required to enter in the values and labels:

```
#include <stdio.h>
#include <string.h>
#include <stdlib.h>

typedef struct barTAG
{
   double value;
   struct barTAG * nextbar;
}bar;

int main()
{
   bar barlist, *lastbar = NULL;
   char value[80];

   do
   {
      printf("Enter the value of the bar, use quit to end: ");
      gets(value);

/* Compare the value typed with quit, if not the same then create new bar, */
/* convert value to double and save in the new bar                         */

      if(strcmp(value, "quit") == 0) break;

      if(lastbar == NULL)
      {
         barlist.value = atof(value);
         barlist.nextbar = NULL;
         lastbar = &barlist;
      }
      else
      {
         if((lastbar->nextbar = malloc(sizeof(bar))) == NULL)
         {
            printf("Oops! Couldn't allocate memory\n");
            return 0;
         }
         lastbar = lastbar->nextbar;
         lastbar->value = atof(value);
         lastbar->nextbar = NULL;
      }
   }while(1);
   return 0;
}
```

We have made **main()** an integer return type as we have used **return 0;** to exit the program, if for some reason the computer can't assign the memory we need for the new structure. This is a little naughty as we haven't freed the memory we have assigned before exiting. In fact the program doesn't do this anyway, so let's do that now.

```
#include <stdio.h>
#include <string.h>
#include <stdlib.h>

typedef struct barTAG
{
   double value;
   struct barTAG * nextbar;
}bar;

int main()
{
   bar barlist, *lastbar = NULL;
   char value[80];

   do
   {
      printf("Enter the value of the bar, use quit to end: ");
      gets(value);

/* Compare the value typed with quit, if not the same then create new bar, */
/* convert value to double and save in the new bar                         */

      if(strcmp(value, "quit") == 0) break;

      if(lastbar == NULL)
      {
         barlist.value = atof(value);
         barlist.nextbar = NULL;
         lastbar = &barlist;
      }
      else
      {
         if((lastbar->nextbar = malloc(sizeof(bar))) == NULL)
         {
            printf("Oops! Couldn't allocate memory\n");
            while(barlist.nextbar != NULL)
            {
               lastbar = barlist.nextbar;
               barlist.nextbar = lastbar->nextbar;
               free(lastbar);
            }
            return 0;
```

```
            }
        lastbar = lastbar->nextbar;
        lastbar->value = atof(value);
        lastbar->nextbar = NULL;
        }
    }while(1);
        /* Call function bar-chart() here */
    while(barlist.nextbar != NULL)
    {
      lastbar = barlist.nextbar;
      barlist.nextbar = lastbar->nextbar;
      free(lastbar);
    }
    return  0;
}
```

The **main()** function is now almost complete. All that remains to be done is call the bar-chart function once we have written it.

2 Now we can actually start working on the function. We know what information we want to pass:

> A pointer to a **NULL** terminated linked list of bars

> Two **int**s which indicate the vertical and horizontal character extent of the page

> Two **double**s which indicate the vertical scale (if these are both zero, then it auto-scales)

> A pointer to a string for the title

> An integer defining the space between columns

> An integer defining column width

We can do the declaration of the function and also declare a new type (with **typedef**), as we will be using **unsigned int**s a lot:

```
#include <stdio.h>
#include <string.h>
#include <stdlib.h>

typedef struct barTAG
{
    double value;
    struct barTAG * nextbar;
}bar;
typedef unsigned int uint;
```

```
int bar_chart();
```

```
int main()
{
...
}
```

```
int bar_chart(bar *barlist, int hori, int vert, int space, int width,
              double vert_max, double vert_min, char *title)
{
}
```

The parameters we are passing, in addition to the address of the first structure are

hori:	Horizontal width of chart. Can be zero if bar width is specified.
vert:	Height of chart in characters
space:	Space between bars in characters
width:	Width of bar in characters
vert_max:	Maximum bar value (if zero function will calculate value)
vert_min:	Minimum bar value (if zero function will calculate value)
title:	Title string for chart

We have defined the function to return an integer so that we can notify the calling function if there has been an error in the passed parameters. This is actually what we will work on next. There are several things we can work on straight away. For instance if the number of bars won't fit on the width of the display, or if the vertical size is less than 2:

```
#include <stdio.h>
#include <string.h>
#include <stdlib.h>

typedef struct barTAG
{
   double value;
   struct barTAG * nextbar;
}bar;
typedef unsigned int uint;

int bar_chart();

int main()
{
...
}
```

```
int bar_chart(bar *barlist, uint hori, uint vert, uint space, uint width,
              double vert_max, double vert_min, char *title)
{
    uint bar_count;
    bar *lastbar;
    double max, min;

    if(vert <= 2) return -1;
    if(width == 0 && hori == 0) return -2;

    bar_count = 1;
    lastbar = barlist;
    max = min = lastbar->value;
    while((lastbar = lastbar->nextbar) != NULL)
    {
        bar_count++;
        max = (max < lastbar->value)? lastbar->value : max;
        min = (min > lastbar->value)? lastbar->value : min;
    }
    if(hori != 0 && bar_count * (space + width) >= hori) return -3;
    if(vert_max != 0.0 && vert_max < max) return -4;
    if(vert_min != 0.0 && vert_min > min) return -5;
}
```

We have used different return values so that if you use the program, you can check to see what's wrong. If some of the data is to be typed in by a user, then based on the return value, you can display different error messages, or get the user to retype the information. We will probably be extending the number of errors as we go along, but it's OK for the time being.

Now we have to calculate all the values that we are going to need in the rest of the function, and also the two string that will be used to make up the bars.

```
#include <stdio.h>
#include <string.h>
#include <stdlib.h>

typedef struct barTAG
{
    double value;
    struct barTAG * nextbar;
}bar;
typedef unsigned int uint;

int bar_chart(bar*, uint, nint, nint, nint, double, double, chart);
```

```
int main()
{
...
}

int bar_chart(bar *barlist, uint hori, uint vert, uint space, uint width,
              double vert_max, double vert_min, char *title)
{
   uint bar_count;
   bar *lastbar;
   double max, min, vert_scale;
   char *column, *blank;

   if(vert <= 2) return -1;
   if(width == 0 && hori == 0) return -2;

   bar_count = 1;
   lastbar = barlist;
   max = min = lastbar->value;
   while((lastbar = lastbar->nextbar) != NULL)
   {
      bar_count++;
      max = (max < lastbar->value)? lastbar->value : max;
      min = (min > lastbar->value)? lastbar->value : min;
   }
   if(hori != 0 && bar_count * (space + width) >= hori) return -3;
   if(vert_max != 0.0 && vert_max < max) return -4;
   if(vert_min != 0.0 && vert_min > min) return -5;

   if(hori == 0) hori = bar_count * (space + width);
   if(width == 0) width = hori / bar_count - space;
   if(vert_max == 0.0) vert_max = max;
   if(vert_min == 0.0 && min < 0.0) vert_min = min;
/* Need to remove 2 from the vertical size so it will fit on the page */
   vert -= 2;
   vert_scale = (vert_max - vert_min) / vert;

/* Set up a string which will be used to build the columns */
   column = malloc((width + space + 1) * sizeof(char));
   for(counter = 0; counter < space; counter++)
   *(column+counter)+' ';
   for(;counter < space+width; counter++)
   *(column+counter)='#';
   *(column+counter) = '\0';

/* Set up a string which will be used as a blank column */
   blank = malloc((width + space) * sizeof(char));
   for(counter = 0;counter < space+width; counter++)
   blank+counter = ' ';
   *(blank+counter) = '\0';
}
```

433

With all of this information we can now output the basic bar-chart without any labels:

```c
#include <stdio.h>
#include <string.h>
#include <stdlib.h>

typedef struct barTAG
{
    double value;
    struct barTAG * nextbar;
}bar;
typedef unsigned int uint;

int bar_chart();

int main()
{
...
}

int bar_chart(bar *barlist, uint hori, uint vert, uint space, uint width,
              double vert_max, double vert_min, char *title)
{
    uint bar_count, counter, bars;
    bar *lastbar;
    double max, min, vert_scale;
    char *column, *blank;

    if(vert <= 2) return -1;
    if(width == 0 && hori == 0) return -2;

    bar_count = 1;
    lastbar = barlist;
    max = min = lastbar->value;
    while((lastbar = lastbar->nextbar) != NULL)
    {
        bar_count++;
        max = (max < lastbar->value)? lastbar->value : max;
        min = (min > lastbar->value)? lastbar->value : min;
    }
    if(hori != 0 && bar_count * (space + width) >= hori) return -3;
    if(vert_max != 0.0 && vert_max < max) return -4;
    if(vert_min != 0.0 && vert_min > min) return -5;

    if(hori == 0) hori = bar_count * (space + width);
    if(width == 0) width = hori / bar_count - space;
    if(vert_max == 0.0) vert_max = max;
    if(vert_min == 0.0 && min < 0.0) vert_min = min;
```

```
/* Need to remove 2 from the vertical size so it will fit on the page */
   vert -= 2;
   vert_scale = (vert_max - vert_min) / vert;

/* Set up a string which will be used to build the columns */
   column = malloc((width + space + 1) * sizeof(char));
   for(counter = 0; counter < space; counter++)
   *(column+counter)=' ';
   for(;counter < space+width; counter++)
   *(column+counter)='#';
   *(column+counter) = '\0';

/* Set up a string which will be used as a blank column */
   blank = malloc((width + space + 1) * sizeof(char));
   for(counter = 0;counter < space+width; counter++)
   *(blank+counter) = ' ';
   *(blank+counter) = '\0';
```

```
    printf("^   %s\n", title);
    for(counter = 0; counter <= vert; counter++)
    {
       printf("|");
       lastbar = barlist;
       for(bars = 1; bars <= bar_count; bars++)
       {
          if((vert-counter) * vert_scale + vert_min <= lastbar->value)
             printf("%s", column);
          else
             printf("%s", blank);
          lastbar = lastbar->nextbar;
       }
       printf("\n");
    }

    free(blank);
    free(column);
    return 0;
}
```

We have added to the bottom of the function two calls of the function **free()** to free the dynamically allocated space we obtained for the two strings for the columns, and also returned zero to the calling function to indicate that no errors have occurred.

This is fine until you try to use negative data. Then it doesn't work properly. We also haven't drawn the horizontal axis yet, so we'll fix those problems now:

```c
#include <stdio.h>
#include <string.h>
#include <stdlib.h>

typedef struct barTAG
{
   double value;
   struct barTAG * nextbar;
}bar;
typedef unsigned int uint;

int bar_chart();

int main()
{
...
}

int bar_chart(bar *barlist, uint hori, uint vert, uint space, uint width,
              double vert_max, double vert_min, char *title)
{
   uint bar_count, counter, bars;
   bar *lastbar;
   double max, min, vert_scale;
   char *column, *blank, axis = 'n';

   if(vert <= 2) return -1;
   if(width == 0 && hori == 0) return -2;

   bar_count = 1;
   lastbar = barlist;
   max = min = lastbar->value;
   while((lastbar = lastbar->nextbar) != NULL)
   {
      bar_count++;
      max = (max < lastbar->value)? lastbar->value : max;
      min = (min > lastbar->value)? lastbar->value : min;
   }
   if(hori != 0 && bar_count * (space + width) >= hori) return -3;
   if(vert_max != 0.0 && vert_max < max) return -4;
   if(vert_min != 0.0 && vert_min > min) return -5;

   if(hori == 0) hori = bar_count * (space + width);
   if(width == 0) width = hori / bar_count - space;
   if(vert_max == 0.0) vert_max = max;
   if(vert_min == 0.0 && min < 0.0) vert_min = min;
```

```
/* Need to remove 2 from the vertical size so it will fit on the page */
   vert -= 2;
   vert_scale = (vert_max - vert_min) / vert;

/* Set up a string which will be used to build the columns */
   column = malloc((width + space + 1) * sizeof(char));
   for(counter = 0; counter < space; counter++)
   *(column+counter)=' ';
   for(;counter < space+width; counter++)
   *(column+counter)='#';
   *(column+counter) = '\0';

/* Set up a string which will be used as a blank column */
   blank = malloc((width + space + 1) * sizeof(char));
   for(counter = 0;counter < space+width; counter++)
   *(blank+counter) = ' ';
   *(blank+counter) = '\0';

   printf("^ %s\n", title);
   for(counter = 0; counter <= vert; counter++)
   {
       if((vert-counter) * vert_scale + vert_min <= 0.0 && axis == 'n')
       {
           printf("+");
           for(bars = 0; bars < bar_count*(width+space); bars++)printf("-");
           printf(">\n");
           axis = 'y';
           continue;
       }
       printf("|");
       lastbar = barlist;
       for(bars = 1; bars <= bar_count; bars++)
       {
/*         if((vert-counter) * vert_scale + vert_min <= lastbar->value)  */
/*             printf("%s", column);                                     */
/*         else                                                          */
/*             printf("%s", blank);                                      */
           if((vert-counter) * vert_scale + vert_min <= lastbar->value
               && lastbar->value >= 0.0
               && (vert-counter) * vert_scale + vert_min >= 0.0)
           {
               printf("%s", column);
               lastbar = lastbar->nextbar;
               continue;
           }
           if((vert-counter) * vert_scale + vert_min >= lastbar->value
               && lastbar->value <= 0.0
               && (vert-counter) * vert_scale + vert_min <= 0.0)
           {
               printf("%s", column);
               lastbar = lastbar->nextbar;
               continue;
           }
```

```
        printf("%s", blank);
        lastbar = lastbar->nextbar;
    }
    printf("\n");
}
if(axis == 'n')
{
    printf("+");
    for(bars = 0; bars < bar_count*(width+space); bars++)printf("-");
    printf(">\n");
}

free(blank);
free(column);
return 0;
}
```

As you can see, the tests for printing either a column or a blank are a lot more difficult. For positive values, we have to make sure the value is positive, that the position on the chart is less than the value and that the position is not less than zero. For negative values, we have to check the opposite of this. To draw the axis we check to see if the position on the chart is less than zero, and that we haven't already drawn the axis.

All that remains is to add a line to `main()` to actually print the chart from the values typed in.

```
bar_chart(&barlist, 0, 10, 2, 4, 0.0, 0.0, "Test");
```

The values can be almost anything you wish, but the above line produces the following chart:

```
Enter the value of the bar, use quit to end: 5
Enter the value of the bar, use quit to end: -2
Enter the value of the bar, use quit to end: 8
Enter the value of the bar, use quit to end: quit
^ Test
|               ####
|               ####
|               ####
|   ####        ####
|   ####        ####
|   ####        ####
|   ####        ####
+------------------->
|        ####
```

Summary

This has been something of a marathon chapter, but the topic is extremely important. Having a good grasp of structures rates alongside pointers and functions as being fundamental to effective use of C. Most real world applications deal with things such as people, or cars, or materials which require several different values to represent them, and structures in C provide a ready tool for dealing with these. Although some of the operations may seem a little complicated, remember that you are dealing with complicated entities.

If you have ambitions to move on to C++ eventually, you will find that if you are comfortable with the application of structures in C, you will have few problems in understanding the basics of object-oriented programming. The syntax which provides these facilities is based very much on the ideas inherent in structures. The idea of a user-defined type that behaves as a built-in type is also fundamental to the ideas behind the object-oriented approach.

CHAPTER 12

Managing Large Amounts of Data

If your PC could only ever process data stored within the main memory of the machine, the scope and variety of applications you could deal with would be severely limited. Virtually all serious business applications require more data than would fit into main memory, and depend on the ability to process data that's stored on an external device such as a fixed disk drive. This chapter is going to cover processing data stored on an external device.

C provides a range of functions in the header file **STDIO.H** for writing to, and reading from, an external device. The external device is typically a fixed disk drive or a floppy disk, but not exclusively. Since, consistent with the philosophy of the C language, the facilities we shall use are device independent, they apply to virtually any external storage device. However, we shall assume in our examples that we are dealing with disk files throughout.

In this chapter you will:

- Understand what a file is in C
- Understand how files are processed
- Learn about writing and reading formatted files and binary files
- Learn about random access to data in a file
- Understand how to use temporary work files in a program
- Write a file viewer program

The Concept of a File

With all the examples we have seen up to now, any data you entered when the program was executed was lost once the program had finished running. At the moment, if you want to run the program with the same data, you have to enter it again each time. There are lots of occasions when this is not just inconvenient, it actually makes what you want to do quite impossible. If you want to maintain a directory of names, addresses and telephone numbers, for instance, a program where you have to enter all the names, addresses and telephone numbers each time is worse than useless. The answer is to arrange to store data on permanent storage that continues to be maintained after your computer is switched off. This is called a **file**, and is usually stored on a hard disk.

You are probably familiar with the basic mechanics of how a disk works. If so, this can be helpful in recognizing when a particular approach to file usage is efficient, and when it isn't. On the other hand, if you know nothing about disk file mechanics, don't worry at this point. There's nothing in the concept of file processing in C that depends on knowledge of any physical storage device.

A file in C is essentially a serial sequence of bytes, as illustrated in the following figure.

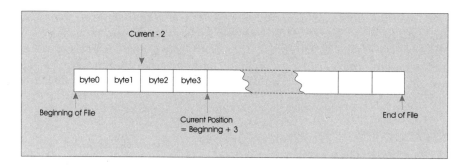

It has a beginning and an end, and it has a current position, typically defined as so many bytes from the beginning. The current position is where any file action, a read or a write, will take place. You can move the current position to any other point in the file. A new current position can be specified as an offset from the beginning of the file, or, in some circumstances, as a positive or negative offset from the current position.

Of course, you can write any data you like to a file. As we shall see, there are various ways that data can be written to a file, but it ends up as just a series of bytes in the end. This means that when the file is read, the program must know what sort of data the file represents. As we have seen often, what a series of bytes represents is dependent on how you interpret it. A sequence of twelve bytes could be twelve ASCII characters, twelve 8-bit signed integers, twelve 8-bit unsigned integers, six 16-bit signed integers, and so on. All of these will be perfectly valid interpretations of the data, so it's important that a program reading a file has the correct built-in assumptions about how it was written.

Processing Files

The files resident on your disk drive each have a name. On a PC running DOS for example, the name is up to eight characters, which can be followed by a period and an extension of up to three characters. When you write a program to process this file, it wouldn't be particularly convenient if the program would only work with a specific file with a particular name. If it did you would need to produce a different program for each file you might want to process. For this reason, when you process a file in C your program references a file through a file pointer. The file pointer is associated with a particular file when the program is run, so that on different occasions the program can work with different files.

If you want to use several files simultaneously, you will need a separate file pointer for each file, although, as soon as you have finished using a file, you can associate the file pointer with another file. So if you need to process several files, but you will be working with them one at a time, you really only need one file pointer.

Opening a File

You associate a specific external file name with an internal file pointer variable, through a process referred to as **opening** a file. This is achieved through the function **fopen()** which returns the file pointer for a specific external file. The function **fopen()** is defined in **STDIO.H**. It has the prototype:

```
FILE *fopen(  char *name, char* mode );
```

The first argument to the function **fopen()** is a pointer to the name of the external file that you want to process, stored as a text string. Obviously, you could specify the name explicitly as an argument, or you could use an array, or a pointer to a `char` variable, in which you would have stored the character string defining the file name. You would typically have obtained the name through some external means, defined as a constant at the beginning of the program, or by reading it in from the keyboard for example.

The second argument to the function `fopen()` is a character string which specifies what you want to do with the file. This is called the file **mode**. As we shall see this spans a whole range of possibilities, but for the moment we shall look at just three, which nonetheless comprise the basic set of operations on a file:

▶ `"w"`   open file for write operations
▶ `"a"`   open file for append operations (for example, adding to the end of the file)
▶ `"r"`   open file for read operations

Notice that these mode specifiers are character strings defined between double quotes, not single characters defined between single quotes.

Assuming the call to `fopen()` is successful, it returns a pointer that you can now use to reference the file in further input/output operations, using other functions in the library. This pointer is referred to as a file pointer, or a stream pointer. So, a call to `fopen()` does two things for you: it creates a file pointer indicating the specific file your program is going to operate on, and it determines what you can do with the file within your program.

The pointer returned by `fopen()` is of type 'pointer to `FILE`', where `FILE` specifies a structure that has been predefined in the header file `STDIO.H` through a `typedef`. Because it has been defined using a `typedef`, a declaration of a file pointer only requires the use of the keyword `FILE`. The structure associated with a file pointer will contain information about the file. This could be the mode specified, the address of the buffer in memory to be used, and a pointer to the current position in the file for the next operation. You don't need to worry about the contents of this structure in practice. It's all taken care of by the input/output functions. However, if you really want to know, you can browse through the library header file. As we have said, if you want to have several files open at once, they must each have their own file pointer variable declared, and they are each opened with a separate call to `fopen()` with the value returned stored in a separate file pointer.

If we suppose we wanted to write to an existing file with the name
MYFILE.TXT, we would use the statements:

```
FILE *pfile = NULL;                    /* Declaration of file pointer   */
pfile = fopen( "MYFILE.TXT", "w" ); /* Open file MYFILE.TXT to write it */
```

The first statement is a declaration for our file pointer of type **FILE**. We have
initialized the pointer to **NULL** to be on the safe side. The second statement
opens the file and associates the physical file specified by the file name
MYFILE.TXT with our internal pointer **pfile**. Because we have specified the
mode as **"w"**, we can only write to the file, we can't read from it. If the file
name **MYFILE.TXT** doesn't already exist, the function **fopen()** will create it.
So here we have the facility to create a new file. Simply call **fopen()** with
mode **"w"**, with the first argument specifying the name you want to assign to
the new file. On opening a file for writing, the file is positioned at the
beginning of any existing data for the first operation. This means that any
data previous written to the file will be overwritten when you initiate any
write operations.

If you want to add to an existing file rather than overwrite it, you should
specify mode **"a"**, which is the append mode of operation. This positions the
file at the end of any previously written data. If the file specified doesn't
exist, as in the case of mode **"w"**, a new file will be created. Using the file
pointer we declared above, to open the file to add data to the end, we
would use the statement:

```
pfile = fopen( "MYFILE.TXT", "a" ); /* Open file MYFILE.TXT to add to it  */
```

If we want to read a file, once we have declared our file pointer, we would
open it using the statement:

```
pfile = fopen( "myfile.txt", "r" );
```

Because we have specified the mode argument as **"r"**, indicating we want to
read the file, we can't write to this file. The file will be positioned at the
beginning of the data in the file. Clearly, if we are going to read the file, it
must already exist. If you inadvertently try to open a file for reading that
doesn't exist, **fopen()** will return **NULL**. It's therefore a good idea to check
the value returned from **fopen()** in an **if** statement, to make sure we are
accessing the file we want.

Writing to a File

Once we have opened a file for writing we can write to it any time from anywhere in our program, provided we have access to the pointer for the file which has been set by `fopen()`. So, if you want to be able to access a file anywhere in a program containing multiple functions, you need to ensure the file pointer has global scope. As you will recall, this is achieved by placing the declaration outside of all of the functions, usually at the beginning of the program code.

The simplest write operation is provided by the function `fputc()` which writes a single character to a file. It has the prototype:

```
int putc( int c, FILE *pfile );
```

It writes the character specified by the first argument to the file defined by the file pointer which is entered as the second argument. If the write is successful, it returns the character written. Otherwise it returns `EOF`, which is a special character called the 'end of file' character. In fact, `EOF` is defined in `STDIO.H` and usually has the value -1. However, this is not necessary always the case, so you should use `EOF` in your programs rather than an explicit value.

In practice, characters aren't written to the physical file one by one. This would be extremely inefficient. Hidden from your program and managed by the output routine, output characters are written to an area of memory called a **buffer** until a reasonable number have been accumulated, when they are written to the file in one go. This mechanism is illustrated in the next figure.

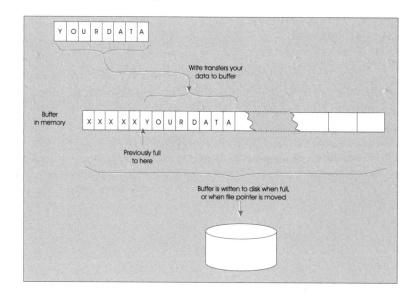

Reading From a File

The function complementary to `putc()` is `getc()` which reads a character from a file that has been opened for reading. It takes the file pointer as its only argument, and returns the character read as an `int` type if the read is successful, otherwise it returns `EOF`. Typical use of `getc()` is illustrated by the statement:

```
mchar = getc( pfile );  /* Reads a character into mchar    */
```

The variable `mchar` is assumed to have been declared as of type `int`. Behind the scenes, the actual mechanism for reading a file is the inverse of writing to a file. A whole block of characters are read into a buffer. They are then handed over to your program one at a time as you request them until the buffer is empty, whereupon another block is read. This makes the process very fast since most `getc()` operations won't involve reading the disk, but simply moving a character from the buffer in main memory to the place where you want to store it.

Don't confuse `getc()` with the function `gets()` which is quite different in operation. We saw `gets()` in Chapter 8.

Closing a File

When we have finished with a file we need to tell the operating system that this is the case, and free up our file pointer. This is referred to as **closing** a file. We do this through the function `fclose()`, which accepts a file pointer as an argument and returns an `int` value which is set to `EOF` if an error occurs and 0 otherwise. Typical usage would be:

```
fclose( pfile ); /* Close the file associated with pfile    */
```

The result is that the connection between the pointer `pfile` and the physical file name is broken and `pfile` can no longer be used to access the physical file it represented. If the file was being written, the contents of the output buffer are written to the file to ensure data is not lost.

It's good programming practice to close a file as soon as you have finished with it. This protects against losing output data, which could occur if an error in another part of your program caused the execution to be stopped in an abnormal fashion. This could result in the contents of the output buffer to be lost as the file wouldn't be closed properly. Another reason for closing files as soon as you have finished with them is that the operating system will usually limit the number of files you may have open at one time. Closing files as soon as you have finished with them will minimize the chances of you falling foul of the operating system in this respect.

There is a function in `STDIO.H` which will force any unwritten data left in a buffer to be written to a file. This is the function `fflush()`. With our file pointer `pfile`, we could cause any data left in the output buffer to be written to the file by using the statement:

```
fflush(pfile);
```

The function returns a value of type `int`, which is normally zero, but will be set to `EOF` if an error occurs.

Try It Out - Using a Simple File

We now have enough knowledge of the file input/output capabilities in C to write a simple program to write and use a simple file, so let's do just that:

```c
/* Example 12.1 Writing a file a character at a time        */
#include <stdio.h>
#include <string.h>

void main()
{
  char mystr[80];               /* Input string                        */
  int i = 0, lstr = 0;          /* Counter, & length of input string   */
  int mychar = 0;               /* Character for output                */
  FILE *pfile = NULL;           /* File pointer                        */

  printf("\nEnter an interesting string.\n");
  gets(mystr );                 /* Read in a string                    */

  pfile = fopen("C:\MYFILE.TXT", "w" ); /* Create a new file we can write */
  lstr = strlen( mystr );

  for( i = lstr-1 ; i >= 0 ; i-- )
    putc( mystr[ i ], pfile );        /* Write string to file backwards   */

  fclose( pfile );                    /* Close file                       */
  pfile = fopen( "c:\myfile.txt", "r" );   /* Open file for reading       */

  while( ( mychar = getc( pfile ) ) != EOF )
    putchar( mychar );                /* Output character from the file   */

  fclose( pfile );
  remove( "c:\myfile.txt" );          /* Delete the physical file         */
}
```

How It Works

Before running this program, or indeed any of the examples working with files, make sure you don't have an existing file of the same name. If you have, you should change the file name in the example otherwise your existing file will be overwritten. This program provides a very simple illustration of writing a file character by character.

After displaying a prompt, the program reads a string from the keyboard. It then executes the statement:

```
pfile = fopen("C:\MYFILE.TXT", "w" );/* Create a new file we can write */
```

This calls `fopen()` to create the new file `MYFILE.TXT` on drive C, and open it for writing. The second argument to `fopen()` determines the mode as writing the file.

After determining the length of the string using `strlen()` and storing the result in `lstr`, we have a loop defined by the statements:

```
for( i = lstr-1 ; i >= 0 ; i-- )
   putc( mystr[ i ], pfile );        /* Write string to file backwards    */
```

The loop index is varied from a value corresponding to the last character in the string, `lstr-1`, back to zero. Therefore, the `putc()` function call within the loop writes to the new file character by character, in reverse order. The particular file we are writing is specified by the pointer `pfile` as the second argument to the function call.

After closing the file with a call to `fclose()`, it is re-opened for reading by the statement:

```
pfile = fopen( "c:\myfile.txt", "r" );   /* Open file for reading         */
```

Here the mode specification "r" indicates that we intend to read the file, so the file is positioned at the beginning.

Within the loop:

```
while( ( mychar = getc( pfile ) ) != EOF )
   putchar( mychar );               /* Output character from the file   */
```

The file is read character by character, the read operation actually takes place within the loop continuation condition. As each character is read, it's displayed on the screen using the function `putc()` within the loop. The process stops when `EOF` is returned by `getc()` at the end of the file.

The last two statements in the program are:

```
fclose( pfile );
remove( "c:\myfile.txt" );              /* Delete the physical file     */
```

These provide the necessary final tidying up, now we have finished with the file. After closing the file the program calls a new function, `remove()`, which deletes the file we have created, to avoid cluttering up the disk with stray files.

Writing a String to a File

Analogous to the function `puts()` for writing a string to `stdout`, we have the function `fputs()` for writing a string to a file. Its prototype is:

```
int fputs(char *pstr, FILE *pfile );
```

This accepts as arguments, a pointer to the character string to be output, and the file pointer. The operation of the function is slightly odd, in that it continues to copy a string until it reaches a `'\0'` character, which it doesn't copy to the file. This can complicate reading of variable length strings. It returns `EOF` if an error occurs and 0 under normal circumstances. It is used in the same way as `puts()`, for example:

```
fputs("The higher the fewer", pfile );
```

will output the string appearing as the first argument to the file pointed to by `pfile`.

Reading a String from a File

Complementing `fputs()` is the function `fgets()` for reading a string from a file. It has the prototype:

```
char *fgets( char *pstr, int nchars, FILE *pfile );
```

It differs from `fputs()` in that it has three parameters. The function will read a string into the area pointed to by **pstr**, from the file specified by **pfile**. Characters are read from the file until a **'\n'** is read, or a maximum of **nchars-1** characters have been read from the file. If a newline character is read, it is retained in the string and **'\0'** is appended to the end of the string in memory. If there is no error it will return the pointer **pstr**, otherwise **NULL** is returned.

Try It Out - Transferring Strings To and From a File

We could exercise the functions to transfer strings to and from a file in an example which also uses the append mode:

```
/* Example 12.2 As the saying goes...it comes back! */
#include <stdio.h>

void main()
{
  char *proverbs[ ] =
  { "Many a mickle makes a muckle.\n",
    "Too many cooks spoil the broth.\n",
    "He who laughs last didn't get the joke in the first place.\n"
  };
  char more[ 60 ] = "A nod is a good as a wink to a blind horse.\n";
  FILE *pfile;                        /* File pointer              */
  int i = 0;                          /* Loop counter             */

/* Create a new file( if myfile.txt does not exist  */
  pfile = fopen("c:\myfile.txt", "w" );

/* Write our first three sayings.    */
  for( i = 0 ; i < sizeof( proverbs )/ sizeof( proverbs[0] ) ; i++ )
    fputs( proverbs[ i ], pfile );

  fclose( pfile );                            /* Close the file          */

  pfile = fopen("C:\MYFILE.TXT", "a" );  /* Open it again to append data */
  fputs( more, pfile );                  /* Write another proverb        */
  fclose( pfile );                       /* Close the file               */

  pfile = fopen("C:\MYFILE.TXT", "r" );  /* Open the file to read it      */

  while( fgets( more, 60, pfile ) != NULL )
    printf("\n%s", more );

  fclose( pfile );                            /* Close the file          */
  remove("c:\myfile.txt");
}
```

Try It Out!

451

How It Works

In this example we have used a novel way of initializing the array of pointers `proverbs[ ]` in the statement:

```
char *proverbs[ ] =
{ "Many a mickle makes a muckle.\n",
  "Too many cooks spoil the broth.\n",
  "He who laughs last didn't get the joke in the first place.\n"
};
```

We specify the three sayings as initial values, which causes the compiler to allocate the space necessary to store each string, and then put the address of the space allocated for each in the appropriate element of the pointer array. The compiler will automatically fill in the dimension for the array to provide sufficient pointers for the number of strings specified as initializers. Each string has `'\n'` as the last character so that `fgets()` will be able to recognize the end of each string.

We have a further declaration:

```
char more[ 60 ] = "A nod is a good as a wink to a blind horse.\n";
```

This initializes a conventional `char` array with another proverb. We also include `'\n'` at the end for the same reason as before.

After creating and opening a file on drive `c:` for writing, the program executed the loop:

```
for( i = 0 ; i < sizeof( proverbs )/ sizeof( proverbs[0] ) ; i++ )
  fputs( proverbs[ i ], pfile );
```

The contents of each of the memory areas pointed to by elements of the `proverbs[]` array are written to the file in the `for` loop using the function `fputs()`. This function is extremely easy to use, just requiring a pointer to the string as the first argument, and a pointer to the file as the second.

The number of iterations is set with the expression:

```
sizeof( proverbs )/ sizeof( proverbs[0] )
```

`sizeof( proverbs )` will evaluate to the total number of bytes occupied by the complete array, and `sizeof( proverbs[ 0 ] )` will result in the number of bytes required for a single pointer in one element of the array. Therefore, the whole expression will evaluate to the number of elements in the pointer array. We could have manually counted how many initializing strings we supplied, of course, but doing it this way means that the correct number of iterations is determined automatically, and this expression will still be correct even if the array dimension is changed.

Once the first set of proverbs has been written the file is closed, and then re-opened with the statement:

```
pfile = fopen("C:\MYFILE.TXT", "a" ); /* Open it again to append data */
```

Because we have the mode specified as "a", the file is opened in append mode. Note that the current position for the file is automatically set at the end of the file in this mode.

We then write to the file with the statement:

```
fputs( more, pfile );                  /* Write another proverb        */
```

The additional proverb stored in the character array `more[]` is then written to the file using `fputs()`. As you see, the function `fputs()` is just as easy to use with an array as it is with a pointer. Since we are in append mode, the new proverb will be added at the end of the existing data in the file.

Having written the file, it is closed and then re-opened for reading using the mode specifier `"r"`. We then have the loop:

```
while( fgets( more, 60, pfile ) != NULL )
  printf("\n%s", more );
```

Strings are read successively into the array `more[]` within the loop continuation condition. After each is read, it is displayed on the screen by the call to `printf()` within the loop. The reading of each proverb by `fgets()` is terminated by detecting the `'\n'` character at the end of each string. The loop terminates when the function `fgets()` returns `NULL`.

Finally, the file is closed, and then deleted from drive C: using the function `remove()` in the same fashion as in the previous example.

Formatted File Input and Output

Writing files one character at a time isn't really adequate for most purposes, neither is the ability to output a string as in **fputs()**. You will generally want to store away big chunks of data at a time, which will usually run the whole gamut of data types. You may also want to ensure the output is structured in a very specific manner. One mechanism for doing just this, is provided by the functions for formatted file input and output.

Formatted Output to a File

We have already met the function for formatted output to a file when we discussed standard streams back in Chapter 10. It is virtually the same as the **printf()** statement, with one extra parameter and a slight name change. Its typical usage is:

```
fprintf( pfile, "%12d%12d%14f", num1, num2, fnum1 );
```

As you can see, the function name has an additional **f** (for file), compared with **printf()**, and the first argument is a file pointer specifying the destination of the output. The file pointer obviously needs to be set through a call to **fopen()** first. The remaining arguments are identical to that of **printf()**. This example writes the values of the three variables **num1**, **num2**, and **num3**, to the file specified by the file pointer **pfile**, under control of the format string specified as the second argument. Therefore, the first two variables are of type **int** and are to be output with a field width of 12, and the third variable is of type **float**, and is to be written to the file with a field width of 14.

Formatted Input From a File

Formatted input from a file is accomplished using the function **fscanf()**. To read three variable values from a file **pfile** you would write:

```
fscanf( pfile, "%12d%12d%14f", &num1, &num2, &fnum1 );
```

This function works in exactly the same way as **scanf()** does with **stdin**, except that here we are obtaining input from a file specified by the first argument. The same rules govern the specification of the format string and the operation of the function, as apply to **scanf()**. The function returns **EOF** if an error occurs such that no input is read, otherwise it returns the number of values read as an **int** value.

Try It Out - Using Formatted Input and Output Functions

We could exercise the formatted input and output functions with an example that will also demonstrate what is happening to the data in these operations:

```
/* Example 12.3 Messing about with formatted file I/O    */
#include <stdio.h>

void main()
{
  long num1 = 234567, num2 = 345123, num3 = 789234;   /* Input values       */
   long num4 = 0, num5 = 0, num6 = 0;           /* Values read from the file */
   float fnum = 0.0;                            /* Value read from the file  */
   int   ival[ 6 ] = { 0 };                     /* Values read from the file */
   int i = 0;                                   /* Counter                   */
   FILE *pfile = NULL;                          /* File pointer              */

   pfile = fopen("C:\MYFILE.TXT", "w" );        /* Create file to be write   */
   fprintf( pfile, "%6ld%6ld%6ld", num1, num2, num3 );/* Write file          */
   fclose( pfile );                                  /* Close file           */
   printf("\n %6ld %6ld %6ld", num1, num2, num3 );/* Display values written*/

   pfile = fopen("C:\MYFILE.TXT", "r" );             /* Open file to read    */
   fscanf( pfile, "%6ld%6ld%6ld", &num4, &num5 ,&num6)  ;/* Read back        */
   printf("\n %6ld %6ld %6ld", num4, num5, num6 );  /* Display what we got */

   rewind( pfile );                         /* Go to the beginning of the file */

  fscanf( pfile, "%2d%3d%3d%3d%2d%2d%3f",        /* Read again            */
     &ival[ 0 ], &ival[ 1 ], &ival[ 2 ], &ival[ 3 ],
     &ival[ 4 ] , &ival[ 5 ], &fnum );
   fclose( pfile );                             /* Close the file and       */
   remove( "C:\MYFILE.TXT" );                   /* delete physical file.    */
   printf( "\n\n");

   for( i = 0 ; i < 6 ; i++ )
     printf( "%sival[i] = %d", i == 4 ? "\n\t" : "\t", i, ival[ i ] );
   printf( "\nfnum = %f", fnum );

}
```

Output from this example would be:

```
234567 345123 789234
234567 345123 789234

        ival[i] = 0    ival[i] = 1    ival[i] = 2    ival[i] =3
        ival[i] = 4    ival[i] = 5
fnum = 234.000000
```

How It Works

This example writes the values of `num1`, `num2`, and `num3`, which are defined and assigned values in their declaration, to the file `MYFILE.TXT` on drive `c:`. This is referenced through the pointer `pfile`. The file is closed and re-opened for reading, and the values are read from the file in the same format as they were written. We then have the statement:

```
rewind( pfile );                      /* Go to the beginning of the file   */
```

This calls the function `rewind()` which simply moves the current position back to the beginning of the file so that we can read it again. We could have achieved the same thing by closing the file then re-opening it again, but with `rewind()` we do it with one function call.

Having repositioned the file, we read the file again with the statement:

```
fscanf( pfile, "%2d%3d%3d%3d%2d%2d%3f",          /* Read again        */
    &ival[ 0 ], &ival[ 1 ], &ival[ 2 ], &ival[ 3 ],
    &ival[ 4 ] , &ival[ 5 ], &fnum );
```

This reads the same data into the array `ival[]`, and the variable `fnum`, but with different formats to those used for writing the file. You can see from the effects of this that the file consists of just a string of characters once it has been written, exactly the same as the output to the screen from `printf()`. You can lose information if you choose a format specifier which outputs fewer digits precision than the stored value holds You can see that the values you get back from the file when you read it will depend on both the format string that you use, and the variable list you specify in the `fscanf()` function.

None of the intrinsic source information that existed when you wrote the file is necessarily maintained. Once the data is in the file it is just a sequence of bytes where the meaning is determined by how you interpret them. This is demonstrated quite clearly by our example, where we have converted our original three values into eight new values.

Finally, we leave everything neat and tidy by closing the file and using the function `remove()` to delete it from drive `c:`.

Dealing With Errors

Our examples haven't included much in the way of error checking and reporting, since it tends to take up a lot of space in the book, and make the programs look rather complicated. In real world programs it is essential that you do check for error returns from library functions. Generally, you should write your error messages to **stderr** which is automatically available to your program, and always points to your display screen. Even though **stdout** may be redirected to a file by an operating system command, **stderr** continues to be assigned to the screen. It is particularly important to check that a file you want to read does exist. It is a good idea to define your file names as string constants, then you can refer to them in your error output. For example, to check that the file **MYFILE.TXT** on drive **c:** has been successfully opened, you could use the code:

```
char * myfile = "C:\MYFILE.TXT";                /* File name       */
FILE *pfile;                                     /* File pointer    */
....
if( pfile = fopen( myfile, "r" ) == NULL )
  fprintf( stderr, "\nCannot open %s.", myfile );
```

It's wise to include some basic error checking and reporting code in all of your programs. Once you have written a few programs, you will find including some standard bits of code for each type of operation warranting error checks, is no hardship. With a standard approach, you can copy most of what you need from one program to another.

Further File Operation Modes

We have only processed files as text files so far, where information is written as strings of characters. Text mode is generally the default mode of operation, but you can specify explicitly that file operations are in text mode if you want to be sure about it. You do this by adding a **t** at the end of the existing specifiers. This gives us mode specifiers **"wt"**, **"rt"**, and **"at"** instead of our original three.

We can also open a file for update, that is for both reading and writing, using the specifier **"r+"**. If you wanted the mode to be specified explicitly as a text operation, it would become **"r+t"** or **"rt+"**. Either specification for the file mode is perfectly acceptable. You can also specify the mode **"w+"** if you want to both read and write a file. To specify text mode explicitly this would become **"wb+"** or **"w+b"**.

457

As we have said, in update mode you can both read and write the file, but you can't write to the file immediately after reading it, or read from the file immediately after writing it, unless EOF has been reached, or the position in the file has been changed by some means. (This involves a function such as rewind(), or some other functions which we will see later in this chapter.) The reason for this is that, as we have already mentioned, writing to a file doesn't necessarily write the data to the external device. It simply transfers it to a buffer in memory which is written to the file once it is full, or when some other event causes it to be written. Similarly, the first read from a file will fill a buffer area in memory, and subsequent reads will transfer data from the buffer until it is empty, whereupon another file read to fill the buffer will be initiated. This is illustrated in the following figure.

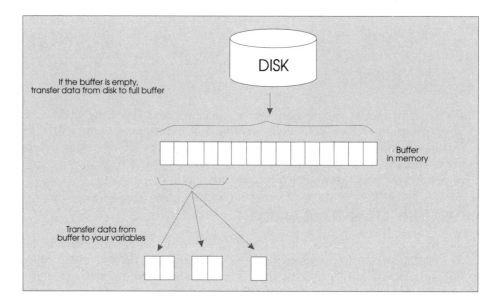

This means that if you switch immediately from write to read, data will be lost since it will be left in the buffer. In the case of switching from read to write, the current position in the file may be different to what you imagine, and you may inadvertently overwrite data on the file. A switch from read to write or vice versa, therefore, requires an intervening event which implicitly flushes the buffers. The function fflush() we mentioned earlier in this chapter will cause bytes remaining in an output buffer to be written to an output file.

Unformatted File Input/Output

The alternative to text mode operations on a file is binary mode. In this mode, no transformation of the data takes place and there is no need for a format string to control input or output, so it's much simpler than text mode. The binary data as it appears in memory is transferred directly to the file. Characters such as `'\n'` and `'\0'` which have specific significance in text mode, are of no consequence in binary mode. Binary mode has the advantage that no data is transformed, or precision lost, as can happen with text mode due to the formatting process. It's also somewhat faster than text mode because no transformation operations are performed. The two modes are contrasted in the next figure.

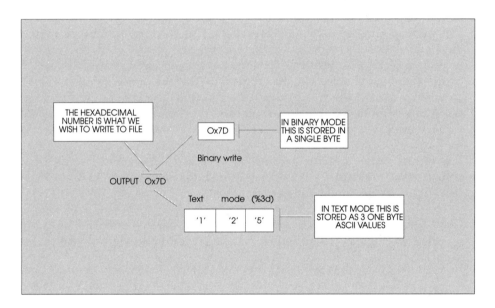

Specifying Binary Mode

Binary mode is specified by appending a **b** to the basic mode specifiers, giving us the additional specifiers **"wb"** for writing a binary file, **"rb"** to read a binary file, **"ab"** to append data to the end of a binary file, and **"rb+"** to enable reading and writing of a binary file.

Since binary mode involves handling the data to be transferred to and from the file in a different way from text mode, we have a new set of functions to perform input and output.

Writing a Binary File

To write a binary file, you use the function `fwrite()`. This is best explained using an illustrative example of its use. Assuming we open the file to be written with the statement:

```
pfile = fopen( "C:\MYFILE.TXT", "wb" );
```

where `pfile` has been declared as a pointer to an object of type `FILE` as before, then we could write to the file with the statement:

```
wcount = fwrite( pdata, size, num_items, pfile);
```

The function operates on the principle of writing a specified number of objects to a file, where each object is a given number of bytes long. The first argument, `pdata`, is a pointer containing the starting address in memory of the data objects to be written. The second argument, `size`, specifies the size of each object to be written. The third argument, `num_items`, defines a count of the number of objects to be written to the file specified by the last argument, `pfile`, the file pointer. The function `fwrite()` returns the count of the number of items actually written. If the operation was unsuccessful, this value will be less than `num_items`.

The return value, and the arguments `size` and `num_items` are all of the same type as that returned by the `sizeof` operator, defined as `size_t`, which is essentially an unsigned integer type.

If we were to assume that we want to write objects stored at an address specified by `pdata`, where `pdata` has been declared as a pointer to `long` with a declaration such as:

```
long *pdata;
```

Once `pdata` has been assigned a suitable valid address, we can specify the write operation from the area pointed to by `pdata` as:

```
wcount = fwrite( pdata, sizeof( long ), num_items, pfile );
```

Therefore, we can use the `sizeof` operator to specify the size in bytes of the objects to be transferred. This is a good way of specifying this value, particularly for structures where it isn't always obvious how many bytes are involved. Of course, in a real context we should also check the return value in `wcount`, to be sure the write was successful.

This means our function for binary writes to a file is geared to writing a number of objects of any length. You can write in units of your own structures as easily as you can write **int**s, **double**s, or sequences of individual bytes.

Reading a Binary File

To read a binary file once it has been opened in read mode, you use the function **fread()**. Using the same variables as in our example of writing a binary file, to read the file we would use a statement such as:

```
wcount = fread( pdata, size, num_items, pfile );
```

This operates exactly as the inverse of the write operation. Starting at the address specified by **pdata**, the function reads **num_items** objects, each of size **size** bytes, and returns the count of the number of objects read. If the read isn't completely successful, the count will be less than the number of objects requested.

Try It Out - Reading a Binary File

We could apply the binary file operations to a program we first saw in Chapter 7 for calculating primes. This time we will use a disk file as a buffer to calculate a larger number of primes. As this program consists of several functions, let's first take a look at **main()**:

```
/* Example 12.4   A prime example using binary files          */
#include <stdio.h>
#include <stdlib.h>
#include <math.h >

#define MEM_PRIMES 100              /* Count of number of primes in memory   */

int test_prime( unsigned long );              /* Function prototype       */
void put_primes(void);                        /* Function prototype       */
void put_buffer( unsigned long *, int );      /* Function prototype       */
int check(unsigned long *, int, unsigned long ); /* Function prototype */

char myfile[] = "C:\\MYFILE.BIN";             /* Physical file name       */
FILE *pfile;                                  /* File pointer             */

unsigned long primes[ MEM_PRIMES ] = { 2UL,3UL,5UL };
int index = 3;                     /* Index of free location in array primes */
int nrec = 0;                                 /* Number of file records   */

void main()
{
```

```
unsigned long trial = 5UL;                    /* Prime candidate         */
long num_primes = 3L, total = 0L;     /* Prime count, total required */

   printf("How many primes would you like?  ");
   scanf("%ld", &total);

  /* Prime finding and storing loop */
  while(num_primes < total )          /* Loop until we get total required */
  {
     trial += 2;                      /* Next value for checking      */

     if( test_prime( trial ) )    /* Check if trial is prime          */
       {                          /* Positive value means prime       */
           primes[ index++ ] = trial;
           num_primes++;            /* Total number of primes         */

           if( index == MEM_PRIMES )     /* Check if memory full      */
           {
               pfile = fopen( myfile, "ab" );
               fwrite( primes, sizeof (long), MEM_PRIMES, pfile);
               fclose( pfile );
               index = 0;          /* Reset count of primes in memory */
               nrec++;             /* Increment file record count     */
           }

       }

  };
  put_primes();
  put_buffer( primes, index );
}
```

How It Works

After the usual `#include` statements, we have the definition for MEM_PRIMES which is the maximum number of primes to be held in memory. Once more than this number of primes has been computed, the primes in memory will be written to a disk file automatically by the program. If you request less than this number, none will be written to disk.

The prototypes for four functions used in the program are:

```
int test_prime( unsigned long  )                 /* Function prototype  */
void put_primes(void);                           /* Function prototype  */
void put_buffer( unsigned long *, int  );        /* Function prototype  */
int check(unsigned long *, int, unsigned long ); /* Function prototype  */
```

Within the prototypes, just the parameter types are specified, without using a parameter name. Function prototypes can be written either with or without parameter names, but the parameter types must be specified.

The following statements are the declarations for the global variables:

```
char myfile[] = "C:\\MYFILE.BIN";              /* Physical file name     */
FILE *pfile;                                    /* File pointer           */

unsigned long primes[ MEM_PRIMES ] = { 2UL,3UL,5UL };
int index = 3;                    /* Index of free location in array primes */
int nrec = 0;                                   /* Number of file records  */
```

These can all be accessed by any function in the program. The first declaration defines a **char** array containing the name of the external file to be used. You need the double backslash to get a backslash character in the string.

We have included the file pointer **pfile**, and the character array **myfile** holding the external file name as globals, to allow input and output operations on the file from anywhere in the program. This allows the function **put_primes()** to be defined without parameters. We also define the array to hold primes in memory as global, and insert the first three primes as initial values.

The function **main()** starts, following the global declarations. When the program executes, you enter the number of primes you want to find, and this value controls the main iteration for testing prime candidates. Checking for a prime is performed by the function **test_prime()** which is called within the loop. It returns 1 if the value tested is prime, and 0 otherwise. If a prime is found we execute the statements:

```
    primes[ index++ ] = trial;
    num_primes++;                              /* Total number of primes   */
```

The first statement here stores the value found in the **primes** array. We keep track of how many primes we have in total with the variable **num_primes**, and the variable **index** counts how many we have in memory.

Every time we find a prime and add it to the primes array, we perform the following check:

```
        if( index == MEM_PRIMES )              /* Check if memory full    */
        {
            pfile = fopen( myfile, "ab" );
            fwrite( primes, sizeof (long), MEM_PRIMES, pfile);
            fclose( pfile );
            index = 0;              /* Reset count of primes in memory */
            nrec++;                 /* Increment file record count     */
        }
```

If we have filled the array **primes**, the **if** condition will be **True** and we will execute the associated statement block. In this case the file is opened in binary mode to append data. The first time this occurs, a new file will be created. On subsequent file opens to append data, the file will be positioned at the end of any existing data in the file, ready for the next block to be written. After writing a block the file is closed, as it will be necessary to open it for reading in the function that performs the checking of prime candidates.

Finally in this group of statements, the count of the number of primes in memory is reset to zero, since they have all been safely stowed away, and the count of the number of blocks of primes written to the file is incremented.

When sufficient primes have been found to fulfill the number requested, two output routines are called. The first outputs to the display screen all the primes from the file, and the second outputs any still remaining in memory that were not written to the file.

The function to check whether a value is prime or not is as follows:

```
/* Function to test if a number is prime using primes in memory and on file */
/* Returns a positive value for a prime found, zero otherwise              */

int test_prime( unsigned long N )
{
    unsigned long buffer[ MEM_PRIMES ];      /* local buffer for primes from the
                                                                         file   */
    int i = 0, k = 0;

    if( nrec > 0 )
    {
                                             /* If we have some records written   */
        pfile = fopen( myfile, "rb" );   /*    open the file.                 */

        for( i = 0; i < nrec ; i++ )
        {                                    /* Check against primes on file first */
            fread( buffer, sizeof (long), MEM_PRIMES, pfile );

            if( (k = check( buffer, MEM_PRIMES, N )) >= 0)
            {
                fclose( pfile );
                return k;
            }

        }
```

```
        fclose( pfile );
    }

    if( k = check( primes, index, N ) )    /* Check against primes in memory */
        return k;                          /* Prime found                     */

    return 0;                              /* Not a prime                     */
}
```

The function `test_prime()` accepts a candidate value as an argument, and returns 1 if it is prime, and 0 if it isn't.

If we have written anything to the file, indicated by a positive value of `nrec`, the primes in the file need to be used as divisors first, since they are lower than those in memory as we compute them in sequence. As you may remember, a prime is a number with no factors other than 1 and itself. It is sufficient to check whether a number is divisible by any of the primes less than the square root of the number, to verify it is prime. This follows from the simple logic that any exact divisor greater than the square root, must have an associated factor (the result of the division) that is less than the square root.

To read the file, the function executes the statement:

```
fread( buffer, sizeof (long), MEM_PRIMES, pfile );
```

This reads one block of primes from the file into the array `buffer`. The second argument defines the size of each object to be read, and `MEM_PRIMES` defines the number of objects of the specified size to be read.

Having read a block, the following check is executed:

```
if( (k = check( buffer, MEM_PRIMES, N )) >= 0)
{
    fclose( pfile );
    return k;
}
```

Within the `if` condition, the function `check()` is called to determine whether any of them divide into the prime candidate with no remainder. This function returns 0 if an exact division is found indicating the candidate is not prime. If no exact division is found with primes up to the square root of the candidate value, 1 is returned indicating that the candidate is prime. If the value returned from `check()` is 0 or 1, in both cases we have finished checking so the file is closed and the same value is returned to `main()`.

The value -1 is returned from `check()` if no exact division has been found, but the square root of the test value has not been exceeded. We don't need to check for the -1 return explicitly, since it is the only possibility left if it isn't 0 or 1. In this case the next block, if there is one, is read from the file by the function `test_prime()`.

If the contents of the file have been exhausted, the statements:

```
if( k = check( primes, index, N ) )   /* Check against primes in memory   */
   return k;                          /* Prime found                      */

return 0;                             /* Not a prime                      */
```

will be executed. Here, the test value is tried against any primes in the array `primes` in memory by the function `check()`. If a prime is found check will return 1 and this value will be returned. Otherwise zero is returned.

The code for the function `check()` is as follows:

```
/* Function to check for division by an array of primes                   */
/* Returns 1 if a prime found, zero if not a prime, -1 for more checks    */
int check( unsigned long *pbuffer, int count, unsigned long N )
{
  unsigned long *pend = &pbuffer[ count - 1 ];
  unsigned long root_N = 0UL;

  root_N = 1.0 + sqrt( (double) N );        /* Upper limit for checking     */

  while( pbuffer++ != pend )
  {

    if( N % *( pbuffer ) == 0UL )           /* Check for exact division     */
      return 0;                             /* If so not a prime...         */

    if( *pbuffer > root_N )     /* Check whether divisor exceeds square root */
      return 1;                             /* If so must be a prime        */

  }

  return -1;                                /* More checks necessary...     */
}
```

The role of this function is to check whether any of the primes contained in the area pointed to by **pbuffer**, divide exactly into the test value supplied as the second argument. The local variables in the function are declared in the statements:

```
unsigned long *pend = &pbuffer[ count - 1 ];
unsigned long root_N = 0UL;
```

Because the computation will be carried out using pointers, a pointer to **long**, **pend**, is defined which points to the last prime in the block that is passed as a parameter. The integer variable **root_N** will hold the upper limit for divisors to be checked against the trial value. Only divisors less than the square root of the test value **N** are tried.

The checking mechanism is controlled by the loop condition:

```
while( pbuffer++ != pend )
```

On each iteration the pointer **pbuffer** is incremented to point to the next prime. This occurs on the first iteration too, so we automatically avoid making the unnecessary check with the first prime which is 2. When **pbuffer** contains the same address as **pend** the loop is terminated since all the primes in the current block have been used as test divisors.

Checking for exact division is done by the statement:

```
if( N % *( pbuffer ) == 0UL )       /* Check for exact division   */
    return 0;                       /* If so not a prime...       */
```

The current contents of the address pointed to by **pbuffer** are divide into **N**, and if the result is zero then **N** is not prime. In this case zero is returned.

If the test division isn't exact, then the following statement is executed:

```
if( *pbuffer > root_N )   /* Check whether divisor exceeds square root */
    return 1;             /* If so must be a prime                     */
```

This checks whether the current divisor is greater than the square root of **N**. If it is we have a prime and we are done, so 1 is returned. Otherwise testing continues with the next prime.

The next function is designed to output all the primes written to the file:

```c
/* Function to output primes from the file */
void put_primes(void)
{
  unsigned long buffer[ MEM_PRIMES ];
  int i = 0;

  pfile = fopen( myfile, "rb" );

  for ( i = 0 ; i< nrec ; i++ )
  {
    fread( buffer, sizeof (long), MEM_PRIMES, pfile );
    put_buffer( buffer, MEM_PRIMES );
  }

  fclose( pfile );
  remove( myfile );
}
```

The operation of the function `put_primes()` is very simple. Once the file is opened, blocks of primes are read into the array `buffer`, and as each is read, the function `put_buffer()` is called to output the values on `stdout`. After all records have been read, the file is closed and deleted.

The last function in our program transfers primes stored in the buffer pointed to by the first argument, to the display screen in lines of five. The number of primes to be output is specified by the second argument. The code for the program is as follows:

```c
/* Function to display an array of primes  */
void put_buffer( unsigned long *buffer, int K )
{
  int i = 0;

  for ( i = 0 ; i < 5*(K/5) ; i += 5 ) /* print multiple of 5 items 5-up   */
    printf ("\n%12lu%12lu%12lu%12lu%12lu",
      *(buffer+i),*(buffer+i+1), *(buffer+i+2), *(buffer+i+3), *(buffer+i+4));

  if( ( K % 5 ) == 0 )
    return;

  printf("\n");                              /* Newline for any stragglers   */

  for (i = 5*( K / 5); i< K ; i++)
    printf("%12lu",*(buffer+i));             /* Display any left             */

}
```

This operates virtually identically to the output mechanism in the original sample program for calculating primes, except that there is a slightly different way of working out the indexing of the leftover primes to be displayed at the end.

To run the program you need to key in all the functions we have described into a single file, and compile it. Assuming you have keyed it correctly, you should be able to get as many primes as your computer and your patience will permit.

A disadvantage of this program when you have a large number of primes, is that the output whizzes by on the screen before you can inspect it. Several things could be done to fix this. You could write the output to the printer for a permanent record instead of writing it to the screen. Or perhaps you could arrange for the program to display a prompt and wait for the user to press a key, between the output of one block and the next. There is also room for improving the efficiency of the calculation.

Moving Around in a File

For many applications you will need to be able to access data in a file, other than in the sequential order we have used up to now. You can always find some information stored in the middle of a file by reading from the beginning, and continuing in sequence until you find what you want. But if you have written a few million items to the file, this may take some time.

Of course, to access data in random sequence requires that you have some means of knowing where the data you would like to retrieve is stored in the file. Arranging for this is a complicated topic in general. There are many different ways of constructing pointers or indexes to make direct access to the data in a file faster and easier. The basic idea is similar to that of an index to a book. You have a table of keys which identify the contents of each record in the file you might want, and each key has an associated position in the file defined where the data is stored.

We will only cover the basic tools in the library necessary to enable you to understand file input/output, and leave further research as a follow on project for you once you get to the end of the book, and are therefore on your way to being an accomplished C programmer.

File Positioning Operations

There are two aspects to file positioning, finding out where you are at a given point in a file, and moving to a given point in a file. The former is basic to the latter. If you never know where you are, you can never decide where you want to go, but remember the old saying, 'wherever you go, there you are'.

A random point in a file can be accessed regardless of whether the file concerned was written in binary or text mode. However, working with text mode files gets rather complicated. This results from the fact that the number of characters recorded in the file can be greater than the number you actually wrote. This is due to a '\n' character in memory translating into two characters when written to a file in text mode (carriage return - CR, and line feed - LF). Of course your C library sorts everything out when you read the data back. The problem arises when you think a point in the file is a 100 bytes from the beginning. If you subsequently write different data which is the same length in memory, it will only be the same length on the file if it contains the same number of '\n' characters. For this reason we shall side-step the complications of moving about in text files and concentrate our examples on the much more useful - and easier - context of binary files.

Finding Out Where You Are

We have two functions to tell us where we are, which are both very similar in what they do, but not identical. They each complement a different positioning function. The first is the function `ftell()` which has the prototype:

```
long ftell( FILE *pfile );
```

so it accepts as an argument a file pointer, and returns a `long` integer value which specifies the current position in the file. This would be used with the file referenced by the pointer `pfile` we have used previously, as in the statement:

```
fpos = ftell( pfile );
```

The `long` variable `fpos` now holds the current position in the file, and as we shall see, we can use this in a function call to return to this position at any subsequent time. For a binary file the value is actually the offset in bytes from the beginning of the file.

The second function providing information on the current file position, is a little more complicated. The prototype of the function is:

```
int fgetpos( FILE *pfile, fpos_t *position );
```

The first parameter is our old friend the file pointer. The second parameter is a pointer to a type predefined in STDIO.H , with the type name fpos_t. The type name is defined in STDIO.H if you want to know exactly what it looks like, but you don't need to worry about it. This function is designed to be used with the positioning function fsetpos() which we will come to very shortly. The function fgetpos() returns zero if the operation is successful, and a non-zero integer value otherwise. Given we have declared the variable position to be of type fpos_t*, we would use the function as in the statement:

```
fgetpos( pfile, position );
```

This records the current file position in our variable position.

Setting a Position in a File

As a complement to ftell() we have the function fseek() with the prototype:

```
int fseek( FILE *, long, int );
```

The first parameter is a pointer to the file we are repositioning. The second and third parameters define where we want to go to. The second parameter is an offset from a reference point specified by the third parameter. The reference point can be one of three values which are specified by the predefined names SEEK_SET which defines the beginning of the file, SEEK_CUR which defines the current position in the file, and SEEK_END which, as you might guess, defines the end of the file. For a text mode file, the second argument must be a value returned by ftell() if you are to avoid getting lost. The third argument for text mode files must be SEEK_SET. So for text mode files all operations with fseek() are performed with reference to the beginning of the file. For binary files you can do what you like, as long as you know what you are doing. The offset argument in binary files is simply a relative byte count. You can therefore supply positive or negative values for the offset when the reference point is specified as SEEK_CUR.

To go with `fgetpos()`, as we said we have `fsetpos()`. This has the rather straightforward prototype:

```
int fsetpos( FILE *, fpos_t * );
```

The first parameter is a pointer to the file set up with `fopen()`, and the second is a pointer of the type you can see, where the value was derived with a call to `fsetpos()`. You can't go far wrong with this one really. We would use it with a statement such as:

```
fsetpos( pfile, position);
```

where the variable position was previously set by a call to `fgetpos()`. As with `fgetpos()`, a non-zero value is returned on error. Since this function is designed to work with a value returned by `fgetpos()`, you can only use it to get to a place in a file you have been to before, whereas `fseek()` allows you to go to any specific position.

Note that the verb seek is used to refer to operations of moving the read/write heads of a disk drive directly to a specific position in the file. This is why the function `fseek()` is so named. With a file that you have opened for update, by specifying the mode as `"rb+"` or `"wb+"` for example, either a read or a write may be safely carried out on the file after executing either of the file positioning functions, `fsetpos()` or `fseek()`. This is regardless of what the previous operation on the file was.

Try It Out - Random File Access

To exercise our new found skills with files, we could modify a program from the previous chapter, to allow us to keep a dossier on family members. In this case we will create a file containing data on all of them, and then process the file to output data on each of them and their parents. This example has been coded to illustrate aspects of using the C language, rather than elegance or consistency in usage. The structures used only extend to a minimum range of members in each case. You can of course embellish these to hold any kind of scuttlebutt you like on your relatives.

Let's look at the function `main()` first:

```
/*    Example 12.5    Investigating the family.       */
#include <stdio.h>
#include <stdlib.h>
#include <string.h>

char myfile[] = "C:\\MYFILE.BIN";                /* Physical file name      */
FILE *pfile;                                     /* File pointer            */

struct Date
     {
         int    day,
                month,
                year;
     };

typedef struct family                            /* Family structure declaration   */
     {
             struct Date     dob;
             char    name[20],
                     pa_name[20],
                     ma_name[20];
     }Family;

int get_person( Family * );              /* Prototype for input function    */
void show_person_data( void );           /* Prototype for function for output */
void get_parent_dob( Family * );  /* Prototype for function to find pa & ma */

void main()
{
   Family member, *pmember = &member;

   pfile = fopen( myfile, "wb" );

   while( get_person( pmember ) )         /* As long as we have input,       */
      fwrite( pmember, 1, sizeof( member ), pfile );   /* write it away.     */

   fclose( pfile );                       /* Close the file now its written  */
   show_person_data();                    /* Show what we can find out.      */
   remove( myfile );
}
```

How It Works

After the `#include` statements, we have the global variables and structure definitions. You have seen all of these in previous examples. `Family` is not a variable, but has been declared as a type name for the structure `family`. This will allow us to declare `Family` type objects without having to use the keyword `struct`. Following the structure declarations, we have the prototypes for the three functions we are using in addition to `main()`.

473

Since we want to use the file positioning functions as well as the basic read and write operations, the example has been designed to exercise these as well. Input is read on one person as a time in the function `get_person()`, the structure being stored in the structure pointed to by `pmember`. Each structure is written to the file as soon as it has been received, and the input process ceases when the function `get_person()` returns zero.

The input file is closed and the function `show_person_data()` is called. Within this function we use the file position getting and setting functions. Finally, the file is deleted from the disk by the function `remove()`.

The code for the input function, `get_person()`, look like:

```
/*    Function to input data on Family members    */
int get_person( Family *temp )
{
    static char test = '\0';                 /* Test value for ending input    */

    printf("\nDo you want to enter details of a%s person (Y or N)? "
                    , test != '\0'?"nother " : "" );
    scanf(" %c", &test );

    if(test == 'N' || test == 'n')
         return 0;

    printf("\nEnter the name of the person: " );
    scanf("%s", temp -> name );              /* Read the Family's name         */

    printf("\nEnter %s's date of birth (day month year); ", temp->name );
    scanf("%d %d %d", &temp->dob.day, &temp->dob.month, &temp->dob.year );

    printf("\nWho is %s's father? ", temp->name );
    scanf("%s", temp->pa_name );             /* Get the father's name          */

    printf("\nWho is %s's mother? ", temp->name );
    scanf("%s", temp->ma_name );             /* Get the mother's name          */

    return 1;
}
```

This function is fairly self-explanatory. None of the mechanisms involved in this function are new to you. An indicator `test` controls whether reading data continues or not, and it is set by the input following the first prompt. It is defined as `static` so the variable and its value persists in the program from one call of `get_person()` to the next. This allows the prompt to work correctly in selecting a slightly different message for the second and subsequent iterations.

If no data input takes place, triggered when `'N'` has been entered in response to the initial prompt in the function, 0 is returned. If more data entry occurs, it is entered into the appropriate structure members and 1 is returned.

The next function generates output for each person, including the date of birth of both parents, if they have been recorded. The code for this function is as follows:

```
/* Function to output data on people on file   */
void show_person_data( void )
{
   Family member, *pmember = &member;
   fpos_t *current = NULL;              /* File position pointer            */

   pfile = fopen( myfile, "rb+" ); /* Open file for binary read & write    */

   while( fread( pmember, sizeof( member ), 1, pfile ) ) /* Read data on person*/
   {
      fgetpos( pfile, current );   /* Save current position               */
      printf("\n\n%s's father is %s, and mother is %s.",
         pmember->name, pmember->pa_name, pmember->ma_name );
      get_parent_dob( pmember );   /* Get parent data                     */
      fsetpos( pfile, current );   /* Position file to read next.         */
   }

   fclose( pfile );
   return;
}
```

This function processes each structure in sequence from the file. At the outset two objects of type **Family** are declared in the statement:

```
   Family member, *pmember = &member;
```

The first variable declared is **member**, and the second is of type pointer to **Family** and is initialized with the address of the first variable declared, **member**. The variable **member** has space allocated for the structure type, and **pmember** provides a convenient working pointer.

Next, a local variable **current** is declared with the statement:

```
   fpos_t *current = NULL;         /* File position pointer                */
```

This declares current as type pointer to `fpos_t`. This will be used to remember the current position in the file. The function `get_parent_dob()` is called later in this function which also accesses the file. It is therefore necessary to remember the file position of the next structure to be read on each iteration before calling `get_parent_dob()`.

All of the processing takes place in a loop controlled by:

```
while( fread( pmember, sizeof( member ), 1, pfile ) ) /* Read data on person*/
```

This uses the technique of reading the file within the loop condition, and using the value returned by the function `fread()` as the determinant of whether the loop continues or not. If the function returns 1, the loop continues, and when 0 is returned the loop is terminated.

Within the loop we have the statements:

```
fgetpos( pfile, current );                /* Save current position      */
printf("\n\n%s's father is %s, and mother is %s.",
    pmember->name, pmember->pa_name, pmember->ma_name );
get_parent_dob( pmember );                /* Get parent data            */
fsetpos( pfile, current );                /* Position file to read next. */
```

First, the current position in the file is saved and the parents of the current person pointed to by `pmember` is displayed. We than call the function `get_parent_dob()`, which will search the file for parent entries. On returning after the call to this function, the file position is unknown, so a call to `fsetpos()` is made to restore it to the position required for the next structure to be read. After all the structures have been processed, the `while` loop terminates and the file is closed.

The function to find the dates of birth for the parents of an individual is as follows:

```
/* Function to find parents' dates of birth.      */
void get_parent_dob( Family *pmember )
{
    Family testmem, *ptestmem = &testmem; /* Workspace for reading in    */
                                          /* relative data               */
    int num_found = 0;                    /* Count of relatives found    */

    rewind( pfile );                      /* Set file to the beginning   */

    /* Get the stuff on a relative      */
    while( fread( ptestmem, sizeof( Family ), 1, pfile ) )
    {
```

```
     if(strcmp( pmember->pa_name, ptestmem->name ) == 0 )
     {             /* We have found dear old dad   */
        printf("\n Pa was born on %d/%d/%d.",
           ptestmem->dob.day, ptestmem->dob.month, ptestmem->dob.year );

        if( ++num_found == 2 )        /* Increment parent count    */
           return;                    /* We got both so go back home   */

     }

     if(strcmp( pmember->ma_name, ptestmem->name ) == 0 )
     {             /* We have found dear old ma       */
        printf("\n Ma was born on %d/%d/%d.",
           ptestmem->dob.day, ptestmem->dob.month, ptestmem->dob.year );

        if( ++num_found == 2 )        /* Increment parent count    */
           return;                    /* We got both so go back home   */

     }

  }
  return;                            /* No more records so return    */
}
```

As the file has already been opened by the calling program, it's only necessary to set it back to the beginning with the `rewind()` function before beginning processing. The file is then read sequentially, searching each structure read for a match with either parent name. The search mechanism is contained in the statements:

```
     if(strcmp( pmember->pa_name, ptestmem->name ) == 0 )
     {             /* We have found dear old dad   */
        printf("\n Pa was born on %d/%d/%d.",
           ptestmem->dob.day, ptestmem->dob.month, ptestmem->dob.year );

        if( ++num_found == 2 )        /* Increment parent count    */
           return;                    /* We got both so go back home   */

     }
```

The name entry for the father of the person indicated by **pmember** is compared with the name member in the structure indicated by **ptestmem**. The pointer **ptestmem** has the address of the family structure last read as a candidate parent. If the father check fails, the function continues with an identical mother check.

If a parent is found, the date of birth information is displayed. A count is kept in **num_found** of the number of parents discovered in the file, and the function is exited if both have been found. Return occurs in any event after all structures have been read from the file.

477

To run this program you need to enter `main()` and the other functions called into a single file. You can then compile and execute it. Of course, the example could have been written equally well using `ftell()` and `fseek()` as positioning functions.

As in the previous examples in this chapter, the program uses a specific file name, on the assumption that the file doesn't already exist when the program is run. There is a way in C to create temporary files that get around this.

Using Temporary Work Files

Very often you will need a workfile just for the duration of a program. It will only be used to store intermediate results and can be thrown away when the program is finished. Our example calculating primes in this chapter is a good example. We really only needed the file during the calculation.

We have a choice of two functions to help with temporary file usage, and they each have their advantages and disadvantages.

Creating a Temporary Workfile

The first function will create a temporary file automatically. Its prototype is:

```
FILE *tmpfile( void );
```

It takes no arguments and returns a pointer to the temporary file. If the file cannot be created for any reason, for example if the disk is full, the function returns **NULL**. The file is created and opened for update, so it can be written and read, but obviously it needs to be in that order. The file is automatically deleted on exit from your program, so there is no need to worry about any mess left behind. You will never know what the file is called, and since it doesn't last, it doesn't matter.

The disadvantage of this function is that the file will be deleted as soon as you close it. This means you cannot close the file, having written it in one part of the program, and then reopen it in another part of the program to read the data. You must keep the file open for as long as you need access to the data. A simple illustration of creating a temporary file is provided by the statements:

```
FILE *pfile;
pfile = tmpfile();
```

Creating a Unique File Name

The second possibility is to use a function that provides you with a unique file name. Whether this ends up as a temporary file or not is up to you. The prototype for this function is:

```
char *tmpnam( char * );
```

If the argument to the function is **NULL**, the file name is generated in an internal static object and a pointer to that object is returned. If you want the name stored in a **char** array that you declare yourself, it must be at least **L_tmpnam** characters long, where **L_tmpnam** is a constant predefined in **STDIO.H**. In this case, the file name is stored in the array you specify as an argument, and a pointer to your array is also returned. So, to take the first possibility, we can create a unique file with the statements:

```
FILE *pfile = NULL;
char *filename = NULL;
pfile = fopen( filename = tmpnam( NULL ), "wb+" );
```

Here we have declared our file pointer **pfile**, and our pointer filename which will contain the address of the temporary file name. We have combined the call to **tmpnam()** with the call to open the file by putting the assignment as the first argument to **fopen()**. Because the argument to **tmpnam()** is **NULL** the file name will be generated as an internal static object whose address will be placed in our pointer **filename**.

Don't be tempted to write:

```
pfile = fopen( tmpnam( NULL ), "rb+" );
```

If you do, you no longer have access to the file name, so you cannot use **remove()** to delete the file.

If you want to create the array to hold the file name yourself, you could write:

```
FILE *pfile = NULL;
char filename[ L_tmpnam ];
pfile = fopen( tmpnam( filename ), "rb+" );
```

Remember the assistance we have obtained from the library is just to provide a unique name. It is your responsibility to delete any files created. You should also note that you will be limited to a maximum number of unique names from this function in your program, but it will be at least 25, and with some implementations a great deal more.

Designing a Program

Now we have come to the end of this chapter we can put what we have learnt into practice with our final program.

The Problem

The problem we are going to solve is to write a file viewer program. This will display any file in hexadecimal representation and as ASCII characters.

The Analysis

The program will open the file as binary read-only, then display the information in two columns, the first being the hexadecimal representation of the bytes in the file, the second being the bytes represented as ASCII characters. The file name will be supplied as either a command line argument, or if that isn't supplied, then the program will ask for the file name.

The stages are then:

1   If not supplied, get the file name from the user.

2   Open the file.

3   Read and display the contents of the file.

The Solution

1   We can easily check to see if the file name appears on the command line by specifying that the function `main()`has parameters. Up to now we have chosen to ignore the possibility of parameters passed to `main()`, but when `main()` is called, two parameters are passed. The first parameter is an integer indicating the number of words in the command line, and the second is an array of pointers to objects of type `char`. The first of these objects is usually a string containing the name used to start the program on the command line, and the remaining objects are strings corresponding to the other words appearing on the command line. If the value of the first argument is only 1, then there are no words on the command line other than the program name, so we have to ask for the file name to be entered:

```c
#include <stdio.h>

int main(int argc, char *argv[])
{
    char filename[80];

    if(argc == 1)
    {
        printf("Please enter a filename: ");
        gets(filename);
    }
}
```

2   If the first argument to `main()` is not 1, then we have at least one more argument which we assume is the file name. We therefore copy the string pointed to by `argv[1]` to the variable `openfile`. Assuming we have a valid file name, we can open the file ready to start reading in the bytes:

```c
#include <stdio.h>

int main(int argc, char *argv[])
{
    char filename[80];
    FILE *openfile;

    if(argc == 1)
    {
        printf("Please enter a filename: ");
        gets(filename);
```

```
   }
   else
      strcpy(filename, argv[1]);
   if((openfile = fopen(filename, "rb")) == NULL)
   {
      printf("Sorry, can't open that file");
      return -1;
   }

   fclose(openfile);
}
```

We have put in the `fclose()` function at the end of the program so that we don't forget about it later. Also, we have used a return value for the program to indicate when an error has occurred.

3   We can now output the file contents. We do this by reading the file one byte at a time, and saving this data in a buffer. Once the buffer is full, or the end of file has been reached we output the buffer in the format we want. When we output the ASCII version of the data we must first check that the character is printable, otherwise strange things may start happening to the screen. We use the function `isprint()` from `CTYPE.H` for this. If the character is not printable, we will print a period instead.

```
#include <stdio.h>
#include <ctype.h>

#define DISPLAY 80

int main(int argc, char *argv[])
{
   char filename[80];
   unsigned char buffer[DISPLAY/4 - 1], byte;
   int counter = 0, final_line;
   FILE *openfile;

   if(argc == 1)
   {
      printf("Please enter a filename: ");
      gets(filename);
   }
   else
      strcpy(filename, argv[1]);
   if((openfile = fopen(filename, "rb")) == NULL)
   {
      printf("Sorry, can't open that file");
      return -1;
   }
```

```
    while(!feof(openfile))
    {
       byte = (unsigned char)fgetc(openfile);
       if(counter < DISPLAY/4 - 1)
          buffer[counter++] = byte;
       else
       {
          for(counter = 0; counter < DISPLAY/4 - 1; counter++)
            printf("%02X ", buffer[counter]);
          printf("| ");
          for(counter = 0; counter < DISPLAY/4 - 1; counter++)
             printf("%c", (isprint(buffer[counter]) != 0)?buffer[counter]:'.');
          printf("\n");
          counter = 0;
          buffer[counter++] = byte;
       }
    }
    for(final_line = 0; final_line < DISPLAY/4 - 1; final_line++)
       (final_line < counter)?printf("%02X ", buffer[final_line]):printf("
");
    printf("| ");
    for(final_line = 0; final_line < DISPLAY/4 - 1; final_line++)
       (final_line < counter)?
          printf("%c",(isprint(buffer[final_line])!=
0)?buffer[final_line]:'.'):
          printf(" ");
    printf("\n");

    fclose(openfile);
}
```

The final couple of `for()` loops look a bit complicated, but simply display the final line of the file. The reason for the use of the `?:` operators in these lines is to pad the lines with spaces so that the last line of output lines up properly. An example of the output is shown on the next page; it shows part of the executable file generated by a DOS compiler of the self-same program.

```
00 8B F0 0B F0 75 05 33 C0 EB 13 90 56 FF 76 0A FF 76 08 | .....u.3....V.v..v.
FF 76 06 9A 36 09 18 00 83 C4 08 5E 8B E5 5D CB 90 55 8B | .v..6......^..]..U.
EC 33 C0 50 FF 76 08 FF 76 06 9A B6 06 18 00 8B E5 5D CB | .3.P.v..v........].
90 55 8B EC 83 EC 04 57 56 BE 3C 01 56 E8 5B 03 83 C4 02 | .U.....WV.<.V.[....
8B F8 8D 46 08 50 FF 76 06 B8 3C 01 50 9A 5E 0C 18 00 83 | ...F.P.v..<.P.^....
C4 06 89 46 FC B8 3C 01 50 57 E8 AB 03 83 C4 04 8B 46 FC | ...F..<.PW.......F.
5E 5F 8B E5 5D CB 55 8B EC 9A DC 0B 18 00 A0 0B 01 0A C0 | ^_..].U...........
74 05 9A 62 16 18 00 5D CB 55 8B EC 56 57 8B 76 06 8A 44 | t..b...].U..VW.v..D
06 A8 83 74 59 A8 40 75 55 A8 02 75 42 0C 01 88 44 06 8B | ...tY.@uU..uB...D..
FE 81 EF 34 01 81 C7 D4 01 A8 0C 75 0A F6 05 01 75 05 56 | ...4.......u....u.V
E8 73 01 58 8B 44 04 89 04 FF 75 02 50 33 DB 8A 5C 07 53 | .s.X.D....u.P3..\.S
0E E8 59 0C 83 C4 06 0B C0 74 11 83 F8 FF 75 1A 80 4C 06 | ..Y......t....u..L.
20 EB 0A 80 4C 06 20 EB 09 80 4C 06 10 C7 44 02 00 00 B8 | ...L. ...L...D....
FF FF EB 24 8A BF E4 00 80 E7 82 80 FF 82 75 0B 8A 7C 06 | ...$..........u..|.
F6 C7 82 75 03 80 0D 20 48 89 44 02 8B 1C 33 C0 8A 07 43 | ...u... H.D...3...C
89 1C 5F 5E 5D CB 00 55 8B EC 56 57 8B 76 08 8A 44 06 A8 | .._^]..U..VW.v..D..
82 74 69 A8 40 75 65 C7 44 02 00 00 A8 01 74 0B A8 10 74 | .ti.@ue.D.....t...t
58 8B 4C 04 89 0C 24 FE 0C 02 24 EF 88 44 06 8B FE 81 EF | X.L...$...$..D.....
34 01 81 C7 D4 01 33 DB 8A 5C 07 A8 08 75 4D A8 04 75 1E | 4.....3..\...uM..u.
F6 05 01 75 44 81 FE 3C 01 74 0C 81 FE 44 01 74 06 81 FE | ...uD..<.t...D.t...
54 01 75 25 F6 87 E4 00 40 74 1E B9 01 00 8D 7E 06 51 57 | T.u%....@t.....~.QW
53 0E E8 5C 0F 83 C4 06 B9 01 00 EB 3F B8 FF FF 80 4C 06 | S..\........?....L.
20 EB 5E 53 56 E8 8A 00 5B 5B F6 44 06 08 74 D5 8B 0C 8B | .^SV...[[.D..t....
```

Summary

Within this chapter we have covered all of the basic tools necessary to provide you with the ability to program the complete spectrum of file functions. The degree to which these have been demonstrated in examples has been, of necessity, relatively limited. There are many ways of applying these tools to provide more sophisticated ways of managing and retrieving information in a file. For example, it's possible to write index information into the file, either as a specific index at a known place in the file, often the beginning, or as position pointers within the blocks of data, rather like the pointers in a linked list. You should experiment with file operations until you feel confident of your understanding of the mechanisms involved.

While the functions we have discussed are quite comprehensive, they are not exhaustive. You should find that the input/output library provided with your compiler provides quite a few additional functions which provide even more options in how you handle your file operations.

CHAPTER 13

Supporting Facilities

At this point you have covered the complete C language, as well as the important library functions. You should be reasonably confident in programming all aspects of the language. If you aren't, that's simply because you need more practice. We can teach you the elements of the language, but to really understand about programming you have to spend time at your computer. After all, that's what programming is all about.

In this final chapter we will drag together a few loose ends, consisting mainly of the pre-processor which you are likely to be dimly aware of by now since we have referred to it from time to time, plus a few further library functions which you will find to be useful.

In this chapter you will:

- Learn about the pre-processor and its operation
- Write pre-processor macros
- Learn about logical pre-processor directives
- Conditional compilation
- Debugging methods
- Some additional library functions

The Pre-processor

The pre-processor is a facility provided by your compiler that is exercised before your C program code is compiled to machine instructions. It can execute a range of service operations specified by pre-processor directives which are recognized by the symbol **#**, the first character of each pre-processor directive. The pre-processor provides a means of manipulating and modifying your C source code prior to compilation. Once the pre-processor phase is completed, and all pre-processor directives have been analyzed and executed, the compiler continues with the compile phase proper, which generates the machine code equivalent of your program.

We have already used pre-processor directives in all our examples, and you are familiar with both the **#include** and **#define** directives. There are a number of other directives which add considerable flexibility to the way in which you specify your programs. Keep in mind, as we proceed, that all these are pre-processor operations that occur before your program is compiled. They modify the set of statements that constitute your program. They aren't involved in the execution of your program at all.

Including Header Files in Your Programs

A header file is any external file, usually stored on disk, whose contents are included into your program by use of the **#include** pre-processor directive. We are completely familiar with statements such as:

```
#include < stdio.h >
```

which fetches the standard library header file supporting input/output operations into your program. This is a particular case of the general statement for including standard libraries into your program:

```
#include < standard_library_file_name >
```

where any library header file name can appear between the angled brackets. If you include a header file that you don't use, the only effect, apart from slightly confusing anyone reading the program, is to extend the compilation time.

You can include your own source files into your program with a slightly different **#include** statement. A typical example might be:

```
#include "MYFILE.H"
```

This statement will introduce the contents of the file named between double quotes into the program in place of the `#include` directive. The contents of any file can be included into your program by this means. You simply specify the name of the file between quotes as we have shown in the example. With the majority of compilers you can specify the file name with either upper or lower-case characters.

You can also call the file whatever name you like. You don't have to use the extension `.H`, although it's a convention commonly adhered to by most programmers in C. The difference between using this form and using angled brackets lies in the source assumed for the required file. The precise operation is compiler dependent and will be described in the compiler documentation, but usually the first form will search the default header file directory for the required file, whereas the second will search the source directory followed by the default header file directory.

You can use this mechanism for dividing your program into several files, and of course for managing any library functions of your own. A very common use of this facility is to create a header file containing all the function prototypes and global variables. These can then be managed as a separate unit and included at the beginning of the program. You need to avoid duplicating information if you include more than one file into your program. Duplicate code will often cause compilation errors. We shall see later in this chapter how the pre-processor provides some facilities for ensuring that any given block of code will appear only once in your program, even if you inadvertently include it several times.

A file introduced into your program by an `#include` statement may also contain another `#include` statement. If so, the pre-processor will process the second `#include` in the same way as the first, and continue processing until there are no more `#include` statements in the program.

External Variables and Functions

With a program made up of several files, you will frequently find that you want to use a global variable that is defined in another file. You can do this by declaring the variable as external to the current file using the `extern` keyword. For example, if we have variables defined in another file as global using the statements:

```
int number = 0;
long array[ 20 ];
```

Then in the function where we want to access these, we can declare them using the statements:

```
extern int number;
extern long array[20];
```

If you want to make the variables accessible to all functions within the current file, then you can declare them as external at the beginning of the file. With programs comprising several files, it's common practice to place all global variables at the beginning of one file, and all the **extern** statements in a header file. They can then be incorporated into any subsequent program file using an include statement.

> Only one definition of each global variable is allowed. Of course they may be declared as external, in as many files as necessary.

Substitutions in Your Program

The simplest kind of symbol substitution you can make, is one we have already seen. For example, the pre-processor directive to substitute the specified numeric value, wherever the character string **PI** occurs, is as follows:

```
#define PI 3.14159265
```

Apart from the fact that **PI** *looks* like a variable, this has nothing to do with variables. Here the identifier **PI** is a token, rather like a voucher, which is exchanged for the sequence of digits specified. When your program is ready to be compiled after pre-processing has been completed, the string **PI** will no longer appear, having been substituted with its definition every time it appears by the pre-processor. The general form of this sort of pre-processor directive is:

```
#define identifier sequence_of_characters
```

Here **identifier** conforms to the usual definition of an identifier in C, as any sequence of letters and digits, the first of which is a letter, and where the underline character counts as a letter. A very common use of the **#define** directive is to define array dimensions by way of a substitution, to allow a number of array dimensions to be determined by a single token. Only one directive in the program then needs to be modified, to alter the dimensions of a number of arrays in the program. This helps considerably in minimizing errors when such changes are necessary. For example:

```
#define DIMENSION 50
int array1[ DIMENSION ], array2[ DIMENSION ], array3[ DIMENSION ];
```

Here the dimensions of all three arrays can be changed by modifying the single #define statement, and of course the array declarations affected can be anywhere in the program file. The advantages of this approach in a large program involving dozens or even hundreds of functions should be obvious. Not only is it easy to make a change, but using this approach ensures that the same value is being used through a program. This is especially important with large projects involving several programmers working together to produce the final end product.

We have used numerical substitution in the last two examples, but you are in no way limited to this. You could write for example:

```
#define Black White
```

to cause any occurrence of Black in your program to be replaced by White. The sequence of characters which are to replace the token identifier can be anything at all.

Macro Substitutions

A macro is based on the ideas implicit in the #define directive examples we have seen so far, but provides a greater range of possible results by allowing what might be called multiple parameterized substitutions. This not only involves substitution of a fixed sequence of characters for a token identifier, but also allows parameters to be specified, which may themselves be replaced by argument values, wherever the parameter appears in the substitution sequence. Let's look at an example:

```
#define Print( My_var) printf( "%d", myvar )
```

This directive provides for two levels of substitution. There is the substitution for Print(My_var) by the string immediately following it in the #define statement, and there is the possible substitution of alternatives for **My_var**. You could write, for example:

```
Print( ival );
```

which will be converted to the statement:

```
printf( "%d", ival );
```

You could use this directive to specify a **printf()** statement for an integer variable at various points in your program. A very common use for this kind of macro is to allow a very simple representation of a complicated function call, in order to enhance the readability of a program.

Macros that Look Like Functions

The general form of the kind of substitution directive we have just discussed is:

```
#define identifier( list_of_identifiers ) substitution_string
```

This shows that in the general case, multiple parameters are permitted, so we are able to define more complex substitutions.

> You mustn't leave a space between the first identifier and the left parenthesis.

To illustrate how you use this, we can define a macro for producing the maximum of two values with:

```
#define max( x, y ) x>y ? x : y
```

so that we can then put the statement in our program:

```
result = max( myval, 99 );
```

which will be expanded by the pre-processor to:

```
result = myval>99 ? myval : 99;
```

It is important to be conscious of the substitution taking place, and not to assume that this is a function. You can get some strange results otherwise, particularly if your substitution identifiers include an explicit or implicit assignment. For example, the following modest extension of our last example can produce an erroneous result:

```
result = max( myval++, 99 );
```

The substitution process will generate the statement:

```
result = myval++>99 ? myval++ : 99;
```

so that if the value of `myval` is larger than 99, `myval` will be incremented twice.

You need to be very cautious if you are writing any macros that generate expressions of any kind. In addition to the multiple substitution trap we have just seen, precedence rules can also catch you out. A simple example will illustrate this. Suppose we write a macro for the product of two parameters:

```
#define product( m, n ) m*n
```

We then try to use this macro with the statement:

```
product( x, y + 1 )
```

Of course everything works fine but we don't get the result we want as the macro expands to:

```
x*y + 1
```

It could take a long time to discover that we aren't getting the product of the two parameters at all in this case, as there is no external indication of what's going on. There is just a more or less erroneous value propagating through our program. The solution is very simple. If you use macros to generate expressions, put parentheses around everything. So if we rewrite our example as:

```
#define product( m, n ) (( m )*( n ))
```

everything will work as it should. The inclusion of the outer parentheses may seem excessive, but since you don't know the context in which the macro expansion will be placed, it is better to include them. If you write a macro to sum its parameters, you will easily see that without the outer parentheses, there are many contexts in which you will get a result that is different from what you expect.

Pre-processor Directives on Multiple Lines

A pre-processor directive must be a single logical line, but this doesn't prevent you from using the statement continuation character \, that we have already seen in the context of spreading a C language statement over several lines. We could write:

```
#define min( x, y ) \
    x<y ? x : y
```

Here the directive definition continues on the second line with the first non-blank character found, so you can position the text on the second line wherever you feel looks the nicest arrangement. Note that the \ must be the last character on the line, immediately before you press *Enter*.

Strings as Macro Arguments

String constants are a potential source of confusion when used with macros. The simplest string substitution is a single level definition such as:

```
#define MYSTR "This string"
```

If you now write the statement:

```
printf"%s", MYSTR );
```

this will be converted into the statement:

```
printf("%s", "This string" );
```

which should be what you are expecting. You couldn't use the **#define** statement without the quotes in the substitution sequence and expect to be able to put the quotes in your program text instead. For example, if you write:

```
#defineMYSTR This string
...
printf("%s", "MYSTR" );
```

there will be no substitution for MYSTR in the `printf()` function. Anything in quotes in your program is assumed to be a literal string, and so the pre-processor won't analyze it.

There is also a special way of specifying that the substitution for a macro argument is to be implemented as a string. For example, you could specify a macro to display a string using the function `printf()` as:

```
#define PrintStr( arg ) printf( "%s", #arg )
```

The character `#` preceding the appearance of the parameter `arg`, in the macro expansion, indicates the argument is to be surrounded by double quotes when the substitution is generated. Therefore, if you write the statement in your program:

```
PrintStr( Output );
```

this will be converted by the pre-processor to:

```
printf( "%s", "Output" );
```

You may be wondering why this apparent complication has been introduced into pre-processing. Well, without this facility you wouldn't be able to include a variable string in a macro definition at all. If you were to put the double quotes around the macro parameter, the pre-processor wouldn't interpret this as a variable, merely a string with quotes around it. On the other hand, if you put the quotes in the macro expansion, the string between the quotes wouldn't be interpreted as a parameter variable identifier, it would be just a string constant. So what might appear to be an unnecessary complication at first sight, is actually an essential tool for creating macros which allow strings between quotes to be created.

A common use of this mechanism is for converting a variable name to a string, such as in the directive:

```
show( var ) printf("\n%s = %d", #var, var );
```

If we now write:

```
show( number );
```

this will generate the statement:

```
printf("\n%s = %d", "number", number);
```

You can also generate a substitution that would allow you to display a string with double quotes included. Assuming we have defined the macro PrintStr as above, and you write the statement:

```
PrintStr( "Output" );
```

it will be pre-processed into the statement:

```
printf( "%s", "\"Output\"" );
```

This is possible because the pre-processor is clever enough to recognize the need to put \" at each end to get a string including double quotes to be displayed correctly.

Joining Two Results of a Macro Expansion

There are times when you may wish to generate two results in a macro and join them together with no spaces between them. Suppose we try to define a macro to do this as:

```
#define join( a, b ) ab
```

This can't work as we need it to. The definition of the expansion will be interpreted as ab, not as the parameter a followed by the parameter b. If we separate them with a blank, the result will be separated with a blank, which isn't what we want either. The pre-processor provides us with another operator to solve this problem. The solution is to specify the macro as:

```
#define join( a, b ) a##b
```

The presence of the operator comprising the two characters ## serve to separate the parameters, and to indicate to the pre-processor that the result of the two substitutions are to be joined. For example, writing the statement:

```
strlen( join( var, 123 ) );
```

will result in the statement:

```
strlen( var123 );
```

This might be applied to synthesizing a variable name for some reason, or generating a format control string from two or more macro parameters.

Logical Pre-Processor Directives

The last example we looked at appears to be of limited value, since it's hard to envisage when you would want to simply join **var** to **123**, since you could always use one parameter, and write **var123** as the argument. One aspect of pre-processing facilities that adds considerably more potential to the previous example, is the possibility for multiple macro substitution, where the arguments for one macro are derived from substitutions defined in another. In our last example, both arguments to the **join()** macro could have been generated by other **#define** substitutions or macros. The pre-processor also supports directives which provide a logical **if** capability, which vastly expands the scope of what you can do with the pre-processor.

Conditional Compilation

The first logical directive we shall discuss allows you to test whether an identifier exists as a result of having been created in a previous **#define** statement. It takes the form:

```
#if defined identifier
```

If the specified **identifier** has been defined, then statements following the **#if** are executed until the statement:

```
#endif
```

is reached. If the identifier hasn't been defined, the statements between the **#if** and the **#endif** will be skipped. This is the same logical process we use in C programming, except that here we are applying it to the generation of modified program statements.

You can also test for the absence of an identifier. In fact, this tends to be used more frequently than the form we have just seen. The general form of this directive is:

```
#if !defined identifier
```

Here the statements following the `#if` down to the `#endif` will be executed if the identifier hasn't previously been defined. This provides you with a method of avoiding duplicating functions, or other blocks of code and directives, in a program consisting of several files, or to ensure bits of code that may occur repeatedly in different libraries aren't repeated when the `#include` statements in your program are processed. The mechanism is simply to top and tail the block of code you want to avoid duplicating as follows:

```
#if !defined block1
#define block1
/* Block of code you do not   */
/* want to be repeated.       */
#endif
```

If the identifier `block1` hasn't been defined, the block following the `#if` will be processed and `block1` will be defined. The following block of code down to the `#endif` will also be included in your program. Any subsequent occurrence of the same group of statements won't be included since the identifier `block1` now exists.

The `#define` directive doesn't need to specify a substitution value in this case. For the conditional directives to operate it's sufficient for `block1` to appear in a `#define` directive. You can now include this block of code anywhere where you think you might need it, with the assurance that it will never be duplicated within a program. The pre-processor directives ensure this can't happen.

It's a good idea to get into the habit of protecting code in your own libraries in this fashion. You will be surprised how easy it is, once you have collected a few libraries of your own functions, to end up duplicating blocks of code accidentally.

You aren't limited to testing just one value with the pre-processor `#if`. You can use logical operators to test whether multiple identifiers have been defined. For example, the statement:

```
#if defined block1 && defined block2
```

will evaluate to True if both `block1` and `block2` have previously been defined, and so the code that follows such a directive won't be included unless this is the case.

A further extension of the flexibility in applying the pre-processor conditional directives, is the ability to undefine an identifier you have previously defined. This is achieved using a directive such as:

```
#undef block1
```

Now, if `block1` had previous been defined, after this directive it is no longer defined. These can all be combined to useful effect as an exercise of your ingenuity.

There are alternative ways of writing these which are slightly briefer. You can use whichever of the following forms you prefer:

```
#if defined or #ifdef
#if !defined or #ifndef
```

Directives Testing For Specific Values

You can also use a form of the `#if` directive to test the value of a constant expression. If the value of the constant expression is non-zero, the following statements down to the next `#endif` are executed. If the constant expression evaluates to zero, the following statements down to the next `#endif` are skipped. The general form of the `#if` directive is:

```
#if constant_expression
```

This is most frequently applied to test for a specific value being assigned to an identifier by a previous pre-processor directive. We might have the following sequence of statements for example:

```
#if CPU == 486
printf("\nPerformance should be good." );
#endif
```

The `printf()` statement will only be included in the program here if the identifier `CPU` has been defined as 486 in a previous `#define` directive.

Multiple Choice Selections

To complement the `#if` directives, we have the `#else` directive. This works exactly the same way as the `else` statement does, in that it identifies a group of directives to be executed, or statements to be included, if the `#if` condition fails. For example:

```
#if CPU == 486
printf("\nPerformance should be good." );
#else
printf("\nPerformance may not be so good." );
#endif
```

In this case, one or other of the `printf()` statements will be included depending on whether `CPU` has been defined as `486` or not.

The pre-processor also supports a special form of the `#if` for multiple choice selections, where only one of several choices of statements for inclusion in the program is required. This is the `#elif` directive, which has the general form:

```
#elif constant_expression
```

An example of using this would be:

```
#define US 0
#define UK 1
#define Australia 2
#define Country US
#if Country == US
#define Greeting #Howdy, stranger.
#elif Country == UK
#define Greeting #Wotcher, mate.
#elif Country == Australia
#define Greeting #G'day, sport."
#endif
printf("\n%s", Greeting );
```

With this sequence of directives the output of the `printf()` statement will depend on the value assigned to the identifier `Country`, in this case `US`.

Standard Pre-processor Macros

There are a variety of standard macros defined by the pre-processor. There are usually a considerable number of these, which you will find described in your compiler documentation. We will just mention two which are of general interest, and which are available to you.

The macro __DATE__ provides a string representation of the date when it's invoked in your program, in the form "Mmm dd yyyy". Here Mmm is the month in characters, such as Jan, Feb, and so on. The pair of characters dd is the day in the form of a pair of digits 1 to 31, where single digit days are preceded by a blank. Finally yyyy is the year as four digits, 1994 for example.

A similar macro, __TIME__ provides a string containing the value of the time when it is invoked, in the form "hh:mm:ss", which is evidently a string containing pairs of digits for hours, minutes and seconds, separated by colons.

You could use this to record when your program was last compiled with a statement such as:

```
printf("\nProgram last compiled at %s on %s", __TIME__, __DATE__ );
```

Once the program has been compiled, the values output by the `printf()` statement are fixed until you compile it again. On subsequent executions of the program the then current time and date will be output. Don't confuse these macros with the time function we will discuss later in this chapter.

Debugging Methods

Most of your programs will contain errors, or bugs, when you first complete them. Removing such bugs from a program can represent a substantial proportion of the time required to write a program. The larger and more complex the program, the more bugs it's likely to contain, and the more time it will take to get it to run properly. With very large programs, such as typified by operating systems or complex applications such as word processing systems, or even C program development systems, they can be so complex that all the bugs can never be eliminated. You may already have experience of this in practice with some of the systems on your own computer. Usually these kinds of residual bugs are relatively minor, with ways in the system to work around them.

Your approach to writing a program can significantly affect how difficult it will be to test. A well-structured program consisting of compact functions, each with a well-defined purpose is much easier to test than one without these attributes. Finding bugs will also be easier with a program that has extensive comments documenting the operation and purpose of its component functions, and that has well chosen variable and function names. Good use of indentation and statement layout can also make testing and fault finding simpler.

It is beyond the scope of this book to deal with debugging comprehensively, but we will introduce the basic ideas that you need to be aware of. Then when it comes to it, you will know which direction you are heading and what tools should be available.

Integrated Debuggers

Many compilers are supplied with extensive debugging tools built into the program development environment. These can be very powerful facilities that can dramatically reduce the time required to get a program working. They typically provide a varied range of aids to testing a program that include:

> **Tracing Program Flow**
> This capability allows you to execute your program one source statement at a time. It operates by pausing execution after each statement is executed, and continuing with the next statement after you press a designated key. Other provisions of the debug environment will usually allow you to display information at ease, pausing to show you what's happening to the data in your program.

Setting Breakpoints

Executing a large or complex program one statement at a time can be very tedious. It may even be impossible in a reasonable period of time. All you need is a loop which executes 10,000 times to make it an unrealistic proposition. Breakpoints provide an excellent alternative. Here you define specific selected statements in your program where a pause should occur to allow you to check what's happening. Execution continues to the next breakpoint when you press a specified key.

Setting Watches

This sort of facility will allow you to identify variables that you want to track the value of as execution progresses. The value of the variables you select are displayed at each pause point in your program. If you step through your program statement by statement, you can see the exact point at which values are changed, or perhaps not changed when you expect them to be.

Inspecting Program Elements

It may also be possible to examine a wide variety of program components. For example, at breakpoints inspection can show details of a function such as its return type and its arguments. You can also see details of pointers in terms of their address, the address they contain, and the data stored at the address contained in the pointer. Seeing the values of expressions and modifying variables may also be provided for. Modifying variables can help to bypass problem areas to allow other areas to be executed with correct data, even though an earlier part of the program may not be working properly.

The Pre-processor in Debugging

Using conditional pre-processor statements you can arrange for blocks of code to be included in your program to assist in testing. In spite of the power of the debug facilities included with many C and C++ development systems, the addition of tracing code of your own can still be useful. You have complete control of the formatting of data to be displayed for debugging purposes, and you can even arrange for the kind of output to vary according to conditions or relationships within the program.

Try It Out - Debugging Using the Pre-processor

We can illustrate how this can be done using a slightly modified version of a previous program which calls functions through an array of function pointers:

```
/* Example 13.1 Debugging using the pre-processor    */
#include <stdio.h>
#include <stdlib.h>

#define random( NumValues ) (int)(((long)rand()*(NumValues))/(RAND_MAX+1))
#define test
#define testf

/* Function prototypes */
int sum( int, int );
int product( int, int );
int difference( int, int );

void main()
{
  int i = 0;                 /* Loop counter                              */
  int j = 0;                 /* Index for function selection              */
  int a = 10, b = 5;         /* Starting values                           */
  int result = 0;            /* Storage for results                       */
  int ( *pfun[ 3 ] ) (int, int ); /* Function pointer array declaration   */

/* Initialize pointers */
  pfun[0] = sum;
  pfun[1] = product;
  pfun[2] = difference;

/* Execute each function pointed to */
  for( i = 0 ; i < 10 ; i++ )
  {
    j = random( 3 );              /* Generate random index 0 to 2         */

    #ifdef test
    printf("\nRandom number = %d", j );
    if( j>2 )
    {
      printf("\nInvalid array index = %d", j);
      break;
    }
    #endif

    result = pfun[j]( a , b );   /* Call random function                  */
```

```
   printf("\nresult = %d", result );
 }
 result = pfun[1]( pfun[0]( a , b ), pfun[2]( a , b ) );
 printf("\n\nThe product of the sum and the difference = %d", result );

}

/* Definition of the function sum */
int sum( int x, int y )
{

 #ifdef testf
 printf("\nFunction sum called." );
 #endif

 return x + y;
}

/* Definition of the function product*/
int product( int x, int y )
{

 #ifdef testf
 printf("\nFunction product called." );
 #endif

 return x * y;
}

/* Definition of the function difference*/
int difference( int x, int y )
{

 #ifdef testf
 printf("\nFunction difference called." );
 #endif

 return x - y;
}
```

How It Works

We have a macro defined at the beginning of the program:

```
#define random( NumValues ) (int)(((long)rand()*NumValues/(RAND_MAX+1))
```

This defines the macro **random** in terms of a function **rand()** from **STDLIB.H**. The function **rand()** generates random numbers in the range 0 to **RAND_MAX**, which is a constant defined in **STDLIB.H**. Our macro maps values from this range to produce values from 0 to **NumValues-1**. We cast the value from **rand()** to **long** to ensure that we can accommodate the result of multiplying it by **NumValues**, and cast the result overall to **int** because that is what we want in our program. It is quite likely that your **STDLIB.H** will already contain a macro for **random**. If so you will get an error message as the compiler will not allow two different definitions of the same macro. In this case just delete the definition from the program.

Look at the loop in **main()**:

```
for( i = 0 ; i < 10 ; i++ )
{
  j = random( 3 );                    /* Generate random index 0 to 2    */

  #ifdef test
  printf("\nRandom number = %d", j );
  if( j>2 )
  {
    printf("\nInvalid array index = %d", j);
    break;
  }
  #endif

  result = pfun[j]( a , b );          /* Call random function            */

  printf("\nresult = %d", result );
}
```

This has been modified compared to the previous version, by indexing the function pointer array using the variable j which has its value generated by the macro call **random(3)**.This will generate a random value between 0 and 2. This makes the example more interesting since we now don't know beforehand what the sequence of function calls is going to be. It depends on what sequence of random index values is generated.

Within the loop we have two statements included if **test** is defined. The first displays the value of the index j. We might well want to see this value when the program is being tested. The second statement, the **if**, is just a precaution. If by some means, we obtained a value for j which was outside the range of valid indexes for the array **pfun**, who knows what might happen.

If we look at one of the functions that may be called, `product()` for example:

```
/* Definition of the function product*/
int product( int x, int y )
{

  #ifdef testf
  printf("\nFunction product called." );
  #endif

  return x * y;
}
```

this also has some code included if `testf` is defined. We can therefore control whether the statements in the `#ifdef` block are included here, independently from the block in `main()`. With the program as written above with both `test` and `testf` defined, we will get trace output for the random index values generated and a message from each function as it is called, so we can follow the sequence of calls in the program exactly.

You can have as many different symbolic constants defined as you wish, as we have seen previously in this chapter, you can combine them into logical expressions using the `#if defined` form of the conditional directive.

Using the assert Macro

The assert macro is contained in the standard ANSI C library `ASSERT.H`. This enables you to insert tests of arbitrary logical expressions in your program, which cause the program to be terminated with a diagnostic message if a specified logical expression is **False**.

Try It Out - Demonstrating the assert Macro

We can demonstrate how this works with a simple example:

```
/* Example 13.2 Demonstrating assertions       */
#include <stdio.h>
#include <assert.h>
void main()
{
  int x = 0, y = 5;
  for( x=0 ; x< 20 ; x++ )
  {
    printf("\nx = %d\ty = %d", x, y );
    assert( x<y );
  }
}
```

Compiling and executing this with a Borland compiler produces the output:

```
x = 0 y = 5
x = 1 y = 5
x = 2 y = 5
x = 3 y = 5
x = 4 y = 5
x = 5 y = 5
Assertion failed: x<y , file EX13_02.C, line 10
```

How It Works

At this point apart from the **assert** statement, the program shouldn't need much explanation as it simply prints the values of **x** and **y** in the **for** loop.

The program is terminated by the **assert** macro which calls **abort()** as soon as the condition **x<y** becomes False. As you can see from the output, this is when **x** reaches the value 5. The macro displays the output on **stderr** which is always the display screen. Not only do you get the condition that failed displayed, but you also get the file name and line number in the file where the failure occurred. This is particularly useful with multi-file programs, where the source of the error is pinpointed exactly.

Assertions are often used for critical conditions in a program where, if certain conditions are not met, disaster will surely ensue. You would want to be sure that the program won't continue if such errors arise. Example 13.1 contains exactly this kind of situation, where we are generating index values using a random number generator. With this sort of technique there is always the possibility of a bug somewhere resulting in an invalid index value. If the index is outside the limits of the array **pfun**, the result is pretty much guaranteed to be catastrophic, as we will be trying to execute a non-existent function at a spurious address. Instead of the **#ifdef** block we could simply have put:

```
assert ( j<= 2 );
```

It is very simple and effective, and provides sufficient information to pin down where the program is terminated if an error occurs.

You can also switch off the assertion mechanism by adding to a program the definition:

```
#define NDEBUG
```

This will cause all assertions to be ignored. It must be placed before the #include statement for **ASSERT.H** to be effective though. If you add this #define at the beginning of Example 13.2, you will see that we get output for all the values of **x** from 0 to 19, and no diagnostic message.

Additional Library Functions

The library functions are basic to the power of the C language. While we have covered quite a range of standard library functions so far, it's impossible within the scope of this book to discuss all the standard libraries. However, we can introduce a few more of the most commonly used functions we haven't dealt with in detail up to now.

The Date and Time Function Library

Because time is an important parameter to measure, C includes a standard library of functions called **TIME.H,** dealing with time and the date. They provide output in various forms from the hardware timer in your PC. The simplest function has the prototype;

```
clock_t clock( void );
```

This function returns the processor time (not the elapsed time) used by the program since execution began, as a value of type **clock_t**. The type **clock_t** is defined in **TIME.H** and is equivalent to **long**. The value is measured in clock ticks. To convert the value returned by the function **clock()** to seconds, you divide it by the constant **CLOCKS_PER_SEC** also defined in the library **TIME.H**. The function returns -1 if an error occurs.

The function **time()** returns the calendar time as a value of type **time_t**. The current calendar time is the time in seconds since a fixed time and date. The fixed time and date is 00:00:00GMT on 1st January 1970 in Borland libraries for example. The prototype of the function time is:

```
time_t time( time_t * );
```

If the argument is not **NULL**, the current calendar time is also stored in the location pointed to by the pointer to **time_t** argument. The type **time_t** is defined in the library, and is equivalent to **long**. To calculate elapsed time in seconds between two successive `time_t` values returned by `time()`, you can use the function `difftime()`, which has the prototype:

```
double difftime( time_t T2, time_t T1 );
```

The function will return the value `T2 - T1` expressed in seconds as a value of type `double`.

Try It Out - Using Time Functions

We could define a function to log the elapsed time and processor time used between successive calls, by using functions from `TIME.H` as follows:

```
/* Example 13.3 Test our timer function        */
#include <stdio.h>
#include <time.h>

typedef struct {
    double CPU,              /* CPU time in seconds              */
           Elapsed;          /* Elapsed time in seconds          */
    } Mytime;

Mytime timer( void );        /* Timer function prototype         */

void main()
{
  Mytime tval;
  long count = 1000000L,
  i = 0;
  double x = 0.0;

  timer();                   /* Set start time                  */

  for ( i=0 ; i<count ; i++ )
    x = 3.4567 * 4.5678;     /* Multiply 1m times               */

  tval = timer();            /* Get time for 1m multiplies       */
  printf("\nCPU time for one million multiplies is %lf", tval.CPU );
  tval = timer();            /* Get time since last call.        */
  printf("\nElapsed time to execute the previous printf is %lf",
                      tval.Elapsed );
}

/* Timer function  */
Mytime timer( void )
{
  Mytime tval = { 0.0,0.0 }; /* struct to be returned initialised to zero */
  static time_t El_last = 0; /* Holds calendar time from last call        */
```

```
   time_t El_this = 0;
   static clock_t CPU_last = 0; /* Holds clock value from last call     */
   clock_t CPU_this = 0;

   if( El_last > 0.0 )
   {
     El_this = time( NULL );
     CPU_this = clock();
     tval.CPU = ( CPU_this - CPU_last )/ CLOCKS_PER_SEC;
     tval.Elapsed = difftime( El_this, El_last );
     CPU_last = CPU_this;
     El_last = El_this;
     return tval;
   }

   El_last = time( NULL );   /* We only execute this bit first time around  */
   CPU_last = clock();
   return tval;
}
```

How It Works

This program serves to illustrate the use of the functions clock(), time(), and difftime(). The timing of the processor usage for the multiply operations won't be very precise. There are instructions other than just multiply involved in the loop and the computation, and the resolution of the timing mechanism isn't very accurate. Similarly, the elapsed time may not be very precise. The function time() returns the current time in seconds, so we won't get values less than a second. It's possible to get more accurate results but this is outside the scope of this book. If your machine is fairly fast the value of the elapsed time to execute some functions may turn out to be apparently zero, but you can see the principles involved.

As a global, we have the declaration:

```
typedef struct{
     double CPU,            /* CPU time in seconds        */
          Elapsed;          /* Elapsed time in seconds    */
     }Mytime;
```

This defines the type name, Mytime, corresponding to the structure shown. The structure has just two members of type double, CPU and Elapsed.

Within our function `timer()`, the values returned by the library functions `clock()` and `time()` are saved in **static** variables `CPU_last` and `El_last`. This is to ensure that they will be available, and their values will persist for use the next time our function is called. This allows the increments since last time to be computed.

Also within the function, the statement:

```
if( El_last > 0.0 )
```

checks whether the static variable `El_last` has a value greater than zero. On the first call to the function it will still have its initial value of zero since there is no history. Therefore, the statements in the `if` block won't be executed. Instead we execute the statements:

```
El_last = time( NULL );   /* We only execute this bit first time around   */
CPU_last = clock();
return tval;
```

This sets `El_last` to the current value returned by the function `time()`, and initializes the value of `CPU_last`.

On second and subsequent calls `El_last` will contain a positive value, in which case elapsed time since the last call can be calculated, along with the processor time used. This is done by executing the block:

```
{
  El_this = time( NULL );
  CPU_this = clock();
  tval.CPU = ( CPU_this - CPU_last )/ CLOCKS_PER_SEC;
  tval.Elapsed = difftime( El_this, El_last );
  CPU_last = CPU_this;
  El_last = El_this;
  return tval;
}
```

The first two statements get the current elapsed time value and the current processor time. The processor time is calculated as the difference between the value just obtained, and the value from the last call of the function, divided by the library constant `CLOCKS_PER_SEC` to get the result in seconds as a decimal value. The elapsed time is then obtained using the function `difftime()`. The result is in whole seconds. We then update the values of `CPU_last` and `El_last` to the current values, to enable the increments in processor time and elapsed time to be calculated on the next call.

The function `main()` uses the function `timer()` to evaluate the processor time used for one million floating multiply operations within the loop, and then to calculate the elapsed time to execute the `printf()` function.

Getting the Date

Having the time in seconds since a date around a quarter of a century ago is interesting, but it is often more convenient to get today's date. We can do this with the function `ctime()` which has the prototype:

```
char *ctime( time_t * );
```

The function accepts a pointer to a `time_t` value as an argument, and returns a pointer to a 26 character string containing the day, the date, the time and the year, and is terminated by a newline and a `'\0'`. A typical string returned might be:

```
Mon May 2  10:45:56 1994\n\0
```

The argument is the address of a value supplied by the `time()` function.

You can also get at the various components of the time and date using the library function `localtime()`. This function has the prototype:

```
struct tm *localtime( time_t * );
```

This function accepts a pointer to a `time_t` type value and returns a pointer to a structure type `tm`, which is defined in the library. The structure contains the members:

int tm_sec	Seconds	
int tm_min	Minutes	Time on 24 hour clock
int tm_hour	Hours	
int tm_mday	Day of the month (1 to 31)	
int tm_mon	Month (0 to 11)	
int tm_year	Year (Current year minus 1900)	
int tm_wday	Weekday (Sunday is 0, to Saturday is 6)	
int tm_yday	Day of year (0 to 365)	
int tm_isdst	Daylight Saving flag (0 for daylight saving time)	

This structure is a **static** structure so it's overwritten with each call to the function. If you want to keep any of the member values, you need to copy them elsewhere before the next call to **localtime()**. You could create your own **time_t** structure and save the whole lot if you really need to.

Try It Out - Getting the Date

It's very easy to pick out the members you want from the structure of type **tm** returned from the function **localtime()**. We can demonstrate this with the following example:

```
/* Example 13.4 Getting date data with ease        */
#include <stdio.h>
#include <time.h>
void main()
{
  char *Day[ 7 ] = { "Sunday" , "Monday", "Tuesday", "Wednesday",
    "Thursday", "Friday", "Saturday" };
  char * Month[ 12 ] = { "January", "February", "March", "April",
    "May", "June", "July", "August",
    "September", "October", "November", "December" };

  char *Suffix[ 4 ] = { "st", "nd", "rd", "th" };
  int i = 3;                    /* Day suffix index                 */
  struct tm *OurT = NULL;    /* Pointer for the time structure      */
  time_t Tval = 0;

  Tval = time( NULL );
  OurT = localtime( &Tval );

  switch( OurT->tm_mday )
  {
    case 1: case 21: case 31: i= 0;                    /* Select "st" */
      break;
    case 2: case 22: i = 1;                            /* Select "nd" */
      break;
    case 3: case 23: i = 2;                            /* Select "rd" */
      break;
    default: i = 3;                                    /* Select "th" */
      break;
  }

  printf("\nToday is %s the %d%s %s %d", Day[ OurT->tm_wday ],
    OurT->tm_mday, Suffix[ i ], Month[ OurT->tm_mon ], 1900 + OurT->tm_year );
  printf("\nThe time is %d : %d : %d", OurT->tm_hour, OurT->tm_min, OurT-
>tm_sec );
}
```

How It Works

In this example, the first declarations in `main()` are:

```
char *Day[ 7 ] = { "Sunday" , "Monday", "Tuesday", "Wednesday",
  "Thursday", "Friday", "Saturday" };
char * Month[ 12 ] = { "January", "February", "March", "April",
  "May", "June", "July", "August",
  "September", "October", "November", "December" };

char *Suffix[ 4 ] = { "st", "nd", "rd", "th" };
```

These both define an array of pointers to `char`. The first holds the days of the week and the second holds suffixes to numerical values for the day in the month when representing dates. We could have left out the array dimensions and the compiler would have computed them for us, but in this case we can be sure we haven't made an error, as we are reasonably confident about both these numbers.

We also declare a structure variable in the declaration:

```
struct tm *OurT = NULL;    /* Pointer for the time structure        */
```

This provides space to store the structure returned by the function `local_time()`.

We first obtain the current time in `Tval` using the function `time()`. We then use this value to generate the values of the members of the structure returned by the function `localtime()`. Once we have the structure from `local_time()`, we execute the `switch`:

```
switch( OurT->tm_mday )
{
  case 1: case 21: case 31: i= 0;                     /* Select "st" */
    break;
  case 2: case 22: i = 1;                             /* Select "nd" */
    break;
  case 3: case 23: i = 2;                             /* Select "rd" */
    break;
  default: i = 3;                                     /* Select "th" */
    break;
  }
```

Based on the member `tm_mday`, the `switch` selects an index to the array `Suffix` for use when outputting the date.

The day, the date, and the time are displayed, with the day and month strings being obtained by indexing the appropriate array with the corresponding structure member value. The addition of 1900 to the value of the member `tm_year` is because this value is measured relative to the year 1900.

Variable Argument Lists

It can't have escaped your notice that some functions in the standard libraries accept a variable number of arguments. The functions `printf()` and `scanf()` are obvious examples. You may come up with a need to do this yourself from time to time, so the standard library `STDARG.H` provides you with routines to write some of your own.

The immediately obvious problem with writing a function with a variable number of parameters is how to specify its prototype. Suppose we are going to produce a function to calculate the average of two or more values of type `double`. Clearly, calculating the average of less than two values wouldn't make much sense. The prototype would be written:

```
double average( double, double, ...);
```

The ellipses (that is the fancy name for the three periods after the second parameter type) indicate that a variable number of arguments may follow the first two fixed arguments. You must have at least one fixed argument. The remaining specifications are as you would usually find with a function prototype. The first two arguments are `double`, and it returns a `double` result.

The second problem with variable argument lists that hits you between the eyes next, is how you reference them when writing the function. Since you don't know how many there are you can't give them names. The only possibility is an indirect method through routines supplied by the library `STDARG.H`. The library provides you with three routines which are usually implemented as macros, but they look and operate like functions so we will discuss them as though they were. You need to use all three when implementing your own function with a variable number of arguments. They are called `va_start()`, `va_arg()`, and `va_end()`. The first of these has the form:

```
void va_start( va_list parg, last_fixed_arg );
```

The name of the function is obtained from variable argument **start**. This function accepts two arguments, a pointer **parg** of type **va_list** and the last fixed argument specified for the function we are writing. So using our function **average()** as an illustration, if we can start to write the function as:

```
double average( double A1, double A2,...)
{
  va_list parg;           /* Pointer for variable argument list         */

  va_start( parg, A2);

}
```

We have first declared the variable **parg** of type **va_list**. We then call **va_start()** with this as the first argument, and specify our last fixed parameter **A2** as the second argument. The effect of the call to **va_start()** is to set the variable **parg** to point to the first variable argument.

We now need to know how to access the value of the variable arguments, so let's show how this is done by completing the function **average()**.

```
/* Function to calculate the average of a variable number of arguments */
double average( double A1, double A2,...)
{
  va_list parg;                          /* Pointer for variable argument list */
  double sum = A1+A2;                         /* Accumulate sum of the arguments */
  double value = 0;                                     /* Argument value */
  int count = 2;                               /* Count of number of arguments */

  va_start( parg,A2 );                         /* Initialize argument pointer */

  while( (value = va_arg(parg, double) )!=0.0 )
  {
    sum += value;
    count++;
  }
  va_end(parg);                        /* Terminate variable argument process */
  return sum/count;
}
```

We can work our way through this step by step. After declaring **parg**, we declare the variable **sum** as **double**, and as being initialized with the sum of the first two fixed arguments, **A1** and **A2**. We will accumulate the sum of all the argument values in **sum**. The next variable, **value**, declared as **double** will be used to store the values of the variable arguments as we obtain them one by one. We then declare a counter, `count`, for the total number of arguments, and initialize this with the value 2 since we know we have at least that many values from the fixed arguments. After calling `va_start()` to initialize `parg`, most of the action takes place within the `while` loop. Look at the loop condition:

```
while( (value = va_arg(parg, double) )!=0.0 )
```

The loop condition calls another routine from `stdarg.h`, `va_arg()`. The first argument to `va_arg()` is the variable `parg` which we initialized through the call to `va_start()`. The second argument is a specification of the type of the argument we expect to find. The function `va_arg()` returns the value of the current argument specified by `parg` and this is stored in `value`. It also updates the pointer `parg` to point to the next argument in the list, based on the type you specified in the call. It's essential to have some means of determining the types of the variable arguments. If you don't specify the correct type, you won't be able to obtain the next argument correctly. In our case the function is written assuming they are all `double`. Another assumption we are making is that all the arguments will be non-zero except for the last. This is reflected in the condition for continuing the loop being that `value` is not equal to zero. Within the loop we have familiar statements for accumulating the sum in `sum`, and for incrementing `count`.

When an argument value obtained is zero the loop ends and we execute the statement:

```
va_end(parg);
```

The call to `va_arg()` is essential to tidy up loose ends that are left around by the process. If you omit this call your program may not work properly. Once the tidying up is complete we can return the required result with the statement:

```
return sum/count;
```

Try It Out - Using Variable Argument Lists

Having written the function `average()` it would be a good idea to exercise it in a little program:

```
/* Example 13.5 Calculating an average using variable argument lists */
#include <stdio.h>
#include <stdarg.h>

double average(double , double,...);      /* Function prototype          */

void main()
{
  double Val1 = 10.5, Val2 = 2.5;
  int num1 = 6, num2 = 5;
  long num3 = 12, num4 = 20;
  printf("\n Average = %lf", average(Val1, 3.5, Val2, 4.5, 0.0) );
  printf("\n Average = %lf", average(1.0, 2.0, 0.0) );
  printf("\n Average = %lf", average( (double)num2, Val2,(double) num1,
                 (double) num4,(double) num3, 0.0) );
}

/* Function to calculate the average of a variable number of arguments */
double average( double A1, double A2,...)
{
  va_list parg;              /* Argument pointer                  */
  double sum = A1+A2;        /* Accumulate sum of the arguments   */
  double value = 0;          /* Argument value                    */
  int count = 2;             /* Count of number of arguments      */

  va_start( parg,A2 );       /* Initialize argument pointer       */

  while( (value = va_arg(parg, double) )!=0.0 )
  {
    sum += value;
    count++;
  }
  va_end(parg);              /* Terminate variable argument process */
  return sum/count;
}
```

If you compile and run this, you should get the output:

```
Average = 5.25
Average = 1.5
Average = 9.1
```

How It Works

This output is as a result of three calls to average with different numbers of arguments. Remember, we need to ensure that we cast our variable arguments to the type **double**, assumed by the function **average()**.

You might be wondering how **printf()** manages to handle a mix of types. Well, remember it has a control string with format specifiers. This supplies the information necessary to determine the type of the arguments. We have seen how things don't work out right if we specify the wrong format for the type of variable we want to output.

Basic Rules

We could summarize the basic rules and requirements for writing functions to be called with a variable number of arguments:

- There needs to be at least one fixed argument in a function accepting a variable number of arguments.

- You must call **va_start()** to initialize the value of the variable argument list pointer in your function. This pointer also needs to be declared as of type **va_list**.

- There needs to be a mechanism to determine the type of each argument. Either there can be a default type assumed, or there can be a parameter which allows the argument type to be determined. For example, in our function **average()**, we could have an extra fixed argument which would have the value 0 if the variable arguments were **double**, and 1 if they were **long**. If the argument type specified in the call to **va_arg()** isn't correct for the argument value specified when your function is called, your function won't work properly.

- You have to arrange for there to be some way to determine when the list of arguments is exhausted. For example, the last argument in the variable argument list could have a fixed value that can be detected because it's different from all the others, or a fixed argument could contain a count of the number of arguments in total, or in the variable part of the argument list.

- There are restrictions on the types of variable arguments you are allowed to use. You can't use **char**, unsigned **char**, or **float** types with **va_arg()**. Check the documentation for your compiler for full details.

- You must call **va_end()** before you exit a function with a variable number of arguments. If you fail to do so the function won't work properly.

You could try ringing the changes on Example 13.3 to understand this process better. Put some output in the function **average()** and see what happens if you change a few things. For example, you could display **value** and **count** in the loop in the function **average()**. You could then modify **main()** to use an argument that isn't **double**, or introduce a function call where the last argument is not zero.

Summary

You should now be a fully-fledged C programmer. C program code will be meat and drink to you by this stage.

Your header files are an excellent source of examples of coding pre-processor statements. You can view these examples with any text editor. Virtually all of the capabilities of the pre-processor are used in the libraries, and you will find lots of C source code there too. It's also useful to familiarize yourself with the contents of the libraries, as many things not necessarily described in the library documentation will be found here. If you are not sure what the type **clock_t** is for example, just look in the library **time.h** where you will find the definition.

To get better at programming, there is no alternative to practice. 'Practice makes perfect' the old saying goes, but unfortunately it doesn't apply to programming. You can always get better but you will never make perfection. However, every time you get a new piece of code to work as it should, it always generates a thrill and a feeling of satisfaction. Enjoy your programming!

Computer Arithmetic

In the chapters of the book, we have deliberately kept discussion of arithmetic to a minimum. However, it is important, so we are going to quickly go over the subject in this appendix. If you feel confident at math this will all be old hat to you. If you find the math parts tough, then this section should show you how easy it really is.

Binary Numbers

First let's consider what we mean when we write a common everyday number such as 321, or the number of the beast 666. Well, obviously what we mean is three hundred and twenty one, and six hundred and sixty six - reputedly tattooed on the back of young Damian's head. Put more precisely we mean:

321 is   3 x 10 x 10   +   2 x 10 + 1

666 is   6 x 10 x 10   +   6 x 10 + 6

Because it is built around powers of ten we call it the decimal system (derived from the Latin *decimalis* meaning *of tithes*, which was a tax of 10% - ah, those were the days...).

Representing numbers in this way is very handy for people with ten fingers and toes, or ten of any kind of appendage for that matter. However, your PC is quite unhandy, being built mainly of switches that are either on or off, which is OK for counting up to two, but not spectacular at counting to ten.

For this reason your computer represents numbers to base 2 rather than base 10. This is called the **binary** system of counting. Digits can only be 0 or 1, ideal when you only have on/off switches to represent them. In an exact analogy to our usual base 10 counting, the binary number 1101 is therefore:

$$1 \times 2 \times 2 \times 2 + 1 \times 2 \times 2 + 0 \times 2 + 1$$

which amounts to 13 in the decimal system. In the following figure you can see the decimal equivalents of 8 bit binary numbers illustrated.

Binary	Decimal	Binary	Decimal
0000 0000	0	1000 0000	128
0000 0001	1	1000 0001	129
0000 0010	2	1000 0010	130
...	...	...	...
0001 0000	16	1001 0000	144
0001 0001	17	1001 0001	145
...	...	...	...
0111 1100	124	1111 1100	252
0111 1101	125	1111 1101	253
0111 1110	126	1111 1110	254
0111 1111	127	1111 1111	255

Note that using the first 7 bits we can represent numbers from 0 to 127 which is a total of 2^7 numbers, and using all 8 bits we get 256, or 2^8 numbers. In general, if we have n bits we can represent 2^n integers from 0 to 2^n-1.

Hexadecimal Numbers

When we get to larger binary numbers, for example:

1111 0101 1011 1001 1110 0001

the notation starts to be a little cumbersome, particularly when you consider that if you apply the same method to work out what this in decimal, it's only 16,103,905 - a miserable 8 digits. You can sit more angels on a pinhead than that. Well, as it happens, we have an excellent alternative.

Arithmetic to base 16 is a very convenient option. Each digit can have values from 0 to 15 (the digits from 10 to 15 being represented by letters A to F as shown in the next figure) and values from 0 to 15 correspond quite nicely with the range of values that four binary digits can represent.

We can therefore represent the binary number above as a hexadecimal number, just by taking groups of four binary digits starting from the right, and writing the equivalent base 16 (also called hexadecimal) digit for each group. The binary number:

1111 0101 1011 1001 1110 0001

will therefore come out as:

F5B9E1

We have six hexadecimal digits corresponding to the six groups of four binary digits. Just to show it all works out with no cheating we can convert this number directly from hexadecimal to decimal, by again using the analogy with the meaning of a decimal number, as follows:

F5B9E1 is 15 x 16 x 16 x 16 x 16 x 16 +   5 x 16 x 16 x 16 x 16 +
11 x 16 x 16 x 16   +   9 x 16 x 16   +   14 x 16   +   1

This in turn turns out to be:

15,728,640 +   327,680   +   45,056   +   2304 +   224   +   1

Hexadecimal	Decimal	Binary
0	0	0000
1	1	0001
2	2	0010
...	...	...
9	9	1001
A	10	1010
B	11	1011
C	12	1100
D	13	1101
E	14	1110
F	15	1111

which fortunately totals to the same number we got when converting the equivalent binary number to a decimal value.

Negative Binary Numbers

There is another aspect to binary arithmetic that you need to understand - negative numbers. So far we have assumed everything is positive - the optimist's view if you will - our glass is still half full. But we can't avoid the negative side of life - the pessimist's perspective that our glass is already half empty - forever. How do we indicate a negative number? Well we only have binary digits at our disposal and indeed they contain the solution.

For numbers that we want to have the possibility of negative values (referred to as **signed** numbers) we must first decide on a fixed length (in other words, the number of binary digits) and then designate the leftmost binary digit as a sign bit. We have to fix the length in order to avoid any confusion about which bit is the sign bit.

Of course, we can have some numbers with 8 bits, and some with 16 bits, or whatever, as long as we know what the length is in each case. If the sign bit is 0 the number is positive, and if it is 1 it is negative. This would seem to solve our problem, but not quite. If we add -8 in binary to +12 we would really like to get the answer +4. If we do that simplistically, just putting the sign bit of the positive value to 1 to make it negative, and then doing the arithmetic with conventional carries, it doesn't quite work:

```
12  in binary is              0000 1100
-8 in binary we suppose is    1000 1000
```

since +8 is 0000 1000. If we now add these together we get:

```
1001 0100
```

This seems to be -20 which is not what we wanted at all. It's definitely not +4 which we know is 0000 0100. Ah, I hear you say, you can't treat a sign just like another digit. But that is just what we do have to do when dealing with computers because, dumb things that they are, they have trouble coping with anything else. So we really need a different representation for negative numbers. Well, we could try subtracting +12 from +4 since the result should be -8:

```
+4 is              0000 0100
Take away +12      0000 1100
```

and we get   1111 1000

For each digit from the fourth from the right onwards we had to borrow 1 to do the sum, analogously to our usual decimal method for subtraction. This supposedly is -8, and even though it doesn't look like it - it is. Just try adding it to +12 or +15 in binary and you will see that it works. So what is it? It turns out that the answer is what is called the two's complement representation of negative binary numbers.

Now here we are going to demand a little faith on your part and avoid getting into explanations of why it works. We will just show you how 2's complement form of a negative number can be constructed from a positive value, and that it does work you can prove to yourself. Let's return to our previous example where we need the 2's complement representation of -8. We start with +8 in binary:

0000 1000

We now flip each digit - if it is one make it zero, and vice versa:

1111 0111

This is called the 1's complement form, and if we now add 1 to this we will get the 2's complement form:

	1111 0111
Add one to this	0000 0001
and we get:	1111 1000

Now this looks pretty similar to our representation of -8 we got from subtracting +12 from +4. So just to be sure, let's try the original sum of adding -8 to +12:

+12 is	0000 1100
Our version of -8 is	1111 1000
and we get:	0000 0100

So the answer is 4 - magic. It works! The carry propagates through all the left most 1s setting them back to zero. One fell off the end, but we shouldn't worry about that. It's probably the one we borrowed from off the end in the subtraction sum we did to get -8. In fact what is happening is that we are making the assumption that the sign bit, 1 or 0, repeats forever to the left. Try a few examples of your own, you will find it always works quite automatically. The really great thing is, it makes arithmetic very easy (and fast) for your PC.

Floating Point Numbers

We often have to deal with very large numbers, the number of protons in the universe for example which needs around 79 decimal digits. Clearly there are lots of situations where we need more than the 10 decimal digits we get from a 4 byte binary number. Equally, there are lots of very small numbers. The amount of time in minutes it takes the typical car salesman to accept your offer on his 1982 Ford LTD (and only covered 380,000 miles...). A mechanism for handling both these kinds of numbers is - as you will have guessed - **floating point** numbers.

A floating point representation of a number is a decimal point followed by a fixed number of digits, multiplied by a power of 10 to get the number you want. It's easier to demonstrate than explain, so let's take some examples. The number 365 in normal decimal notation would be written in floating point form as:

.365E03

where the E stands for "exponent" and is the power of ten that the .365 (the mantissa) is multiplied by to get the required value. That is:

.365 x 10 x 10 x 10

which is clearly 365.

Now we can look at a small number:

.365E-04

is evaluated as $.365 \times 10^{-4}$ which is .0000365 - exactly the time in minutes required by the car salesman to accept your cash.

Suppose we have a large number such as 2,134,311,179. How does this look as a floating point number? Well, it looks like:

.2134311E03

It's not quite the same. We have lost three low order digits and we have approximated our original value as 2,134,311,000. This is a small price to pay for being able to handle such a vast range of numbers, typically from 10^{-38} to 10^{+38} either positive or negative, as well having an extended representation which goes from a minute 10^{-308} to a mighty 10^{+308}. They are called floating point numbers for the fairly obvious reason that the decimal point "floats" depending on the exponent value.

Aside from the fixed precision limitation in terms of accuracy, there is another aspect you may need to be conscious of. You need to take great care when adding or subtracting numbers of significantly different magnitudes. A simple example will demonstrate the kind of problem. We can first consider adding .365E-3 to .365E+7. We can write this as a decimal sum:

.000365 + 3,650,000

This produces the result:

3,650,000.000365

Which when converted back to floating point becomes:

.3650000E+7

So we might as well not have bothered. The problem lies directly with the fact that we only carry 7 digits precision. The 7 digits of the larger number are not affected by any of the digits of the smaller number because they are all further to the right. Funnily enough, you must also take care when the numbers are very nearly equal. If you compute the difference between such numbers you may end up with a result which only has one or two digits precision. It is quite easy in such circumstances to end up computing with numbers that are totally garbage.

ASCII Character Code Definition

ASCII: American Standard Code for Information Interchange

The first 32 ASCII characters provide control functions. Many of these have not been referenced in this book but are included here for completeness. In the following table, only the first 128 characters have been included. The remaining 128 characters include further special symbols and letters for national character sets.

Decimal	Hexadecimal	Character	Control
000	00	null	NUL
001	01	☺	SOH
002	02	●	STX
003	03	♥	ETX
004	04	♦	EOT
005	05	♣	ENQ
006	06	♠	ACK
007	07	•	BEL (Audible bell)
008	08		Backspace
009	09		HT
010	0A		LF (Line feed)
011	0B		VT (Vertical tab)
012	0C		FF (Form feed)
013	0D		CR (Carriage return)
014	0E		SO
015	0F	¤	SI

Continued

Decimal	Hexadecimal	Character	Control
016	10		DLE
017	11		DC1
018	12		DC2
019	13		DC3
020	14		DC4
021	15		NAK
022	16		SYN
023	17		ETB
024	18		CAN
025	19		EM
026	1A	→	SUB
027	1B	←	ESC (Escape)
028	1C	L	FS
029	1D		GS
030	1E		RS
031	1F		US
032	20		space
033	21	!	
034	22	"	
035	23	#	
036	24	$	
037	25	%	
038	26	&	
039	27	'	
040	28	(	
041	29	)	
042	2A	*	
043	2B	+	
044	2C	,	
045	2D	-	
046	2E	.	
047	2F	/	
048	30	0	
049	31	1	
050	32	2	
051	33	3	
052	34	4	
053	35	5	
054	36	6	

Continued

Decimal	Hexadecimal	Character	Control
055	37	7	
056	38	8	
057	39	9	
058	3A	:	
059	3B	;	
060	3C	<	
061	3D	=	
062	3E	>	
063	3F	?	
064	40	@	
065	41	A	
066	42	B	
067	43	C	
068	44	D	
069	45	E	
070	46	F	
071	47	G	
072	48	H	
073	49	I	
074	4A	J	
075	4B	K	
076	4C	L	
077	4D	M	
078	4E	N	
079	4F	O	
080	50	P	
081	51	Q	
082	52	R	
083	53	S	
084	54	T	
085	55	U	
086	56	V	
087	57	W	
088	58	X	
089	59	Y	
090	5A	Z	
091	5B	[	
092	5C	\	
093	5D	]	

Continued

Decimal	Hexadecimal	Character	Control
094	5E	^	
095	5F	_	
096	60	`	
097	61	a	
098	62	b	
099	63	c	
100	64	d	
101	65	e	
102	66	f	
103	67	g	
104	68	h	
105	69	i	
106	6A	j	
107	6B	k	
108	6C	l	
109	6D	m	
110	6E	n	
111	6F	o	
112	70	p	
113	71	q	
114	72	r	
115	73	s	
116	74	t	
117	75	u	
118	76	v	
119	77	w	
120	78	x	
121	79	y	
122	7A	z	
123	7B	{	
124	7C			
125	7D	}	
126	7E	~	
127	7F	delete	

Reserved Words in C

The following list of words are C keywords and may not be used and can't be used as variable names or for any other purpose.

auto	int
break	long
case	register
char	return
const	short
continue	signed
default	sizeof
do	static
double	struct
else	switch
enum	typedef
extern	union
float	unsigned
for	void
goto	volatile
if	while

INDEX

C++ is widely taught as a first programming

language because of its power and simplicity.

This book provides wide coverage of the

language and is aimed squarely at the

beginner to C++.

Author: Ian Wilks Price $19.95 ISBN 1-874416-29-X

INSTANT....................

Designed as a rapid introduction to the programming

language, these books deliver fundamental, essential

knowledge in an entertaining, painless way. These

books are ideal for students looking for a swift

grounding, or indeed for anyone wanting to make a

quick breakthrough into programming proficiency

The Book

Author: Ben Ezzell (Includes disk)
Price $39.95 ISBN 1-874416-22-2

The Revolutionary Guide to Visual C ++ provides the reader with a

comprehensive understanding of objects, thus making Windows programming with the MFC an easier

task to accomplish. Section One allows the C programmer to quickly get to terms with the difference

between C and C++, including the concepts involved in object oriented design and programming. In

Sections Two and Three, you are guided through the various steps required to produce complete

Windows applications.

The Series

REVOLUTIONARY GUIDE TO ....

Learn the programming techniques of the industry experts with the Revolutionary Guides. This series guide

you through the latest technology to bring your skills right up to date. Example applications are used t

illustrate new concepts and to give you practical experience in the language.

The Book

The Beginner's Guide to C++

This Beginners Guide contains comprehensive coverage of the language syntax. It teaches first

procedural and then object oriented programming and is the ideal start for the newcomer

to the world of programming languages.

Author: O. Yaroshenko Price $29.95 (includes disk) ISBN 1-874416-26-5

The Series

BEGINNER'S GUIDE TO ....

These guides are designed for beginners to the particular language or to

programming in general. The style is friendly and the emphasis is on

learning by doing. The chapters focus on useful examples that illustrate

important areas of the language. The wealth of examples and figures

help make the transition from beginner to programmer

both easy and successful

Authors: Various Price: $44.99 ISBN 1-874416-34-6

The Book

Assembly Language Master Class covers the 386,

486 and Pentium processors. This guide gives

aspiring experts a tutorial covering subjects such as

direct SVGA access, serial communications, device

drivers, protected mode and Windows, and virus

protection secrets.

............MASTER CLASS

The Series

The aim of this series is to bring together the ideas of a

number of the leading edge experts in one indispensable

book. Each chapter has a defined objective built around

the key application areas of the language.

WIN FREE BOOKS

TELL US WHAT YOU THINK!

Complete and return the bounce back card and you will:

- Help us create the books you want.
- Receive an update on all Wrox titles.
- Enter the draw for 5 Wrox titles of your choice.

FILL THIS OUT to enter the draw for free Wrox titles

Name _____

Address _____

_____

_____

_____ Postcode/Zip _____

Occupation _____

How did you hear about this book ?

☐ Book review (name) _____

☐ Advertisement (name) _____

☐ Recommendation

☐ Catalogue

☐ Other _____

Where did you buy this book ?

☐ Bookstore (name) _____

☐ Computer Store (name) _____

☐ Mail Order

☐ Other _____

What influenced you in the purchase of this book ?

☐ Cover Design

☐ Contents

☐ Use of Color

☐ Other (please specify)

How did you rate the overall contents of this book ?

☐ Excellent

☐ Good

☐ Average

☐ Poor

What did you find most useful about this book ?

_____

What did you find least useful about this book ?

_____

Please add any additional comments. _____

_____

What other subjects will you buy a computer book on soon ?

_____

What is the best computer book you have used this year ? _____

WROX PRESS INC.

Wrox writes books for you. Any suggestions, or ideas about how you want information given in your ideal book will be studied by our team. Your comments are always valued at WROX.

Free phone from USA 1 800 814 3461
Fax (312) 465 4063

Compuserve 100063,2152.
UK Tel. (4421) 706 6826   Fax   (4421) 706 2967

Computer Book Publishers

NB. If you post the bounce back card below in the UK, please send it to:
Wrox Press Ltd. 1334 Warwick Road, Birmingham, B27 6PR